BOXWALLAHS

Cawnpore chimneys: Raghavindrajit Singh.

ENDPAPERS
View from the gates of Elgin Mills

BOXWALLAHS

The British in Cawnpore
1857-1901

ZOË YALLAND

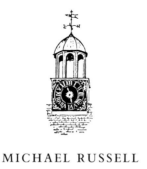

MICHAEL RUSSELL

© Zoë Yalland 1994

First published in Great Britain 1994
by Michael Russell (Publishing) Ltd
Wilby Hall, Wilby, Norwich NR16 2JP

Typeset by The Typesetting Bureau
Wimborne, Dorset
Printed and bound in Great Britain
by Biddles Ltd, Guildford and King's Lynn

ISBN 0 85955 206 3

In memory of my father and mother

Contents

—

Illustration Sources

The late E. T. H. Alexander, 358 (Shand); author's collection, 6, 41, 57, 114a, 114b, 125, 137 (Atkinson); 4, 35, 271a, 271b, 381 (photographs taken by the author); 2, 249, 250a, 250b, 266, 268, 342, 343, 345a, 345b, 373, 377, 425, 426 (Butterworth album); 360 (Cherry family); 344 (the late Mrs Nuna Davey); 169 (collection Mrs Forster); 16, 37, 45, 82b, 95, 105, 143, 171, 208 (Bourne), 242 (Gangi Sah), 249, 335, 338a, 338b, 388, 414 (miscellaneous); 157 (collection the late Mrs Joyce Umfreville); 145, 265, 379, 389, 424, 428b, endpapers (Mrs Margaret Vernon); Kathleen Bannerman, 428; Mrs Audrey Baylis, 158 (Rust); Dr Stanley Black, 410; British Library, 63; photograph Ewen Caldwell, 431; Colindale Newspaper Library, extracts from the *Pioneer*, 161, 162, 164, 176, 184, 199, 218b, 220, 396, 458, Appendix; collection Giles Eyre, 28; collection Michael Garnett, 265 (Dagg); photograph Reggie Ginns, 415; collection Ian Grant, 241, 342; the late Alice Horsman, 261; collection Henry Horsman, 417a, 417b; the late Mrs Noel Kilby, 91 (Bourne & Shepherd), 132a, 132b, 141b, 153, 189; MacRobert Archives, 283, 286a, 292, 294 (Bourne & Shepherd), 295, 298a, 298b, 302a, 302b, 303, 304, 309, 371, 403 (Bourne & Shepherd), 412, 413, 419, 422, 423; Mrs Mollie Mallaby, 20, 26, 198a, 198b, 212, 407; collection James Maxwell, jun., 207, 372; Lieutenant-Colonel P. St G. Maxwell, MC, 132c, 141a, 155 (Clarke), 182, 191, 193, 194, 344, 355, 357, 361, 363, 392, 409; S. P. Mehra, 432; National Army Museum, 61 (and thanks to Raghavindrajit Singh and P. J. O. Taylor), 73; collection Dr Munishwar Nigam, 258; Norohna family, 55 (Sharma & Co., Cawnpore); Ordnance Equipment Factory, Kanpur, 270; Oriental and India Office Collection, 43 (Dr Murray), 70 (Ahmed Ali Khan); P & O, 321; Major Nick Pocock, MC, 418; Raghavindrajit Singh, i, 107; photograph Mrs Mabel Ridsdale, 429; the late Major John Stewart, 100; John Stewart, 110a, 110b, 126, 408; Tannery and Footwear Corporation of India, 218b; Board of Trustees of the Victoria and Albert Museum, 109; Victoria Museum, Calcutta, 48-9;

Mrs Lorna Lancaster Wells and Nigel Smith, 274, 416; collection Anne West, 252; collection Theon Wilkinson, 80, 82a (by an Indian artist); photograph Wynyard Wilkinson, 237.

Author's Note

═══════

Over the years the spelling of many words and place names has changed: I have used the earlier spelling wherever possible, as being more in keeping with the times. Early letters are peppered with capital letters, which have been left in the text – as has the inconsistent spelling: sometimes, even in one letter, several versions of the same word are used.

While respecting my Indian friends' modern preference for the 'First War of Independence', I felt it appropriate to describe the stirring events of the sepoy revolt of 1857 as the 'Mutiny'.

Indian words and words of Indian origin which found their way into the everyday conversation of the British in India are in italics. A glossary is included at the end of the book.

The following abbreviations have been adopted:

BL   British Library
OIOC   Oriental and India Office Collection
NAI   National Archives India, New Delhi
NAM   National Army Museum
V&A   Victoria and Albert Museum
VM   Victoria Memorial, Calcutta

Cawnpore was spelt thus, occasionally Cawnpoor, for nearly 200 years, but after Independence it became Kanpur. In referring to it after 1947 I have used that spelling.

'Anglo-Indian' here is used in the modern sense for people of mixed parentage.

Finally a word about the title:

Box-wal(l)a(h) 19C Anglo-Indian hybrid from box + wala. Origin, an Indian itinerant pedlar or packman: later a shop-keeper, retailer or businessman, Indian or European. [From Ivor Lewis, *Sahibs, Nabobs and Boxwallahs*, OUP, Bombay, 1991.]

Boxwallah – a derogatory term for European businessman derived from door-to-door salesmen. [From Charles Allen, *Plain Tales from the Raj*, André Deutsch, 1975.]

The ordinary routine of daily life was occasionally broken by the arrival of a boxwallah or travelling pedlar, who kept a store of miscellaneous articles. It was pleasant therefore to hear the salutation, 'Salaam, Mem-Sahib, I your old *boxwallah*', and in reply to the query, 'What have you got?' 'Everything, Mem, powder, powder-puff, pen-ink, paper, enbelop, inkstand, corkiscrew, toot-broosh, very good isoap, cotton-tape-button-hook tilet vinegar; everything MemSahib want, *that* I give.' Of course the MemSahib did want something, if only for the pleasure of ransacking the pedlar's box, such visits, like those of angels, being few and far between. [From Mrs Herbert Reynolds, *At Home in India*. H. Drane, London, 1903, from chapter relating to 1865-74.]

This India is a dreadful country for people in his position. You must be 'in the service', that is either a Military man or a Civilian, to be thought anything of. If you are an outsider, a railway engineer, or an Indigo Planter or anything else, you are supposed to be not a gentleman, and society makes a dead set against you and excludes you – unless you have introductions and are known to be of good family and are pleasant, agreeable, and gentlemanly in manners – and still in spite of all this you'll sometimes hear people say deprecatingly, 'Oh, he's not in the service'. [From a letter written by Tina Roberts to her Aunt Marjory dated 16 September 1862 referring to their friend A. G. Murray who was on the railways. Stewart family papers.]

I was a *boxwallah* – a somewhat derogatory term for anyone who earned a living trading. And then again sub-divided into 'mercantile' (in office) or 'trade' (selling in shop). [Article in *Indo-British Review* 1994 by James Murray. Note by Theon Wilkinson – 'I always thought the actual handling of money was the touchstone in determining whether mercantile or not!']

Among the girls' circle of friends was Mr Allen, George Berney Allen, in charge of the Boot Factory. He was rather a serious young man and confided his liking for poetry to Lilian. Lilian wrote to her Aunt Tina, 'Browning's poem of *Aurora Leigh* was lent to me the other day by Mr Allen, son of the Pioneer man and I like it very much indeed. . .' However, John Stewart's comment to Tina is a reminder how deep the prejudice against 'trade' and the 'boxwallah' was. 'Mr Allen aged 20, son of my friend of the Pioneer who married a sister of Justice Turner is a very gentlemanly young man, well educated and fond of poetry etc. But he is connected with Boots and his father was Peake and Allen originally though he is now head of the Press in India, a CIE, a capitalist, and a member of Simla Society.' [From the Stewart family letters.]

Acknowledgements

―――――

My research into the British families in Cawnpore began in 1968. As I wrote in the Acknowledgements for my first book *Traders and Nabobs*, this research material covered virtually all the information I needed to draw upon to write all three proposed books in the series of which *Boxwallahs* is the second. With that in mind I fully acknowledged in *Traders* the help many, many kind friends and professional bodies had contributed. I would like each and every one of those names to know I appreciate their part not only in *Traders and Nabobs* but also in *Boxwallahs*.

However, I must make special mention of some who have been particularly closely involved with the *Boxwallahs* saga. The MacRobert Trustees once again in a generous gesture have made it possible for this volume to be so copiously illustrated. Mrs Mollie Mallaby made available personal papers and possessions of her grandfather Gavin Jones and has been a staunch supporter over many years. The late Joyce Umfreville lent me the Maxwell letters to transcribe and Antony Werner Fanny Tracy's letters and diary. Colonel Peter Maxwell shared details of Ralph Maxwell's sportsmanship while Pop Fuller, Charles Ker, R. A. Everett, and E. T. H. Alexander gave me details on pigsticking and the Cawnpore Tent Club.

The late Major John Stewart, Sandy Stewart and John Stewart most generously made available their collection of Stewart letters to enable me to transcribe thirty years of letters written by John and Millie in Cawnpore and which included the valuable letters from Sir George Allen and Gavin Jones. Charles Allen and the late Major Idris Williams gave useful family details about Sir George Allen and I am grateful to John Rhatigan of the Administrative Department of Colindale Newspaper Library for the opportunity to study the *Pioneer* newspapers. Malcolm Barnes and Edward Bishop, Mrs Peter Corneille and W. P. Ogilvie helped over Allen Bros London office. Rosalind Cattanach of the London Spiritual Mission, Kensington, and the late J. Stanley Beard, FRIBA, were particularly helpful about Sir William Cooper, while M. D. Percival and Robert Percival had details of Hume Towers. Accrington Public Library provided information on John Harwood.

My very special thanks to Tony West for the working notebooks and diaries of his grandfather Atherton West when he was working at the Elgin Mills. Thanks to Ian Gibson, Principal Keeper of Technical and Industrial History, Lancashire County Council and Helmshore Museum for original plans for the Elgin Mills and many important technical details on the supply of machinery and early working practices; also to Mr Dabral, Mr Sharma, Madge Vernon and Peggy Vernon on Elgin information. The Butterworth material comes from our family anecdotes and my father's 'Notes on the Family of Butterworth'. Margaret Cooke and Michael Garnett helped with early details of the Cawnpore Volunteers. Richard Horsman, the late Alice Horsman and Henry Horsman told me about the Horsman family and Major Nick Pocock, Gussie Bevis and Mabel Ridsdale provided delightful contemporary anecdotes.

Mr Chopra showed me the first Muir Mills Minute Book with a wealth of unusual detail, including the light it throws on Gavin Jones and Sir Henry Ledgard. Rhodes House, Oxford, helped with SPG records and the Revd George Slater, Canon Michael Storrs Fox and the Bishop of Durham guided me on the chapter on Foss and George Westcott.

Ian Mitchell, the late archivist of the MacRobert Trusts Museum at Tarland was an invaluable help in assessing the material on the life and work of Sir Alexander McRobert and his first wife Georgina. Dr Charlie Milne, F. Brightman and T. V. Baddeley contributed lively personal anecdotes.

I should also like to thank the following people for their encouragement and support, sometimes in providing or checking material, or photographs, for hospitality I enjoyed while travelling, or for help in some practical form. I am very grateful to them. At the OIOC Anthony Farrington, Deputy Director (India Office), Pat Kattenhorn of Prints and Drawings, Tim Thomas of the Readers' Service Team and Gita Venugopal Reprographic Customer Service; at the NAM Dr Peter Royden, Head of Archives. In India, Ram Advani, Atma Prakash Gupta, Pushy Khanna, Santosh Mahendrajit Singh, S. P. Mehra, Dr Munishwar Nigam, Raghavindrajit Singh, Anita Rewal, Dr Chandrakanta Rohatgi and Dr Kanchan Rohatgi, H. K. Srivastava and Thomas Smith. In the United Kingdom, Louise Adorian, James and

Barbara Anson, John and Kathleen Bannerman, Audrey Baylis, Ewen Caldwell, Judith Cameron, Elizabeth Christie, Francis Cherry, Salli Dyson, Phyllis Forster, Cecil Gash, Reggie Ginns, Ian Grant, Fiona Greenwood, Christopher Hawes, Harold Hobson, Lorna Lancaster Wells, Dr Rosie Llewellyn-Jones, Betsy Macdonald, Ian MacMaster, Alastair Macpherson, honorary archivist of Haileybury College, Paul Norris, Stephen Rabson, P & O archivist, Tigger Ramsay Brown, Michael Satow, Catherine Sears, Nigel Smith, E. A. Stromeyer, Elizabeth Talbot Rice, Peter Taylor, Anne West, Kenneth Wilcox, and Wynyard Wilkinson. In the United States, Reggie Bason, Professor Peter Fay, and Andrew Ward; and in Canada, Gordon Hughes.

I should like to thank my publisher for work extending over four years that has gone into the production of this companion volume to *Traders and Nabobs*, his sure professional touch and attention to pleasing detail; Lynda Deane for putting the manuscript onto disc; and Joanna Motion for proof-reading and careful work on the index.

My brother Theon Wilkinson has been a constant supporter, never too busy to discuss or answer queries or look things up from his wide source library. Within my family it is the loving support and wholehearted encouragement of my children, Hugo, Jonathan and Joanna, who have helped in so many practical and important ways, and of my husband Basil Yalland that has made this endeavour possible. I thank you all most warmly.

Preface

This is the second volume in a series of three books on the saga of the British families in Cawnpore. Readers of the first book *Traders and Nabobs: The British in Cawnpore 1765-1857,* may perhaps recall that my family were associated with the mills in Cawnpore for three generations, on my mother's side since 1882 and on my father's side since 1912.

As a small girl, for the first eight years of my life I woke every morning to hear the hooters of the Elgin Mills calling the men to work. It was a glorious childhood. Sunshine and shadows, brilliant colours and endless horizons, multitudes of people, magic and mystery, strong scents and violent deaths, fabulous journeys and dreadful partings – oh, those partings! At eight came the trauma experienced by the great majority of the children born to English families working in India, boarding school in England. Grey skies, chilblains, doors that shut, tight formal clothes and aloneness.

In my second term at school in England, one late afternoon in September, the headmistress sent for me and said my father had come to say goodbye because he was returning to India. He had been shown into the private dining-room. The curtains were drawn and the room seemed overcrowded with the oval dining table and chairs set round it. My father was wearing a new Huntsman suit, a grey check with waistcoat, the bottom button undone. His hair was smoothed close to his head and his face had a tight look. I hardly looked at him; I felt as wooden as the table. What was there to say? I don't recall what my father said, but he called me 'darling' and then to my horror and astonishment I saw the tears roll down his cheeks and he took out his handkerchief and blew his nose, embraced me and quickly turned to go. I did not see him again for three years.

My father's bookstand remains an icon of those lengthy, unquestioned separations. It was a neat contraption on which to prop open a book while eating. There are clips to hold back the pages and hinges to adjust the angle of the book so that the best light falls on the page. Every year when my brother and I were at school in England my mother would travel 'home' to be with us for the Easter and summer holidays. She booked her passage well in advance, the P & O sending her a plan of the ship so that she could choose an L-shaped cabin with a porthole on the cool side of the ship and travel in the style expected of the wife of a director of Begg Sutherland & Co. Eight months of every year my father was therefore alone. His office work and many committees kept him busy, his delight in his beautiful garden was a pleasure but the evenings were difficult, especially at mealtimes. He sat alone at the head of a huge table, chosen so that it would seat twelve at Christmas parties, and in front of his place was the book stand. In order not to hurry too much over the food, passed to him by the silent bearers, he forced himself to read through each meal.

Many years later, after India had gained Independence and one by one the European mill owners and managers had sold up or handed over to Indian colleagues, and we too had left India for good, I often found myself haunted by those memories, calling England our home and yet living in India where in fact I had the only home I knew for thirty-five years. My father's self-imposed solitariness, my mother's loneliness — since she could only be with her children during school holidays: I wondered what possible reason my father could have had to stay and work in India when it imposed such restrictions on family life. What was there in Cawnpore that could sufficiently compensate for the agony of that separation? Did Cawnpore offer money? Opportunity? The good life?

Then one day I was walking in London in winter and glanced up at the tall chimneys of the red brick Victorian houses along Gower Street and I found myself transported to the thrill and excitement of arriving by train at Cawnpore as a child. The great steam engine had pounded and shouted its way through the Bombay ghats and the vast empty horizons of India. One moment and the sun burned a hole in the sky, then suddenly it had gone, the sky emptied and there was a hushed moment before nightfall when all time seemed to have stopped as the train approached Cawnpore. In the rapidly darkening sky I could see first one mill chimney and then another: Atherton West, Lalimli, Muir, New Victoria, Cooper Allen, the Power House and . . . beloved Elgin. Each a landmark, each a proud and grimy monument to men long dead. But who were they? Why did they come to Cawnpore? Where did they come from? What was there before they came?

From that moment the decision to research and collect material and

write the story of the British families at Cawnpore was taken. I have
been marvellously supported and encouraged in this long endeavour by
my family and by family friends. Many people have been immensely
generous with making personal papers and photographs available to me.
It is this original and hitherto unpublished material – letters, diaries, mill
records – that has shaped this unique picture of the daily life of the
'Boxwallahs' and the memsahibs of Cawnpore.

   Traders and Nabobs set the scene, describing Cawnpore in its 'palmy
days', the influence of the Maxwell family, ending with the disaster of
the massacre and destruction of the city at the time of the Mutiny.
Boxwallahs carries on the story, beginning with the thrilling escape of
Gavin Jones and the restoration of law and order; how into the vacuum
created by the Mutiny, the coming of the railway and the boom in
cotton prices gave the impetus for the genius of Gavin Jones and the
stability of Hugh Maxwell to combine in putting up the first up-country
cotton mill in India. From this early start all subsequent industrialisation
stemmed and names that will be familiar with India hands emerge.
Colonel John Stewart of the Harness & Saddlery Factory, Sir George
Allen of the *Pioneer* and his partners at Cooper Allen, Sir William
Cooper and Sir Henry Ledgard; the first technicians – my grandfather
among them – Atherton West, Alfred Butterworth, Albert Horsman;
the distinguished churchmen Foss and George Westcott and the most
remarkable of all, the man who was to take over the mantle from Gavin
Jones and become the 'uncrowned king' of Cawnpore, Sir Alexander
McRobert. *Boxwallahs* takes the reader to the turn of the century and
ends with the death of Queen Victoria. The epilogue rounds off the lives
of the main players and looks briefly ahead to my planned third volume
and the events that led to 1947 and Independence.

Prologue

═══════

The Legend of Cawnpore

My Great-Aunt Emma, on a two-year trip round the world, arrived in India from Melbourne in 1897 and travelled up-country to Cawnpore to spend four weeks with my grandparents, Alfred and Polly Butterworth. Her diary entry for Monday, 13 December is headed 'At last at Cawnpore'.

It was forty years since the Mutiny of 1857 and the terrible massacre that had made the name of Cawnpore notorious, yet on her very first afternoon, every European visitor to Cawnpore, Great-Aunt Emma,[1] chiffon scarf wrapped over her small bonnet and tied tightly under her chin, set out in the family carriage to pay her respects to the Angel of the Well in Memorial Well Gardens, the well that stood guardian to the legend of Cawnpore. The carriage with its chestnut mare, Nancy, in smart harness and trappings all made from Cawnpore leather, bowled briskly along the Mall. Stretches of sand on either side of the wide road kicked up into dust that even on this cold December day turned the dense foliage of the neem trees white.

Great-Aunt Emma, twice widowed, with small blue eyes that twinkled behind steel-rimmed glasses, looked about her, determined to miss nothing of the horrors of the story. Beside her sat my little grandmama, the curves of her body hidden by a full high-yoked dress, a sweet rather vague smile on her face, a pretty face that had earned for her the sobriquet of 'The Rose of Lancashire'. She had had six children and now after a lapse of six years was pregnant again. This child was to be my mother, the darling and favourite of her parents. Opposite sat my grandfather, short, well-built, with a full drooping moustache, proud of his job as manager at the Cawnpore Woollen Mills, proud of his fifteen years in Cawnpore and the progress in the city. As they clip-clopped along through Parade Bazaar crowded with Indian people, he pointed

Alfred and Polly Butterworth driving through the Memorial Gardens, returning from tennis – c. 1885.

out the main buildings: Christ Church with its square tower, a pre-Mutiny building; the Prince of Wales Hospital; several new bank buildings. Opposite 'Baker, Anson, Coachbuilders and Auctioneers' and 'Charles and Co., Chemists (established 1863)', where two large flasks, one red, one blue, stood in the windows on either side of the door, the carriage pulled up at the imposing main gates of the Gardens. Only one Indian at a time – accompanied by a European – was allowed in the Gardens. The Indian syce, decked out in huge *puggri* and dark serge coat, climbed down and the coachman drove on at walking pace.[2]

This drive through the Gardens on the way to church service was a regular ritual. (Fifty years later it was Ram Swaroop, the grandson of that coachman, who drove me in the white Armstrong-Siddeley to Christ Church for my wedding.) Proceeding at a slow walk between the avenue of bottle palms, the carriage approached the Gothic screen that surrounded the shrine of the Well. The Angel, made by Baron Marochetti[3] to a design inspired by Lady Canning, is holding fronds of crossed palm. She has an expression on her face of sadness when viewed from one side and of severity when viewed from the other. A soldier on custodian duty unlocked the beautiful wrought-iron gate, fashioned from a captured mutineers' cannon. The fact that the Angel was set back within a deep moat-like drop, distancing it from the walkway, contributed to the sombreness of the setting. In the distance swarms of flying foxes squabbled in the branches of huge banyan trees, hanging upside down in unconscious mimicry of those rebels who had been summarily strung up on improvised gallows when Havelock's army drove the Nana Sahib out of Cawnpore and avenged the massacre of the unfortunate women and children at the Bebee Ghur. Cawnpore had its fame through the stories of horror and valour that attended the deeds of the Mutiny period. The Poet Laureate composed an ode, poems and ballads appeared in the *Pioneer* newspaper. The Mutiny had definitely put Cawnpore on the map as a tourist attraction.

By 1897 Cawnpore was a thriving industrial city. People like my grandfather, reading newspaper advertisements in the English papers offering jobs to technicians at the newly established mills, rushed to Leadenhall Street, London. They booked passages on one of the fleet of forty P & O ships for the fortnightly sailing to Calcutta and came flocking out to Cawnpore with dreams of making a fortune, or at least living the good life.[4] Tourists like Great-Aunt Emma and young men on the Grand Tour made a point of breaking their journey while in India to visit the Mutiny sites, in much the same way that young people nowadays queue to see the Chamber of Horrors at Madame Tussaud's. Joe Lee, a cheeky Mutiny veteran with many a yarn to tell, made a good living out of it.[5] He ran Lee's Railway Hotel near the EIR station and his visitors' book lists bigwigs and people of distinction – it was a society impressed by titles. They came from not only all over India but also from the cities of America, from Hawaii, Australia, Norway, Germany and Russia. Thomas Cook and Sons ran a Round the World Party that included Cawnpore on its itinerary. For a consideration Joe Lee would take you on a tour of Wheeler's entrenchment and down to Massacre Ghat, show you the very spot where the Nana Sahib had ordered his prisoners trampled to death by his favourite elephant (which had not wanted to hurt the victims and had to be prodded to carry out its brutal task); and all this with tears in his eyes.

At the mess house of the Volunteer Rifles, amateur soldiers, Englishmen and Anglo-Indians, men who worked in the mills by day, met regularly to practise defence and attack 'in case of need', and stories were recounted again and again of Mutiny adventures. But the Mutiny veterans themselves, while modestly accepting their roles as heroes, seldom spoke of what they had witnessed and endured. It was a form of self-defence to blot it all out. But it was not surprising perhaps that the man who was hailed as the 'Father of Cawnpore', the man who was behind practically every new industrial development in Cawnpore, was also the hero of a thrilling Mutiny escape. When so many of his own family and friends had met their death at the hands of the rebels and with almost the entire European population of Cawnpore killed and murdered, for him alone to have survived suggested that fate had singled out Gavin Jones for a special destiny.

The Angel of the Well.

I

The Making of a Hero

━━━━━

Gavin Jones's Escape from Fatehgarh to Cawnpore

It had long been rumoured that the rule of the East India Company would come to an end in 1857, exactly one hundred years from the date of the Battle of Plassey when Clive defeated the Nawab of Bengal and assumed authority for the government of Bengal.

Well-intentioned liberal reforms had disturbed the high-ranking Bramhins, undermining their traditional influence, while unwise policies of annexation, rumours of enforced Christianity and the introduction of the suspected Enfield rifle all caused disquiet and discontent. When it was announced that the title of King of Delhi was to lapse with the death of the old Moghul Emperor Bahadur Shah, the peoples of northern India were drawn together in a common cause to throw out the British. Nevertheless in the three Presidencies only the Presidency of Bengal was affected and even in Bengal Calcutta remained calm. It was the old Moghul heartland where the uprising took place, in an area between Delhi, Lucknow and Cawnpore; and there the violence was horrific.

The outbreak occurred on 10 May 1857 at Meerut, a garrison town not far from Delhi. There on a Sunday, the troopers of the 3rd Light Cavalry murdered their officers as they came out of church, set free the prisoners and, leaving Meerut in flames, marched to Delhi to pledge themselves to the Emperor. The entire native garrison at Delhi rose in sympathy and in the Ganges valley throughout northern India no Englishman was safe.

At the start of the hot weather of 1857 Gavin Jones joined his brother John Moore Jones on the family indigo estates near Fatehgarh. This was a town about seventy-five miles north of Cawnpore, close to Farrukhabad, which had become a military cantonment in the early 1800s when the East India Company granted amnesties to the adventurers serving with the Mahratta armies. The town was dominated by the fort, an area of

Repulse of a Sortie: *Captain G. F. Atkinson,* Campaign in India, 1857-58.

twenty acres surrounded by thick mud walls and semi-circular bastions, protected on three sides by a dry ditch and on the fourth by the River Ganges.

Hearing of the uprising at Meerut, the European community, mostly indigo planters, merchants, missionaries and traders, made plans to escape by boat to Cawnpore. The news of the mutiny of the 9th Native Infantry at Aligarh on 4 June aroused fears that the 10th Native Infantry at Fatehgarh would rise in sympathy, so the Europeans took to the boats under the protection of a friendly zemindar, Hardeo Buksh, who supplied a guard of matchlockmen. The boats cast off silently in the darkness and glided into the main stream. But at daybreak the passengers found themselves in danger. Villagers, believing the 'Sahib log' carried treasure and valuables, gathered along the banks firing and trying to trap the clumsy flat-bottomed boats into shallow channels where they would become stranded and easy to loot. At the mouth of the Ramganga, a tributary of the Ganges, the fugitives pulled in to the shore for a desperate counsel, joined by Hardeo Buksh himself. Foreseeing the dangers, he urged the party to return with him to his fort deep in the jungle where he would guarantee to keep them safe. All but forty of the party, however, terrified by recent events, were afraid to place themselves in the power of an Indian and chose instead to push on to Cawnpore. When their boats reached the town seven or eight days later, they found General Wheeler and the entire European population besieged by the Nana Sahib. The bridge of boats to Allahabad was closed against them and they were cornered on an island. The men were shot in front of their families and the women and children led away as prisoners to the Savada Kothi.

Among the forty people who decided to trust themselves to Hardeo Buksh was Gavin Jones. His group travelled two days through the jungle to the promised sanctuary but found nothing of a fort about it – no facilities for defence and no accommodation or shelter. The women and children lodged as best they could under trees and in small thatched sheds, bitterly regretting not having gone with the rest of the party in the boats.

Then, unexpectedly, news came that the sepoys at Fatehgarh had not risen on the arrival of the rebels from Aligarh and the town was quiet. Accordingly preparations were made to leave the jungle and return to Fatehgarh. Hardeo Buksh repeatedly warned them that the sepoys were not to be trusted but only Edwards, a fugitive magistrate, and Probyn with his wife and four children elected to remain under the old zemindar's protection. Gavin Jones and the rest of the small party returned to the fort at Fatehgarh where everything appeared orderly.

Gavin Jones's own account of his escape, which was published in *Blackwood's*,[1] makes it clear why he came to be seen as a hero to the people of Cawnpore.

Alas! it was merely the 'lull before the storm'. Barely had our fears been lulled into repose, when all sense of security suddenly vanished at the intelligence that the 41st Native Infantry mutineers from Sitapur, Oudh, had intimated to the 10th their intention to visit Fatehgarh on their way to Delhi, and expected them to join. It was a day of intense anxiety and excitement, knowing the temper of the 10th, and the conditions on which they had sworn allegiance. Every precaution was immediately taken to prevent the rebels crossing the Ganges; the bridge-of-boats was destroyed, and every boat within several miles on either side of the river burnt or sunk. The 10th worked with a will, and, to the casual observer, displayed genuine alacrity in the service; but the experienced in native character saw in this very circumstance the withering of all their hopes. Two days passed in profound suspense; we hoped that the difficulty of obtaining the means of crossing might induce the rebels to change their course and leave us unmolested; but on the third day our worst fears were terribly realised. Early on the morning of the 18th of June, the 41st, after making a circuitous journey, crossed the river higher up, and entered the city of Farrukabad from the north-west. There they raised the standard of rebellion, and proclaimed Nawab Tafazul Hosain Khan, ruler of the province, and sent a messenger to the 10th, demanding surrender of the treasure and the heads of the officers and European residents of the station. The 10th who had evidently been in communication with the 41st, whilst temporising with them, deceived us with a display of zealous loyalty distrustful of the intruders, and anxious to secure the contents of the treasure-chests, which they held in their possession, they warned off the officers, and plundered the money before the 41st could arrive on the scene to claim a share. They next proceeded to the jail and liberated all the prisoners, offering, however, no violence to the officers and residents, but leaving us completely to the tender mercy of the invaders and the fanatic rabble of the Nawab.

Before daybreak, when most of us lay unconscious of all that was transpiring outside of the fort, wherein we lay slumbering in the open air on the bank of the river, an officer of the 10th came in breathless from the sepoys' lines, with a countenance boding no good, and announced the terrible news that the 10th had mutinied and the 41st were expected in the station every minute. The alarm produced simply defies description. We were at the time in the presence of a strong detachment of the 10th Regiment which garrisoned the Fort; our movements, therefore, were paralysed, and we were reduced to the most abject state of helplessness, expecting every moment to see the men turn upon us and massacre us. The suspense was simply appalling as we stood, ladies and children, young and old, in the presence of the sepoys in small groups, without arms and no possible means of escape, watching their every movement with intense interest and no little trepidation. Contrary, however, to all expectations, the men began to leave the fort in small numbers, more anxious to obtain a share of the plunder of the treasury outside than the disposal of our worthless lives. In a few minutes the entire body departed, leaving us helpless but in sole possession of the fort. The exit of the last man became the signal for action; not a moment was lost in closing the gate and taking measures for the protection of the ladies and children whom, but a moment's reflection convinced us, it was impossible, with our limited means and small numbers, to escort to Agra or any other place of safety. Search was instantly made for arms and ammunition, and between two and three hundred muskets, some cases of ball ammunition and a few boxes of blank cartridges were found in the guard-room; a 24-pounder howitzer, charged with scrap metal, was hurriedly dragged out of the pattern shop and laid fronting the gateway to guard the passage. By this time we were joined by Colonel Smith, who came in fagged and dispirited, escorted by three or four of his most attached men, who hung about him sobbing like children. At the imminent peril of his life, the gallant old Colonel had used every effort to keep his regiment together and to recall the men to a sense of their duty, exposing himself recklessly in the midst of a disorganised and infuriated mass, to win them back. The sepoys, however, were beyond control. Blinded by the sight of the piles of silver, and the fear of its falling into the hands of the 41st, they raved for the plunder, and disregarded the appeals and threats of their Commander. It was sufficient for them that the British Raj was at an end, the magic link was severed; they had therefore now no fear of consequences, and each did as his desire dictated; the men loaded themselves with as much coin as they could carry, and those who had ponies and bullocks brought them into requisition, and thus prepared crossed into Oudh, with the object of making their way to their homes, before the 41st had time to come up to snatch from them their long-preserved loot. The faithful escort implored the Colonel to allow them to remain with him and share his dangers and fate, but he looked upon their presence in the midst of us as rather a source of danger than protection, as it was liable to draw upon us the vengeance of their comrades, therefore yielding to the wishes of the Colonel, they reluctantly took their departure, and the gates were finally closed upon them and barricaded. The refugees were forthwith mustered, and the garrison of thirty-five men, old and young, divided into three bodies, and told off, each under the command of Colonels Goldie, Smith and Tucker. Measures were at once adopted to render our position defensible.

The fort had been the workshop of the Government Gun Carriage Agency. In defence of the bastions, light guns were now dragged into position and dummy guns to draw the enemy fire cunningly constructed from blackboards stuck with gun muzzle stops, mounted on carriages and placed in commanding positions. There was no ammunition for the guns, so scrap iron and sledgehammers tied up in gunny bags had to serve. With a large area to protect and few men to guard it, the defence became a matter of ingenuity. In the exposed woodyard they pretended to lay a mine and so well was it set up that no attack came from that quarter. As for a few more days the rebels still held back, stores of gram, rice and dal were brought in from the nearby bazaar. Crouched at the low breastworks, the defending pickets watched and waited for the attack. They saw the sepoys parading up and down galloping the horses and swanking in the carriages that had belonged to their officers. In the evening the band regaled them with familiar airs, invariably ending up, from force of habit, with 'God Save the Queen'.

On the morning of the 26th of June 1857, just a week after the 10th deserted their colours, the enemy advanced as they had threatened in full force, whilst it was yet dark with their guns, cavalry, and infantry drawn up in battle array making a most imposing display, and commenced the attack with their artillery. The sudden booming of the guns and the whiz of the shots over our heads startled all sleepers to consciousness, and in a moment we were at our posts to meet the desperate and unequal encounter. In breathless silence we kneeled behind the breast-work in the dark hour of the morning clutching our muskets, unable to see the enemy, but painfully conscious of our weakness, and oppressed with a sense of the inevitable doom that seemingly awaited us and the helpless ones with us. We could not hope to survive the day, for our spies had reported but the day before that the sepoys were going to attack with fifty scaling ladders simultaneously from all directions. It was impossible to repel such an attack with our slender force, some of the bastions being necessarily left undefended, while many could only be manned by one or at most two men, and the intervening walls depended entirely on the cross fire of the flanking bastions for their defence, the strength of the garrison being concentrated at the angles, which were naturally the weakest points, and where we mustered six and eight strong in each. The booming of the guns in the profound silence of the early hour alone told us of the presence of the rebels in our vicinity; not a sound or a movement else could be seen or heard as we eagerly watched in silence. Presently the fire abruptly ceased, the rebels having discovered that the guns were producing no effect – for without exception the shots had all flown past over the fort into the Ganges in the rear – till daylight came to their aid, when they resumed the work of destruction, we now began to see the imposing array of the rebel force. The cavalry trotted briskly forward and drew up behind a large tope of trees covering the roadway, and the artillery were posted in another large tope in front about 1,500 yards distant, whence they maintained a steady cannonade with their 6-pounder field pieces, whilst the infantry advanced in open order, skirmishing and covering the assaulting parties who were slowly creeping up with their huge ladders. About a dozen or more came in sight simultaneously, almost within range of our muskets, when the order was passed round to the posts, as the short rattle of the musketry rent the air and made our blood creep. 'Reserve your fire and be careful of your ammunition.' On they came slowly but steadily, yelling and gesticulating like fiends, and emboldened by our silence dashed forward as they neared the fort walls in the hope of securing a safe lodgment before we could offer them any effectual check. They were, however, mistaken; our guns opened with scrap and our musketry began to play with visible effect on the ladder bearers within a hundred yards range; the fellows fell right and left, and as none advanced to fill up the gaps, they wavered, dropped their unwieldy burdens, and fled to cover. This was an unexpected result; in place of despondency our spirits rose with every success, and a very little time sufficed to see our valiant assailants, after a few abortive attempts, give up the game and retire disconcerted and disappointed. The defence had not been equally successful in all directions. At the south-west corner, the scalers had succeeded in planting three ladders against the bastion, where our cross fire had been feeble and ineffective; fortunately for us the rebels had not taken into calculation the depth of the ditch that surrounded the walls, and the ladders were consequently just so much too short to reach the top, so when the men mounted and tried to scramble up, their glittering blades reflected in the sunlight above the breastworks betrayed their presence to the defenders. As quick as thought our men rolled down upon them the heavy half-wrought gunnywheel naves we had piled up to raise the breastwork for our better protection against musketry fire; the heavy logs swept the ladders of the assailants, and a concentrated fire of musketry completed their discomfiture. At nightfall the ladders were hauled into the fort. The contest raged with unabated vigour for about two hours, when the enemy began to lose heart and waver; their fire gradually slackened in all directions, and very soon after they withdrew; leaving a number of their dead and wounded scattered over the plain, and ourselves jubilant for the time being over the triumph. In the afternoon the attack was renewed, but the failure of the morning had considerably damped the ardour of Jack sepoy, whilst we, no longer paralysed with the anxiety and uncertainty of the results which oppressed us in the morning, met the advance calmly, and drove the rebels back with considerable loss, without sustaining any harm ourselves.

As these half-hearted attempts to take the fort became more and more feeble daily, so rose our spirits and hope, for our spies reported that discontent was rife among the sepoys, who were deserting in large numbers, and the Nawab and his retainers were taunting them for their want of success, which tended the more to dispirit them. Our casualties thus far were trifling, notwithstanding the incessant fire maintained against us night and day, allowing us no intervals of peace and forbidding sleep except in snatches, under fatigue and exposure to the burning sun; but our spirits were buoyant, and the favourable turn affairs had taken enabled us to endure all cheerfully. Unhappily for us the Nawab of Farrukhabad, who was deeply implicated in the rebellion, and was therefore personally interested in the expulsion of the English, his authority and the stability of his Nawabdom depending upon it, observing that the courage of the sepoys was flagging, summoned the aid of the Pathans of Shamshabad and Mhow. By this means he excited a spirit of rivalry between the different parties, and stimulated their zeal with an offer of a lakh of rupees to the successful captors. Thus reinforced by a host of fanatical Mussalmans, accustomed to the exercise of arms from their infancy, the leaders combined to exterminate the common enemy and advanced to the attack with renewed resolution and more confidence, conducting their operations with more tact and method. Their first move was to occupy all the lofty houses of the adjoining bazar that stood within range, and commanded the interior of the fort and our positions; the rifle company of the 41st thus covered us from every position of vantage and crippled our movements, as we no longer could expose our heads above the breastwork with impunity, and they proved such expert marksmen, that few of the men in the nearest picket had escaped without two, three, or more shots through their sola hats, which the enemy caught sight of moving above the breastworks. Seeing that an exposed hat top invited a shower of rifle bullets, we took advantage of it and made it a regular practice of drawing their fire by holding up an empty hat just above the walls; the plan proved a great success, till someone more enthusiastic than prudent riased his hat too high above the breastwork and a riffle bullet carrying it away exposed the stick that supported it, betraying the trick. The manoeuvres of the cavalry and artillery were repeated, both taking up their old ground which they had occupied on the first day of the siege; the latter opened fire on us while the sepoys advanced covering the Pathans, who boldly advanced armed with swords only, led by a daring fanatic; the ladders which still lay scattered over the plain, where they had been abandoned by the sepoys, were picked up and the men pressed forward, heedless for a while of the havoc our musketry was creating among them, but our steady and deliberate fire was telling among their ranks slowly but surely, when confusion began to show itself at every step, and presently in less time than it takes me to write this, the Pathans broke in disorder, dropped their burdens and retired en masse out of range of our muskets.

The contest for our little garrison proved a most severe one, and but for the fact of each man being armed with six and eight muskets apiece, which we kept always ready loaded by our sides, it would have gone hard with us, for it is certain we could not have checked the determined attack of a force that outnumbered us at least sixty times. The riflemen, however, had done their work among us and rendered some of our most exposed positions untenable. Our little store of ammunition was greatly reduced, and our guns were no longer able to reply with effect; but few cartridges remained which were husbanded with the utmost care for the last struggle, which it was manifest was now rapidly drawing upon us, for we felt ourselves incapable of offering further effectual resistance if similar attacks to the last were to be repeated by the enemy. Several of our best men had fallen, nevertheless the nature of our position and the surrounding circumstances made us cling the more stubbornly to the defence, and we continued to hold our own in spite of the overwhelming odds against us. Again and again the rebels were repulsed till it became evident to the leaders that other plans would have to be adopted to dislodge us and take the fort. Accordingly, one morning we found the usual mode of attack discontinued and beyond the continual crack of the rifles, which knew no cessation, all was silent; the change to us was gloomy and ominous in the extreme, some more hopeful than others regarded it as a favourable sign, indicating failure of the siege, others instinctively felt that it boded evil, and that the worst was yet to come. As the day advanced occasional feints were made, and the night alarms became more frequent, which kept us on the alert and wearied us for want of rest, whilst their insidious plans were being carried out unsuspected and unknown to us beneath the fort walls.

The rebels burrowed under the foundations of the fort and laid a mine which they exploded at daybreak. Just before the mine was sprung, Gavin Jones had been taking his turn of duty at a loophole. He saw the fuse smouldering, then was half stunned by the thunder of the explosion. In the smoke and darkness and confusion two or three of the defenders rushed to try to close the breach. Jones stood with Bhairo, his brother's bearer, beside him, loading and unloading his muskets, firing down into the mass of the storming party, shooting as fast as he could, shifting the musket from one shoulder to another as the recoil became too painful. Just as he found he could carry on no longer the rebels turned and began to retreat. Gavin's brother John Moore Jones was among the first to be killed, mortally wounded by a bullet in the head. They carried him down from the ramparts and buried him at nightfall.

In the fierce midday heat of noon a second attack was made and repulsed. But that night the ominous sounds of further mining were distinctly heard and it was decided the only chance of saving the women and children was to take to the boats. Three boats tied below the walls of the fort were prepared and at midnight all was in readiness. At a given signal two men crept out to spike the guns and destroy the remaining ammunition.

Silence in the fort was profound, broken only by the crack of the enemies' rifles, the cry of the children, and howling of dogs we were abandoning as we silently took our places in the boats. By two, as the moon dipped in the horizon, the aged Colonel Goldie stepped forward in his boat, and in a stentorian voice gave the command 'All ready? Let go.' The last with an emphasis that awoke the echoes and alarmed us not a little lest the signal should reach the ears of the enemy and give the alarm. Slowly we dropped down with the sluggish stream, every heart throbbing almost audibly, as we cleared the shelter of the fort and stood out in the open in full sight of the enemy; the poor children crowded within, moaned and cried piteously to the infinite distress of their parents, who sought in vain to quiet them. It was a solemn spectacle; the prayers of the helpless went up on high to the Almighty for strength and deliverance from the awful ordeal we had to face as we floated down dejected and almost hopeless, but resolved with the courage of despair by God's help to encounter it manfully.

The river was very low, the depth of water barely sufficient to float the boats over the numerous bars and sandbanks. Jones was in the third boat, manned only by Europeans unfamiliar with the heavy unwieldy country craft. He lay stretched at full length steering, keeping his head well down while the oarsmen tried to get out of reach of the shore. The bank was thronged with assailants, their shots pitting the water and rattling against the bamboos of the boat. The three boats turned for safety away from the main channel and into a side cutting. Here they were out of reach of the mob but soon the leading boat stuck fast and had to be abandoned, the people on board wading in the shallows to join the other two boats.

Once again they were confronted by a sandbank. The leading boat managed to float across it but the boat Jones was steering, lying low in the water weighed down with the human cargo, grounded.

Thus unintentionally abandoned we were left to our own resources, every man got into the water and applied their backs and shoulders to push her into deep water, but both wind and current were against us, and all our efforts failed to clear the bend which would have floated us into the channel. The crisis had now come, though we could not realize it. The rabble which had gained strength as they followed us down, being reinforced by the villagers on the way, swarmed in hundreds, kept up an unceasing yell, and assailed us from every available direction with their matchlocks and showers of arrows. At this time two boats, apparently empty, with their solitary steersmen on each, were seen slowly dropping down with the stream towards us, their inoffensive exterior disarmed suspicion, and we paid no heed to them but continued our futile efforts to push off our boat, contending

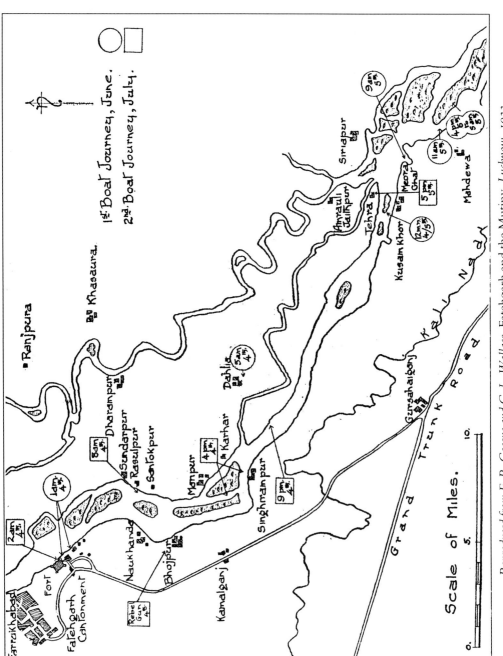

1st Boat Journey, June.

2nd Boat Journey, July.

Scale of Miles.

0.   5.   10.

Reproduced from F. R. Cosens and C. L. Wallace, Fatehgarh and the Mutiny, Lucknow, 1933.

hopelessly with the current, the wind, and the merciless rabble who were only kept at bay by our muskets. The surprise was complete; at about 20 yards the sepoys unmasked and poured in a volley into us, and, ere we could recover from the suddenness of the attack, the boats were alongside. Resistance was useless, but rather than yield to the savage ruffians, we called to the ladies to follow us into the river. The summons, however, was unnecessary, for the instant the rebels boarded, it became the signal for a general rush to the water, into which they plunged, praying aloud to the Almighty for mercy and succour in their dire extremity. The scene which followed, it is impossible for me to depict, little groups formed in the lea of the boat of wives and children clinging to their husbands and parents, the irresistible current swept past till they disappeared in the deep, either shot down by the sepoys' muskets, or mercifully engulfed by the river. Others driven frantic, rushed madly hither and thither in wild despair in the hope of eluding the fire of the murderers till exhausted or shot, death relieved them of their agony, and the sacred Ganges claimed their mortal frames. In their insatiable thirst for blood and plunder, the rebels pursued the fugitives, breast deep in water, while from the more humane shouts could be heard to the ladies that they sought not their lives, nor those of their children, but the foul butchery that was being perpetrated by their comrades sufficiently gave them the lie and the appeal was unheeded. At this crisis I was hit on the right shoulder by a musket ball.

For a moment I felt bewildered and helpless, and knew not what to do under the circumstances; death was certain, and the idea of attempting to escape never entered my mind. Some others, like myself, stood hopeless and resigned by the side of the boat being unarmed, unable to make any resistance. Suddenly my eyes fell on Bhairo issuing from the side of the boat, with my poor brother's only child in his arms, imploring the mob to spare her life and that of her mother, who followed, both apparently severely wounded. 'God help them', I exclaimed in an agony of grief, and sprung up into the boat, resolved to sell my life. I hastened in for my rifle and revolver which were near the stern, but both were in the possession of the enemy; hurrying back I came upon Captain Fitzgerald whose wife and child were clinging to him weeping bitterly, and besought him to give me the musket he held in his hand, but he was too agonised to attend to my appeals, and I turned round to search elsewhere, when I seized one from the hands of an Eurasian drum-mer, who was that instant emerging from beneath the floor, and dashed astern, where the sepoys were looting. I appeared just in time to see the thatched roof of the enemies' boat alongside left, and the hairy chest of a powerful sepoy stand displayed before me, a score of muzzles protruded simultaneously at my feet, quick as thought I levelled my piece, without shouldering, and discharged the contents into his breast. He fell with a heavy thud, and the roof dropped with him leaving me an interval to re-load. I had not, however, time to snatch a percussion cap from the ammunition box, before I was forced to beat a retreat. I rushed from one side to the other in search of a cap, but could find none, nor could I obtain one from any of those who still lingered in the boat; feeling myself helpless and incapable of defending myself, my heart sickened at the sight of the wounded and dying, and a feeling of horror seized me at the thought of the torture and mutilation that awaited them, and of which I too might be a victim. I flung the useless musket aside and hastened to fly from the boat, when my first thought was that, if struck, I should find a peaceable end in the water and escape the terrible possibility of being wounded and captured. On my way out my eyes fell on a gourd which lay in a corner in my path, instinctively I seized it and sprang overboard. The gourd had been captured floating down the river the day before by a servant, who had carefully stowed it away for an emergency; little did I imagine at the time that it would prove of service to me. Casting a last look at the boat, and the struggling groups in the water, I turned my head, sickened at the sight, towards midstream and swam out with all my might to get out of range.

Swimming strongly, Jones struck out for midstream. The shrieks of terror from the boats receded and he knew he was out of immediate danger. He swam with more leisurely strokes, floating from time to time to conserve his strength and keeping tight hold of the precious gourd that buoyed him up. He wondered whether he might catch up with the leading boat that had floated over the sand bar. Then a fierce storm broke, with torrents of rain lashing the water into choppy waves. Little fish pestered the wound in his shoulder and he was in constant fear that he might attract the attention of an alligator. As the gourd kept filling with water he had to empty it. He felt his strength ebbing away; then, just as he felt certain he must drown, again and again, as if by divine providence, he found his feet touching ground and he was able to rest and recover his breath. After what seemed like many hours in the water the large outline of the boat came into sight and with one last desperate effort he swam out to try to reach it.

Silently he came up to the boat where all was still as death. An indescribable gloom seemed to hang in the air. 'How did it go with you?' whispered two or three voices as he floundered alongside, unable to raise his numbed hands to climb on board. 'All, I'm afraid, killed,' he replied. They helped him aboard. Exhausted, he threw himself down on a mattress and slept, only to be wakened by a heavy splash as Conductor Rohan's body was consigned to the deep water.

> With heavy hearts we proceeded on our voyage; the day was beautiful with just enough cloud to temper the sun's fierce heat, and the night's rain had completely altered the parched aspect of the landscape. All nature seemed to smile in its serenity and beauty, contrasting strangely with our wretchedness and misery; hunted as we were more like wild beasts than civilized beings, and forsooth but six weeks before the masters of the land. The villagers too seemed to repose in profound peace, as if ignorant of the revolution that convulsed the Empire. The change from the awful excitement of the past and unusual quiet reigning around us was wonderfully soothing as we smoothly glided down the river without the sound even of a ripple to break the silence: it was the first quiet day that we had experienced after the terrible ordeal of the past fortnight, for which, I am sure, we were all heartily grateful.

In the afternoon the high cliffs of Kusam Khor came into sight and to avoid attack from that village the boat steered towards the Oude bank, only to find a group of forty or so wild-looking men standing in silence watching. Once again the boat was driven on to a sandbar. Jumping out, the hunted men struggled to drag it into a deeper channel that would lead to the main stream. Men from Kusam Khor had crossed to an island and were approaching to attack, when to the surprise of the desperate men struggling with the boat the Oude villagers raised the alarm and four Thakurs swam across and helped to pull the boat through. Oude had a reputation for lawlessness and allegiance to the old Moghul empire. It had come under Company rule only in the last twelve months. Yet here were these villagers seeming to be genuinely friendly with offerings of milk and cooked food. Their chief, Balgobind, conferred with the party and it was arranged that his villagers would guard the

Gavin Sibbald Jones, 1865.

boat overnight and then with the protection of a new crew of boatsmen
it could proceed next day. Thankful for this unexpected good fortune,
the Fatehgarh fugitives prepared to sleep. But they were desperately
cramped, seventy-five in a boat built to accommodate twenty. Jones's
wound was now festering, his back and shoulders were burnt and blis-
tered by the sun. Unable to get comfortable, he decided to try to find
somewhere ashore more comfortable to sleep and rest.

Stepping ashore I asked the first man I met if he would conduct me to his village and procure me some food. Bhabhutising Thakur, who proved a staunch friend afterward, the individual interrogated, readily replied 'han, challo' (yes, come on), and leading the way bade me follow in the pitchy darkness along the narrow footpath, skirting the fields. Ten minutes' walk brought us to his humble hut; seating me at the foot of a tree, my kind-hearted host walked into his house and fetched me out a *thali* (brass dish) of *dal* and *chapaties* (thick lentil soup and hand-bread), which had been prepared for himself and placed it before me, bidding me eat. It was an unusual and very bold proceeding on the part of the Rajput thus to disregard the prejudices of his high caste, by offering a Christian food in a vessel he used himself, aware of the prejudice of the Hindus, and the hostility such an act was likely to provoke among his caste brethren, I showed my reluctance to take advantage of his kindness, which would subject him to the necessity of a course of purification to render the vessel fit for his use again, by refusing to eat out of it, and desired him to transfer the contents into a platter of leaves, stating my reasons for suggesting the change. The man was evidently pleased and not a little surprised, and smiling at my considerate request, observed to the bystanders, 'the sahibs, too, understand our prejudices,' a remark which was received with expressions of approval. It was a great point gained, and I determined to make the most of my fortuitous success: so after satisfying the cravings of hunger, I asked my host if he could find me a charpoy to enable me to rest for the night, the ground being too damp to lie on. After a little search one was produced. It was an old rickety discarded piece of furniture in tatters and otherwise uninviting in the extreme; but on the principle of never to look a gift horse in the mouth, I gratefully accepted it and tried to find relief on it. Such, however, was out of the question; to begin with, it was a foot and a half too short for my long body, and the loose broken stringing hung like a sailor's hammock under my weight, the hard grass cordage cutting keenly into my tender back. Nevertheless it was better than the wet ground, and I was comparatively safe from the attacks of creeping vermin which make repose on mother earth so dangerous at this time of the year. Oh, for a little straw I sighed; but such a luxury was beyond the resources of the little village, and sleep refused to visit my eyes; it was impossible, without something to alleviate the roughness of the grass cordage which buried itself into my tender flesh, to find repose, and I was terribly tired, and longing for a little sleep before I rejoined the boat. I struggled in vain against the difficulties; at last I got up in despair and begged some of the men to fetch me anything in the shape of straw; to ask for a sheet or bedding of any kind was out of the question. One of them walked off to an old deserted hut and fetched me an armful of thatching, the only material procurable, and spread it thickly over the charpoy. Those who know what rough stuff thatching grass is to lie on with a bare back will form some idea of its comfort, nevertheless, it was a decided improvement, and overcome by sheer exhaustion, I fell into a deep sleep, in spite of the attacks of myriads of mosquitoes that swarmed about me. At midnight a heavy hand on my shoulder shook me to consciousness, and the jingling of steel ramrods about me roused me thoroughly. Starting to my feet, I asked what was the cause of the warlike preparations. 'The Colonel sahib had sent for you to join the boat at once,' was the answer. I arose at once to follow, the idea occurring to me that perhaps the Colonel had determined to clear the coast before the hostile natives were up; but on rising to walk I found I was stiff and sore and almost incapable of exertion; not even the prospect of being left behind, aroused me to make the effort to get to the boat. Callous and indifferent, I fell back on my straw bed, and bade the messenger to inform the Colonel that I was unable to join him. After the absence of a few minutes the man returned with a more urgent request for me to return to the boat at once, as he was about to leave; but I felt too weak and indifferent about myself to heed the warning, and dismissed the messenger to say that I could not join him. The good-hearted old Colonel, however, appeared unwilling to abandon me, and fearing that I might be detained by treachery, despatched the man a third time; this time armed with a note; happily for me the man got mixed up in a fray on his way to the village and lost the letter, and the boat cast off without me. It subsequently transpired that the presence of the boat had attracted the villagers from the neighbourhood, who, from cupidity, assumed a hostile bearing, showing a strong disposition to overpower and loot the boat. Observing this tendency, the Colonel determined to quit the place, particularly as Balgobind seemed powerless to restrain his own people. The sight of a few hundred rupees (Rs 1,100) paid to some boatmen engaged for the voyage – a large sum in the eyes of the villagers – brought matters to a climax, and the intruders fell to looting the small band that had engaged to go down with the boat and proceeded to attack the boat; when the lashing was severed and the outrage prevented, the boat glided down safely enough; but, alas! to meet its doom later on at Cawnpore, where every soul, over seventy-five in number, of the unhappy fugitives perished by the hand of the execrable Nana and his minions.

Next morning the profound and strange quiet of the village, and the absence of familiar faces which were wont to greet me, together with my own personal helplessness, produced a strong reaction, and contributed to make me feel the utter desolation of my condition. I was a stranger among men, in whom love of money and thirst for blood had extinguished the nobler sentiments of humanity. Any reckless vagabond, wishing to gain the favour of the Nawab and reap a handsome reward, might with impunity strike off my head and carry it off triumphant to that chief. Being separated from friends and relations, with not the remotest prospect of ever seeing them again, oppressed my thoughts and depressed my feelings beyond control. 'Why did I in a moment of weakness throw away the only chance I had of life?' It seemed strange inexplicable infatuation, and I could not help upbraiding my folly. No longer able to restrain my feelings, I retired to the darkest corner of the hovel and sought relief in tears, and consolation in prayer to the Almighty Father who had thus far wonderfully preserved me, when so many of my friends and companions had perished violently. At this moment Balgobind unexpectedly and unperceived entered the shed, and noticing my plight the Brahmin was evidently touched with compassion; taking me by the hand gently, he said, 'Weep not, no man dare touch a hair of your head, while Balgobind has a drop of blood in his body.'

Life in the little village of Terah was gloomy and monotonous. Shut off from any news of events in the outside world, Jones shared a dilapidated shed with the cattle. He was wracked with fever from his suppurating wounds, plagued with sandflies and mosquitoes and exhausted by the hot clammy weather of the early monsoon. One of the Thakurs made him an ointment of oil, wax and charcoal of herbs, but it was no relief. Eventually a puppy he had befriended by offering it scraps of food licked clean his wounds. This gave some improvement. Occasionally there was a visit from Balgobind to relieve the solitude.

Balgobind, who was a shrewd, sensible fellow, had throughout unswervingly maintained that the arms of the British would ultimately triumph, which I often thought was said to me by way of consolation; but as our intimacy grew closer, I was tempted to ask him his reason for entertaining such favourable views of our situation. The simple but sagacious Brahmin looking me full in the face, and nodding his head significantly, replied – 'Listen, our countrymen have neither wisdom nor leaders competent to turn their advantages to account'; moreover, he added 'they are destitute of justice and truth; they had imbued their hands in the innocent blood of women and children. Ram will never prosper their cause.' A few days after this conversation I was surprised to see Balgobind walking up to my hut at an unusually early hour, his countenance beaming with pleasurable excitement, which he was hardly able to suppress. 'Khush ho,' said he, 'khush ho, ab ayeh' (rejoice, rejoice, they have arrived) alluding to the advance of the Europeans under the immortal Havelock, who had driven out the Nana and his hordes and recaptured Cawnpore

This news had a marked effect. Jones noticed that the men of the neighbouring village who had scarcely deigned to notice him were now lavish in their attentions. Now a message came from Hardeo Buksh suggesting that Jones make his way secretly to rejoin him where Edwards and Probyn were concealed. Taking Balgobind into his confidence, Jones discussed the whole scheme and together they worked out the best method of escape from the village. Balgobind promised to mislead the villagers as to which direction they had set off.

The guide having appointed a rendezvous under a solitary bush in the middle of a large open field took his leave and bade me join him after dark when the villagers retired to rest. I retired to the darkness and smoke of my quarters earlier than usual, and patiently watched the long hours till the last of the villagers gathered up his *hukah* and *chillum* (pipe) and left the village *chabutra* (raised platform) for his hut, quietly I slunk out of my hiding and dropped myself over a low wall which screened me from observation, and following the direction given me by the guide, made my way to the spot indicated, where I found him waiting with a pony for my accommodation. I mounted without loss of a moment, and we hurried away as fast as the inundated state of the country and the pace of my steed, which was never beyond a walk, permitted, avoiding by circuitous

by-paths every village that lay on our road. The howling and bark-
ing of the village dogs at our heels caused us no little uneasiness, lest
the noise might alarm the villagers and send them in pursuit; our
fears, however, were groundless, for the slumbering villagers paid
no heed to the noise, such alarms of dogs not being unusual (to
disturb the midnight repose of the slow aryan brother). We passed
on undiscovered and unchallenged in the bright moonlight that
lighted our path, the brilliancy of which we often felt we could
dispense with with more safety to ourselves.

After an uncomfortable hour's ride with feet dangling without stir-
rups they abandoned the ponies and pushed on by foot, feeling their way
cautiously through flooded fields and ravines until they came to a plateau
where there were cattle grazing. A group of fierce-looking herdsmen
came and demanded to know who they were and where they were going.

'Who are you?' asked the foremost as we neared him. 'Hardeo
Buksh's sepahi,' answered the guide. 'And who is that with you?'
inquired another as he deliberately walked up to me and removed
the blanket off my face to scrutinise me. Not satisfied with the
guide's evasion. 'Ha! Ha! Ha! Ha!' laughed out the fellow, half in
jest, half in derision as he discovered a white face. 'Is this the fellow
who was with Balgobind at Terah?' 'The same,' I replied, finding
it useless any longer to maintain the disguise. My prompt reply
evidently tickled them, and to my surprise won their sympathy,
for the man immediately added with a mixture of commiseration
and contempt – 'Jao, bhagaya' ('Go, you have escaped'), and good-
naturedly tapping me on the shoulder . . . bade us adieu.

Thankful to leave such dangerous friends behind, they hurried on,
anxious to reach Dharampur, Hurdeo Buksh's headquarters, before
dawn. They arrived at three o'clock. Cautiously the guide led the way
through the winding footpaths to the entrance. Here they were joined
by a second man and they secretly crept along until they reached the
Ramgunga and crossed over in the ferry to the village of Khasowra.
Dawn was breaking as they swam the last *nullah* and Jones found himself
once more with his own countrymen. It was Edwards, who with the
Probyns had been in hiding for two months. Writing afterwards in his
Personal Adventures, Edwards described the meeting:[2]

I was roused this morning before dawn by a noise in the enclosure,
and on looking up saw a tall spectral looking figure standing before

me naked, except a piece of cloth wrapped round his waist, much emaciated and dripping with water. I recognised him as young Mr Jones, who, Hurdeo Buksh had informed us, had been saved from the boat captured by the sepoys. He had until then been hidden in one of Hurdeo Buksh's villages, and, in consequence of the good news, of the successful advance of our troops, had been permitted to join us. He was very weak, and when I recognised and spoke to him, burst into tears at hearing his own language again, and seeing one of his own countrymen.

The welcome given to Gavin Jones was full of kindness. Probyn provided him with an old shirt and trousers. Mrs Probyn, almost broken with the hardships of her situation and anxiety for her little children, busied herself to prepare a little cooked food. After two months of living in hourly fear of death this comparative security was like the gift of life and all the hardships experienced seemed for the moment to be buried in the joy of being rescued and with friends. One evening as the little group of fugitives prepared for sleep Jones began softly to sing 'Old Folks at

Gavin Jones's pants: 'This is the only clothing I escaped with when I swam for life from the boat captured by the rebels in which we attempted to escape to Cawnpore, 4 July 1875.'

Home'. It may have been the quality of his fine Welsh voice or the poignancy of their situation, with memories of all they had once known and enjoyed, but they were all deeply moved and never heard the song again without recalling the singer and the circumstances of that night.

The days and long nights at Khasowra dragged out in fearful suspense, alternating between hope and despair, waiting, waiting for news of the restoration of the Company Raj that would make escape possible. It was a time of rumours and inflammatory proclamations put out by the rebel leaders calling up all rajahs, *talookdars* and chiefs in Oude to join in the extermination of the common enemy, with large rewards offered for the heads of the Englishmen. Hardeo Buksh, who had been so determinedly loyal, now came under great pressure from his relatives who considered they stood in danger of losing their ancestral rights and possessions for his act of 'madness' in harbouring the English. Hardeo Buksh warned the fugitives never to show themselves by daylight in the little enclosure outside their rooms and to keep strict guard at night, and have guns and pistols always ready beside them.

At last news came of Havelock's arrival in Cawnpore but this was followed by a rumour that the Gwaliors were advancing on Agra and that Delhi was abandoned. On 22 August Hardeo Buksh visited them again, full of apprehension and insisting that they must now escape while there was still time. He had heard that the common people had been stirred up by the proclamation and were thirsting for revenge against the English. The river now was in full flood and offered a comparatively safe route and Hardeo Buksh promised to supply a boat. All agreed to make the attempt to reach Cawnpore.

The fugitives sent a secret message to Havelock. Written on a tiny scrap of paper with a small stub of precious lead pencil dipped in milk to render it invisible, it was rolled inside a quill, sealed at both ends and carried in the mouth of the messenger. It was dangerous work; their messenger reported having seen three men caught carrying messages for Europeans blown away from rebel guns. General Havelock in his reply urged them to remain in hiding a little longer as the rebels infested nearly all the roads and made travelling dangerous. But after months cooped up the longing for action was too strong and all decided to take their chance on the river.

They rose early. It was Sunday, dull and rainy, the boat ready moored at the Ramgunga and crowded with its eleven matchlockmen and eight boatmen all provided by the good Hardeo Buksh and placed under the command of Pirthi Singh. The Probyns took one last long look at the

A talookdar of Oude.

spot where they had buried two of their infants, the only piece of dry ground they had been able to find. For several miles Hardeo Buksh accompanied the boat on horseback along the bank. He had taken the precaution of seizing the ferry boats plying across the Ganges so that as the boat made its way along the Ramgunga to the Ganges it would not be intercepted. When finally he took his leave he warned them on no account to expose themselves to view. With protestations of thanks for his bravery, hospitality and practical help, they parted from their benefactor.

The change and near prospect of joining friends was most gratifying, our hearts were light, and looked alone to the bright side of things, casting all fears and gloom to the winds, as the boat sped along on the swift flowing Ramganga; the banks were narrow and brimful to overflowing, so that our boat stood level with the land, but as we were passing through Hardeo Buksh's villages we had nothing to fear, and enjoyed the fresh air and speed of our motion through the inundated scenery around us. At about twenty miles from our start-ing point the boat missed the main channel, which the boatmen failed to avoid, as the flow was too swift to pull past the cross current, which bore us away almost in the twinkling of an eye ever a rapid, on the edge of which we stranded, and ran the imminent risk of being wrecked. It was a most trying moment for us all, as we dare not leave our concealment, and for five or ten minutes the boat seemed to be forced higher and faster on the bar by the rushing water, which stood piled up in a high wave on one side, giving her an uncomfortable angle; the boatmen were utterly helpless, as they could obtain no foothold in the rushing water, to land and help her off, so there we remained tilted dangerously on one side, the water roaring and surging fiercely around us with great force. The torrent, however, which was a source of such dread, proved our best friend, for it rapidly scoured away the land from beneath the boat, and every now and again the boat gave an uneasy jerk, bumped heavily, and gradually worked her way through the bar by a series of rapid thuds which threatened destruction, ending at last in a plunge, and we glided into deep water to our infinite relief and the joy of the men, who simultaneously cheered '*Jaim jai, Ganga Maye*' (Blessed be Mother Ganges). On we sped at the rate of five or six miles an hour down the winding channel without further mishap, thankful to have escaped a danger no one had anticipated.

Now, once again, they found themselves approaching the unfriendly heights of Kusam Khor. This time the river was in full flood and the boat stood out in midstream, a safe distance from musket fire. The men crowded at the ferry challenged them, 'Who are you?' Pirthi Singh stood up and shouted that he was taking his family to Tirwal Pallia, a village further along. They yelled to him to pull ashore and a voice called out, 'You have *feringhis* (Europeans) on board!' The Thakur had a ready answer: 'I wish we had and we should soon dispose of them and get their plunder.' Cries of 'Stop and come ashore' were repeated but the river was flowing so swiftly the boat was soon out of reach and no pursuit was attempted.

At about ten o'clock that night the boat reached the rendezvous where Hardeo Buksh had arranged for a Rajput chief, Dhanna Singh, to meet them and convey them on the last most dangerous part of their journey. The boat *luggaoed* midstream to an island overgrown with grass and *jhow*. Here under cover of darkness the boatmen cooked themselves some food and Jones and his party walked about, stretching cramped limbs and discussing how far they could trust their new protector. They knew from his reputation that he had carried out many armed attacks, raiding villages in the Doab. Hardeo Buksh had impressed upon Dhanna Singh that his dacoity and looting expeditions would draw retribution and severe punishment upon himself once the British were back in power, but if he saved the lives of these fugitives he would earn a pardon and a handsome reward. Dhanna Singh pledged his honour as a Rajput to convey the party safely to Cawnpore.

Dhanna Singh's wild appearance gave some cause for alarm. Self-possessed and confident, he took his place in the boat, his flowing beard tinged with grey, his physique wiry and athletic. From the folds of his waistband he took out a dagger which he sheathed and unsheathed, toying with it as everyone watched him uncomfortably. Then in a gesture of friendliness he passed it round. As Edwards admired its fine workmanship he could not help wondering how many victims it had claimed.

The boat floated smoothly along. Dhanna Singh's name, called out in a powerful harsh voice, satisfied any challengers. Edwards records:

At one village, however, much embarrassment was caused by the party challenging being intimate with Dhanna Singh, expressing great satisfaction at his arrival, begging him to come ashore and take them on board. Dhanna Singh showed great readiness and presence of mind in this difficulty. He answered the hail with great apparent cordiality, and, telling the rowers to stop pulling, began asking questions about different persons and places; he thus held the party in conversation till we had floated well past the village, when he called out that he could not stop just then, as he wanted his family to be at the ghat in time to bathe before the morning, but that on his return in two or three days he would make a point of stopping in the village. On saying this he ordered the men to give way as fast as possible, and we passed on without further notice.

Soon they passed Mendhi Ghat, the indigo factory where Gavin and John Moore Jones had been living when they fled to Fatehgarh for safety. It was a dangerous spot, the chief ferry into Oude. The passengers were afraid they would be detected but a heavy bank of cloud swept across the face of the moon and in the darkness the boat slipped safely past.

Ten miles further on was Bithoor, the stronghold of the Nana Sahib, bristling with his soldiers and guns. The sun shone down from an un-clouded sky. Suddenly rounding a corner the boat was close under a high cliff, so close to the soldiers ashore that Edwards and Probyn held a hand across the children's mouths for fear they would speak and give them away. The Muslims were celebrating the Mohurrum festival with hundreds of men loitering round the buildings on the high bank firing off their *feu de joie*. Fortunately Dhanna Singh was known to the Nana's men and he called out to the challengers reassuring them with friendly warnings to beware the 'goras' – the European soldiers – who were in force below Bithoor. Meanwhile the boat sped on its way.

The excitement and anxiety while passing Bithur was intense. We were within a few miles from our own people, and half an hour would see us out of the reach of the merciless enemy, yet the slightest suspicion might have wrecked all our hopes and expecta-tions in a moment. Much of our good fortune was due to the loyalty of Hardeo Buksh's men, and the admirable manner in which Dhanna Singh acted his part, coupled with the fact that he was but recently a noted rebel himself. Thus disarming all suspicion of the character of the expedition, and under God's providence we escaped unharmed from the midst of all danger. After leaving Bithur a couple of miles behind us, the spire of the old church at Cawnpore came in sight in the distance, sending a thrill of joy into our hearts, which filled us with the most grateful expectations. It was impossible to realise that we had run the gauntlet for a hundred and fifty miles and were at last within sight of our own people. The danger, however, was not yet all past, a strong west wind had sprung up and blew us across the river close under the lea of the Oudh shore, in spite of the efforts of the rowers, and revealed to our astonished gaze the camp of the rebels within musket range, who occupied the road to Lucknow, and were massed along the river shore to oppose the crossing of the British force. The sight of the boat created quite a stir among the sepoys, and we could hear the drums beating and bugles sounding the alarm, and expected every moment to be intercepted, but not a shot was fired, and we escaped past with nothing worse than an unpleasant fright. Soon after the old magazine was sighted, and we could see a picket of Sikhs scrambling down the heights, evidently greatly excited, for they were loading their muskets and taking up positions of vantage at the water's edge. We had been mistaken for the enemy, as friends coming down the river in these times was out of the question, and they were ready to give us a warm reception; but before a shot was fired, observing their hostile proceedings, Probyn lifted his sola hat off his head and waved it to the men who, fortunately for us, recognised the British head-dress, and Wazir Singh, Mr Edwards's faithful servant, hailed them in their own dialect, informing them who we were. The native officer in command and all the men then came forward to congratulate us on our escape, at which they seemed as heartily rejoiced as if they had been our own countrymen.

The Sikhs gesticulated and grinned with delight, describing to each other how they were on the point of firing into us, seeing the matchlock men on the top of the boat, whom they took for rebels, when the sight of the sahibs in the front revealed who we were and prevented a catastrophe. We therefore congratulated ourselves that Cawnpore was entered in broad daylight, and not in the darkness of night when the consequences might have been disastrous under the circumstances, for we could not have communicated with them before mischief was done. The Sikhs gave us directions where to proceed, and that we should find the troops entrenched a couple of miles lower down, below the steamer, which we should find moored on the way.

They landed at 2 p.m. on 31 August, the first boat for over two months that had appeared on the river. They had run the gauntlet for more than 150 miles of river-way through the midst of the enemy's territory. A picket of HM's 84th Regiment was on duty at the *ghat* and hands reached out to steady them as they stepped ashore to warm greetings and congratulations. The Probyn children were lifted up and carried tenderly up the bank to where Sherer, the acting magistrate – Cawnpore being under military rule – held office in a small tent.

Sherer barely recognised them in their Indian attire. Jones carried his arm in a sling, Probyn looked starved and in poor health. Edwards, in sheer relief, fainted and fell to the ground. They heard for the first time of the terrible events that had taken place at Cawnpore, how the entire European population – about 1,000 people – had taken shelter in General Wheeler's hastily prepared entrenchment where they had withstood the attacks of the Nana Sahib's army for twenty-one days in the height of the hot weather. And how when the old general had accepted truce terms from the Nana Sahib for safe transport to Allahabad, he and his force while boarding the boats at Suttee Chowra Ghat had been treacherously slaughtered, only four men surviving to tell the tale. Many of the women and children were taken captive to the Bebee Ghur where only hours before Havelock arrived to rescue them they were massacred and their bodies thrown into the well. Jones hardly dared to ask the fate of the earlier fugitives from Fatehghar and heard that not one had survived. As they were led to rooms at Mahomed's Hotel they could scarcely believe that out of that large number of people, men, women and children, all known to them, they four with the children were the sole survivors.

Mahomed's Hotel had been the Nana Sahib's headquarters and only a hundred yards from the Bebee Ghur. They were shown the room in which the Nana had slept and another room, fitted up with *choolhas* for cooking his food. When they found themselves in a house again for the first time in three months they instinctively knelt down to bless God who had so wonderfully delivered them from death.

Jones ends his story of his escape from Fatehgarh with a sad tribute to Bhairo, the man who had been his brother's devoted servant for over twenty years. Bhairo had remained in concealment at Fatehgarh but when he learned that Gavin Jones was alive and in hiding at Terah made preparations to help him escape to Agra. He procured clothes for disguise and borrowed a few rupees from fellow servants, but the very day he planned to set out he was seized with an attack of cholera and died.

2

Suppression of the Uprising
1857 - 1859

___

Cawnpore under Military Occupation

Gavin Jones found himself in a Cawnpore under military occupation. When Havelock's army entered the city the Nana Sahib had withdrawn to Bithoor and now Havelock's immediate objective was to march to Lucknow to relieve the Residency and prevent a disaster mirroring the fate of Cawnpore under General Wheeler. General Havelock set out for Lucknow, followed by General Neill and later General Outram, their advance made possible by the construction of a bridge of boats fording the Ganges at Cawnpore and the creation of a strong entrenchment to guard the approach to it. The line of communication for supplies and reinforcement coming up from Calcutta was vital.

The senior civilian was J.W. Sherer, who had accompanied Havelock's army when it entered Cawnpore to find the women and children imprisoned at the Bebee Ghur had been slaughtered and their bodies, 'the living with the dead', cast into the well. Sherer, with no official recognition, had to keep a low profile, confining himself chiefly to negotiating with sympathetic Indian merchants for the supply of food. Captain Herbert Bruce had been put in charge of the city and cantonment with the specific duty of raising a military police force. The entrenchment with a force of about 500 men was under the command of Colonel Wilson.

At a point a little upstream of where the Lucknow Bridge stands today, work on the bridge of boats commenced. A small steamer went back and forth and the river was surveyed. The main stream ran fast on the Cawnpore side but on the Lucknow bank there were three sandy islands with deep 30-foot-wide channels between them. Grass was trodden into the mud and wooden platforms stored from the old bridge dragged across the sand. Boats had to be found and boatmen persuaded

Anchor from Havelock's bridge of boats: at the old H & S superintendent's bungalow.

to position them at anchor before timber could be laid across them. Crommelin, the man in charge, worked night and day, up to his waist in water often under fire, until at last the causeway consisting of seventy-five boats was complete. It was many weeks, however, before it was strengthened sufficiently to take the weight of heavy artillery.

The entrenchment guarding the bridge on either shore was strongly constructed with well-planned earthworks – a very different affair from Wheeler's entrenchment. Every coolie in Cawnpore seemed to be at work; men were paid four annas a day, women two annas and even children capable of carrying a basket earned six pice a day. Over 7,000 people were involved. Bales of cotton were built into the ramparts, a host of different containers, even soldiers' knapsacks were filled with earth and stacked up into the breastworks. Mowbray Thomson, Delafosse, Sullivan and Murphy,[1] the four survivors from Wheeler's entrenchment and the treachery at the boats, returned to Cawnpore as heroes. Thomson was put in charge of the fortifications of the entrenchment and Delafosse joined Bruce in raising a police force. They returned to work as if nothing extraordinary had happened to them.

The length of the entrenchment to the north was guarded by the River Ganges while to the south a huge area in front of the entrenchment was cleared of ruined buildings and trees to prevent surprise attack, with one or two buildings alongside fortified as outposts. From the entrenchment there was a clear view to the low line of buildings along the main street and the only object standing in the foreground was the temporary wooden cross over the well at the Bebee Ghur. The small defensive force was camped under canvas within the entrenchment.

Twelve days after Jones reached the safety of Cawnpore, Bruce wrote a report to General Outram setting down all he had been able to do to establish order within Cawnpore and the outlying districts.[2] Sherer describes the first time he met Bruce. He came into his tent dressed in khaki[3] and holding out his hand, introduced himself: 'I am Herbert Bruce, I hope we shall be friends and work cordially together.' Sherer found himself looking into pale blue eyes in a colourless face. Everything about him was pale from his khaki uniform to his light coloured hair under an ash-coloured helmet. But it was his air of determination that impressed Sherer most.

To quote from Bruce's report to Outram, dated 12 September 1857:

Upon the arrival of General Havelock at Cawnpore, about 10 days before I took charge, Mr Sherer, the Collector of Futtehpore, who had accompanied the force from Allahabad, raised a small temporary Police by aid of the respectable Mahajuns of the City, just of sufficient strength to aid in procuring supplies for the Army.

4 The great difficulty was in getting men; for influential persons who had taken no part in the rebellion against us held back at this early stage of our re-occupation.

5 I had some trouble in raising a sufficiency of men, which I accomplished through the aid of those of the large neighbouring Zemindars who reside in the City, and a week after I assumed charge, the City and Cantonment Police had been completed to its original strength, and has since been working successfully.

6 Simultaneously with the above, steps were taken to collect as much of the plundered European property as possible, this property was strewed over an area of 70 square miles of country, every house had been gutted and every lane and street was overspread with every description of European goods.

7 An immense deal of this property has been saved, that which can be recognized is put aside for restoration to the owners, or sold for

Portrait of Sir Henry Havelock.

the benefit of deceased estates, and the rest disposed of by Public Auction.

8 A proclamation was then issued by General Neill, threatening even the punishment of death to any person who after the expiration of one week was discovered to have European plundered property in possession, this order had an excellent effect, quantities of things were found placed out in the streets for the first 3 nights after the issue of the order, and it also assisted us in adjusting cases in which plundered property was subsequently seized.

9 The Assembly Rooms was chosen as a fit place for all this property to be massed, and Lieutenant Delafosse of the 53rd was placed under me to look after it, and superintend the sales which are still going on.

10 Besides the above recovered property, I have seized, confiscated, and sold the property of the Principal Citizens who joined the 'Nana' and are now absent, taking care that articles relating to either the Commissariat or Ordnance, were handed over to those Departments. A great deal of valuable property has been thus secured, and the proceeds of the sales carried to Government credit; the work has not yet ended, although most of the principal cases have been disposed of. . .

17 An intelligence department was organized and has been improving on its working ever since, but no one knows better than yourself the difficulties of obtaining reliable information, especially in a country where a great many of the inhabitants are against us, as well as the mutinous troops.

18 I believe however that the information which has from time to time been supplied has been generally correct, good, and timely, and that both Generals Havelock and Neill are satisfied with the efforts that have been made.

19 The Police arrangements having been completed for the city, Cantonments, and Suburbs of Cawnpore, I was on the 26th August directed by General Havelock at the suggestion of General Neill, to extend the Police arrangements into the adjacent Purgunnahs, which had been quite out of our control, all the old Police having either joined in the rebellion, or been destroyed by the rebels, and the Civil Authorities had not succeeded in replacing them.

20 The task was one of some difficulty, because General Havelock was unable to detach troops to aid, and even those of the Zemindars in the districts who had taken no part against us, appeared to think that the time had hardly arrived for active co-operation.

21 The first place I took in hand was Bittoor, because not only was the dread of the 'Nana' there, very great, but independent of this the place itself is looked upon as unsafe, by reason of the Ganges just above being almost fordable in the autumn, and I know that if I succeeded there, I should be successful elsewhere; and secondly, because Bittoor was the place best suited for the application of my scheme, should the loyal people of the neighbourhood continue to hold back as I anticipated.

22 No one responded to my call for Police men, and I therefore set to work and enlisted 100 sweepers, appointing their Chowdrie, Thannadar of Bittoor. The object was this, the Bunggys elated beyond measure at the idea of being raised so high, did not demur at going to Bittoor, because they know very well that no good Hindoo or Mussulman even would run the risk of being killed by a sweeper in attacking them, whereas the lower castes have no scruples whatever in fighting any who may oppose them they have been doing well there ever since.

23 The effect was like magic, all thought that the system would be extended throughout the whole district, and if they did not afford zealous aid, they would in like manner be ruled by unclean men.

24 Next day I suppose at least 100 respectable persons were produced by the Zemindars, who promised to be security for all who were enlisted in the Police, and in three or four days from the time, I was ordered to extend my jurisdiction, strong Police posts had been radiated into those of the surrounding Purgunnahs, I was ordered to look after, and we are now able to command supplies, and in fact the resources of the country to a considerable distance. . .

32 The next question is confiscation of landed estates. Many of the large and influential Zemindars who have rebelled have houses and valuable property in the Chief Cities, these together with any credits in the hands of the Bankers as regards Cawnpore, have been confiscated and the proceeds credited to Government, but still no one possesses power over the estates, and the holders though absent and in open rebellion against the Government, are still realizing the rents and thus providing themselves with the means of prolonged opposition to Government. I applied to Mr Sherer, the Senior Civilian, upon this subject but he informed me he had no power to alter the existing system regarding landed registration.

33 Doubtless it may require time to re-organize a revenue system, but at any rate the payment of rents should be suspended to people who are openly and notoriously hostile to us.

34 The system of public sales of lands in satisfaction of decrees is unquestionably telling against us very much now, for it is not in India as elsewhere that money and influence go together, hereditary rights give a political weight and influence which no money can purchase, and the men who are doing us most mischief now are those who have been sold up, and the auction purchasers who are generally loyal are of no use in this crisis. . .

35 The few men who have been able as well as willing to aid us most here, are those who have retained their feudal influence as well as their estates. . .

38 In conclusion, I beg to mention that in all the work I have carried out here, I was only aided by one Native, who was made over to my by General Neill.

39 I believe this man, Tussildar Pursaud Narain, afforded valuable aid in organizing the new Police and re-establishing order at Allahabad, and I can safely say he has performed excellent service here. I was stranger to this part of the country, and all the former Civil and Police Officers, both European and Native had either been killed or had fled with the 'Nana' and the first great difficulty was to find one or more trustworthy employees. Pursaud Narain has been most zealous throughout, and I beg to recommend him to notice, and hope his exertions may be rewarded by immediate promotion.

Bruce went on to recommend that no man should be enlisted 'who will not eat in Messes like the Seikhs', arguing that this would lessen the amount of baggage on the march by about fifteen cooking pots a man, which would reduce the carriage of a regiment by fifty camels. He considered two cooks should be allowed to each company. He also summed up his policy of employing low-caste men. 'There is no Native Government which would exalt them and if we once give them a position they would very soon see that the only way of maintaining it is by fidelity to the only ruler who would dream of upholding them.'[4]

Major Anson's Account

Major O. H. St G. Anson, a first cousin of Major-General George Anson, who had been Commander-in-Chief at the time of the uprising at Meerut, marched with his regiment, the 9th Lancers, along the Grand Trunk Road. Delhi had been recaptured from the mutineers and now the Lancers, accompanied by the Sikhs and the artillery, were dispersing the enemy in the Doab as they advanced to join forces with Havelock for the relief of Lucknow.

In Cawnpore they camped on the Grand Parade, the old cavalry parade ground, the camp extending over a huge area from Christ Church to the Subadar's Tank. First came a vast congregation of camels,

*Mutineers surprised by Her Majesty's 9th Lancers on the march from Umballa to Delhi:
Captain G. F. Atkinson,* Campaign in India 1857-58.

a wonderful confusion of vehicles and animals with a motley crowd of
camp followers in attendance – this in response to an urgent request for
camels and *hackeries*. Then came the Sikh Cavalry, the Sikhs black-
bearded, broad-shouldered and slender-limbed, fine-looking people
dressed in a wonderful diversity of costume and armed with a variety of
Oriental weaponry. These were followed by the lines of the 9th Lancers,
the Bengal Artillery and the European Foot, horses neatly picketed
nibbling at their fodder, tents pitched in streets.[5]

Anson's wife and children were up in the hills, at Kusauli.. It was
seven months since he had seen them; he tried after each day's long
march to write every day, 'scratching away at a letter with the perspira-
tion streaming and the ink drying up at the end of every second word'.[6]
There was no *dak*, no postage stamps; the only means of smuggling a
letter through the rebel lines was to bribe a man with a donkey to stuff its
saddle with letters. So many poor fellows had been caught, however,
and punished by having their hands and noses cut off, that few would
attempt it. Yet many letters got through and were lovingly preserved.

Like every European soldier writing from Cawnpore, Anson first described the horrors of the Bebee Ghur and the astonishing vulnerability of Wheeler's entrenchment. But he also described other aspects of Cawnpore.[7] Anson and his wife Frances both knew it well. It was where they had been married and where her father Colonel James Manson had settled in retirement after many years as commissioner in Bithoor with Bajee Rao, the ex-Peishwa of Poona. In fact Anson had been married in Cawnpore twice, both times at Christ Church, the building where his father-in-law James Wemyss of the Bengal Civil Service had presided over the laying of the foundation stone.

Camp Cawnpore
October 27th, 1857

Yesterday I went to see the house where so many of our unfortunate women and children were murdered. It is a low, flat-roofed house, about 100 yards to the left front of the assembly-rooms, close to the northern gateway of the general's house.[8] It is a villainous-looking place, and will be more famous in history than the Black Hole of Calcutta. We saw lots of remnants of gowns, shoes, and garments dyed in blood, and blood upon the walls in different places. Outside in the compound there was a skull of a woman, and hair about on the bushes. Oh! what pain, and grief, and fear must have reigned there! Oh! what tearful eyes and aching breasts must there have throbbed! From there I went to see Sir H. Wheeler's entrenchment, and found it to be our old hospital surrounded by a trench. Such despicable cowards, however, were the awful savages, that what would have taken us a couple of days to level with the ground, they in twenty-two days damaged only the exterior walls of, very few of their shot penetrating the outside wall. Our fire from the entrenchment seems to have kept them completely at bay, and had not provisions and ammunition failed, they would have held out till H.'s arrival. This morning I walked to see the Spiers' house,[9] and a most melancholy sight it presented. The trees all round scorched and killed by the tremendous blaze of the bungalow, which, with its fine verandah, pillars still standing, looked noble in its very desolation. From there I went to your old house, to the gate of it, for I did not venture in, being all alone, walking with only a stick in my hand. It was in an admirable state of preservation, and lots of people were cutting the grass in the compound. Further than this I did not go, much as I wished to see the Wemyss's

Ruined hospital in General Wheeler's entrenchment.

house; it was hardly safe for a lone European, unarmed, to go so far. . . *Wednesday, 28th* I should like you to see the assembly-rooms and compound. In the latter are carriages and buggies of every sort, and howdahs and palanquins, and broken-up furniture. In the former there is every conceivable description of household property and clothing, from the magnificent pier-glass to a mouse-trap. We are now to halt here, or just on the other side of the river, till the arrival of Sir Colin Campbell on the 1st or 2nd prox. Nearly 400 of the 93rd Highlanders arrived yesterday. It is an uncommonly fine-looking regiment, in splendid discipline.

Camp Cawnpore
Thursday, October 29th, 1857

I walked through the Gwaltolah bazaar this morning to the magazine, and found the bazaar in good order, except here and there where a house had been looted. It is the nicest most shady, and respectable bazaar in Cawnpore. The magazine presented a most ruinous spectacle, the buildings inside being all more or less tumbled down, and the strong wall of the place itself in some parts laid low. The compound inside was filled with the *débris* of magazine stores. When I surveyed the surroundings of the place I came to the con-clusion that Wheeler was quite right in not shutting himself up in it.

Lucknow

Troops fresh from England began rapidly pushing up country to Cawnpore to gather under Sir Colin Campbell, the new Commander-in-Chief. Havelock and Outram, with only 3,179 men and 14 guns, had fought their way through the narrow streets of Lucknow, suffering severe losses in their struggle to rescue the defenders of the Residency; but while they had succeeded in reaching the Residency they in their turn were surrounded and besieged. Sir Colin Campbell planned a second relief.

The 93rd Highlanders and an advance party of Sir William Peel's Naval Brigade were among the first fresh troops to arrive at Cawnpore. Lieutenant George Cracklow, of the Royal Artillery[10] was amused at the impression they created:

> The 93rd Highlanders have arrived and form a subject of intense delight and astonishment to the Sikhs who have never seen anything of the sort before, they say that the Bagpipes are the Lungee-Baja (that is War Music) and at once applied to their Commanding Officer to be supplied with them as also the Highland bonnets which divide their admiration with the Pipes. Their astonishment at the Highlanders had hardly subsided when Peel's Naval Brigade with the Heavy Guns arrived. The tall hairy old Sikhs could not make out these square-made oddly dressed little sailors and said they must be the spirits of the women who were murdered come back to avenge themselves.

Major Anson did not hold such a good impression of the Highlanders:

> I cannot keep the Highlanders and other troops of sorts out of my buggy in the line of march. They fall out, pillage some mess or officer's hackery, get drunk, and then tumble into the first conveyance they find on the road. So great and shocking have been the irregularities committed that the Commander-in-Chief has ordered a roll-call every two hours, and two parades a day, and enjoined the provost-marshals to the rigid performance of their duty.

Marching with the 93rd Highlanders and the 9th Lancers when they set out for Lucknow was Lieutenant Frederick Roberts of the Bengal Artillery, a tiny figure, little taller than a boy. This was the future field-marshal. The fact that he had been born in Cawnpore and was to win the

Roberts winning the VC at Khudaganj, 2 January 1856: by R. Caton Woodville.

VC near Cawnpore made it possible in years to come, during his campaigns in Afghanistan and the Boer War, for the Cawnpore mills to cultivate this association and ask his patronage from Government for orders of Army uniforms and supplies.[11]

When Campbell finally fought his way through to the Residency in Lucknow and joined up with Havelock and Outram, the immediate priority was to evacuate the women and children and wounded from Lucknow and send them down river to Calcutta. Roberts was among those who first met the defenders. He summed up his impressions:

> The more I saw, the more I wondered at what had been achieved by such a mere handful of men against such vast numbers. It was

specially pleasant to me to listen to the praises bestowed on the officers of my own regiment, of whom nine were present when the siege commenced, and only one escaped to the end unwounded, while five were killed or died of their injuries. Of the other three, one was wounded three different times, and both the others once.

All were loud, too, in their praises of the Engineer officers. During the latter part of the siege the rebels finding they could not carry the position by assault, tried hard to undermine the defences; but our Engineers were ever on the watch, and countermined so successfully that they were able to frustrate the enemy's designs on almost every occasion.

The wonderful manner in which the Hindustani soldiers held their ground, notwithstanding that they were incessantly taunted by their mutinous comrades for aiding the Feringhis against their own people, was also much dilated upon.

The casualties during the siege were extremely heavy. When it commenced on the 1st of July, the strength of the garrison was 927 Europeans and 765 Natives. Of the former, 163 were civilians – brave and useful, but untrained to arms; of the latter, 118 were pensioners, many of whom were old and decrepit. Up to the arrival of Outram and Havelock (a period of 87 days), 350 Europeans and 133 natives were either killed or died of wounds and disease. Of the noble and unselfish conduct of the ladies and soldiers' wives, every-one spoke in the highest terms and with the warmest appreciation. They suffered, without a murmur, the most terrible hardships; they devoted themselves to the sick and wounded in the hospital, and were ever ready to help in any way that was useful. Two ladies were killed, and nine died, during the siege.

The contemplation of the defence of Lucknow, and the realiza-tion of the noble qualities it called forth in the defenders, cannot but excite in the breast of every British man and woman, as it did in mine, feelings of pride and admiration.[12]

In recognition of this the Union Jack was never lowered at night.

The Evacuation to Cawnpore

Arrangements for the evacuation from the Residency and the march escorting the women and children to Cawnpore, on the first stage of their journey to Allahabad and safety, took several days to complete. On 27 November the twelve-mile column of wheeled carriages, with elephants, camels, bullock carts, grasscutters' ponies and *doolies* with the wounded, was ready to set out. The families were carefully guarded; Major Anson's letter of 25 November 1857 shows how fraught with danger the operation was.

> The very great work of relieving the garrison of Lucknow is so far complete. Both yesterday and to-day have been very busy days. The labour of removing 428 women and children, besides some 1,000 sick and wounded, has been immense, and attended with no little risk. We had not evacuated the Martinière fifteen minutes to-day before it was swarming with Pandies[13] like a nest of ants. The same with Dilkooshah. The Commander-in-Chief's column arrived here yesterday; Outram's to-day. I arrived in camp here yesterday at 7 p.m., having been the whole day out, and at 1 a.m. this morning I returned to the Dilkooshah on escort duty, and formed, with others, the rear guard of Outram's column. The Pandies followed us up for about half a mile, and then ceased to molest our formidable array of British troops. Poor General Havelock died about eleven o'clock yesterday, at the Dilkooshah, and was buried here this morning. He died of an acute attack of dysentery, brought on, I verily believe, by running nearly three-quarters of a mile, under fire, from the residency, to meet the Commander-in-Chief, and greet him as his deliverer. His son, poor fellow, is terribly cut up by the blow. We march to-morrow *en route* to Cawnpore with the ladies, &c., &c., and sick and wounded.

The joy of the rescued women and children was tempered with the sad news of Havelock's death. The story was often told of how Jessie Brown, a sergeant's wife, lying sick with fever in the Tykhana, the huge, cool underground chamber at the Residency, crowded with women and children, had been the first to hear the thrilling sounds of Havelock's bagpipes and started up with 'Dinna ye hear them? Dinna ye hear them? the pipes of Havelock!'[14] Havelock had been immortalised by the first relief of Lucknow. Worn out by the campaign, he had died of dysentery and was buried at Alumbagh, a walled garden on the outskirts of Lucknow. There is hardly a cantonment town in India even today that does not have a Havelock Road.

OVERLEAF: *Arrival at Cawnpore of the relieved garrison of Lucknow, 28 November 1857. Print by T. McLean 1859, after Sarsfield Green.*

But the march had its lighter moments. A sergeant of the 93rd High-landers, William Forbes-Mitchell, was on guard duty at Bunnee Bridge, as the convoy moved off from Lucknow, to see all the baggage carts safely across and was witness of an amusing incident.[15]

A commissariat cart, a common country hackery, loaded with bis-cuits, got upset, and its wheel broke just as we were moving it on to the road. The only person near it belonging to the Commissariat Department was a young *baboo* named Hera Lall Chatterjee, a boy of about seventeen or eighteen years of age, who defended his charge as long as he could, but he was soon put on one side, the biscuit-bags were ripped open, and the men commenced filling their haversacks from them. Just at this time, an escort of the Ninth Lancers, with some staff-officers, rode up from the rear. It was the Commander-in-Chief and his staff. Hera Lall seeing him rushed up and called out: 'O my Lord, you are my father and my mother! what shall I tell you! These wild Highlanders will not hear me but are stealing commissariat biscuits like fine fun.' Sir Colin pulled up, and asked the *baboo* if there was no officer present; to which Hera Lall replied, 'No officer sir, only one corporal, and he tell me, "Shut up, or I'll shoot you, same like rebel mutineer."' Hearing this I stepped out of the crowd and saluting Sir Colin, told him that all the officers of my company were wounded except Captain Daw-son, who was in front; that I and a party of men had been left to see the last of the carts on to the road; that this cart had broken down, and as there was no other means of carrying the biscuits, the men had filled their haversacks with them rather than leave them on the ground. On hearing that, Hera Lall again came to the front with clasped hands, saying 'O my Lord, if one cart of biscuits short, Major Fitzgerald not listen to me, but will order thirty lashes with provost-marshal's cat! What can a poor *baboo* do with such wild Highlanders?' Sir Colin replied: 'Yes, *baboo*, I know these High-landers are very wild fellows when hungry; let them have the bis-cuits'; and turning to one of the staff, he directed him to give a voucher to the *baboo* that a cart loaded with biscuits had broken down and the contents had been divided among the rear-guard by order of the Commander-in-Chief. Sir Colin then turned to us and said: 'Men, I give you the biscuits; divide them with your comrades in front; but you must promise me should a cart loaded with rum break down, you will not interfere with it.' We all replied: 'No, no,

Sir Colin, if rum breaks down we'll not touch it.' 'All right,' said Sir Colin, 'remember I trust you,' and looking round he said, 'I know every one of you,' and rode on. We very soon found room for the biscuits until we got up to the rest of the company when we honestly shared them. I may add that *baboo* Hera Lall Chatterjee is still living, and is the only native employee I know who served through the second relief of Lucknow. He now holds the post of cashier in the offices of Messrs. Neill and Co., of Clive Ghat Street, Calcutta, which doubtless he finds more congenial employment than defending commissariat stores from hungry wild Highlanders, with the prospect of the provost-marshal's cat as the only reward for doing his best to defend his charge.

Action against the Gwaliors

The Commander-in-Chief had set out for Lucknow leaving General Windham in Cawnpore to command Colonel Wilson's force of 500 men. His instructions were explicit: Windham was to play only a defensive role, guarding the bridge of boats and the vital line of communications. Then disquieting news came in. The considerable army of the Gwalior Contingent, a crack force of Mahratta soldiers trained by Company officers, had been held loyal by the Maharaja, but now they had broken away. Joined by the rebels dispersing south after the fall of Delhi and the soldiers of the charismatic Rani of Jhansi,[16] the Gwaliors, led by the able General Tantia Tope, were rumoured to be approaching across the Jumna to join the Nana Sahib's forces and attack Cawnpore. Sir Colin Campbell gambled that he could relieve the siege of the Residency and return in time from Lucknow to prevent this.

Fresh convoys arrived daily at Cawnpore until there were over 2,000 troops camped in and around the entrenchment. Encouraged by the number of reinforcements and anxious to attack the Gwaliors before they joined the Nana and reached the city, Windham unwisely decided to disobey orders and take the offensive. He sent a letter to the Commander-in-Chief outlining his plan and seeking approval to go ahead, but the letter never reached Sir Colin Campbell. Windham meanwhile drew up plans for an attack.

On 26 November Windham fought a successful battle against the advance guard of the Gwaliors at Pundoo Nuddee, but as night fell his men found themselves six miles out of Cawnpore in a vulnerable position. Next morning they faced the might of the whole well-drilled Gwalior army with its powerful field artillery. Windham ordered the retreat but as the men came under murderous cannonade the retreat turned into a rout, with some of the younger, untried soldiers dropping their weapons and running for the entrenchment, much to the disgust of their Sikh companions. An old Sikh sirdar at the gate tried to halt the rush and panic and form them up into some sort of order. 'Don't run, don't be afraid, there is nothing to hurt you.' But as they pushed past him he shrugged in despair. 'You are not the brothers of the men who beat the Khalsa army and conquered the Punjab.'

Within the entrenchment as everyone hurried for shelter all was panic and confusion. Trains of elephants, camels, horses and bullock wagons came in at the main gate, all heavily laden. The fort covered three or four acres yet there was scarcely room to move. Around the scattered buildings within the entrenchment animals were tethered by stakes among huge piles of trunks, beds, chairs and an amazing assortment of furniture and baggage.

> Mounted officers were galloping across the rough ground between the inner and outer entrenchments, and doolie after doolie, with its red curtains down, concealing some poor victim, passed on to the hospitals. The poor fellows were brought in, shot, shattered, and wounded in every imaginable way; and as they went by, raw stumps might be seen hanging over the sides of the doolies, literally like torn butcher's meat... The surgeons who did their utmost, were so overworked that many sufferers lay bleeding for hours before it was possible to attend to them.[17]

At nightfall a handful of biscuits and some rum and water were served round for supper and the men slept on the ground rolled up in their cloaks, each man at his post. Only Windham remained awake, calm, conscious of the importance of holding the bridge. The city and cantonments were in the hands of the Gwaliors and they were able to bring forward their guns until the bridge of boats was within their range of fire. Next day Windham sent out a small detachment of 14 officers and 160 men under Colonel Wilson to spike these guns. Colonel Wilson and his men of the 64th Regiment planned to take the guns on the high ground above the Kacheri Cemetery by surprise attack, while the 34th Regiment was detailed to give them cover by guarding the bridge near the theatre.[18] The action that took place on the bridge is described by a young cadet of the 34th Regiment. He was eighteen; the fight at the Pandoo Nuddee had been his baptism of fire.[19]

In the early morning we were marched out by companies, and piled arms under some trees just beyond the glacis of the entrenchment. We were to have another hard day, it was said. Very soon came the command in a hoarse whisper, 'Fall in! Stand to your arms!' And off we marched, to occupy and dispute the passage of the main roads leading to the entrenchment. My regiment was stationed close by the bridge over a small stream, beyond which lay the church of Cawnpore – or, rather, its walls, for the church had been plundered and wrecked during the first defence under General Wheeler.

Company after company defiled right and left along the bank, and we comprehended that the stream was to be our line of defence, and this bridge the key of the position. On the far side of the stream extended a wide sandy plain, with no cover but the church walls and some mud huts, and clumps of trees at about 800 yards' distance, among which we could see figures moving. We were soon employed in making a barricade across the bridge-way by means of broken carts, with planks, railings, or whatever we could lay our hands on. I and some others were carrying the wheel of a cart to add to the obstruction, when whiz! a round shot came into the midst of us, and we fell about like a heap of wooden soldiers. I staggered to my feet again, much surprised at finding myself alive, and even more astonished that none of my comrades were hurt. We had been knocked over by the rushing wind of the shot, which must have passed right through the midst of us. Among the distant trees we could see the enemy's guns, which thenceforth kept up a steady fire on our position, and we watched the round shot as sometimes, after striking the ground, they came hopping towards us like lively cricket-balls.

'Arrah! the playful little varmints! they hops about like St Patrick's pig in a thunderstorm,' quoth an Irishman who was sitting close by under cover of a mud wall; when crash came one of the 'varmints' through the wall, knocking him head over heels, and breaking his fire-lock 'all to smithereens', as he expressed it, but without doing him any further injury. The fire grew hotter as the day wore on, and we on the bridge were ordered to lie down, while two Madras guns were brought up to return the fire, without much effect in checking that of our opponents.

Towards four o'clock we began to get the worst of it, and being largely outnumbered, our small force was driven in on both flanks. The enemy now came pouring down, and occupied the church on our left, where they brought a gun to bear on the bridge at close quarters, loading with grape, pushing the gun out round the corner to fire, and drawing it back to reload under cover. From the church, from the houses, from every available cover, the fire concentrated on the bridge, while our men replied with spirit, although we had many casualties. Three of our subalterns were hit, one killed. The noise of the firing, the shouts and cries, were terrible. The men, so long exposed to this terrific fire, began to waver.

'They are surrounding us!' came the cry.

'Never mind, my boys!' cried the Colonel. 'We've got to keep this bridge, if we die for it!' and he, standing up in the midst of the shower of bullets, lit a cheroot as quietly as if he had been at home. I admired that man, and he certainly gave us new courage. The hardest sort of fighting is to stand still and be shot at. One can fight or fire, but to do nothing is a severe ordeal for nerve and courage.

Our surgeon had established himself under cover of a mud wall hard by, and was tending the wounded as calmly as if he were in Netley Hospital. The Brigadier, General Carthew, was brought in to have his wound dressed, just as I was helping to carry one of our poor fellows who had been badly hit. I ran off to fetch water for him, glad to have anything active to do, instead of waiting passively among the bullets.

It was getting towards sundown when we got our orders to retire to the entrenchment. An Englishman does anything better than retreat, and when the order to fall back was given, most of the men ran for it; but they had held a difficult position under heavy and deadly fire during the whole weary day, and this disorderly retreat was covered by a small party of officers, non-commissioned officers, and a few of the best men. Fortunately, our opponents were not inclined for close quarters, and we all reached the fort in safety. How any of us survived that storm of death on the bridge is still a mystery to me, and the feeling of finding myself alive and unhurt that night was little short of ecstasy. In our regiment alone we had three officers killed and eight wounded, with a heavy list of killed and wounded among the men.

I shall never forget that Bridge at Cawnpore as long as I live. The bullets whizzed past as if the air was alive with them.

The young cadet was Thomas Lewin, who survived to tell the tale. Colonel Wilson was less fortunate.

The Gwaliors took possession of Christ Church and the Assembly Rooms and formed a complete cordon that stretched past the high ground at Kirk and Co.'s premises,[20] where four guns were hidden, past the old cemetery and Duhan's Hotel to the river. Their gunfire closed in on the outpost at Henry Martyn's church held by thirty men of the 64th Queens and threatened the entrenchment. Colonel Wilson had been sent out to spike the enemy guns.[21]

If Wilson had taken the road nearer the river, skirting the graveyard, he could have approached the Gwaliors' guns unseen. As it was, he chose the wrong turn and his men had to skirmish up the steep slope where they were quickly cut down. Wilson and six of his officers died with eighteen of his men, and many more were wounded. The firing was so fierce that the 64th were driven back and had to abandon the bodies of their companions. Wilson's body was found among the dead next day and brought into the entrenchment for burial, carried on a hospital doolie, 'reverently covered up, and attended by a favourite Portuguese servant'.[22] This was Manuel Xavier de Noronha It is not certain

M. X. de Noronha with wife Anna and children William and Mary.

what brought Noronha to Cawnpore – one source says that he came as a photographer from Goa, another that he had been state engineer at Tonk. There are several tales of his Mutiny exploits, that he saved the lives of eighty men, that he went out of the entrenchment unarmed to rescue a young wounded ensign calling out for water; but whatever the truth, in recognition of his loyal and gallant services, he was given a site in Sudder Bazaar. He built Manuel House and the Noronha family settled down to live and work in Cawnpore.[23]

A Taste of Battle

Padre Moore, chaplain to Windham's forces, had barely arrived in Cawnpore when the attack by the Gwaliors took place and he had to take refuge in the entrenchment. Here he had his first experience of warfare and living among rough soldiers. He saw 'scenes of blood and wounds and death, and encountered personal dangers, and heard the most blasphemous oaths such as fall to the lot of few reverend divines to experience'. He lived in a tent with a field gun only three yards from his bed but 'I am so used to the fire now that even a night attack does not disturb my slumbers'.

His main task was visiting the sick and burying the dead. Hastily improvised hospitals had been set up.

> 200 in hospital some 2 miles behind the Commander-in-Chief's camp. I went out this morning at 7 am, had 3 funerals there and did not get back to my tent until past 11 – breakfast – out again in my hospitals until 2.30. . . They continually fire upon me whenever my duty compels me to go outside beyond the ramparts for burial. No graves are dug and we cannot spare men from the rampart but lower the dead into old wells with my own hands and get my own spades and go round for volunteers to fill them in. Sick and wounded cannot have been less than 500.[24]

Padre Moore described conditions in camp. He lost all his supplies and books – 'no Bible or Prayer Book, 150 cheroots and a few bottles of Porter from the Commissariat indifferent meat' – but no amount of work tired him. He was undismayed by scenes of death and drunkenness: 'I am the most cheerful fellow in camp. I never felt happier in my life.' The behaviour of the troops within the camp, however, was a cause for anxiety. They broke open every place for drink: private stores and

Our Padre; *from* Curry and Rice *by Captain G. F. Atkinson, Royal Engineers.*

baggage were looted, even the hospital comforts were broken open and carried off. The whole place was a scene of direst confusion.

> ... All my wine, Brandy was stolen by Europeans. All my tables chairs 2 beds easy chair and book table, number of papers all my cooking vessels, 20 rupees in hands of Khansamah – I have saved 9/10 of my crockery, nearly all my clothes except what the dhoby had, communion plate and bed clothes, my hat and revolver which never leaves me, my Rifle (given me) my pony and saddle, since looted by Europeans.

But he ends his letter cheerfully. 'Fear not wifey. I am doing my duty to the best of my ability.'

When the chance to return into the town came once more he reported,

> The rebels have burnt every house they could fire, nothing has escaped except the Theatre which is pucka. The school room and

contents all burnt. . . House walls blackened, doors broken, holes in the walls where brackets torn down, plaster broken from 3 ft round the room, boxes and beds litter the place. Fireplace broken. Floor all broken by gun balls. . .

Another version corroborates Padre Moore's account. When events at Cawnpore reached the men camped outside Lucknow at Alumbagh, Francis Collins,[25] an assistant surgeon with the 5th Fusiliers, wrote home:

Alum Bagh Dec 5 1857 We have news that Sir Colin did not reach Cawnpore until they [the Gwaliors] had done considerable damage there. We hear that they got into the town and set the Assembly Rooms on fire in which were all our mess stores and regimental and private baggage, including our band instruments were stored. Everything is reported as destroyed that was left there. . . The baggage and stores belonging to our Head Quarters were originally left in the entrenched camp at Cawnpore, but were removed to the Assembly Rooms because there was not room for the large quantity of Commissariat stores and munitions of war, which had to be considered first. All regiments are suffering alike and there will be a great scarcity of clothing for some time to come.

Alum Bagh 7 January 1858 It is only by scraps that we hear of all the mischief the Gwaliors did when they made their raid upon Cawnpore. They did much plundering in the town and carried off the mess plate of the 90th Regiment, some of which is said to have been found in a well at Bithoor, the residence of that miscreant the Nana Sahib. . .

Amongst things our Regiment has lost at Cawnpore is our Drum Major's staff. . . captured from a French regiment at the storming of Badajos and since used by the regiment. The tassels also have been cut off our Colours. When our baggage was moved from the entrenchment, these things were placed in the guardroom under the charge of the guard. We are told that one day during the panic that occured when the Gwaliors attacked the station, the Drum Major's staff was found to have been cut in two, and the silver head stolen. The tassels were cut off our Colours at the same time. The 88th Regiment is said to have furnished the guard that day.

Among the many who crowded for shelter in the entrenchment was James Clement Jones and his country-born wife Caroline. Jones was a bandsman, a competent flautist, and he and his Anglo-Indian family had survived the massacre at Cawnpore by being disguised and hidden by a loyal servant in a nearby village. Caroline Jones, though illiterate, spoke English and being a good cook was put to work helping with the messing at the fort hospital. One day a cannon ball fell into the *dechi* in which she was cooking the rice, scattering the contents everywhere and terrifying the poor woman. Her husband, who was later put in charge of the bridge of boats, ultimately – by dealing in house property and real estate which was big business after the Mutiny – made enough money to establish himself in an auctioneer's business, Baker Anson and Co. It was his son, Albert, who later ran Baker Anson.[26]

Campbell to the Fore

For seven days the city and cantonment of Cawnpore was in the hands of the Gwaliors. They streamed into the narrow streets of the bazaar from the Kalpi Road and laid waste such buildings as were still standing. Meanwhile the Nana's forces approached from the old civil station at Nawabganj, alongside the river, through cantonments until the entrenchment was menaced and the bridge of boats in grave danger. The rebels made huge bonfires of the equipment stored in the Assembly Rooms and burnt Windham's hurriedly abandoned camp on the Kalpi Road, gleefully looting the kit. Christ Church and nearby houses where much property had been stacked were also set alight. They then directed their guns against the bridge of boats and a fireboat was sent downstream but somehow the attack on the bridge became dissipated by the wholesale destruction being wreaked on the town.

On the road from Lucknow, Sir Colin Campbell hurried on at the head of his convoy from the Residency. He had had no news from Cawnpore for ten days and now the ominous sound of distant heavy gunfire warned him that Windham was under attack. An urgent note written in Greek from Windham pleading for help was smuggled into camp. Windham reported that there had been hard fighting and his troops had been forced to retire within the entrenchment. There was a real danger they could not hold the bridge.

Lieutenant Roberts was sent ahead to ride as fast as he could to learn the exact position. The bridge, guarded by a small detachment, was still open but the men confessed to being 'at their last gasp'. He crossed into the entrenchment to seek out General Windham. Suddenly loud cheers broke out. The Commander-in-Chief, anxious and impatient, had followed closely behind Roberts and now, accompanied by his staff officers, appeared in person. The men, many of whom had fought under Campbell in the Crimea, clustered toward him, elated.

The morale in the entrenchment changed dramatically as defensive positions were taken up, piquets and outposts occupied. Campbell's own position was constantly under attack, fire rafts were floated one after another down the river, but over two days the entire convoy was brought safely across the river. By fortunate chance the enemy had not crossed the canal and the road to Allahabad was still open. After a few days' rest, while the rough country carts were prepared for the journey and while the children played with improvised toys, the survivors of the Residency set off with a suitable escort for the next stage of their journey to Allahabad. Freed from this responsibility Campbell made his plans to fight the Gwalior Contingent.

December 6th dawned a glorious winter's day, clear and cool with not a cloud in the sky, as the Commander-in-Chief prepared to do battle with the Gwaliors and drive them out of Cawnpore. Fresh reinforcements had arrived from Allahabad, including another Highland regiment that marched in, bagpipes playing. Campbell's army now numbered 5,000 infantry, 600 cavalry and 35 guns. He divided the infantry into four brigades supported by the cavalry and artillery, leaving Windham in charge of the entrenchment.

The army of the Gwaliors, 25,000 men with 40 guns, was camped at the junction of the Kalpi Road and the Grand Trunk Road. It was divided into two distinct bodies, the Mahrattas guarding the road to Kalpi and the Nana Sahib's troops holding the ground between the city and the river, covering the retreat to Bithoor. Tantia Tope was in overall command.

Campbell knew how to get the best out of his men. As they formed up in columns, hidden from the enemy by the half-ruined barracks, he rode up to tell them that the women and children had reached Allahabad in safety, that they were facing strong well-disciplined forces and he warned them that if they found casks of rum in the enemy's camp they must not touch a drop because it was reported to have been drugged.

The men paraded at 4 a.m. At 9 a.m. every gun in the entrenchment opened fire and at 11 o'clock the signal to advance was given. The enemy opened a tremendous cannonade, round shot, shell and grape, but colours in front, pipers playing, the line steadily advanced, determined to show the Gwaliors these were different men from those they met under

Mutiny Cavalry Attacking an Infantry Square at the Battle of Cawnpore: *from Charles Ball's* History of the Indian Mutiny. *Presented in 1937 to All Souls Memorial Church, Cawnpore, by Major-General C. S. B. Hay, Commander Lucknow District.*

Windham. A great fight took place to gain the crossing over the canal, in the face of thirty guns and outnumbered ten to one. The men showed their spirit by singing as they advanced a song made famous in the Crimea to the tune of 'The British Grenadiers'.

After crossing the canal and re-forming, the men came on the enemy's camp. The casks of rum stood invitingly knocked open but the troops resisted temptation and marched on. Now came the crucial action. On a huge open plain red-coated sepoys, unaware of the guns, formed into squares of brigades ready to face the cavalry, holding their fire until the cavalry were within 300 yards. But at the last minute Grant's order was shouted for the cavalry to wheel outwards and for Bouchier's guns, held in readiness, to fire into the squares. At a range of 250 yards the grape cut a swathe of dead five yards wide. Once the enemy realised they were facing the guns and not the cavalry they fled, pursued by both cavalry and infantry for fourteen miles. The enemy were routed, their camp, ordnance and thirty-two guns were captured, while Campbell lost only ninety-nine killed and wounded.

Next morning it was found the Gwaliors had left the city. When Campbell's men marched through the streets they met no enemy and

the townspeople came out with food and water, seemingly glad to
see the Europeans in occupation again. But while half the Gwaliors
had been defeated, those under the Nana Sahib had escaped towards
Bithoor and the tired troops were once more required to chase the
enemy. They set off along the Grand Trunk Road until word came
that the Nana Sahib and his army were attempting to cross the river
into Oude. The cavalry and horse artillery galloped through ploughed
fields to cut him off and advanced to the banks of the river. The Nana's
boat was the first to push off and got safely away but many waggons of
ammunition and a hundred carts filled with the plunder of Cawnpore
were taken.

That night the quartermaster divided a lot of shirts and underclothing
among the soldiers and they were allowed to go by wings to undress and
bathe in the Ganges. It was the first time for twenty-seven days that the
men had been able to take their clothes off their backs. 'The condition of
our flannel shirts is best left undescribed, while our bodies round our
waists, where held tight by our belts, were eaten to raw flesh. We sent
our shirts afloat on the sacred waters of Mother Gunga, glad to be rid of
them, and that night we slept in comfort.'[27]

In Cawnpore cannon balls no longer fell into the entrenchment but a
hectic air prevailed. It affected even the worthy Padre Moore, who had
been given orders to get the church ready for 800 men on Christmas
Day. He had acquired a buggy but no horse so he commandeered six
coolies to pull it.

Off to Brigade Major to get authority and permission to do according to my own sweet will – viz seize all the material I wanted. . . off
to the Collector to seize benches and timber etc. Church going on
bravely night and day, all my men gone, my house can wait. Got
bands together to practise hymns for Xmas Day. My decoration at
Church will be as good as last years at the Free School.

I have stolen all my wood. Dangerfield goes out and loots for
me.

Dangerfield has bought an old side board and table and 4 purdahs for 2/4 for me. I have bought Nickel's horse for 40/-, very old
but better than my tat.

I have as good singing as in any church in India – all are
volunteers from different regiments. The Band Master told me they
spent two hours every day in practice over the Te Deum, Jubilate,
hymns etc.

The Christmas Day service took place at 10.30 a.m. A tremendous congregation turned out – 'the natives are astonished to see 1,200 troops European, assembled at a Church twice burnt down in 6 months'. Young Lewin found the circumstances almost unreal.

It was with truly thankful hearts that we fell in for church parade on Christmas Day, and well do I recall the cheerful strains of the band playing, 'Hark to the merry Christchurch bells', as the Colonel walked through our open ranks making his inspection. The message of 'Peace and goodwill towards men' was read to us by the white-robed clergyman in the roofless church, whence, a short time previous, the rebels had trained their guns on the bridge, and I gazed curiously on the blackened and shot-torn walls of the building, which I had last seen filled with the dusky redcoated enemy, and sending forth volleys of fire and smoke. After the

The Revd Moore's drawing of Christ Church.

service, I with two or three more, went to the corner round which they had slewed on us that accursed 9 pounder gun. The marks of its wheels still showed plainly on the ground.[28]

Major Anson, who had spent three Christmases in Cawnpore, was not so impressed with Mr Moore as a preacher, accusing him of great insensitivity in preaching a charity sermon, rattling away asking the congregation to give their money to some coal and blanket association at home instead of giving them a sermon appropriate to the circumstances. But, Mr Moore did not care. He was doing a good trade in employing twelve men to make little crosses and confessed he could not keep up with the demand. Everyone wanted mementoes of the grisly events at Cawnpore.[29]

The Nana Sahib

The Nana Sahib was a hunted fugitive with a ransom on his head. Every man in Campbell's army dreamed of capturing him dead or alive. Rumours of sightings of him were constantly coming in and many expeditions were sent out to try to flush him out of hiding. He was said to be leading a wretched existence, seldom sleeping two nights in the same place, dressed as a fakir with his head all shaved. Lieutenant George Cracklow's letter is typical. It was written on 14 February 1858, from 'Seorajpore 20 miles from Cawnpore on the GT Road'.

I have been sent out after the Nana Sahib who is supposed to be trying to escape from Oudh to cross the Ganges somewhere near this and get thence to Calpee. We started again this morning at 3 o'clock and came into this place expecting to have a fight and everyone of us having privately made up his mind to catch the Nana himself, but as yet bad luck to the miscreant, we have seen nothing of him or his followers, he is supposed to have received intelligence of our being on the look out for him, and has not crossed yet. I do not think we have the slightest chance of catching him as the country is so covered with clumps of trees and high crops that a mounted man can disappear in a few minutes. . . The Nana is in rather a desperate way, he is about 5 miles from us, but on the opposite side of the river, all the Ghats and places where the river can be crossed are watched and we have lots of Troops in the vicinity on the look out for him, the only thing wanted is for him to cross. Sir Colin's force is on the opposite side of the river and I can't think why he does not attack him and either catch him himself or drive him over to us. The intelligence brought by our spies was that he intended coming over today, but our arrival had made him alter his plans. We have tolerably good information regarding him, he keeps a horse saddled night and day ready to fly, a 5,000 reward is on his head and altogether I think his life must be a burden to him.[30]

Having failed to capture the Nana Sahib, the troops were ordered to Bithoor to raze the Nana's palace to the ground. Lieutenant Roberts was one of the first to reach Bithoor, which, while not a large town, was a holy place and had associations with ancient Hindu mythology. For a brief period it had been the headquarters of the East India Company's civil administration of Cawnpore but more recently it had been the home of the ex-Peishwa of Poona, Bajee Rao, and his adopted son Nana Sahib, when he was settled there in exile at the close of the Mahratta wars. The Peishwa had brought with him many of his retainers and there were several handsome houses in the town decorated with wooden carvings in the style of Poona mansions. Roberts was surprised to find the palace in good order and virtually untouched. In one room he found letters written to Azimullah Khan, the Nana's chief adviser. Some were from his English fiancée, the girl he had met and courted in England, others from a Frenchman. There were even letters addressed to Constantinople written by Azimullah Khan but not dispatched, all of which seemed to indicate to Roberts that the Nana had been intriguing with the King of Delhi and the Nawab of Oude for the overthrow of the Company rule.

Tales of the fabulous wealth of the ex-Peishwa of Poona and the Nana Sahib were common gossip. Now, during the destruction of the palace, soldiers were given orders to empty the wells and search for possible treasure that had been hidden in them. Believing they would share in the spoils the soldiers worked with a will.

Rupees to the amount of thirty *lakhs* were recovered, which had been packed in ammunition-boxes and sunk in a well; also a very large amount of gold and silver plate and other valuables, among other articles a silver howdah which had been the state howdah of the ex-Peishwa. Besides the rupees, the plate and other valuables recovered were said to be worth more than a million sterling, and it was circulated in the force that each private soldier would receive over a thousand rupees in prize money. But we never got a *pie*! All we did get was hard work. The well was large. Four strong frames were erected on the top of it by the sappers, and large leathern buckets with strong iron frames, with ropes attached, were brought from Cawnpore; then a squad of twenty-five men was put on to each rope, and relieved every three hours, two buckets keeping the water down and two drawing up treasure. Thus we worked day and night from the 15th to the 26th December, the Forty-Second, Fifty-Third, and Ninety-Third supplying the working-parties for pulling, and the Bengal Sappers furnishing the men to work in the well; these last, having to stand in the water all the time, were relieved every hour. It was no light work to keep the water down, so as to allow the sappers to sling the boxes containing the rupees; and to lift three million rupees, or thirty *lakhs*, out from a deep well required considerable labour. But the men, believing that the whole would be divided as prize-money, worked with a will. A paternal Government, however, ignored our general's assurance on this head, on the plea that we had merely recovered the treasure carried off by the Nana from Cawnpore. The plate and jewellery belonging to the ex-Peishwa were also claimed by the Government as State property, and the troops got – nothing! We had even to pay from our own pockets for the replacement of our kits which were taken by the Gwalior Contingent when they captured Wyndham's [*sic*] camp.[31]

Back in Cawnpore Major Anson indulged in a little quiet looting on his own account but he justified it to himself on the grounds that the house and contents had originally been the home of his wife. He wote to her describing his visit there:

> Nawaub Gunge, Cawnpore
> Saturday, December 19th, 1857
>
> ... I went to your old house yesterday morning, and bore away from the walls four handsomely carved Fenoose-holders and three or four punkah ornaments. Since they were the wretch Nana's property I had the less scruple in taking them. In the little corner bottle khana on the left as you enter, there had been a grand smash of bottles, and of a cabinet holding them. I was very nearly meeting with the reward of looting, for, just as I was about knocking off another Fenoose holder, I discovered that a lot of bees had made their nest behind it, so I let it alone. I went into every room of

the house so familiar to you, and found it in better order than I
expected. I have taken three or four pleasant walks in the Company's garden, which, as you may imagine, is fast becoming a wilderness, though it has been so well cared for that it is still most
attractive in its adversity. The Tank, with its pretty trees all around
and within, looks still like a spot that fairies would choose for a
moonlight dance in.

Nothing now remains at Bithoor of the Nana Sahib's palace save a
high brick wall, once enclosing the Peishwa's estate, and a huge well,
possibly the very well from which the thirty lakhs were recovered.
However from time to time objects that had been associated with the
Nana Sahib made their appearance in England and found their way into
museums. But he himself was never captured.

'Jamie Green'

Towards the end of February Campbell had collected sufficient stores
in his advanced fortified camp at Alumbagh to set out to strike what
he hoped would be the final blow, to capture the city of Lucknow
and end the campaign. Convoy after convoy carrying provisions and
military equipment for the anticipated siege had come into Cawnpore
and pushed on to Alumbagh. The length of the bullock trains was sometimes as long as three miles. Lewin counted no less than 1,400 camels and
900 carts in one such convoy.
Cawnpore itself was humming with activity:

Cawnpore is full of the bustle of Military preparation, the engineers
are at work building the Fort barracks, Railway and houses.
Thousands of men are employed making tents, saddlery, harness,
and preparing guns and ammunition for the Troops. The bridges
have been made over the river and the stream of guns, waggons,
carts, soldiers, horses and men scarcely ceases night or day. We shall
have about 15,000 Troops in the Field, put the Camp Followers at
three times that amount which is a very low average and you will
then be able to fancy what provisions for such a multitude for a
month must be.[32]

Approaching Lucknow, Campbell's army 'massed in front of the
doomed city and lay like a huge boa constrictor coiled and ready for its

spring all along the road from Cawnpore to the Alumbagh'. On that road the 93rd Highlanders were camped at Unao where an incident took place that puts one in mind of Kipling's famous verse from 'The Ballad of East and West'.

> Oh, East is East, and West is West, and never the twain shall meet
> Till Earth and Sky stand presently at God's great Judgement seat;
> But there's neither East nor West, border, nor breed, nor birth,
> When two strong men stand face to face, though they come from
>   the ends of the earth!

A man came into camp selling plum cakes. His handsome intelligent looks and clean white clothes indicated he was no usual camp follower but his basket was carried by a villainous-looking coolie. Sergeant Forbes Mitchell called the 'plum-cake wallah' into his tent where the man sat down and eagerly read the English newspapers, explaining away his excellent English by saying he had served as mess *khansama* in an English regiment and been taught in their regimental school. He gave his name as Jamie Green and the coolie's as Micky, an Irishman whose mother 'belongs to the regimental bazaar of the 87th Royal Irish and he lays claim to the whole regiment including the sergeant major's cook for his father'. But next day the news broke that Jamie Green, the plum-cake wallah, had been arrested as a spy from Lucknow and Micky the coolie was one of the butchers at the Bibee Ghur. They were both to hang.

By chance the two prisoners were brought to Forbes-Mitchell's tent and left in his safe keeping all night. Some of the guard made to taunt the prisoners and break their caste by forcing them to eat pork, but Forbes Mitchell angrily prevented it. Something in the bearing of Jamie Green had touched the Scottish soldier's heart. He made up his mind to remain awake all night but, while guarding them carefully, to give the prisoners every possible freedom and consideration for their last night on earth. He unbound their hands to enable them to make their devotions and sent for food from the Mahomedan shopkeepers. When the shopkeepers heard the circumstances they insisted on providing the food free. The prisoners ate well, hookahs were called for and the two men talked long and intimately. Jamie Green protested he was no spy but an officer in the Begum of Oude's army, her chief engineer who had come out to reconnoitre and assess the strength of the siege train.

There must be many Indian families living in Kanpur today whose forebears lived through the terrible days of the Mutiny, yet I have not been able to find anyone who has family legends to tell about those

'JAMIE GREEN' 69

experiences. This story of Jamie Green comes as near to answering many of the unanswered questions about the Nana Sahib and his involvement with the massacre at Cawnpore and it comes across very movingly in Forbes-Mitchell's own words.[33]

'My name is Mahomed Ali Khan. I belong to one of the best families of Rohilcund, and was educated in the Bareilly College, and took the senior place in all English subjects. From Bareilly College I passed to the Government Engineering College at Roorkee, and studied engineering for the Company's service, and passed out the senior student of my year, having gained many marks in excess of all the European pupils, both civil and military. But what was the result? I was nominated to the rank of *jemadar* of the Company's engineers, and sent to serve with a company on detached duty on the hill roads as a native commissioned officer, but actually subordinate to a European sergeant, a man who was my inferior in every way, except, perhaps, in mere brute strength, a man of little or no education, who would never have risen above the grade of a working-joiner in England. Like most ignorant men in authority, he exhibited all the faults of the Europeans which most irritate and disgust us, arrogance, insolence, and selfishness. Unless you learn the language of my countrymen, and mix with the better-educated people of this country, you will never understand nor estimate at its full extent the mischief which one such man does to your national reputation. One such example is enough to confirm all that your worst enemies can say about your national selfishness and arrogance, and makes the people treat your pretensions to liberality and sympathy as mere hypocrisy. I had not joined the Company's service from any desire for wealth, but from the hope of gaining honourable service; yet on the very threshold of that service I met with nothing but disgrace and dishonour, having to serve under a man whom I hated, yea, worse than hated, whom I despised. I wrote to my father, and requested his permission to resign, and he agreed with me that I, the descendant of princes, could not serve the Company under conditions such as I have described. I resigned the service and returned home, intending to offer my services to his late Majesty Nussir-ood-Deen, King of Oude; but just when I reached Lucknow I was informed that His Highness Jung Bahadoor of Nepal who is now at Goruckpore with an army of Goorkhas coming to assist in the loot of Lucknow, was

Queen Akutar Mahall, aged sixteen, Nauwab Raunaq-Ara Begum of Oude. Photo Ahmed Ali Khan, Lucknow, 1855.

about to visit England, and required a secretary well acquainted with the English language. I at once applied for the post, and being well backed by recommendations both from native princes and English officials, I secured the appointment, and in the suite of the Maharaja I landed in England for the first time, and, among other places, we visited Edinburgh, where your regiment, the Ninety-Third Highlanders, formed the guard of honour for the reception of his Highness. Little did I think when I saw a kilted regiment for the first time, that I should ever be a prisoner in their tents in the plains of Hindustan; but who can predict or avoid his fate?

'Well, I returned to India, and filled several posts at different native courts till 1854, when I was again asked to visit England in the suite of Azeemoolla Khan, whose name you must have often heard in connection with this mutiny and rebellion. On the death of the Peishwa, the Nana had appointed Azeemoolla Khan to be his agent. He, like myself, had received a good education in English, under Gunga Deen, head-master of the Government school at Cawnpore. Azeemoolla was confident that, if he could visit England, he would be able to have the decrees of Lord Dalhousie against his master reversed, and when I joined him he was about to start for England, well supplied with money to engage the best lawyers, and also to bribe high officials, if necessary. But I need not give you any account of our mission. You already know that, so far as London drawing-rooms went, it proved a social success, but as far as gaining our end a political failure; and we left England after spending over £50,000, to return to India *via* Constantinople in 1855. From Constantinople we visited the Crimea, where we witnessed the assault and defeat of the English on the 18th of June, and were much struck by the wretched state of both armies in front of Sebastopol. Thence we returned to Constantinople, and there met certain real or pretended Russian agents, who made large promises of material support if Azeemoolla could stir up a rebellion in India. It was then that I and Azeemoolla formed the resolution of attempting to overthrow the Company's Government, and, *Shook'r Khooda!* we have succeeded in doing that; for from the newspapers which you lent me, I see that the Company's *raj* has gone, and that their charter for robbery and confiscation will not be renewed. Although we have failed to wrest the country from the English, I hope we have done some good, and that our lives will not be sacrificed in vain; for I believe direct government under the English parliament will be more just than was that of the Company, and that there is yet a future before my oppressed and down-trodden countrymen, although I shall not live to see it.

'I do not speak, *sahib,* to flatter you or to gain your favour. I have already gained that, and I know that you cannot help me any farther than you are doing, and that if you could, your sense of duty would not let you. I know I must die; but the unexpected kindness which you have shown to me has caused me to speak my mind. I came to this tent with hatred in my heart, and curses on my lips; but your kindness to me, unfortunate, has made me, for the second time since I left Lucknow, ashamed of the atrocities committed during this rebellion. The first time was at Cawnpore a few days ago, when Colonel Napier of the Engineers was directing the blowing up of the Hindoo temples on the Cawnpore *ghat,* and a deputation of Hindoo priests came to him to beg that the temples might not be destroyed. "Now, listen to me," said Colonel Napier in reply to them; "you were all here when our women and children were murdered, and you also well know that we are not destroying these temples for vengeance, but for military considerations connected with the safety of the bridge of boats. But if any man among you can prove to me that he did a single act of kindness to any Christian man, woman, or child, nay, if he can even prove that he uttered one word of intercession for the life of any one of them, I pledge myself to spare the temple where he worships." I was standing in the crowd close to Colonel Napier at the time, and I thought it was bravely spoken. There was no reply, and the cowardly Brahmins slunk away. Napier gave the signal and the temples leaped into the air; and I was so impressed with the justness of Napier's remarks that I too turned away, ashamed.'

On this I asked him, 'Were you in Cawnpore when the Mutiny broke out?" To which he replied: 'No, thank God! I was in my home in Rohilcund; and my hands are unstained by the blood of any one, excepting those who have fallen in the field of battle. I knew that the storm was about to burst, and had gone to place my wife and children in safety, and I was in my village when I heard the news of the mutinies at Meerut and Bareilly. I immediately

OPPOSITE: *Robert Napier (later Lord Napier of Magdala) with his ADC at Lucknow during the Mutiny (detail). Photograph Felice Beato, courtesy of the National Army Museum.*

hastened to join the Bareilly brigade, and marched with them for Delhi. There I was appointed engineer-in-chief, and set about strengthening the defences by the aid of a party of the Company's engineers which had mutinied on the march from Roorkee to Meerut. I remained in Delhi till it was taken by the English in September. I then made my way to Lucknow with as many men as I could collect of the scattered forces. We first marched to Muttra, where we were obliged to halt till I threw a bridge of boats across the Jumna for the retreat of the army. We had still a force of over thirty thousand men under the command of Prince Feroz Shah and General Bukht Khan. As soon as I reached Lucknow I was honoured with the post of chief-engineer. I was in Lucknow in November when your regiment assisted to relieve the Residency. I saw the horrible slaughter in the Secundrabagh. I had directed the defences of that place the night before, and was looking on from the Shah Nujeef when you assaulted it. I had posted over three thousand of the best troops in Lucknow in the Secundrabagh, as it was the key to the position, and not a man escaped. I nearly fainted; my liver turned to water when I saw the green flag pulled down, and a Highland bonnet set up on the flag-staff which I had erected the night before. I knew then that all was over, and directed the guns of the Shah Nujeef to open fire on the Secundrabagh. Since then I have planned and superintended the construction of all the defensive works in and around Lucknow. You will see them when you return, and if the sepoys and artillery men stand firmly behind them, many of the English army will lose the number of their mess, as you call it, before you again become masters of Lucknow.'

I then asked him if it was true that the man he had called Micky on our first acquaintance had been one of the men employed by the Nana to butcher the women and children at Cawnpore in July? To this he replied: 'I believe it is true, but I did not know this when I employed him; he was merely recommended to me as a man on whom I could depend. If I had known then that he was a murderer of women and children, I should have had nothing to do with him, for it is he who has brought bad luck on me; it is my *kismut*, and I must suffer. Your English proverb says, "You cannot touch pitch and escape defilement," and I must suffer; Allah is just. It is the conduct of wretches such as these that has brought the anger of Allah on our cause.' On this I asked him if he knew whether there was any truth in the report of the European women having been dishonoured before being murdered. '*Sahib*,' he replied, 'you are a stranger to this country or you would not ask such a question. Any one who knows anything of the customs of this country and the strict rules of caste, knows that all such stories are lies, invented to stir up race-hatred, as if we had not enough of that on both sides already. That the women and children were cruelly murdered I admit, but not one of them was dishonoured; and all the sentences written on the walls of the houses in Cawnpore, such as "We are at the mercy of savages, who have ravished young and old," and such like, which have appeared in the Indian papers and been copied from them into the English ones, are malicious forgeries, and were written on the walls after the re-occupation of Cawnpore by General Outram's and Havelock's forces. Although I was not there myself, I have spoken with many who were there, and I know that what I tell you is true.'

I then asked him if he could give me any idea of the reason that had led the Nana to order the commission of such a cold-blooded, cowardly crime. 'Asiatics', he said, 'are weak, and their promises are not to be relied on, but that springs more from indifference to obligations than from prearranged treachery. When they make promises they intend to keep them; but when they find them in-convenient, they choose to forget them. And so it was, I believe, with the Nana Sahib. He intended to have spared the women and children, but they had an enemy in his *zenana* in the person of a female fiend who had formerly been a slave-girl, and there were many about the Nana (Azeemoolla Khan for one) who wished to see him so irretrievably implicated in rebellion that there would be no possibility for him to draw back. So this woman was powerfully supported in her evil counsel, and obtained permission to have the English ladies killed; and after the sepoys of the Sixth Native Infantry and the Nana's own guard had refused to do the horrible work, this woman sent and procured the wretches who did it. This information I have from General Tantia Topee, who quarrelled with the Nana on this same matter. What I tell you is true: the murder of the European women and children at Cawnpore was a woman's crime, for there is no fiend equal to a female fiend; but what cause she had for enmity against the unfortunate ladies I don't know – I never inquired.'

Those readers who were in India at the time may remember that something about this slave-girl was said in all the native evidence collected at the time on the subject of the Cawnpore massacre.

I next asked Mahomed Ali Khan if he knew whether there was any truth in the stories about General Wheeler's daughter having shot four or five men with a revolver, and then leaped into the well at Cawnpore. 'All these stories', was his answer, 'are pure inventions with no foundation of truth. General Wheeler's daughter is still alive, and is now in Lucknow; she has become a Mussulmanee, and has married according to Mahommedan law the man who protected her; whether she may ever return to her own people I know not.'

In such conversation I passed the night with my prisoner, and towards daybreak I permitted him to perform his ablutions and morning devotions, after which he once more thanked me, and prayed that Allah might reward me for my kindness to His oppressed servant. Once, and only once, did he show any weakness, in alluding to his wife and two boys in their faraway home in Rohilcund, when he remarked that they would never know the fate of their unfortunate father. But he at once checked himself, saying, 'I have read French history as well as English; I must remember Danton, and show no weakness.' He then produced a gold ring which was concealed among his hair, and asked me if I would accept it and keep it in remembrance of him, in token of his gratitude. It was, he said, the only thing he could give me, as everything of value had been taken from him when he was arrested. He went on to say that the ring in question was only a common one, not worth more than ten rupees, but that it had been given to him by a holy man in Constantinople as a talisman, though the charm had been broken when he had joined the unlucky man who was his fellow-prisoner. I accepted the ring, which he placed on my finger with a blessing and a prayer for my preservation, and he told me to look on it and remember Mahomed Ali Khan when I was in front of the fortifications of Lucknow, and no evil would befall me. He had hardly finished speaking when a guard from the provost-marshal came with an order to take over the prisoners, and I handed this man over with a sincere feeling of pity for his fate.

Immediately after, I received orders that the division would march at sunrise for Lucknow, and that my party was to join the rear-guard, after the ammunition-park and siege-train had moved on. The sun was high in the heavens before we left the encamping-ground, and in passing under a tree on the side of the Cawnpore and Lucknow road, I looked up, and was horrified to see my late prisoner and his companion hanging stark and stiffened corpses! I could hardly repress a tear as I passed. But on the 11th of March, in the assault on the Begum's Kothee, I remembered Mahomed Ali Khan and looked on the ring. I am thankful to say that I went through the rest of the campaign without a scratch, and the thoughts of my kindness to this unfortunate man certainly did not inspire me with any desire to shirk danger. I still have the ring, the only piece of Mutiny plunder I ever possessed, and shall hand it down to my children together with the history of Mahomed Ali Khan.

The Heat of the Day

Letters written from Cawnpore at this time give a variety of contrasting conditions and impressions. Lieutenant George Cracklow, writing to his mother, grumbled that everything he had possessed had been plundered by the mutineers and no tailors or clothes were to be procured. He spent 'a pleasant morning repairing his breeches' – the only pair he had – and went on to paint a picture of himself for her.

I am the most extraordinary figure you can imagine, my face burnt black and all the skin peeling off, we have no uniform – anyone wears whatever they can lay hands on, mine consists of a pair of trousers dyed blue, a coloured shirt and a turban, a sword belt with a tremendous sharp sword and a brace of pistols and a tin pot. This is the most useful article of the whole lot I think, the thirst one suffers from is something terrible and the tin pot comes into use very often. . .

By 10 February Cracklow was able to report that the telegraph was working up to Agra and life gradually returning to normal in the town.

The inhabitants have returned to the villages and everything looks much as it used to do. All the chuprassies and blackguards who were formerly in the Government Service and who have been cutting European throats in the meanwhile are again in the Service. . . here we are taking them back again, paying them wages and pensions and almost patting them on the back because we cannot prove that [censored] committed murder.

The weather was agreeable. Major Anson took part in a cricket match, in which his regiment, the 9th Lancers, scored 190 against the Artillery's 140, he himself having a good innings of 45. He made time to explore the many areas of the town that had once been familiar to him and found the Gwaliors had left it almost unrecognisable.

I took a walk this morning to view the second desolation of the Cantonment. You have no idea what a waste the poor unfortunate station is – compounds eaten up, trees all cut down, walls all broken down – it is quite difficult to find one's way about so utterly changed is the whole aspect of the place. The spirit of judgment and the spirit of burning has passed over it. Familiar as I was with every turn, I was constantly thinking what turn to take. The assembly-room is roofless, and one vast mass of bricks and rubbish inside, with huge beams, charred all over, lying about. Huge shot-holes are visible in nearly every large house. There are wooden benches in the church and a Seirkee roof over it. . . The large trees in the church compound have been well peppered with round shot, and the bridge over the nullah is in a terribly dilapidated state. The canal is dry just now. What splendid cover the brutes had. The well containing the remains of the poor massacred women and children has been puckahed over with a view to some large monument being placed there. Meanwhile the 32nd have raised a small one, with a very pretty Greek cross on it, to the memory of their own women and children. Soldiers are digging away for money and jewels in Wheeler's entrenchment. One found 300 rupees buried there the other day.

In spite of the circumstances of campaigning, the 9th Lancers maintained their elitist traditions. In one letter, while out chasing the Nana Sahib, Major Anson describes breakfasting on the line of march, lying stretched on the ground under the shade of a pretty little grove and enjoying a very good veal pie, the wing of a duck and bread and butter with two cups of coffee and one of tea. And the very day Major Anson took his walk through the desolation of Cawnpore he reported that large quantities of stores had arrived from Allahabad and that their mess was well supplied with everything but champagne.

After a tremendous fight, street by street, building by building, Lucknow fell to Sir Colin Campbell. But the capture of Lucknow did not end the campaign, difficult mopping up operations still continued with constant forays made from Cawnpore. Now, too, the hot weather began in earnest, 'with the sun like a golden ball of fire, all day red hot', the hot winds blowing and the camp smothered in dust. The men were fairly well housed but the officers were often quartered in derelict bungalows with no protection from the sun. Assistant Surgeon Collins enjoyed the luxury of sleeping between sheets for the first time in six months, but it was his letter of 22 April that conveyed, in what he called 'These extraordinary times', the heat the soldiers endured.

Cawnpore April 22 1858

The wind blows hotter and hotter every day. The only comfort we have is our bath which we use at the least twice during the 24 hours, in the morning and evening. It is impossible to stir out with safety between 8 am and 6 pm. The very birds disappear at 9 am and we see nothing more of them till sunset or near that hour. In the morning from 7 to 9 we see them with their beaks wide open panting for breath and it is quite extraordinary how the whole animal creation disappears as the wind gets up, and not a sign of a living creature is to be seen again until sunset. There is an old store near the Canteen that we have turned into a mess room, it is very rough but handy place, built of bricks. It keeps off the horrible wind which as you face it feels like the blast from a furnace, so hot and dry is it that our hands and faces are more chapped than we find them in England in the deepest frost weather. Only a few weeks ago we were complaining of the cold but this is certainly much worse to bear. The cold did not kill, but this kills, often in a few hours, and is usually known as 'sun stroke' but should more properly be called 'heat stroke' for it occurs very frequently during the night, and often during the day, when the person who is attacked is under cover, and not in the direct rays of the sun. Soldiers are rendered insensible while in barracks, and often when in their beds during the night. A man wakes up and hears his neighbour in the next bed breathing heavily. He gets up to see what is the matter and finds that he is insensible, and these cases not infrequently prove fatal. We are badly off for hospital accommodation here, and also for the necessaries required for the less serious cases, so it is no wonder that the more serious cases are more difficult to manage than they should be.

Fred Roberts and Sir William Peel had shared the rigours of the Lucknow attack. Now they were both on their way down to Calcutta, Roberts on sick leave and Peel to rejoin his ship. They came into

On the roof of Alumbagh, Lucknow, 1858.

Cawnpore together on the night of 19 April. Next morning, when Roberts went to bid Peel goodbye, he found him lying in his tent with high fever and some suspicious-looking spots on his face. A surgeon of the 5th Fusiliers – a brother officer of Collins – was urgently summoned and diagnosed smallpox. On the march back from Lucknow, still suffering from a wound, Peel had been carried on a doolie; he had refused a carriage, preferring to be treated like one of his own bluejackets, and it was surmised the doolie had earlier been used for a smallpox victim.

Padre Moore and his wife, who had recently joined him, kindly took Peel into their home to nurse him. (They were now living in the ruins of General Wheeler's old bungalow.) But for all their careful nursing Peel, son of an English Prime Minister, proud possessor of the newly created Victoria Cross won at Sebastopol in the Crimean War, died on 27 April. They buried him at the new cemetery at Mirpur, filling up fast with casualties.[34]

This morning died at Cawnpore Sir William Peel, of small-pox. He was taken ill a week ago having almost recovered from the wound he received during the siege of Lucknow, when the Troops were advancing to the Martinière College. He was on his way down the country to join his ship. By his death the Country has lost one of its best and most gallant officers. Many brave men are born in our little isle, of these few are fit to be mentioned the same day with Peel. . . the Nation will mourn the loss of one it can ill spare.[35]

In June 1858 Cracklow was writing:

The heat and sun is killing these new regiments off at a tremendous rate. We bury about a dozen every night. . . the heat and sun is killing a great many more than the enemy. . . Our life is terrible, not a book to read or even a newspaper. Nothing for it day after day when we get in from our march at about 8 in the morning, but to lie with our head wrapped in a wet towel and long for sunset.

Collins told much the same story:

Cawnpore May 30 1858

Our sick have been daily increasing in number and 4 days ago we had 140 in hospital.[36] Today we have 105. . . no one but those who have experienced it can form any notion of the discomforts of the hot winds, where the proper appliances for counteracting their effects are not to be had. . . .In this building there is one large room in which there are no less than 6 officers living, with their beds all in the centre of the room. On these we pass the greater portion of the day, with nothing in the way of clothing upon us but a pair of the thinnest possible drawers, here called pyjamas, and with wet towels over our chest and heads. The row of beds is known as 'Rotten Row'. . .

It was under those extreme conditions of the hot weather of 1858 that the last battles of the Mutiny took place, men dying of heat stroke and exhaustion on the march, becoming hysterical and delirious for thirst and lack of sleep. In April Jhansi was captured and sacked. In May Campbell defeated the rebels outside Bareilly and in June Gwalior fell. The Rani of Jhansi was killed in battle, Tantia Tope escaped into the jungles. To all intents and purposes the revolt was crushed.

Dramatis Personae

The King of Delhi, the last Moghul emperor, was put on trial before a military court and found guilty of having abetted the mutineers in their crimes. He was sentenced to exile for life in Rangoon. Tantia Topi, betrayed while he slept by the Rajah of Narwar, faced execution by hanging with great courage. Tufts of his hair were removed as gruesome trophies. The Nana Sahib was said to have died in the forests of Nepal but rumours of sightings of him continued for many years. The ruins of a considerable settlement with the central foundations of a large European-style building was discovered in dense forest during the 1920s and was believed to have been the Nana Sahib's hideout.[37]

The Rani of Jhansi.   *The Nana Sahib.*

Gavin Jones for services rendered during the Mutiny was awarded the Mutiny Medal. He served under Sir Colin Campbell during the advance to Fatehgarh and was mentioned in despatches. Padre Moore, in his enthusiasm for the amazing scenes he had witnessed, set them all down on cloth. His rather crudely executed scroll, scene upon scene of events in Cawnpore, can be seen in the transcript room at the British Library.[38] Major Anson, poor Octo, fell ill. The fatigue and exposure he had experienced at Delhi and Lucknow brought on tuberculosis. His wife hurried down from Kasauli to nurse him at Dehra Dun but he died and is buried there in a family enclosure with others of his family, the Wemysses and Muirs. I do not know what happened to George Cracklow but his letters came under the hammer at Robson Lowe's salerooms in London. They were bought by an American collector but I was lucky enough to see them before they left the country.[39]

Lieutenant-Colonel Williams, military secretary to Government North Western Provinces, heard the depositions of forty-two witnesses at Cawnpore.[40] They were drawn from respectable and influentiual residents and from all classes and creeds. It was so long after the events had taken place that it was difficult to assess how far the testimony was to be relied upon. In an earlier report, dated 15 November 1858, he ends:

When the history of the Bengal Army shall be written in a just and candid spirit, it will be cleared of many of the sweeping charges at present hurled against it. It will be seen that while many base acts of cruelty and treachery have attended it, not a few noble acts of devotion and fidelity redeem the hideous darkness of the picture.

3
Restoration of Law and Order
1858 – 1859

───

The Viceroy's Grand Tour

A Royal Proclamation announced to the people of India that Queen
Victoria had abolished the East India Company and placed India under
the direct rule of the British Government. The Queen promised that all
men who had not committed murder were to be forgiven, religions
were to be tolerated and ancient customs respected. Lord Canning, who
was now the first Viceroy, proposed to make a triumphal tour through
Oude, the North Western Provinces and the Punjab, in a spirit of recon-
ciliation, showing the flag and rewarding those who had remained loyal
during the uprising. The British Government wished to demonstrate
their friendliness towards the Indian people.

> No one can gainsay the fact that India will take a long time to settle,
> that will be a work of time... The great work is done and the
> minutiae are left to do. The enemy is beaten up everytime and
> point, he has no means, no forces to make a stand and by degrees
> will come all round to the old thing. There are great preparations
> going on... A great demonstration will be made this cold weather,
> armies and siege trains will march about along the roads, across
> country and in every direction. There will be no opposition and the
> civil powers will soon be strengthened.[1]

Lieutenant Frederick Roberts, after a brief home leave when he got
married in Ireland and had his honeymoon interrupted with a call to
Buckingham Palace to receive the Victoria Cross from Queen Victoria's
own hands, returned to India for further duty. He was appointed to
make all the arrangements for the Viceroy's Grand Tour. It was a formidable undertaking. Roberts worked from Allahabad where he stayed

with a brother officer, Lieutenant John Stewart – they had been at Addis-combe together. Stewart, who was in charge of the arsenal, described the feverish activity at Allahabad.

> Officers are busy constructing public works, collecting supplies for European troops, drilling recruits both European and Native, and every one indents on the Arsenal. We are continually employed making up all kinds of tools, implements, repairing gun carriages and making ammunition of all kinds. In the city every tailor is engaged making light clothing for the troops, the contractors have thousands of men employed in tents, bedding, doolies etc. Every artificer is employed by the Railway making carriages etc. Every mason is building houses, every carpenter roofing, every *bheesty* watering, every sweeper sweeping. . .

The Viceroy, his staff and guests required no less than 150 large tents; the Commander-in-Chief with the officers of the Army headquarters also had to be provided for, along with the post office, telegraph, workshops, commissariat and *toshikhana*. All these were accompanied by an escort of artillery, cavalry and infantry, and the Viceroy's bodyguard. Everything was planned in duplicate so that with each day's march the huge party could move into similar quarters that had been selected and pitched ahead in readiness.

The scale of the undertaking can be gauged from details of the transport equipment: 500 camels, 500 bullocks, 100 bullock carts, 40 riding elephants, 527 coolies to carry the glass windows of the tents, 100 *bhisties* and 40 sweepers for watering and keeping the camp site clean. The camp equipment made up the rear. A motley crowd of followers, totalling, with their women and children, not less than 20,000, were in attendance.

By 16 August Stewart was able to write:

> Here we are past the middle of August and in the middle of the rains, weather very pleasant and country very quiet. A remarkable lull in all operations. The Trunk Road open from Calcutta to Peshawar and a good deal safer than Pall Mall at 1 in the morning! Ladies flying up and down the country all alone and everything coming smooth and pleasant as of old. Lady Canning is on her way to Allahabad by steamer or rather in her barge tugged by a steamer and all the ladies of the Gov Genl's and Commdr in Chief's staff also coming and taking up their abodes in the cantonment of Allahabad.

TOO "CIVIL" BY HALF.
The Governor-General Defending the POOR Sepoy.

The Proclamation was officially announced in every station in India on 1 November 1858. In Cawnpore there was a parade; where 'sufficient numbers of Indians'[2] attended but not a large crowd. Mr Batten, the judge, read the document from an open carriage, a few fireworks were let off and everyone went home.

The durbar, held two days later, was a much grander occasion. The Viceroy went first to Lucknow and on 3 November arrived in state in Cawnpore. The ceremony took place in a double-poled pavilion lined with yellow *kanats*. By two o'clock all were in their places, Lord Canning, seated in the centre, was attended on his right by more than eight princes and *talookdars*, all in their most gorgeous silks and jewels, while the Commander-in-Chief, now created Lord Clyde, his officers and a group of civilians conspicuous in their sombre black clothes, took their place to his left. *Kelats* and gifts were presented, the Chikaree Rajah was given special praise, but it was only the Rajah of Rewah, a tall, fine man accompanied by Willoughby Osborne, who had a gold chain placed around his neck by the Viceroy himself. Lord Canning made the announcement that in future the British Government would recognise the rights of adopted heirs. This news was received with satisfaction.

For a moment the solemnity of the occasion was interrupted. An elderly, toothless bodyguard of a Rajput chief, garbed for the fray, took his sword up to the Viceroy so that it could be touched and blessed. The old soldier announced in a loud voice that if the Lat Sahib's enemy ever gave him trouble he had only to say the word and the sword would be drawn in his defence. 'He quite upset Lord Canning's gravity who held out for some time but at last burst into uncontrolled laughter.'[3]

Lord and Lady Canning, continuing the progress of their durbar, visited Fatehgarh, Agra and Meerut, spending Christmas at Delhi, then on up into the Punjab, to Amballa and Amritsar, and enjoying what were perhaps the most splendid scenes of all at Lahore. There, in reply to the chiefs, the Viceroy made an eloquent speech thanking the nobles and the peoples of the Punjab for their courage and loyalty during the uprising. After six months' march over 1,000 miles, camp broke up and the Viceroy returned to Calcutta. It had been a march as Roberts pointed out 'never likely to be undertaken again by any other Viceroy of India, now that railway trains run from Calcutta to Peshawar, and saloon carriages have taken the place of big tents'.

Sherer's Report

On 13 January 1859 John Walter Sherer, the senior civilian and magistrate of Cawnpore, wrote his official report to Government.[4]

When the convoy of women and children from the Lucknow Residency set out for Allahabad, Sherer received a note from Bruce asking for a meeting. He left the entrenchment by the little temple on the riverside – probably the Bhagwatdas Temple whose effigies still carry reminders of those times – and made his way to the fortified house occupied by Windham and Bruce, dodging the fire from the Gwaliors who had got the range. Only part of the house, which stood unevenly, was safe, but in a small dark hole of a room partially underground, Sherer helped himself to some bread and bacon he found on a shelf, while round shot whizzed overhead. Bruce placed pen and ink before him and asked him to sign acceptance of authority for the city of Cawnpore. Bruce himself had received a new appointment.

Fortunately the enemy were not very good shots, but they carried away part of the balustrade of the roof, twice. I should not think it has happened before for a Magistrate to take charge of a district, a few hundred square yards only which were then in British possession, and to sign the usual papers under a heavy cannonade playing on his predecessor's house.[5]

Following the defeat of the Gwalior Contingent the tension in the town relaxed. The merchants, regaining confidence, were ready to supply money to any amount. Sherer was kept busy with treasury affairs, collecting commissariat stores, constructing carts, corresponding with Agra and paying the troops. The country people and the labourers, after centuries of conquest and warfare, had learnt the importance of siding with success. They began to come into town now, offering milk, eggs and fruit for sale. As soon as they saw they were kindly received and honestly paid, they came forward in great numbers.

Although the district continued to be very disturbed, gradually as the roads became safer it was possible to go out on tour. Some of the zemindars agreed to become sub-collectors of the revenue and, to Sherer's amusement, supplied their own retainers, wild-looking Rajput matchlockmen to guard the sacred revenue. It was made perfectly clear to all that any revenue paid to the Nana would not count against that due to the Company.

Records of every description had been destroyed. With so much confiscated property, which claimant was to be believed? A good recommendation might be worth good money; the danger of corruption was ever-present. The city of Cawnpore itself was fined £30,000 for its too ready acceptance of the Nana's occupation and this sum was raised without an appeal. There was one solitary protest from a goldsmith who claimed he was not a regular resident of Cawnpore, but when he was told he risked personal arrest the protest was withdrawn. Ultimately the fine was used to create the Memorial Well Gardens, laid out as a beautiful park which since Independence in 1947 has returned to the citizens of Kanpur as the Nana Rao Park.

Men suspected of complicity in the uprising or caught with looted property were subjected to summary justice at the gallows. Sherer wrote:

I believe the executions to have been far less numerous here than at most other places which the rebels had possession of. Fair and careful trials were always accorded, and I never heard the natives complain of the result of any, except that of Azim Alee Khan. In that case Captain Bruce asked my opinion, and it confirmed his own, that the Khan Sahib was guilty.

Sherer marvelled at the composure with which the unfortunate men went to their deaths. 'The Mohamedans died with hauteur and angry scorn, the Hindoos with an indifference which was astonishing.' Inevitably unfair and pathetic incidents took place, soldiers stirred to fierce passion by the stories of atrocities at the Bebee Ghar at times took the law into their own hands and many of the common people feared the soldiers more than the authorities. The conduct book of one Fusilier Kelly, who had been in the relief of Cawnpore, notes that he was sentenced to seven days confined to barracks 'for hanging a native without permission'.[6]

Like many of his contemporaries, Sherer commented on the fact that in the East the public mind is affected by disaster or success: a defeat – and everyone deserts. A victory – and all throng to congratulate and support. Sherer's *munshi* reported that during the time when the Gwaliors had overrun Cawnpore he had heard a quarrel between the couple who were his next-door neighbours. The husband threatened the wife with 'You had better be careful; there are no British now, and no reason exists why I should not break your head and thrown you into a well.' Prudently, the lady remained silent.

Things settled down surprisingly quickly. In Sherer's opinion the best people in the town and district of Cawnpore were delighted that the British had returned to power.

I found the ploughman in the field; the boy singing at the well as he urged the bullocks down the slope; the old woman sitting at her door, twisting her little cotton gin (I fear with scarcely velocity enough to compete with the New World) and her daughters grinding the millet, all supremely unconscious of the descendant of Timoor, who with somewhat unseemly haste had made but yesterday a royal progress through their fields and villages.

The taste for misrule has clearly for the time departed. The people have seen that neither Rajah nor Nawab can construct a practicable administration and the old rule seems better than none.

I trust experience may teach us to amend those parts of our administration, which may be oppressive or distasteful to the people, so that they may accept our rule, not only as inevitable, but also as that with which they are best satisfied.[7]

The Maxwells

A letter under the title 'Sufferers at Cawnpore', signed by Captain Herbert Bruce, Superintendent of Police, and dated 31 July 1857, appeared in the *Englishman*[8] appealing for a European familiar with the former residents and able to identify their property to come forward:

> . . .the property of the unfortunate people who lost their lives here has been collected in one spot, and that any which can be recognized will be handed over to the owners, or put up to auction for the benefit of deceased estates, and the rest sold.
>
> There is a good deal of property belonging to the different mercantile firms here, as well as to the heirs of deceased officers & c., but when I mention that every house was gutted, and the property scattered over 60 or 70 square miles of country, it will be apparent how impossible it was to take care of individual interests.
>
> I would recommend any one connected with Cawnpore, to appoint an agent upon the spot, who can recognise the property, and he should be armed with authority to receive charge of it.
>
> Almost all of the former European residents here having been murdered by the miscreant 'Nana Sahib', and no one being forthcoming to recognise or give any information concerning the property that has been saved, it would aid us very much were some European to return, who may be acquainted with the former residents, or be able to point out the property of different owners.

The man who was able to help more than any other was Hugh Maxwell, from a family that had been settled at Cawnpore for over fifty years. Hugh Maxwell was a tall, lean, good-looking man with a serious, almost fierce expression. He was forty-eight when the Mutiny broke out, established as a successful indigo planter, a family man with five young children and a reputation for fairness and steadiness in business dealings and with the Maxwell family's good name behind him.

His father, John Maxwell, was the only son of the Revd John Maxwell, minister of New Machar, near Aberdeen in Scotland. Left fatherless at a very young age and with a mother and a large family of sisters to support John Maxwell had sailed for India on the *William Pitt* in 1786 to seek his fortune as a partner in Davidson and Maxwell, Calcutta Europe Shop. Striving to better himself, he moved on to become editor of the *India Gazette*; then, faced with the restrictions and censorship imposed by

Hugh Maxwell.

Lord Wellesley, he left Calcutta and moved up-country to Taundah where he learnt the production of cotton and indigo. It was when he came to Cawnpore in 1806 as agent to the Army contractor, a lucrative appointment at a time when Cawnpore was Army Headquarters and the largest up-country cantonment in India,[9] that he became successful. In ten years he established himself in cotton, indigo and rum and laid the foundations of the fortune and reputation of the Maxwell family.

John Maxwell's children fall into three groupings. Two children, Agnes and Adam, were born in Calcutta to Indian mothers, a daughter Fanny was born up-country at Aleabad, and four sons were born in Cawnpore to his common-law wife, Elizabeth Nann, daughter of a silversmith. Hugh Maxwell was the second son of the four sons born in

Cawnpore and Cawnpore was the scene of his childhood. The fortified house next to the Kila where Sherer took over authority for the town from Bruce was for many years the Maxwell family home and the boys once played in the garden.

When John Maxwell died the boys were thought too young (Hugh was seven) to attend the funeral at Kacheri Cemetery, the officers' burial ground that had been encircled by the Gwaliors when Colonel Wilson was killed and the 64th Regiment so severely mauled. But twenty-two years later, after an education and upbringing with his father's relatives in Scotland, Hugh Maxwell stood there when they opened up his father's grave, laying to one side the massive granite slab that had come from London with the eulogies to the successes of John Maxwell's life inscribed upon it. Now the coffin of Adam Maxwell, his eldest brother and something of the black sheep of the family, was lowered into it.

It was many years before Adam Maxwell's name could be mentioned without ridicule or censure. Adam had been born to an Indian mother, a chance that gave John Maxwell the opportunity to acquire land; but Adam's mixed blood was a blessing and a curse that nearly lost the family their fortune.[10] His constant evasion of paying the revenue due from his indigo estates and villages infuriated the authorities. They determined to make an example of him and the zealous Mr Reade succeeding in ruining him and it took twenty years for the family fortune to recover. The Maxwells worked hard, however, and gradually prospered again. Three of the brothers, Peter, David and James, were established in the district between Cawnpore and Fatehgarh while Hugh played his part near Mirzapore, maintaining contact with important Calcutta business interests up-country.

Just before the Mutiny Hugh Maxwell moved back into the Cawnpore district. The annexation of Oude in 1856, the removal of the barriers of trade restriction and the proposed railway link to Calcutta were opportunities to be explored. Now, when the Mutiny took place, it was pure chance that saved Hugh Maxwell's life. His wife Charlotte had been in England visiting their children. Leaving the younger ones at school, she returned with Fanny aged eighteen, who was hoping to find a husband and make her own life in India. Hugh Maxwell went down to Calcutta to meet their ship. With the shocking news from Delhi, Lucknow and Cawnpore in the papers each day, he put them on the next ship back to England.

Hugh's elder brother Peter, head of the family since Adam's death, was a prosperous indigo planter. He was appointed opium agent by

Robert Montgomery (grandfather of the celebrated field-marshal) who had described him as a most respected gentleman. Peter was killed at Wheeler's entrenchment leaving a vast amount of his estate to settle. Hugh himself had married in 1839 into the Jones family – Gavin Sibbald Jones was his wife's young brother. While proud of Gavin Jones's escape, Hugh found himself fathering the young man, as well as looking after the affairs of John Moore Jones, killed at Fatehgarh and Edmond Jones, killed at Gopi Gunj, both brothers-in-law. The youngest Maxwell brother, James, had married into the Churcher family at Fatehgarh and Thomas Churcher, another brother-in-law, had been killed there also. Then, besides the personal angle, there was the collapse and loss of business associations. The family of John Kirk and Co., the Cawnpore firm that had handled all the sales of the produce from the Maxwell estates, was wiped out except for one young boy who had been at school in the hills and now needed assistance. People like Greenway Brothers, who had lost nineteen members of their family, appealed to Hugh Maxwell for help, as did his good friend of many years' standing, Dr David Begg, the 'planter's doctor' who had been a big loser in his involvement in Begg Christie and Co.

No record has survived to show if Hugh Maxwell stayed at Mahomed's Hotel, or went to look at Henry Christie's house that had stood close to Suttee Chowra Ghat where the massacre at the boats had taken place, or walked to the ruins of Kirk and Co. to see the nearest point the Gwaliors had brought four guns to play on the Kila. Only the dry details of the inventories of the destruction of Maxwell property give some idea of what was involved.

The Mendhee Ghaut Concern comprised indigo and saltpetre factories and zemindaree estates: 'before the mutinies there were an assistant's bungalow, manufacturing house, drying house, godown, stabling, out offices, 2 reservoirs and 14 pairs of vats and all the necessary implements for producing 1000 pounds of indigo annually all in good condition, but these were all burnt down and the property destroyed or plundered by the rebels in June 1857.' The two-storied dwelling house with kitchen, stabling and offices and garden in the village of Gungaganj, also the saltpetre factory with godowns, boilers and implements complete for producing 200 *maunds* of refined saltpetre *per diem*, were all destroyed. It was the same at the indigo factories at Bilhour and Mokunpore. Mokunpore was the residence of Peter Maxwell, its handsome contents and furniture destroyed or stolen. In Fatehgarh two more family properties were destroyed, a fine old house that had once belonged to Colonel

Gardner and a *kutcha* bungalow intended for Bebee Golaub Jaun, the Cashmere lady who had been Peter Maxwell's *bebee*. It is not known if she survived to enjoy it and the Rs. 80/- per month intended for her welfare.[11]

All that was finally saved from Mokunpore was 'a damaged single-poled tent, an incomplete set of electroplated ware, ninety-six pieces of table crockery, two iron baths, three scotch terriers and a buggy much burnt and damaged by mutineers'.

In Calcutta a public meeting was called and a committee formed to put forward the plight of the sufferers from the Mutiny and rebellion and to press their claims for compensation on Lord Canning. Schedules were drawn up to list the individual heavy losses.

> Your memorialists beg to urge most earnestly on your Lordship the justice of their claim for prompt and full compensation. The Schedule of losses attached, though necessarily incomplete, shows how great their pressure is, delay in the declaration by Government that compensation will be granted adds grievously to the injury already suffered. To many it will prove ruinous, to all a source of much inconvenience, many of the sufferers have an additional claim to consideration in the fact of their having served actively and efficiently against the rebels.[12]

Some claims, such as that from Dr Bruce at Cawnpore, were straightforward. He had left his appointment of medical store keeper to go on home leave. His books, surgical instruments, plate and household effects were all lost.[13] Amelia Horne's claim was more complicated.

> I am one of the survivors of the unfortunate garrison of Cawnpore. When after the capitulation we were taken to the Boats I was forcibly taken ashore again and brought back to Cawnpore. I was subsequently carried into Oude and kept there a captive for 10 months, when lately I succeeded in making my escape to Al-lahabad. The whole of our family must have been cruelly killed and of course all our property is lost. I take the liberty of thus addressing you as I am given to understand that Government has graciously allowed two thousand Co Rupees compensation to all persons situated like myself. . .[14]

Government distanced itself by refusing compensation but wrote that if she was destitute she could, by making application to the civil authorities, receive a pension.

Many applications like the claim by Malcolm and Co., Calcutta agents, were typical of business losses. Thomas H. Churcher in Fatehgarh had been supplying them with country produce and they had been in partnership with Messrs Colesworth and Powell of London for the supply of hides. Bills of exchange were drawn on Calcutta and negotiated in Fatehgarh and goods sent down river by boats 'in accordance with the usual and established practice'.[15] But when the Mutiny broke out, boats laden with hides and goods in transit were destroyed and the books of accounts of the agency, which showed all monthly transactions, goods purchased, money received and invoices of goods despatched, were missing after 30 April. It was not surprising that the deputy magistrate wrote despairingly of his task, protesting at 'the extreme difficulty of obtaining proofs at this station where almost every European was murdered and records of every description destroyed'.[16]

W. M. Russell, the Times *correspondent in India.*

4
The Old Koi Hais

――――

John Stewart: Early Days

Of the several people who played a prominent part in the growth of Cawnpore, three men in particular came from families with pre-Mutiny connections: Hugh Maxwell, Gavin Jones and John Stewart. Their families were long established in India. Their grandparents had lived at the time of Clive and Warren Hastings and their vision of India and themselves in India was the vision of people who felt themselves part of India, to some extent Brahminised. They had absorbed and accepted many facets of Indian life and culture. Those Europeans who came to India after the Mutiny, while respecting and admiring the old *koi hais*,[1] looked at India with more Western eyes. This difference shows up in many ways. For instance, John Stewart in 1859 called Lady Inglis, the wife of the new general at Cawnpore and the senior lady at the station, the Burra Bebee. Future generations would change this to Burra Mem-sahib.

John Stewart was born in India in 1833, one of six brothers and a sister. His father, Major William Murray Stewart of the 22nd Native Infantry, adjutant at the Fort, Chunar, Governor-General's agent at Benares and superintendent of the estates of the Rajah of Benares, lived in a huge old bungalow rented from the Maharajah and was renowned for his hospitality and conviviality.

A letter written by John Stewart to his sister when he was seven years old has survived;

> My dear Missy,
> I love you very much. Toony, Jimmy and Georgy are quite well. Papa has a bad cold. My garden is very pretty, we have got 2 red parrots and a black monkey.
> Mama gave a large dinner the other day and we gave a small

dinner on our little table. I have got a Squirrel just like yours that died last year.

I am your loving brother,

JOHN STEWART

Two years later he was bravely preparing to face the conventional separation from parents and India for years of schooling in England.

His mother was a Debnam, daughter of Major Robert Debnam of the 65th Regiment, later with the 13th Light Infantry, who eventually settled in the Gorukpore district as a grantee opening up the land to indigo. Her brother, George Debnam, was an indigo planter and her sister married the Revd John Justis Tucker, related to H. St G. Tucker, who had travelled as a cadet to India on the *William Pitt* with John Maxwell in 1786, and had risen to become chairman of the East India Company. Unlike the British Army where appointments were by purchase, the Indian Army was entirely officered by patronage of the directors of the East India Company. The way you got on in life was as much due to whom you knew as who or what you were. This fortunate relationship to the chairman of the East India Company was instrumental in Willy, Bob, John and George Stewart all getting their cadetships to Addiscombe.

Addiscombe, situated on the outer fringe of London, at Croydon, was the Sandhurst of the Indian Army. While the majority of Indian Army cadets went straight to India to begin their service, the crack cadets, intended chiefly for the Artillery, passed through Addiscombe on fees of £100 a year. Many of these were drawn from the long-established European families in India where by tradition the family pattern was for the sons to attend school in England and return to take up work in India. They were the sons of military men or affluent men in trade and commerce, or sons of the clergy; only occasionally were they minor aristocrats. Almost without exception they had their sights on a posting to Bengal.

At this time the college was run by the Governor, Major-General Abbott, and his wife. They insisted that, no matter how wealthy a boy's family his pocket money must not exceed 2/6 a week. This would be cheerfully spent at Mother Rose's Tuck Shop, thereby leaving nothing over, so the authorities hoped, for the temptations of drink and gambling.

Stewart failed to shine at Addiscombe. He was a victim of poor health, but kept out of mischief and managed to scrape through his exams to gain a place in the coveted Bengal Artillery. He sailed on 20 February 1852 from Southampton on the P & O steamer *Ripon*. It was a memorable voyage, six Addiscombe 'chums', one of them the future Lord Roberts, their schooldays behind them, returning to India with the promise of adventures ahead. At Alexandria they left the ship to be towed up the canal for ten hours in a large mastless vessel. Then they travelled for sixteen hours by steamer on the Nile to Cairo where they spent a couple of nights at the famous Shepheard's Hotel. Next came the most remarkable part of the journey, across ninety miles of desert, shapeless masses of rock strewn with the skeletons of animals, no road, a mere cutting in the sand that disappeared entirely at night. They trundled along in a conveyance that closely resembled a bathing machine, pulled by mules.[2] Behind followed the camels with the baggage and cargo – even the coal for the ships in the Red Sea came by camel. With an occasional halt for refreshments they reached Suez after eighteen hours and boarded their ship, the *Oriental*. It docked safely in Calcutta on 1 April.

In high spirits at being back in the country of his birth Stewart joined his brother Willy at Dum Dum. He felt instantly at home and in better health.

> Dum Dum 18 April 1852
>
> I am sure Indian climates will agree with me, and I begin to feel quite a native already. I like a Punka though and find it rather hot without one. I think an Indian Evening with moon-light is one of the most splendid things you can imagine, and I like sitting out on a verandah enjoying a cigar on such an evening. If it was not that I had examinations to pass in Hindee, I am afraid I would get into lazy habits; but I am determined to mugg the language and get over them as quickly as possible so I have commenced in earnest with a Moonshie already, and with a little hard work I daresay I will be able to pass the first examination in 4 or 5 months. I have a pretty good Moonshie, at least he is celebrated for passing young men very quickly. He knows how to charge though and won't teach for less than 20 Rupees per month.

The Stewarts found strength in their Scottish heritage and took great pride in their family interdependence and their link with Ardvorlich, the estate in Scotland that had been in the family for over 300 years. On the death in 1853 of Major William Murray Stewart, Willy became the tenth laird and the Stewart brothers joined together to do what was necessary to free Ardvorlich from debt. They corresponded regularly and at length. Tina, the only girl among the six brothers, acted as the central focus for the whole family. It was she to whom they all wrote, and it was she who kept and cherished the letters that survive today. John expressed this family solidarity when he wrote to Tina to console her on the death of their father.

> . . . we his children must all love one another and we must all join hand in hand and support our name and family. You know the story of the Greek father who gave a bundle of sticks to his sons and asked them to break it in two, and when they could not he gave them the sticks one by one and they broke them quite easily, thus proving to them simply that (in a body) they were strong but one by one their strength was nothing. . .[3]

Stewart had married Amelia Webster in July 1857 and was on leave in Scotland when the Mutiny first broke out. Ordered to report for duty, he returned immediately to India to rejoin his unit, leaving Millie behind. It was an anxious voyage: he was sad to be parted from his bride, and fearful for the fate of his four brothers in India. The lack of news was made worse by the frustrating slowness of the ship. 'Wherever we land I rush to the news rooms and carefully con over all the newspapers.' Among the list of those known to be killed was William Stewart, his eldest brother, murdered by the mutineers at Gwalior. But there was no news of Willy's wife and two children. 'Willy's name stares at me in full in every list of the unfortunate killed, but of the others no mention is made and I keep picturing to myself the misery they are undergoing if alive or the atrocities that ended them.'[4]

On arrival at Calcutta Stewart was sent to Allahabad, not to fight and 'get a smash' as he would have liked, but to play his part in the commissary of ordnance, 'to make the excellent arrangement to feed them [the army], to clothe them, to direct them and to supply them with ammunition.'[5] Stewart was at Allahabad when Sir Colin Campbell prepared his forces to attack Lucknow. He wrote to his sister Tina on January 1858:

> This day has been Sunday but such a day! Work work work from morning to night. Three Regiments march at three in the morning and all the arrangements for their departure have had to be made *today*. Although a thin wall is all that separates my quarters from the room in which service is performed I was unable to attend today being called to the Arsenal to arrange about the despatch of a heavy

Engagement photograph of John Stewart and Amelia Webster.

8 inch gun belonging to Captain Peel of the Naval Brigade. This Leviathan had to be moved off to the Railway, with 400 rounds of ammunition weighing in all about 20 tons.

Things are looking uncommonly warlike again and this time again Lucknow is to be the seat of warfare. Everything is kept very quiet but there is no doubt that Sir Colin will hurry down with his large army and be met at Cawnpore with fresh troops from down country — (these very same 3 regiments that march tomorrow) two of cavalry and one of infantry. There are more besides at Cawnpore and Fattehpore, all will join Outram at Alum Bagh and our desperate effort will be made before 3 weeks are out, to capture Lucknow and kill a very large number of the enemy which can be done now the Chief has 4 or 5 regiments of cavalry. Besides the big gun sent up today nine 24 pounders are to go soon and a whole lot about 5,000 rounds of shot and shell with a complete Engineers Park. I am going out again to the terminus of the Railway which is now Khaja to send off all those stores by Bullock Train to Cawnpore. I think it is a good thing the Chief has determined to take Lucknow this cold weather for it will bring the mutiny to a crisis instead of letting the vagabonds nestle in a stronghold and brew mischief a whole Hot season.

I fear my presence is again required down in these parts and I shall see none of the fun, but I am working for John Company and earning my salt. The disappointment is however great to me, for I should like to see a good scrimmage but it won't do and I must look to the future by sticking here I shall get permanently into this department which will perhaps give me many years of affluence and comfort.

When the women and children arrived at Allahabad from Lucknow, sent down from Cawnpore, Stewart had to make the arrangements to complete their journey to Calcutta. He hired country boats from his own stores. He was amused that in spite of the ordeals they had endured 'many of the widows were quite gay and flirted away with the young officers here'. By August he was in charge of ordnance.[6]

I have carried on the working of this large Arsenal now for two months under the nose of all the big wigs and in daily communication with them and my usual luck has carried me through without a mistake, in fact I think with some credit to myself and by means of my official connection and contact with the Chief and his staff I have acquired a personal acquaintance with them all which may tell well for me some day. It has been in my power to do the Chief some favours in the way of getting his guns mounted and his sword put in order in the Arsenal work shops!

When Stewart happened to make a suggestion to the Chief about some guns at Cawnpore, it very much met with approval. He immediately invited him to take 'pot luck' to discuss the idea further, as a result of which Stewart found himself posted to Cawnpore in charge of the Cawnpore magazine. It was the start of nearly thirty years' association and work at Cawnpore and the establishment of Cawnpore as the great leather centre of India.

With the outlook more settled, Stewart wrote to Millie on 2 August 1858 encouraging her to risk the voyage out.

Ladies fly all over the country now and the Stations are becoming cheery and the houses all habitable and comfortable. Luxuries are creeping in again. Carriages and buggies knock about. . . steamers now coming up country bringing up ladies and children. . . marriages are taking place. . . and the newly married pairs are coming up to spend their honeymoons. Two newly married Bengal Artillerymen are coming with their wives to my Quarters to be my guests in a week or two. What do you think of that, and what do you say about the safety or danger of India? It was never safer than it is now for we never had so many Europeans!

By Christmas time Millie had arrived at Calcutta, less than pleased that her husband saw fit to give her instructions as to how to behave on the voyage out. Not to be 'too intimate with any of the passengers' was 'a precaution which I thought would not have been necessary but which I now of course attend to'. She also had misgivings about the news that her husband now wore an immense beard, concerned that it would make him look 'so very dark.' It was a sensitive issue. Stewart had confided to his mother when at school at St Andrews that the boys had mockingly called him 'black' and 'Negro' on account of his dark complexion. But it was no blemish on their reunion. Stewart got leave to go down to Calcutta where they stayed at Wilson's Hotel. The street on which their windows looked out was 'more noisy than Piccadilly.' They set themselves up with 'tongues and hump' from D. Wilson and Co. for the journey and Stewart ordered a case of wine from Colins and Co.[7] Millie could not resist buying some chintz and they invested in a good-looking mirror because Stewart assured her such a thing was not to be had in the north west. They arrived at Cawnpore early in the New Year. It was to be their much-loved home until 1887.

On 4 February 1859 Stewart wrote to his brother-in-law:

More than a month has rolled away since Millie landed in the country and we have rolled 600 miles up the grand trunk road and are comfortably housed and settled for the present in this hated place late the scene of such horrible atrocities. Cawnpore is beginning to wear a more civilized aspect now however carriages and buggies are to be seen driving on the dusty roads, a Band strikes up at 5 pm on a would-be-green maidan and a dozen or so of the fair sex are to be seen gracing the performance. The night before last there was a ball given by the Bachelors to the ladies of the station and notwithstanding the scarcity of the latter dancing was kept up till 3 pm with great spirit and animation.

The calling business is pretty well over but every one has called on us first – that is on Millie for I know them all as a bachelor. It is no joke paying visits in Cawnpore the Civil and Military Lines are 7 miles apart. We return the visits of the Civil community yesterday and the Military today. Our new General has just arrived, General Sir John Inglis with Lady Inglis who will be the Burra Beebee of the place.

Ten days later Millie wrote to Tina:

Our house is in the Fort, a very nice one so large and airy it is by far the nicest house in Cawnpore – this everybody says. It is newly done up and looks cool. The weather just now is delicious and I shouldn't mind if it always continues so. In the mornings we walk out but not very far as Johnnie has always too much work to do to permit of his taking much walking exercise. In the evening we generally take a drive out. Sometimes the Band plays where all the beauty and fashion of the station are to be seen, but unless at the Band we never meet a single carriage – where all the inhabitants drive to is a mystery, this is the usual complaint. The reason is that there is no principal drive so each one goes a different way.

Another St Andrews friend called here the other day, a Dr Wright; he recognized me at the Band. It is very pleasant out here meeting with old friends, for being so far away one likes to speak of home.

The Coming of the Railway

The coming of the railway transformed much of Indian life. From the time the first deed of contract was signed on 17 August 1849 it took six years of hard work to the opening of the first 120 miles of track out of Calcutta. Capital of £2½m. was raised by 11,472 shareholders, almost entirely subscribed in England, and plans were drawn up. Teams of engineers and contractors arrived, land was acquired, the track for the line surveyed. The first locomotives were despatched by ship, taking three or four months to arrive, while workshops were established for the manufacture of carriages and rolling stock based on original patterns sent from England. Huge numbers of labourers were engaged to assist with the earthworks of embankments and masonry work on bridges and tunnels. The long-despised labourer now found himself better paid and more sought after than the well-to-do cultivator.[8]

John Stewart had the opportunity to travel on an experimental run and replied to Tina's eager questioning in a letter from Calcutta dated 4 January 1855.

> You ask me to describe the East Indian Railway. The carriages are much finer, larger, and quite as well made as the English ones. They don't go fast here at present cosny they are *feared*, but they will soon gain confidence and *chal* at a great pace. I came 40 miles in two hours which is not bad considering we had to stop at 4 stations.

Contrast this with the problems involved in even a comparatively short journey before the coming of the railway. John Stewart was laying his plans for a visit to Tina, married to a civil servant at Mirzapore.

> Cawnpore 16th November 1854
> I leave this on Monday night and Allahabad on Tuesday night so that (if all goes well) I ought to be with you on the morning of Wednesday. I am to travel by Dak Gharee as far as Maharajgunge, and then be pulled by bearers to the river. Be a good girl and have a Chuprosse ready waiting for me with a boat to cross over at Newria Ghat, and give me some conveyance from Neuria to your house. I am sending two boxes by Bullock Train to Gopeegunge from where they can be transported by coolies. I daresay there may be some difficulty in their arriving at Mirzapore, but I can't help it, there being no Bullock Train the whole way to your station.

The dak-ghari, *or post-chaise; illustration from James Grant,* Cassell's Illustrated History of India.

The bullock train consisted of a number of lumbering vehicles, some piled high with boxes and stores, others with open sides hung with heavy canvas curtains. The cart was long enough for the traveller to lie full length, his head pillowed on the bullock's sack of bran, while crouched at the other end was the servant sitting on the portmanteau. At night the interior was lit by an oil lamp swinging from a hook. Outside all was silent except for the groaning of the heavy wooden wheels and the rough voice of the driver perched on the pole to which the oxen were yoked, urging on the beasts.

On 4 February 1855 invited guests in Calcutta crossed the Hooghly by ferryboat and Governor-General's barge and boarded the train at Howrah station – then no more than a collection of small huts and sheds. The party travelled in style to mark the official opening. Lord Dalhousie performed the ceremony but was unwell and unable to accompany his guests as they travelled the 120 miles to the coalfields of Raneegunge on the new track of 5'6" gauge.

The outbreak of hostilities in 1857 halted work on the route planned for the East Indian Railway. A twenty-five-year-old civil engineer called Samuel Carrington,[9] who had left his native Cumberland in June to work for the East Indian Railway Company, found the Mutiny had caused terrible havoc, throwing back the work at least three or four years. All the bridges were burnt up-country and between Allahabad and Cawnpore all carriages, stores and engines had been destroyed. Many of the railway engineers had lost their lives in the fighting.

Carrington was at Allahabad when the ladies and children passed through from Lucknow. On 27 November 1857 seventeen engineers dined together at the hotel bungalow and afterwards held a meeting to decide about a memorial to be erected at Cawnpore in memory of their brother engineers who were killed or died of hardship at Cawnpore or on the line during the Mutiny. The names of eighteen were known besides three or four covenanted inspectors from England. 'Everyone there had some intimacy or acquaintance with those who were murdered, £60 was subscribed at the table for the tablet.'

Six months later tremendous progress had been made. The pay for labour had been raised to double and treble the old wage, yet even so the coolies ran away to cut the harvest and glean the fields. For all that, it was hoped to have the line from Allahabad open to Cawnpore by 1 August 1858.

> Every day when the Engine comes to the little Tank for water which takes some time, as it has to be handed up by coolies in large jars called gullars, great crowds of men collect about it, some men out of the village or fellows lounging about the works such as small native contractors and they – all Brahmins – count their beads over and pray and salaam to the Engine. This they do because they see it possesses a power they do not understand. They are not at all afraid of it but only wish to show it respect and get the good will of the something that moves it.

Carrington also wrote a delightful description of the official opening of the line from Allahabad to Futtehpore. He had to be up early as the train was due to start at 6 a.m. The preparations were spectacular:

> 3 grand arches and a large number of flags strung across the platform ... and some grand red bands across the arches with 'Rule Britannia', 'God Save the Queen', 'Welcome', 'The Way to Prosperity', 'Success to the East Indian Railway' etc on them. A pilot engine was to run before to clear the way all covered with flags and festoons. A newly finished engine was ready to convey his Lordship the Governor and all the nobs. This engine was there and then christened Lord Canning by Mrs Irving the Doctor's wife. It looked very smart with fresh paint and polish, garlands of flowers

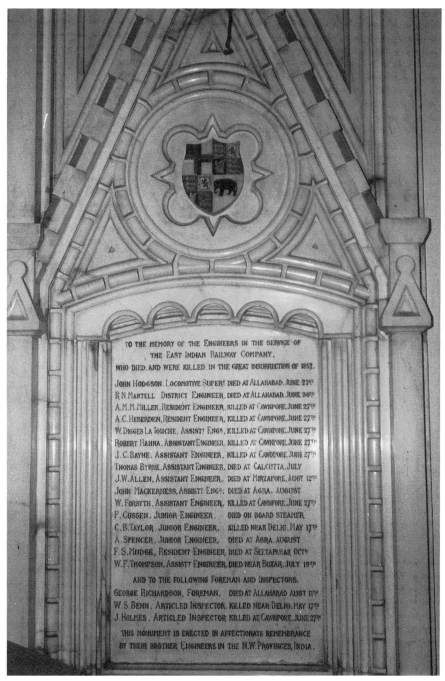

Memorial in All Souls Church to engineers killed at Cawnpore. Photo Raghavindrajit Singh.

and a great crown of red and white stuff in the front of the funnel. At 6.30 am the carriages came up with His Lordship and no end of great people – officers and numerous others. Lord Canning was received by the railway company which was represented by Mr Purser, Mr Rendal, Mr Betagh, Mr Carbery and a few others that wished to have the felicity of being introduced to his Lordship and making a polite bow though yours truly prefered getting on the platform where he could see everything without interruption. His Lordship looked a very mild bland individual, he smiled and bowed to everyone who touched his hat to him. Prayers were then read by Mr Spay and a blessing given on the platform. The Band played 'God Save the Queen', everyone popped into the carriages as fast as they could and away went the train, faster than ever it went before on this line. Got all right to Futtehpore in 3 hours (73 miles). All the guards at the stations at which we stopped were turned out and presented arms. The Seihks at Bahrampore did the same although no one in the train saw them as it passed at the rate of 30 mph. All the Madras troops were out at Futtehpore. The field guns gave a salute and everyone cut across the fields to Mr Edmunstone's house, in half an hour or more the breakfast was ready – now after 11 am. All very good, turkeys, hams, beef, jellys, tarts, cakes and all sorts of things, just as you would see at a grand déjeuner in England with some unknown dishes in addition, iced tea, coffee and champagne – they all took their own knives and forks and plates glasses etc and a *kitmagur*. . .

But travel by rail continued to present many problems.[10] The big hold-up was bridging the river at Allahabad. The journey from Calcutta to Cawnpore in 1859 required 200 miles by train from Calcutta, then three days and nights by carriage and horses, and the fourth night to cover the last 100 miles between Allahabad and Cawnpore by railway.

The line to Delhi was progressing. Tina wrote to John Stewart from Agra on 18 June 1862.

The Railway brought us (from C'pore) a great improvement since I left last year. Indeed the different railways lines all over India are now drawing so nearly to completion that we shall soon have steam carriages all the way from Calcutta to Lahore. No one who has not known India before the era of railways, can tell what a change, what an improvement the introduction is making in the whole character of the country and its people.

Sikh woodcut of a railway train, c.1870.

But oh! the heat of that journey! from Cawnpore to Agra by railway on the 22nd May. Leaving at midday and arriving at sunset! We were obliged to travel by day as no night train had been commenced to be run. The sun, the flies, the Hot Wind, the thirst, the dust, and the woodash from the engine [only wood burnt, coal being a scarcity] all combine to make it anything but a journey of pleasure.

Letters of a Cawnpore Memsahib

'Dear Millie' was a sensible plump Scot who had no illusions about her looks. She knew she was born plain and that John Stewart had only proposed marriage after her elder sister turned him down. But she was a devoted wife and mother to his children. In all the letters exchanged between them there is nothing but affection, pride and mutual regard. Stewart's one weakness was a passion for dancing. As a young man he would travel almost any distance for a good dance and had an eye for an attractive partner. Millie treated all this with indulgence and her natural common sense provided a balance to her husband's ebullience.

Millie came from a military family; her father was Major-General Thomas Webster and two of her brothers were serving in the Indian Army but she herself had never been to India and had very little idea when she first arrived of how to run a large bungalow, manage the domestic arrangements, entertain on the scale her husband expected, look after the children in a hostile climate and aspire to be fashionable. She sensibly accepted Stewart's nudges towards seeking advice on nearly every subject from his sister Tina, married to William Roberts. Tina knew all about life in India, moved in ICS circles and was in herself remarkable. It was to her that Millie's early letters from Cawnpore were written.

Tina Roberts.   *Amelia Stewart.*

The Stewarts lived at first in a bungalow within the compound area of the Fort, the Kila. At that time Tina was in England settling her children into school. Later, when Tina returned to India, Millie wrote to her at Bareilly where Tina's husband was the commissioner and then at Agra. These extracts from Millie's letters cover the first six years of her life at Cawnpore during which time she had a son, Willie, and three daughters.

Cawnpore 14 April 1859 The month of May is the hottest here I believe but I do not expect to feel it so much as I hear people say, for at present, with so many appliances to keep out the heat I feel our rooms too cold and constantly am obliged to shut one of the doors because with the hot winds blowing against the Tatties the rooms are so very cold.

We are going to have some more Theatricals soon, the last ones came off splendidly so I rather look forward with pleasure to them as they are the only kind of amusement we have in Cawnpore. We have now got one road watered to drive upon it is a great improvement and every one seems to take advantage of it. The 48th Regt has just come in, they have got a splendid Band which is to favour us twice or three times a week, so it is very nice.

Cawnpore 13 June 1859 The weather is fearfully hot just now, but it doesn't affect my health in the very least so I ought not to complain; but really the only times enjoyable just now is a little before sun rise when we invariably go out; we are most regular in doing this being up every morning by 4 or ½ past am. We drive first, a little way in the buggy and then get out and walk; at ½ past 6 we have chota hazari when we both enjoy these large Bombay mangoes but until lately I didn't appreciate them at all.

I wonder if you have been busy shopping yet; preparing for India I mean. What do you think of that horrid duty laid upon everything English which arrives in India even to ladies' dresses and bonnets? We had to pay for the crockery which I sent away from Edinburgh in November '57 because it arrived a few days after the duty put on English things had commenced.

Cawnpore 3 July 1859 This perfectly trying weather. . . something terrific the heat so close and muggy, yesterday I think our rains have commenced and already we all feel better. I am a great sufferer from prickly heat, completely covered with it from under the roots of my hair down to my feet. Such an object as I appear Johnnie says he has never seen anyone so bad. I can scarcely sit still a moment and consequently am very idle, and at night I can hardly manage to sleep for it, otherwise dear Tina I am very well indeed – only occasionally fits of headache oblige me to lie down but I do not suffer much from this as I thought I should have done.

Cawnpore 25 August 1859 The weather here is very hot and sultry, very unhealthy as it always is this month and next in India, the cholera is raging everywhere in this Station and many Europeans have died from it. One officer died two days ago and in our compound one European child died and a woman is at present very ill. At Dum Dum we heard that 24 Europeans had died in one day. . .

We have no amusements going on here; two nights ago some amateurs performed in the theatre but it was a great failure and so very warm in the house that I heartily wished I had not gone. The detachment of the 48th Regt who were here have left for Allahabad so now we have only one European Regt., the 80th. The band of the former Regt. was a great acquisition to the station as it played twice every week on the Mall and then there was a little excitement and amusement. The 80th have a band but it is not worth going to hear.

Johnnie is very busy, I seldom see him from 7 o'clock am at chota hazari until five or six in the evening when we always take a drive. Instead of the work decreasing in this Magazine it is fast increasing, what they intend to do with us we can't tell, I hope to remain now at Cawnpore but still we may be ordered off very suddenly.

Cawnpore 2 December 1860 My box which Bob [John's brother at Cachar, Assam] so kindly brought out for me arrived some time ago, with some very nice things, a pretty bonnet and two nice cold weather dresses besides frocks and hats for Willie. Have you got your box yet? Who is getting your things for you? I was on the whole disappointed with my box because Kate [her sister] didn't send the half of what I wanted.

I have got a piano, at least it is on its way now. Johnnie bought it from a lady at Benares who he used to know and as she was a great musician I hope it will be a good one, price Rs 500 very cheap for a good piano.

Cawnpore 9 January 1861 I am afraid you will think I have delayed too long in sending you your mourning but the Kapra Walla promised to come twice and although several messengers went to him he did not come but yesterday afternoon I got the things, 16 yds of alpacca at 2/- a yard and 6 yards of crape at 1/4, they are the best I could get – the alpacca is broader than it usually is and as he had but 16 yards I took all he had – 16. I suppose you want some of it for other purposes than a dress because it is too much for that.

I daresay dear Tina there will be some things in your box which I shall be very thankful to buy from you – have you such a thing as a hat coming in it, gloves or neck ribbons? they forgot to send me some. We can easily dispose of anything you like here. I shall be delighted to do our best in the disposing of them. I hope you will think the alpacca good enough and also the crape, I think 6 yards ought to be enough for flounces or rather tucks.

Cawnpore 16 February 1861 . . . Thank you dearest Tina for offering to let me buy from you some of your nice English things, it is a great catch for me and I am sure I shall avail myself of it. I shall take all the gloves, kid and thread, and if I find I have too many will dispose of them afterwards. The wreath you mention I should like too, I am sure it is not dear and by your account must be very pretty, oaks and acorns I suppose the colors of it are green and white. Why not let me dispose of some of your things here – I am sure I should be delighted to do it and I think they would easily sell there are such heaps of ladies here compared with other stations. I think I would like that black tulle dress you speak of it must be so pretty. I am not too proud dear Tina to accept that brown straw hat you offer me but is it wise in your giving it away when on board ship you will require it. I have not worn a turn up yet but I admire them very much. I got such a pretty little black crape bonnet from a lady at Fattehghur who had brought it out from England and soon after her arrival had to return again. It only cost 16/-, is it not very cheap?

Cawnpore 26 February 1861 I shall be very glad indeed to buy the Box of Cougar Tea from you, also some claret if you will let us know how much you can spare, Johnnie says the Champagne he will not take as we never give grand enough dinners for that. . .

Johnnie is out just now buying books at a sale, the library of some native infantry Regt.

Our weather is getting rather warm now. I have commenced muslins and Johnnie thin coats, the cold weather flies away so soon before one has time to appreciate it.

What about that black dress you are getting out Tina? Are you going to let me take it off your hands? I am badly in want of a nice black dress for wearing at a large party or ball, what I have are only dinner dresses.

Cawnpore 18 November 1861 We were much delighted to receive from Nynee Tall some days ago six maunds of potatoes and five hundred walnuts which Mr Roberts [Tina's husband] had kindly sent us. I am sure it was very good of him to think of us amongst all his arduous duties. I had the potatoes all hung up on Tatties under the stable verandah where they get plenty of air and are quite safe.

I have only succeeded in disposing of your rose coloured barege and the pink wreath. I bought the chintz and damask I think you know as they were sold some time ago, a Mrs Angelo bought your dress, she had been at Mussoorie this year and she told me if I had sent the dresses up there they would certainly have been sold for so many young ladies were married there this season.

You were kind enough to offer to bring me out some things. . . I do not want many things in the shape of clothes, only four muslin dresses of a good kind to do for wearing when a friend or two in at dinner, one muslin cloak, a large kind and a pretty shape and one muslin jacket, made up. I am afraid my list will exceed £20.

ABOVE *'Our Cook Room'*. BELOW *'Our Cloth Merchants'*.

Cawnpore 4 December 1861 We are enjoying our cold weather exceedingly. It is an unusually cold season this and for a month or more we have had large fires every night and we do enjoy sitting round it. My brother Robert is here, he has been with us since the 20th of last month so will have paid us a long visit before he joins his Regt which is expected here on the 6th inst. and is going on to Lucknow. Both Robert and Harry are coming here at Xmas time. I take such long walks now up as far as the Fort of a morning and then Johnnie leaves us there and Robert drives me back in the buggy. I feel so strong and well this cold weather and able to do anything!

We have had a number of visitors lately the last were the Aitkens[11] from Lucknow, they were out in camp a short way from this, and came in to attend the Cawnpore Races. They were very good Races this time and we enjoyed them exceedingly. Johnnie is talking of going over to Lucknow to attend a fancy ball but I think it will be only a talk. . .

Cawnpore 19 December 1861 It is so near Xmas time that I cannot let this mail pass without writing to wish you a Merry Xmas and a happy New Year. You will have one great grief dear Tina when you have to part with your children but you must think of the happy reunion with your husband. . .

How busy you will be dear Tina at the very last. I hope you will not find my box very inconvenient, will you kindly bring me some Nursery Rhymes and some picture books for Willie is very quick to learning little hymns and songs and I can't remember many of them to teach him, he says the Little Busy Bee so nicely.

There has been a great deal of sickness amongst children, in the shape of croup and bronchitis but I am happy to say ours have escaped every thing of that kind. They are out all day long now and they enjoy it very much. We are going to a place called Najafghur on the 26th about 20 miles down by the river, it is for a change of air, and as Johnnie has a week's holiday I think he is wise in taking a little change. A Capt and Mrs Simmonds accompany us, the shooting is very good there so the gentlemen will enjoy that. There is a large house at Najafghur unoccupied so we propose living in it, giving the Simonds one half of it. We are to go down by boat and I am looking forward to this with great pleasure. We are to start at 7 am and get there in time for breakfast at 11 o'clock. Mrs S has a little baby so we shall have plenty amusement with so many children. The Station was quite gay while the Races lasted but now it is very quiet and dull. Numbers of Regts pass and repass but we see nothing of them, they stay such a short time. . .

We had an immense box of tea sent us by Bob, it was grown in his own gardens. It is delicious tea when mixed with China tea.

The garden is looking very nice and the vegetables are very far advanced. Johnnie is growing oats on the opposite side of the river, he has taken two fields for which he pays rent and he has planted oats which are growing very nicely. We shall be able to have regular oatmeal porridge and oatcakes.

Cawnpore 28 June 1862 We have been gay at Cawnpore of late – Such a lot of dinners and a Freemasons' Ball – not the most aristocratic of balls as you may imagine. Consequently few of the ladies from cantonments went to it. I and five others were all that were there, we agreed beforehand to dance nothing but quadrilles but I enjoyed looking on at the funny set of people far better than if I had danced every thing. The Masons were dressed in full tog and altogether it was an amusing enough party, although awfully hot and not a thing fit to eat or drink – *no ice.* Johnnie wouldn't hear of my refusing the invitation because he thought the Freemasons' lot might be offended but I don't think we would even have been missed.

The river has risen most wonderfully, not an island is visible now and the water is close up to our bank. The garden and compound look green and pretty and all the flowers are blooming. The passion flower is a mass of flowers over the centre arch and also at the garden gate.

Cawnpore 7 September 1862 I am busy working for the Cachar Fancy Sale and hope to have some things ready to send up to you by Johnnie to go with your contributions. I am at present working a pair of slippers as Charlotte [Anthony's wife] asked me to do, have finished two mats and intend to do one or two things more. I have ordered some little shoes to be made by Rung Lall and he has commenced them. Can you suggest anything else that I could send for if I knew what to work and could get the materials I shall be only too happy to do so.

Our station has been exceedingly healthy this year, not a single case of cholera amongst the troops. The weather is hot during the day but the mornings and evenings are most delightfully cool.

Cawnpore 4 October 1862 [Johnnie was at Agra] I wrote and told him yesterday of my numerous visitors. In the morning Mrs Hale paid me a long visit, then Mr Billy spent half the day tuning the piano, after he went Mrs Grey came for an hour or two and after she had gone Mrs Simmond – Capt S joined his wife and remained until gunfire when I took a lonely tea and went to bed. I get up exactly at gunfire and go to bed at that hour. . . Today I am going to drive out with Mrs Hoede and she wants me to remain to dinner offering to drive me home by the moonlight.

I am very glad to hear that you found Willie's box in good order and that you like his little smocks, they are very plain and simple but good enough of their kind – he seldom wears anything but low necked smocks so I find it hard to get nice boys' patterns in consequence.

Cawnpore 14 January 1863 Charlotte is quite delighted with the house and thinks Johnnie has done wonders in making up all the furnitures. She and I went out visiting yesterday. We called six places and ended by taking tiffin at the Hales; each place we went to the ball was discussed and it appears to be thought unlikely that it will ever take place – but today we must know for certain as there was a meeting last night to decide about it – the officers are quite disgusted at the number of refusals they have had – only 20 ladies accepted so at the last there will not be so many – it is all on account of that unfortunate Mrs Hay and even the ladies of the 46th seem disinclined to continue their acquaintance. I am afraid Charlotte will hate Cawnpore, there is no amusement of any kind and not a place to go to.

We are going down to the Civil Lines this morning. The Hales are coming into dinner and Major Roberts[12] of the C in C's Camp is coming also, he remains with us until the Chief goes. I wonder if it is true that the Chief has been recalled and that Sir Robert Napier is to succeed him. There was a report here yesterday to that effect. . .

Cawnpore 2 April 1863 I have always forgotten to ask you if you have still some common brown soap to spare me and which I shall be only too happy to take off your hands.

Johnnie left the house as the gun fired this morning and was away until 12 o'clock – he has the office in the compound again which is much nicer than in the Fort. I too got up at gunfire this morning and have been very busy all day trying on muslin dresses etc for it is high time now to wear thin clothing. The heat here is excessive but in the house very bearable. I can't sit very long with out calling for a punkah. Robert sent me some beautiful chintz from Calcutta and we are having the round ottoman covered with it. I also hope to have the sofa done tomorrow, the chintz is a large flowery pattern and will set our room off wonderfully. . .

Cawnpore 18 April 1863 How gay you have been dear Tina, Agra is much more lively than Cawnpore, nothing whatever goes on here and with the exception of driving out with a lady sometimes I never see one. The Mandersons of the Engineers stationed here, and who live quite near us, are under orders to go to Agra, I think she is a very nice person and you will like her very much. Mrs Maxwell went to Mussoorie last Saturday, the 11th Mrs Franks accompanied her – Mrs Vesey leaves in 10 days. She is almost quite convalescent again and the report is that she won't be much marked by small pox. I hope not for her sake poor thing. Col Vesey accompanies her for 6 months.

Cawnpore 19 June 1863 The news about your little ones is delight-ful, they all appear so happy and well, I shall prize their cartes very much dear Tina and thank you much for thinking of giving them to me. I do so long to see a likeness lately taken of all the little pets and shall have great pleasure in placing them in order in my carte book.

We have been so gay here lately, two picnics to the Nawabganje Gardens, the last given by the Maharaja of Gwalior, a large tiffin party at the Artillery Mess and no end of soldiers games at which every one in the Station meets and refreshments and ices are handed round. There is also a Gym Club being got up where people are to meet twice a week and all sorts of games are to be played. The energetic individual who is doing so much for the Station I am sorry to say has received orders to go home where his services in the Horse Artillery have been applied for, he is such a nice man and a great acquisition to the station that everyone will miss him very much.

We have a small dinner of ten people on Tuesday night, I hope it will be a cool evening – the rains commenced on the 15th ultimo and we have had heavy showers ever since but not enough to make the air cool. It is dreadfully hot and muggy when the rain stops. Johnnie is quite well and is making a lot of improvements in those little gardens in front, he is having bricks put all round the edges of the walks and pounded bricks laid down for gravel. It looks very neat and will be a great improvement.

After a visit to Agra Tina saw Millie and her children off at the station; at Toondlah they changed trains.

Cawnpore 21 January 1864 As I said I would I must write and let you know of our adventures since last night – We arrived at Toondlah, Mr Murray kindly procured for us a whole compartment to ourselves of a second class carriage, a very superior one to that you saw us get into at Agra, no holes in the cane work and so clean and nice that I felt quite charmed. Two gentlemen shared the next compartment and as they slept the whole way they could not be much the wiser of our presence next door. It was extremely cold so I at once made up beds for the children and put them into them and both Willie and Mabel slept soundly until we reached Cawnpore which was about ten minutes before 5 o'clock. Baby also gave no trouble and the Dhai enjoyed a pretty good night's rest. I lay down most of the way but didn't sleep. However I felt all right today and not as if I had not been in bed. Johnnie of course was at the station to receive us and so delighted to have us all back again. After all my packages were taken out of the carriage and not one of them was forgotten. We drove home and sat round the fire until day light, then we had chota hazari and as Johnnie had been up until very late and then up so early in the morning he went and lay down for an hour while I unpacked my boxes and now I think I shall soon get everything straight again.

My snuggery is not at all a small room and so cheerful and nice and the passage entering into the dining room is quite large enough to admit two ladies with very extensive crinolines to walk side by side. The house looks very comfortable and as all the walls have been white washed it looks very clean. Johnnie was out at dinner last night and we are expected to dine at the Stampers' [the padre] tomorrow evening.

Johnnie tells me there is a talk of a great deal of gaiety going to take place here. Horse races, a pic nic and a ball, the days are not quite fixed yet. Johnnie has gone to the Fort but is to be back soon to take me to the Band where I am anxious to see a Mrs Brownlow of the 19th Dragoons, that is to say her husband Capt B belongs to that Corps and his wife is I hear particularly stylish and handsome.

Cawnpore 25 January 1864 Johnnie and I took a walk last night with Capt Coghill, Brigade Major. He wanted us to go and see what he thought of that little house next the Church being turned into a Club Room – he is trying to collect funds to buy a billiard table and is going to get up a Reading Room which if they succeed will be a nice amusement for gentlemen during the hot weather – the room appears well suited for this purpose and I have no doubt Capt Coghill will be fortunate in doing all he wants to.

Johnnie goes to the Fort from 11 am to 5 pm – he is there now.

Cawnpore 19 February 1864 I have received Cross and Blackwell's list but I am sorry to say that neither John nor I have looked it over yet, we have been so much occupied lately but I hope in a few days to be able to return it to you with a list of the things we want. Cawnpore has been so uncommonly gay lately and we have had such a houseful that I have found little time for letter writing. Our races on the 11th, 13th and 15th were most successful, the Officers of the 88th take so much interest in racing that they did every thing they could to make the races interesting. The first day there was a grand Tiffin to which everybody in the Station went to, the food was given by contract and of course was bad, but we had games, Aunt Sally croquet and archery – it was great fun. . . We had a ball last Friday at the Artillery Mess house, that thatched bungalow near us on the banks of the river – it was a delightful ball, and everybody appeared to enjoy it. Our party consisted of Dr Young, Dr Inkson, Miss Taylor and Willie and Miss Playfair. Dr Inkson had been with us for a week. Dr Young and his niece Miss Taylor came from Oonou [Unao], the young lady has just arrived from England and is very stylish as well as pretty – she was generally considered the belle of the Ball – her dress was plain white tarlatan but so prettily made. She wore a pink flower on one side of her hair which was dressed in the new way, plaited and worn with a comb. I had on my new dress but before wearing it again I had the skirt taken to pieces, took a breadth and a half out of it and added both tog to make it longer. You have no idea how much this improved it, and it looked so pretty and was very much admired. I managed to unpick the trimmings and put it all on again. Nearly as nicely as you did it for me dear Tina. . .

Cawnpore 28 March 1864 We are going to have theatricals here, and all sorts of fun. There are no lack of ladies in the Station now and none of them leave during the hot season so there is talk of great things being done for their amusement, and I hope something will be got up such as croquet or archery parties.

Cawnpore 27 May 1864 John goes every afternoon to the Club, that little blue house next the Church. It has been added to and is now a nice place and very successful as a club. John enjoys his three hours there very much, sees the papers, plays at whist or billiards and also joins after sunset at that game called Hockey on Horseback. The club is a usual resort every evening for the ladies who go to look on at this game, and on Thursday nights there is a ladies' party. We are invited to go after dinner and generally we number about 14 or 15. I have been sending my piano and there is music and games – the latter consist of drawing room croquet etc etc. Mrs Sydney Chalmers is a grand musician, her singing is exquisite and it is the greatest treat to listen to her. I never heard anyone equal her and she is so good natured and willing to sing whenever asked. One or two other ladies here perform but they do not shine. Mr Wilmer, Capt Logan and some other gentlemen sing well, generally the Christies Minstrels' songs and to these I play accompaniments – this is all my share in the musical way.

Captain Coghill, Brigade Major, is the originator of all this sociability, he is a very nice person and spares himself no trouble or expense. He has lots of money apparently and spends a good deal for others. I have joined Mrs Lance and one or two other ladies in going to a working class for women twice a week. Mrs Lance and I were alone for some time but now others have joined. Mrs Lance has done everything for it, she collected money and bought calico prints flannels etc, these things she had cut out into chemises, dresses, petticoats and versions of the garments for women and children and they are kept in one of the Infantry Barracks where the women meet twice a week and where some ladies are present to distribute them. The women sit and sew for 3 hours and when each garment is finished they take it home and are paid for making it, but at the end of each month the women pay for the article at a very much cheaper rate than they could procure it. One lady reads while the women work, the class has only been commenced but as yet it answers very well. There are some very nice women amongst them and all are very well behaved. I felt afraid at first and thought there would be many disagreeable scenes but this is not the case.

Home Nursing

Health was always in the forefront of people's minds in India. In 1854 Stewart had counted ten medical men in Cawnpore, attending a European community of roughly a thousand. Hospitals were for the soldiers. For everyone else who fell ill sickness was a matter of home nursing, with visits from doctors and devoted ministration by female friends and relations backed up by domestic help. It was not unusual for a kind neighbour to sit with an invalid for two or three hours at a time.

Each year seemed to bring an epidemic of one form or another. Children were especially vulnerable to sudden attacks of fever with high temperature and ague. Vaccination against smallpox was regularly carried out, the pus from the infected arm, taken before the crust formed, used to vaccinate the next child. One year there was an epidemic of sore eyes and the treatment prescribed was the application of four leeches, two to the corner of each eye, until the inflammation went down. On another occasion, to save a little girl suffering from severe convulsions, two doctors applied a fly blister to the back of her neck which, when the blister rose, was lanced.

The start of the rainy season was always an unhealthy period and in August 1864 there were several cases of cholera. 'Today Mr Stamper buried one of the women of our Working Class, it seems she has had diarrhoea for some weeks and never told the Doctor. What foolish people these Barrack women are. Several children of the 88th have died of cholera very suddenly. I trust it will not spread through the Station. . .'

The Stewart letters give a glimpse into the manner in which European women coped with their pregnancies. It would seem from Maxwell and Stewart letters that very little comment was made about the lady being pregnant. Millie was safely delivered of her first child, Willie, in October 1859. Stewart reported delightedly, 'Never was such an easy confinement and such a quick recovery. Dearest Millie is a regular hand at it and makes a first rate nurse and nurses the whole child to her own cheek.' This was all the more remarkable as the household was 'throng' with visitors including Roberts, in preparation for the visit to Cawnpore of the Viceroy and Commander-in-Chief.

A daughter, Mabel, was born a year later. Millie nursed her for six months, but then fell ill herself and the baby suffered an attack of dysentery. She also developed violent convulsions, so bad they left her slightly paralysed. Without the devoted nursing of Tina, the child might not have lived.

It was at the third confinement that things did not go so well. In July 1863 Stewart commented that Millie could hardly bear the jolting of a carriage, although they still seemed to be expecting eleven or twelve to a *burra khanna* that evening. A young European woman had been engaged as a nurse; it was her first post but she was good-tempered and active and too young to have acquired the cocky airs and expensive ways of the usual English nurse. The baby arrived unexpectedly early. 'Millie took us by surprise this forenoon and without any difficulty whatever – and no discomfort brought forth a little daughter. The Doctor was not an hour in the house, the nurse came too late, even the ayah was away at her dinner, so I had to officiate as general nurse. I had just come back from the Fort and saw the Doctor who said it would be over in half an hour!' But then things began to go wrong. Millie's milk did not come, she fell prey to post-natal depression and, convinced she was dying, upset every-one by asking to be prayed for. She was in considerable pain and unable to sleep for three days and had to be 'kept up' with lots of food and wine. Arrangements were quickly made to send for a *dhaee* – a wet nurse – to feed the baby.

Stewart wrote to his sister on 14 October 1863:

We have secured a woman after some trouble – we got one yester-day who was a stunner, with a child of 40 days old – but when it came to eating she positively refused to eat out of any plates but those of her caste and not even to have her dinner cooked in our kitchen. This was too much and she was today changed for another, a more promising one and a more gentle and gareb [humble] woman who makes no bones about dinner, the only ob-jection to her was that her child is 3 months old. She is *Mussel woman* and has had her goosul [bath] and does not look bad. Henny Playfair had some ready made clothes and she is already decked out, more are to be made for her and it is to be hoped she will be a success.

And again on 19 October:

The first Dhaee was sent off when she would not eat our grub – the second appears to have had the evil eye on her milk for today and yesterday she has been nearly dry though she came with lots – Milly gave her a good stiff dose of Castor oil which played old

harry with her and she made her take out some stale milk into a cup
– and the natives say that 'nuzzur hog gya' ['the gift, the blessing
has gone'] but we are in hopes the milk will come back when the
effects of the castor oil have worn off. She's a very nice woman.

A few months later and a third *dhaee* was engaged. 'We got another
Dhaee yesterday who looks a good one, but of course is giving the
usual trouble about Burtans and Kuppra [pots and pans and clothes]. She
turned up her nose at the Dal the first day, because it had too much
Huldee – and the reason she came to us was that she couldn't get enough
to eat at home!' But Millie was delighted with her. The baby, Lilian,
grew tremendously fat and well. Millie told Tina, 'The Dhaee is a very
nice woman quite young and so fond of Baby, her child is thriving
nicely it is being nursed by a Native woman and looks very well. The
child was only 20 days old so she has loads of milk. . .'

Millie's experiences of childbirth were more fortunate than some. In
1864 Cawnpore lost five babies, either born dead or dying soon after
birth. There is not a cemetery in India that does not provide pathetic
reminders of the dangers of childbirth in those days before antiseptics
had been introduced.

'The Burra Mochee'

In a career of thirty years John Stewart built the small arsenal depot at
Cawnpore so effectively into the Government Harness Factory that by
the 1880s it supplied all the leather equipment for the entire British
armies in the East.[13] It was not his first experience of Cawnpore, nor the
family's first association with Cawnpore. As far back as 1775 when it was
little more than an army camp, Surgeon John Stewart, John's great-
uncle, had served in Cawnpore with the 3rd Brigade and had written
shrewd observations about it to the family in Scotland. Stewart himself
spent several months in Cawnpore in the autumn of 1854, tied to a desk
job and taking a poor view of the work expected of a keen young cadet
fresh from Addiscombe.

20 October 1854 Since I arrived here I have been very busy for I have
been receiving over Command of an European Company of Artillery. Such dik and bother I never had in my life. A drunken set of
Europeans to manage and not a soul to help me. Such accounts to
keep, and such sums of money to disburse. The service every day

Scene in Camp: *from Captain G. F. Atkinson* Campaign in India 1857-58.

is requiring more from the officers, we are now in time of peace little better than bankers' clerks as far as the work we have to do is concerned. The officer is obliged to keep the Khansamah's accounts of 80 men, each separately, to pay the men daily, to pay their servants monthly, to sell them liquor and beer and keep their accounts, and be banker for the men generally. Here's work for an officer. I had the command of Europeans at Benares, but there I had a subordinate to do the dirty work, here there's no one, and I am Sirdar Bearer to 80 Europeans. Pleasant!

By 1862 he was nicknamed the 'Burra Mochee'.[14] This achievement was very much a matter of a man with practical gifts seeing a need that existed, perceiving the opportunity at hand to satisfy it, and having the tenacity and drive both to persuade Government to back his scheme and to see it through. There was also an element of luck. He had the ear of Lord Roberts, his Addiscombe 'chum'.

John Stewart.

The original arsenal at Cawnpore was the Cawnpore Magazine that dates from 1786. It was one of the first public buildings to be built when the first British troops to penetrate up-country were encamped at Cawnpore, then little more than a hamlet. With high walls crowned with imposing turrets the Magazine dominated the area and bordered the River Ganges, providing a well-defended position for the storage of military equipment, guns, ammunition, carts, tents, grain, transport animals – everything required for the back-up of the army engaged in war against the Mahrattas.

Labourers from the nearby villages had flocked into Cawnpore seeking the chance to supply the needs of the camp. Many of the labourers were *chamars*, whose caste was at the lowest rung of the social scale. 'Almost every village in the Doab contained one or more families of these necessary adjuncts to a village community which, carrying on agricultural operations entirely by cattle labour, requires the disposal by unclean hands of the animals that died.'[15] Since they were already outcasts they had no hesitation in undertaking the many menial tasks that regimental life required, while the British, having no prejudice against the *chamars*, employed them in ways in which no orthodox Indian would have done at that time.

Many *chamars* found work at the Cawnpore Magazine. Much of the equipment was imported from Europe but there was a steady demand for the manufacture of tents, rope and leather pouches. Buff hides for belts or hinges were also in demand, as was bung leather for barrels, besides the constant repair work that called for carpenters and metal workers. An ordnance report dated 1838 describes the Cawnpore leather as 'rough, coarse and spungy' and the articles in consequence as 'unserviceable'. The leather workers were hampered by the primitive methods of tanning the leather, the only methods they knew.

In the district the babul tree grew wild. It is a small stunted thorn tree with mimosa-like blossom which survives in even the most barren land. The bark from this tree makes tannin from which raw hides can be quickly processed into workable leather. The *chamars*, seeing the need for shoes, boots and harness and saddlery in the camp, set to work to supply the market requirements as best they could. 'Each family set apart a corner of their mud huts to hang a skin or two from the roof, sewn into bags and filled with chopped babul bark and water, the pressure of the water forced the tannin into the texture of the skin and converted it in the brief space of a week or ten days into passable leather.'[16]

Cawnpore quickly won a reputation for leather goods. Mentioned in the inventory of goods sold at the death of Colonel Stainsforth in 1781 (his was the earliest surviving tablet at the Kacheri Cemetery) is a pair of 'new Country shoes'.[17] In 1807 at the death of Richard Nann, Hugh Maxwell's maternal grandfather, '3 pairs of Cawnpore boots and 3 Cawnpore saddles with bridles complete' are listed.[18] Emma Roberts, a journalist who had been in Cawnpore at the time of the opening of the theatre, wrote that Cawnpore was celebrated for its leather goods and spoke admiringly of delicate white kid gloves 'of a very fair quality'.[19]

The *chamars* worked closely with the butchers and the trade in goat hides and sheepskins became substantial. There was a time in the 1830s, however, when the success of the leather trade in Cawnpore had led to serious abuse. 'The great demand for leather in Cawnpore has proved very fatal to troop horses, and those of travellers proceeding to the station.' Many officers were warned of the danger to their horses, but it was some years before the practice was controlled.

> They have the credit in good authority of *poisoning horses*. . . so we picketed ours together and made the syces and grass cutters divide themselves into watches and keep sentry. . . When our Regiment was marching from G – to C –, at the last halt but one there were I think 19 ponies and tatoos dead in the camp from poison, the large horses escaped. The best way to defeat this infamous system is to make a rule to cut the hide of every horse so destroyed into narrow strips and to burn it.[20]

Even Fanny Parks, author of *Wanderings of a Pilgrim in Search of the Picturesque*, had a similar experience. She lived in Cawnpore in what is now the district magistrate's bungalow. She sadly described the loss of two handsome grey carriage horses.

> During this month of June we have lost two very fine grey carriage horses, the first we have lost during a residence of nearly eight years in India; they have been poisoned by the grass-cutters for the sake of their skins, each skin being worth about six rupees. The first stage out of Cawnpore is famous as a place where horses die on their march, and hides are there procurable for tanning. The poison is made into small balls, scarcely bigger than pills, which are thrown into the manger, or into the grass. In the evening I observed about twenty natives surrounding the entrance gate, who had come in the hope of carrying the carcase away, to sell the hide, and to feast themselves upon the flesh, for the people of the Doom caste eat

carrion. They were disappointed in their hope of a repast; we had the horses put into a boat and sunk in the Ganges.[21]

In time, however, this nefarious trade was controlled and the *chamars* concentrated on tanning the leather or in setting up as small manufacturers with workshops in the bazaar. 'These industrious people, the despised of the population, not only contrived to meet local demands but extended their operations in successfully imitating English-made articles, which widened their field.'[22] In 1849 when the collector, Robert Montgomery compiled his list of the population of Cawnpore, out of a total of 6,628 engaged in trades or professions he noted 558 shoe makers, 199 saddlers and 125 tanners.[23]

The Mutiny swept away this local industry entirely. John Stewart, aware that vast amounts of equipment had been destroyed during the fighting and alive to the difficulties of depending on England for the supply of leather equipment for the great number of troops now in India, saw the strategical importance of creating a local supply and utilising the resources of India. His idea was that if he could revive the old skills of the local *chamars* and introduce European methods of tanning and currying leather, it should be possible in time to produce leather articles as good as any imported from Europe.

In 1860 Stewart was selected by the Military Department of the Government of India to organise and establish the supply of harness, saddlery and accoutrements locally to the Army in India. The family letters give few details of how he went about this. In August 1862 he told Tina that 'I am well up in collars of English shape just now having had to make a lot for the R.A.' and only two months earlier he had mentioned 'Mr Elisha Deacon my tanner has arrived'.

On 2 May 1863 he wrote, 'I have gone into the hide market and buy for myself and I am cutting bark in the Jungles which keeps me out a great deal and gives me rides of 12 to 13 miles almost daily. My afternoons are spent in my office which is not very cool.' And by October 1863 his hopes were beginning to be realised:

[To Tina] *Cawnpore 6 October 1863* I have little chance of getting away now till the very end of October – I have been ordered to postpone my leave till a most important Board has assembled which is to decide finally whether a Government Tannery on a large scale is to be established here. The whole of my work here is to undergo scrutiny by 3 old and experienced officers and I could not be happy if I were absent while such a Board was reporting on my proceedings and sealing the fate of my scheme. The Govt has asked the C in C to appoint the Committee and I only hope that they will be quick about it and have it over this month.

The nature of the experiments exercising his ingenuity and his enthusiasm to explore every possible useful avenue are delightfully expressed in his letters to his sister Tina.[24] Here in microcosm is what trade is all about, the supply and exchange of goods as they are required and available. Stewart was frequently asked to help out, commissioned by friends to carry out practical requests, and he made quite a reputation for himself in doing so. His letters also convey his relationship with his work force. Rung Loll, who made so many pairs of shoes, was frequently mentioned.

In 1866, with the blessing of the Government of India, Stewart was sent to England to learn what he could about modern tanning and currying processes and their suitability for Indian hides. He was away for two years.

The Maxwells, Tom Tracy and Gavin Jones

On writing paper headed with the Maxwell family crest, Fanny Maxwell sat down to write to her fiancé. It was December 1860. Their engagement was to be announced the next day. She started her letter 'My dear Mr Tracy' and signed herself, 'Yours very much, Fanny Maxwell'. Above the crest and its motto 'I am ready' she added, 'So am I'.

Mrs Maxwell and her eldest daughter Fanny had returned to India to rejoin Hugh Maxwell. Their domestic arrangements were sufficiently well organised and back to normal for Millie Stewart to be able to say in July 1859: 'They [the Maxwells] appear to have plenty of money, such fine Calcutta furniture and grand carriage and horses and their dinners are always good.'

Tom Tracy as a member of the prestigious Civil Service, the 'heaven born', seemed an eligible enough bachelor to be a son-in-law for the Maxwells. He came from a well-connected family in Southern Ireland and had served in Cawnpore the past couple of years, often touring the district with Sherer. He weighed fourteen stone and was somewhat short-sighted and too easily bored, but Fanny was enchanted with him – or at least with the idea of becoming a married woman.

During the three months of their engagement Tom was frequently away touring in the district – Secundra, Shahjehanpore, Bhoneypore, Akbarpore, places on the old Moghul highway. Fanny wrote him effusive girlish letters describing the daily events and making eager plans for their future. Tom was romantic enough to safeguard these letters, which survive to provide us with the earliest picture of Hugh Maxwell's family at Cawnpore.[25]

The Maxwells lived in a fine bungalow in the centre of Cawnpore and another with a more rustic air about it at Nawabganj. If the worst came to the worst Fanny and her intended could start life together with the Maxwells. But Fanny was keen that she and Tom should find a house of their own. Her letters contain many references to the difficulties of finding a vacant house at a rent they could afford in a town still bearing the scars of recent fighting.

On New Year's Day 1861 Fanny went for a short ride while her mother and Mrs Tresidder, the doctor's newly acquired second wife, drove out in the buggy. They met at Mr Macfarlane's house on the way home.[26] 'It has been newly done up and looks clean and nice!' On closer inspection, however, a few days later, it was discovered the doors were only six foot high. Moreover the contractor, Budloo Soonar, announced it would not be finished for another two and a half months and the rent would be Rs. 100 per month. The only other house vacant was a doctor's, 'Mr Jones's', and no amount of coaxing could get an answer out of Mrs Jones. Fanny was hopeful of securing it for Rs.60 or 70, but even at the end of February nothing could be settled and Fanny wrote despairingly 'I do not know what we are going to do for a house, dearest.'

Through descriptions of balls and dances, of evenings when Fanny wore white tarletan and a wreath of wild roses in her hair, the endless round of morning calls to ladies in the station, of archery competitions and whist, of race meetings and theatricals, Hugh Maxwell comes across as a man deeply engrossed in business affairs. Friends and visitors were regularly entertained but Hugh Maxwell was too busy, for instance, to accompany his wife and daughter to the New Year's Eve Ball or go with them to the theatre. He worked long hours, often until late at night. There were cases he had to attend in Allahabad and Calcutta; important negotiations were taking place between him and would-be prominent citizens of Cawnpore; but if Hugh Maxwell discussed these schemes with his wife she did not mention them to Fanny, who was unaware of what preoccupied her father.

At home Hugh Maxwell was a typical Victorian father. All important

Tom Tracy.   Fanny Maxwell.
The Maxwells' bungalow at Nawabganj where Gavin Jones recovered from smallpox.

decisions affecting the lives of the family were made by him, but he combined this with a kindly interest in their welfare. As soon as the engagement had been announced he made Tom Tracy feel already one of the family and found time to encourage him by giving him advice on how to make the best of camp life. He made arrangements when Tom was out in camp for his mail to be sent out to him; at regular intervals, two coolies were sent off with provisions that included such items as bread and vegetables, English papers and books, and on one occasion gunpowder to enable Tom to make up cartridges for his next shoot.

It was in this role of a father figure that Hugh Maxwell invited his young brother-in-law Gavin Sibbald Jones up from Calcutta. But Gavin had barely arrived before he fell ill and on 23 January the doctor was sent for. A few days later Fanny wrote: 'Poor Gavin's illness has turned out to be small pox and for fear of infection Papa and the Doctor are very anxious to get Mama and myself out of the house.' Hugh Maxwell acted swiftly – his wife Charlotte was pregnant. The dak[27] was laid on for 3 p.m. and by 9 a.m. next day they arrived after a severe jolting all night at Fatehgarh to stay with Charlotte's sister Alice Saunders until it was safe for them to return.

Hugh Maxwell took over the responsibility for nursing Gavin Jones. Fanny's letters echo the news as it reached them from Cawnpore. On 31 January Gavin had regained consciousness and lost his deafness, but looked a 'dreadful figure'. The crisis was reached on 4, 5, and 6 February when he was critically ill. 'Poor Gavin seems to have had small pox very seriously. Mama had a few lines from Papa today, he was very anxious about poor Gavin. They are afraid he will not have strength to get over the disease, it has left him so weak, but they are feeding him up with soup and wine, so we must hope for the best that he may get well through it poor fellow.' Dr Tresidder shook his head and advised calling in another doctor. If Gavin pulled through this crisis all might yet be well. By 8 February he was out of danger, still very weak but getting hungry, a good sign.

The recovery was a long slow progress. Gavin was not well enough until 11 February to have his linen changed. Now he could take eggs and chicken lightly grilled but even a week after that his feet were too painful for him to stand and the crusts on his face were still infectious. It was 26 February before he was able to walk and plans were then made for him to be moved to Mendhi Ghat to recuperate at the old indigo bungalow which was built in an idyllic position on a slight promontory overlooking the Ganges. At night the fireflies danced in the neem leaves, overhead the stars sparkled in a velvet sky. Across the low sand banks the silence was broken by the howling of the jackals.[28]

Meanwhile preparations for Fanny's wedding went ahead. A large bottle of carbolic acid disinfectant, 'as extensively used in the large hospitals in England', arrived from Benares; the house was whitewashed and thoroughly ventilated. Charlotte and Fanny returned home. It was to be a quiet wedding, very different from the weddings that took place ten years later when Fanny's two younger sisters were married. Fanny asked her friend Amy Pereira in Calcutta to carry out some modest commissions for her: to buy crockery and the ornaments for the cake, a few suitable garments and a wreath for her to carry. Fanny planned to wear for her wedding a bonnet she had already worn, and her choice of bridesmaids was limited to mere acquaintances. Two sets of invitation cards were printed, one as invitations, the other for Tom to send out as announcements of the happy event. A dove grey dinner service arrived while the breakfast and tea set were to be white porcelain edged with gold. Charlotte's gold wedding ring was sent off to be used as a pattern.

'The Day' was fixed for Tuesday 12 March. On the 8th Tracy returned from tour and shaved off his beard. On the 9th he bought the licence and on the 11th wrote laconically 'Last day of bachelor existence; cheerful but resigned.' A friend, Carpenter, came up from Futtehpore to see him 'disposed of'. His diary was snatched from him next day by his young wife who made the entry herself. 'Married TBT at 12, came home, had tiffin, cake etc and afterwards drove to Suchendee. N.B. To remember *next time* not to start without money or provisions.'

The honeymoon, spent touring in the district, was not a great success. For two weeks they lived under canvas, moving from Suchendee to Barah, Deegh and Bhogneypore. It was very hot, there was no sense of privacy, Tom was busy with his own work during the day and Fanny, who was not used to life in the countryside, quickly became bored. 'Usual number of meals, nothing else worth chronicling.' Easter fell early that year; by Good Friday they were thoroughly scratchy with each other. 'Hot + Buns. Plenty of + husband.' They decided they had had enough of camp and on Easter Monday at 7 p.m., in the cool of the evening, they started back to Cawnpore in their palkees. 'I have not room to describe my feelings.'

Back in the familiar world of Cawnpore Fanny enjoyed a drive in the buggy with Tracy, pleased to be taken to the band and round the garden of Company Bagh. On 10 April they took possession of their own home, 'Tom's and mine!' For Fanny, this was what marriage was all about.

The hot weather of 1861 had started early. Fanny's enthusiasm flagged and over the weekend of 22 June Tracy took back possession of his diary, 'finding it was not properly kept up.' For the rest of the year his brief daily entries tell something of his work and the life style of a young civil servant, one of the first among the 'Competition Wallahs'. Entrance to the Indian Civil Service was no longer by preferment but had been thrown open to a competitive examination in 1855. Brief quotations in Latin in the margin of the diary indicate Tracy had received a typical classical education.

When on duty in Cawnpore as a joint magistrate he rode to the *cutcherry* every weekday, including Saturday, for magisterial or collectory duties, arriving there at eleven or by noon at the latest. All through this particular year, however, he complains that there is not much work; only on two occasions is there cause to stay and work late at the office. Day after day he comments 'Nothing particular.' There is very little revenue work to do and practically no criminal cases. The court reader, the *peshkar,* prepares files of documents and brings them in to be signed or initialled (often every page had to be signed – one of the earliest tasks as a newcomer was to learn which documents needed a full signature). The hot days drag on, the rains commence. He is ill with diarrhoea, and bored, he complains of being seedy and disgruntled with things in general. He counts the office stationery, writes letters, attends to the records and is glad when the monotony is broken by the meeting of the Road and Ferry Fund or the newly set up Municipal Committee. He draws his salary once a month and devours the lists of new appointments in the *Government Gazette*, praying for promotion or a move to another district. Only when the cold weather begins in October is there anything stimulating in his work. During the whole of 1861 the only events of any moment are three murder cases, a case of suspected poisoning and a few cases of appeal against income tax assessment.

All civil servants had to be proficient on horseback and from the diary entries it is clear how much Tracy depended on his horse. At times he would ride into the city on duty, accessible to any member of the public who might wish to speak with him. His duties also took him riding to Bithoor, Old Kanhpur and Nawabganj. Half his time was spent touring the district on horseback, camping each night at a different place, meeting the villagers, listening to their complaints, reporting back to his superior on the crops and giving an assessment of the revenue.

He moved almost entirely in the small circle of civil servants, frequently driving out with Fanny, occasionally taking a peg at the Artillery mess or attending an auction held by the 54th or the 48th Regiments (it proved to be a mistake to buy their Moselle). Only once does he mention a social visit to an Indian and that was to Nawab Bakur Ali Khan.

The Tracys' bungalow, rented at Rs. 60 per month, was within walking distance of the bandstand in Company Bagh. Generally the Tracys drove out together in their buggy to listen to the band. When Fanny became pregnant Tracy rode alone. He was also known to walk and run with a companion in an attempt to keep his fourteen stone in check. On average they attended Christ Church Sunday services once in three weeks.

Most of the household business was conducted by Tracy, although Fanny paid the staff – coins set out in front of her in neat piles, calling up the servants one by one to make their thumb print, left hand for a man, right hand for a woman. It was her husband who rode to Dalziel's, the only shop of any size, to order the stores. On one occasion he came back with a pork pie hat. The servants received their wages six days after Tracy received his salary, but they seem not to have had the knack – or resources – to attract good staff. Nor were they particularly successful at handling them. The cook is described as a 'swindling' *khansamer*, the mate-bearer as a 'useless cub' who had to be sacked and once Tracy 'licked' the syces, 'lazy brutes', and dismissed them for neglect.

During the year Tracy read *The Mill on the Floss, Anatomy of Central Africa* and *The Ingoldsby Legends*, all bought at Dalziel's. Towards the end of the rainy season he would sometimes go to the baths for a dip on his way to work, and after work he might play battledore or shuttlecock or join a group for archery practice. Very little home entertaining seems to have taken place but they dined regularly with the Maxwells. Once after dinner, when the ladies had retired and the cigars and brandy had been passed, a serious discussion on the prejudices of the Indians took place. A great deal of interest had been aroused by the 'Great Oudh' case at Lucknow. The majority of English people at Cawnpore thought it a clear example of Lord Canning's obsession with clemency towards the Indian people.[29]

The 'Great Oudh Libel Case'[30] was heard at Lucknow and referred entirely to events that took place in Lucknow. But there were reasons why Cawnpore society followed the proceedings with keen interest. Pearson, Tracy's immediate senior, was brought in from Cawnpore to

Our Bath: *from* Curry and Rice *by Captain G.F. Atkinson, Royal Engineers.*

be the special judge, it being considered important to have an impartial outsider on the bench. Mrs Pearson was a family friend of both the Maxwells and Tracy in his bachelor days. Tracy had confided his closest secrets to her. Mrs Pearson responded by acting chaperone to Fanny and playing at match-making. Now she could give them details of the case. Elliott, whose letter formed part of the evidence, was the friend with whom Tracy went exercising to the Company gardens. Of the three Indians involved, Unjore Tewaree's name aroused intense interest in Cawnpore. He had been a sepoy with the 1st Bengal Native Infantry when the Mutiny broke out and saved the lives of a European clerk and his wife at Banda. He joined Havelock's forces as a spy and was several times taken prisoner and tortured. Another time he faithfully carried a letter from Outram at Lucknow to Campbell at Cawnpore, surviving cruel treatment when he fell into the hands of the rebels. But his greatest claim to fame came from the help he gave Lieutenant Fred Roberts in obtaining information in an attempt to capture the Nana Sahib.[31] The Government had rewarded him handsomely, granting him the title of Sirdar Bahadoor, Member of the Order of British India and the gift of Rs. 3,000.

Government had recently brought in a trade tax. This was introduced and accepted in other cities without question but at Lucknow it was openly resisted. The civil servants determined to carry through these new measures had acted somewhat over-zealously. There were whispers of locks being broken open when keys were not brought quickly enough, of respectable women being exposed to threats by underlings, and sweeper women being sent into zenanas to seize the jewels of the inmates. When these suspicions reached the ears of the *Oudh Gazette*, the editor thought fit to bring them to the notice of his readers and accused the collectors of the Trade Tax of 'tyrannous oppression and corruption'. In June 1860 Ramdyal, an extra assistant commissioner at Lucknow, brought an action for libel against the *Oudh Gazette*. This had been backed up by a letter from Elliott, the city magistrate, refuting the charges against Ramdyal.

The police took matters into their own hands, thereby compounding the problem. Captain Chamberlain, the Deputy Superintendent of Police,[32] and Lieutenant Scott, the Superintendent of City Police, made their own investigations privately, encouraging and inviting complaints of oppression which they then passed on to the defence lawyers as evidence against Ramdyal. The three Indians in the case were native officers of the police, Unjore Tewaree, Jugganath Singh and Moula Buksh, brought in as witnesses to the oppressive measures. Unjore Tewaree was defended by a Mr Norris.

The case dragged on for months. In the end Ramdyal was given an honourable acquittal. His loss of temper on two occasions was deemed without significance and no act of oppression was shown to have been committed. The conduct of the police in Lucknow was judged utterly indefensible. Both Chamberlain and Scott were dismissed from service. The three native witnesses were convicted of perjury and sentenced to hard labour in chains. It was supposed that they had been motivated by a desire to support a cause which they believed to be favourably looked upon by their superiors and had deceived them with stories of oppression which they knew to be untrue, and so perjured themselves before a court of justice. At this stage Lord Canning, the Governor-General, intervened.

Although the Governor-General cannot allow any services,

however eminent, to shield a man from the consequences of wilful and deliberate perjury. . . yet in remembrance of the devotion shown and the courageous assistance given by Unjore Tewaree to his Officers, and to others in a time of utmost danger, the Governor-General remits to him the remainder of the imprisonment to which he has been sentenced. . .

Unjore Tewaree was permitted to retain the financial grants that had been made but his name was erased from the Roll of Order, depriving him of his honorary title. He was also dismissed for ever from service of the Government. His two fellow witnesses were also let off but dismissed the service.

Among the Europeans in Cawnpore, judging from Fanny's letter to Tracy, and even extending to the civil servants, this act of clemency was not popular. 'You will be provoked to hear that Mr P has decided the *case* in favor of the *natives!* I suppose it is very much what you expected from him, but it does seem a great shame. He says the evidence was not sufficient to convict them, and that you had got hold of the wrong people! I believe Mr Lance is very much disgusted and says he will leave the Station.'

The last word however rested with Lieutenant Fred Roberts who never forgot Unjore Tewaree's loyal help. Some years later, hearing the brave old man was paralysed and in want Roberts persuaded Lord Napier to give Tewaree a pension for life. Whenever Roberts passed through Cawnpore Tewaree had himself carried to the station to meet Roberts, although he lived some distance away.

Fanny Maxwell writes of Hugh Maxwell being occupied at his '*cutcherry*'. Her use of the word *cutcherry* instead of the more usual word *dufta*, a study, conjures up the prestige, influence and patronage Hugh Maxwell exercised as the senior surviving member of the European community.[33] He did indeed hold 'court'. Here negotiations took place, financial transactions were discussed, bargains struck and new ideas put forward; everyone seemed to want his opinion, help or encouragement. On both sides it was a relief and a bond to have shared in common the happier cordiality and cooperation that had existed between the English and the Indian business communities before the uprising took place.

Dr David Begg had known Hugh Maxwell for over twenty years, since Maxwell had been an indigo planter in Mirzapore. Shortly before the Mutiny Begg had set up Begg Christie and Co., an indigo seed firm at Cawnpore. But with the Christie family all killed, Begg, now retired, sent his brother-in-law Donald Macfarlane to negotiate a new agreement to form a company that became Begg, Maxwell and Co., dealing in country produce.

Frederick Buist, the station master of the East Indian Railway, came with a group of influential Indian backers.[34] They sat round the table, men who commanded lakhs of rupees, some wearing huge wound turbans in pale colours, snow-white gathered *dhotis* under loose shirts, and shoes with turned up toes. They watched Hugh Maxwell closely. They had formed the Cawnpore Cotton Committee in 1860 and now in response to the dramatic rise in cotton prices they were enthusiastically contemplating a scheme to start a cotton mill – rather than send the raw cotton to Calcutta how much more advantageous to weave it into yarn. They needed Hugh Maxwell's name and business authority to head the list of subscribers. They proposed to call it the Cawnpore Cotton Spinning and Weaving Company.

G. E. Lance, the collector and magistrate, sought Hugh Maxwell's advice on the setting up of the Municipal Committee for the 'improvement and better government of Cawnpore'. Ideas were discussed of how to raise the necessary taxes without alarming the people. With the whole of Cawnpore to be rebuilt, good roads, lighting and drainage were of paramount importance. It was proposed that house proprietors should be taxed Rs.15 per acre and in return they would have a say in how affairs were run. This was at a time when only thirty-nine registered house proprietors existed.[35] Tracy was elected secretary at the first meeting of the Municipal Committee; at the second Hugh Maxwell was co-opted and he later brought into the committee his nephew John Tritton.

In a more personal area Maxwell felt responsible for the way in which Gavin Jones's career should develop. After Jones had recovered from smallpox, in view of his bent for engineering it was arranged that he should go to work on the GIP railway where the line was under construction between Jubbalpore and Hoshangabad. Norris and Weller had the contract for building the line, and as Sam Weller had been a personal friend of John Moore Jones, Gavin's eldest brother, he was glad to give the young hero a post.

The Maxwell family still owned Bilsee indigo estate in Rohilkhund and George Debnam, John Stewart's uncle, was another caller at the *cutcherry* – to sign an agreement to go into partnership with Hugh Maxwell. The Society for the Propagation of the Gospel (SPG), also successfully courted him to join their committee in raising funds to rebuild the orphanage on the Grand Trunk Road. Similarly, Indian brokers and

David Maxwell and Sam Weller.

John Tritton.

contractors all waited patiently at Hugh Maxwell's door. They needed his ear to obtain a testimonial of good character so that they might apply for the many opportunities now opening up. They also offered the loan of good money for any worthwhile scheme he might like to recommend to them. History was being made but they were probably all too busy to recognise it.

On the last day of December 1861 Tracy summed up the year with a comment that the only event of much importance to him had been his marriage to Fanny Maxwell, that he had now completed four years' residence in India and been on the whole 'd. . .d'. Cryptically he adds Psalms LXXV.6 – which reads: 'Set up not your horn on high; and speak not with a stiff neck. For promotion cometh neither from the east, nor from the west; nor yet from the south.' Tracy, in despair, added 'East, west, north, south, from none!'

The Cotton Crisis

Civil War broke out in America in 1861; within weeks the Southern ports were blockaded and supplies of cotton on which Manchester mills depended for their production were not available. Suddenly cotton from India was big money. The first importation of cotton from the district between Cawnpore and Agra, from Bundlecund and the Doab, the fertile land between the two rivers, the Ganges and the Jumna, dates from 1783. The cotton was gathered in every evening by the villagers who sold it next morning to cotton dealers, who in their turn made contracts to supply cotton to the merchants.[36]

There are references in the records of 1806 to the huge volume of raw cotton passing through Cawnpore – stopped at the Customs House for duty to be paid, or being steered past in rough country boats, sides raised high to support a great number of bales, making their way to Mirzapore and the port of Calcutta, their cargo destined for Manchester or the East India Company's trade with China.[37]

The Maxwells had been involved with the cotton trade since John Maxwell settled in Cawnpore. He had owned considerable property in cotton go-downs and press houses. In the go-downs some attempt was made to clean the raw cotton which was often full of dead leaves, seed pods, even scraps of fabric and potato skins. It was spread out on the floor and sunned and beaten with twigs to remove particles of dirt. Then it was 'screwed' and compressed into bales and secured with strips of metal. The cotton screws were the pioneers of an immense export of cotton apparatus from England.[38]

Manchester was entirely dependent on imported cotton to keep its mills supplied. Most of that cotton had come from America where the staple was longer than Indian cotton, but about 20 per cent of Manchester's cotton was bought from India.[39] After two bad years, when the supply of raw cotton fell below the demands and capacity of the English mills, the Manchester Cotton Supply Association was formed in Manchester in 1857 to encourage the cultivation of a better quality of cotton from India. When civil war broke out in America they redoubled their efforts and an important conference took place on the need for greater production of cotton at Hingunghat in Central India, famous for its high-quality cotton.

In the past the price of cotton fetched had often been too low to encourage cultivation. Land was taxed according to what was grown on

'Mountains' of raw cotton.

it, so that no crop meant no tax. When cotton prices were low, therefore, there was no inducement to the peasant to grow cotton and risk
paying tax. There was also the considerable cost of carriage, whether
by river or bullock cart. Now suddenly both these disadvantages were
removed with dramatic results.

A resolution passed by the Governor-General in Council was forwarded to all magistrates and circulated to all commercial communities
with translations into 'Ordoo and Hindee'. It caused a sensation in the
Cawnpore district. 'Government will not compete, but will do all she
can to encourage the supply of Indian cotton, to lend money to the
capitalists and to open up and maintain road and water communication
to the sea-board.'[40]

The road and ferry fund in Cawnpore had just completed a good
network of roads around the town, while the railway was open as far as
Allahabad. The ancient trade routes of the rivers that had made Kalpi
and Mirzapore famous markets were now deserted; all produce of the
country – grain, oil, seed, sugar and cotton in vast amounts – came to
Cawnpore to the railhead.

Carts laden with cotton crowded into the town until roads became blocked and bales were stacked higher than the roofs of the houses. The authorities, alarmed, were desperate to provide space, so they brought in elephants to flatten the mud huts of the camp-followers that over the years had sprung up on cantonment land. Even when space had been made, the mountains of cotton created an amazing sight and took months for the railway to transport. With the war in America continuing, the price of cotton was forced up to unprecedented heights, creating a boom in India that enriched both merchant and producer.[41] Cotton sold for Rs. 24 a maund. Entire ships were acquired to transport the precious cargo; in 1861 the *Mary Lord* was let for Liverpool at 2.15s a ton[42] and it was said that the cotton *banias* were 'praying fervently for a continuation of the American war as it would not matter to them if every man in America were destroyed, provided Cotton rose sufficiently high to admit a remunerative rate'.[43]

It was the station master of the East Indian Railway who had the brilliant idea of manufacturing cotton on the spot instead of sending it to Calcutta, since it was around the railhead that the bales of cotton were piled high. Frederick Buist, the station master, who had already formed the Cawnpore Cotton Committee, now discussed the possibility of putting up a mill with some of the leading cotton merchants, wealthy commissariat contractors and agents who were ready to subscribe the capital. Together they went to ask Hugh Maxwell to join them and become one of the directors.

From the date of that first meeting it took five years of planning, discussions and painstaking hard work to bring their ideas to fruition. On 6 February 1865 Hugh Maxwell as chairman gave the first annual report to a small group of interested shareholders. They included two Indian directors and Joseph Strong, the newly arrived resident engineer of the EIR. Capital of 3 lakhs (Rs. 300,000), later increased to 4 lakhs, was raised by the issue of 1,600 shares of Rs. 250, of each, which only 75 per cent had been called up. A site was selected on the river bank, twenty-five acres of land were acquired on which the ruins of the building known as the Old Hospital had stood, situated between the Customs House at Permit Ghat and the old Magazine. It was purchased from the Municipality for Rs. 1,146, which included compensation for the standing crops. The hard-working peasants had not wasted a moment in utilising the ruined site; the crops they had sown sold for Rs.309. Provision was also made for a railway siding to serve the site. In true Victorian style the enterprise was called after the new Viceroy, Lord Elgin, and

Entrance to Elgin Mills.[44]

formally registered on December 1864 as the Elgin Cotton Spinning and Weaving Company.

A simple plan for the construction of the first mill building is among the records of Messrs Platt Brothers of Hartford Works, Oldham, Lancashire, along with details of the first machinery shipped out on the *Vanguard*: 18 throstles of 268 spindles and 8 self-acting mules with 648 spindles were the first on order. The drive shafting and steam engine to power the machinery was ordered from B. Hicks and Sons of Bolton, through their agent Mr R. Newton of Bombay. The erection of the buildings including bungalows for the European staff was contracted with Messrs Doyle and Co. of Calcutta and the foundation stone was laid on 8 December 1864 'in the presence of a numerous assemblage of the residents of Cawnpore and neighbouring stations'.

The *Pioneer* carried full details of the important first Annual General Meeting (see Appendix). The Company's bankers were the Agra and Masterman's Bank, Calcutta, but it is interesting to note that a private Cawnpore banker, Gooropersaud Sookul whose name appeared in the original Cawnpore Cotton Company, offered them 6 per cent on money deposited with him against 2 per cent of the Agra and Masterman's Bank. A list of seventy-eight shareholders is given, which includes thirty-eight military men, five doctors, twenty-two European civilians, one English lady, Mrs Chalmers (whose beautiful singing voice Millie Stewart greatly admired) and one padre. Hugh Maxwell was re-elected chairman with Lala Ishack Lall, Lala Guneshee Lall and Lala Chota Lall and Hugh Maxwell's nephew John Tritton as directors. Everyone at the meeting congratulated him and each other.

Hugh Maxwell, however, was not entirely easy in his mind. Platt Brothers had arranged to engage and send out European staff to fit and work the machinery but Doyle and Co. were very behind with the erection of the mill building. In spite of a heavy penalty clause, in case of any delay, by February – in two and a half months out of the five months stipulated – they had only got up to floor level with the building. Cotton prices had fallen, cotton was selling in the bazaar for Rs. 11/8 and Rs. 10/8 in the district. Several Mahajans had gone bankrupt with over-speculation. The papers reported 'one poor wretch swallowed a diamond and so died; and there are rumours of other suicides occasioned by commercial misfortunes'. Hugh Maxwell was planning to go home on leave. He wished things at the mill were further advanced.

Gavin Jones: Family Background

In the Gavin Jones family few personal papers survived the Mutiny. On the outbreak of hostilities John Moore Jones as head of the family placed all valuables and family records in the fort at Fatehgarh for safety, but these were destroyed by the rebels when the fort fell into their hands. Luckily Gavin's sister Fanny Bell, living at Saugor where she escaped the outbreak, had treasured a small notebook in which their mother had carefully recorded the dates of births and marriages of her children. One entry reads: 'Tuesday 22 December 1835 at 8 am in Featonby's house on the Circular Road Calcutta, born Gavin Sibbald Jones'. He was the eleventh child out of fourteen.

Feetenby's house, Calcutta, is significant. Calcutta was where Gavin's father, John Benjamin Jones grew up and Feetenby's house was at the centre of a bitter quarrel between JBJ and his stepfather. The Jones family had had a comparatively long association with India.[45] JBJ's father, Benjamin Leonard Jones, was a Welshman from Pembroke, a master pilot in the East India Company's service, guiding East Indiamen through the shifting dangerous sandheads at the approach to Calcutta. He had settled in Calcutta with his two brothers, James and David, both merchants, and in 1791 married Ann Hall, aged fifteen, the daughter of a retired sea captain and his Portuguese wife Isabella Roderiques. JBJ never knew his father, who was missing presumed drowned when the boy was only two. Left a widow at twenty in a society where European women were scarce, Ann Jones soon married again. Her second husband was James Feetenby, a kindly older man, a cabinet-maker by profession. JBJ was sent to live with his grandmother at Serampore, the little Danish settlement on the right bank of the Hooghly sixteen miles above Calcutta, opposite Barrackpore and the elegant country seat of the Governor-General. The town was a busy commercial centre, and, being beyond the jurisdiction of the Company, a refuge for debtors or anyone seeking to escape Company law. Here JBJ learnt to write and speak fluent French and Portuguese. Old Mrs Hall, his grandmother, was a devout Roman Catholic with a house full of statues and holy pictures. The priest was a regular visitor. JBJ, however, was sent to Marshman and Carey's recently established school, a mixed Anglican boarding school for English and Anglo-Indian children.[46]

When the first missionaries came to Calcutta, the official attitude to them was so inimical that they were able to remain in India only by taking up residence at Serampore. The old school of Company men believed that they interfered with the established pattern of Indian life, stirred up trouble, and would eventually lose India for the Company. On the other hand, men like Joshua Marshman and William Carey believed fervently in the importance of educating the Indian people and in the supreme value of the message they tried to convey. Whatever one thinks of their opinions, they were remarkable men: learned, inspired, self-disciplined and fiery. They translated the Scriptures into the vernaculars of India and translated into English the Indian epic the *Ramayana*; they published the first Indian vernacular paper and an English language paper *The Friend of India* as vehicles for their advanced ideas. Their experiences went further than academic pursuits: Carey had spent time on an indigo estate and Marshman's father had worked in an English mill producing superfine woollen cloth. These were the men who taught JBJ, exercising a profound influence on his life and affording an education that was astonishingly wide.

The prospectus cited 'reading, writing, book-keeping, geography, etc... Latin, Greek, Hebrew, Persian and Sangscrit [*sic*]'. In addition Carey and Marshman taught modern languages, history, botany, chemistry, astronomy, law and the history of the antiquities of Hindustan. All this at a time when men qualified for Company office if they could read, write and understand double-entry book-keeping.

On the occasions when JBJ stayed at the Feetenby household in Calcutta he must have been made sternly aware of the difficulties of rearing children in India. Four stepbrothers and sisters were born to his mother but none survived beyond the age of eight. When JBJ was fourteen he attended the funeral of a stepbrother who died aged six, accidentally killed by a musket shot. The next year his stepfather died. The following year a stepsister and Feetenby's daughter by an Indian woman who had lived with them died within five days of each other. Feetenby had been comfortably off and in the last years of his life had taken pride and pleasure in overseeing the building of a fine house in extensive grounds at Intally on the Circular Road, which he had put in his wife's name. This was the house that was the centre of bitter disputes and in which Gavin Jones was to be born. JBJ's mother married for the third time on 13 October 1813, a day that was to be doubly unfortunate for the family. It seems likely that her husband, James Brown Moore, a pensioner of the Marine Establishment, married her for her money.

JBJ started his working life with the firm of Palmer and Co., Calcutta. When he was twenty-two he married Fanny Palmer, the daughter of a wealthy merchant, at the Cathedral, Calcutta. The baptism details of their fourteen children chart his commercial progress, from assistant to book-keeper and writer until, by the time his fifth child was born, he was in a position to give up trade. Thereafter he lists his occupation as 'gentleman'. The financial stability and independence he had attained enabled him to take his family home to England for an extended visit of two years. There he had a leisurely, civilised leave, furthering his considerable artistic talent.

It was while he was away that his mother died. She apparently left no will and Moore began spending lavishly from her estate, filing a bill in equity claiming the property left to her in trust by her second husband. On his return to Calcutta JBJ immediately filed a cross suit. It was an acrimonious quarrel, resulting in the whole of Moore's estate being willed to distant relatives on his death. So great was his animosity of JBJ that he gave explicit instructions in his will that although he left some of his wife's jewellery to JBJ's children, 'I furthermore do particularly desire that the said Property be whatever it may be shall not at any time under any circumstance become the property of their Father and Mother.' Moore died in 1834 and it was with a note of triumph and satisfaction that JBJ was able to write that his son Gavin was born in Feetenby's house.

While JBJ had grown up in Calcutta, Gavin's earliest recollections were of the indigo estate at Babcha. Probably the bitterness between JBJ and his stepfather played a part in his decision to leave Calcutta. For some time JBJ had been moving in a circle which had connections with indigo. He moved up-country, first to Tirhoot and then settled at Babcha in the Jaunpore district between Benares and Mirzapore. It was a marvellous existence for a boy. Their home was a magnificent old two-storey house with a high 'keep' and castellated walls that gave it the impression of being fortified. It was set in parkland ablaze with bougainvillea and approached through groves of mango trees. Sometimes Gavin accompanied his father round the estate on his pony, visiting the villages that grew the indigo. They were always received with ceremony and hospitality.

JBJ stood six foot tall, handsome and well built, a wonderful raconteur, with natural charm. The time the children enjoyed the most was the evenings when their parents entertained and the house was full of guests. Gavin Jones described it:

In those prosperous days when indigo had no rival the planters made large fortunes and lived in palatial homes like princes. Christmas week in the delightful cold weather, when work was finished for the season, used to be the time for the gathering of the clans. Planters were wont to meet and make merry. Babcha used to be the rendezvous for the annual gathering. Visitors from surrounding factories, Jaunpore and Benares flocked to the factory and the magistrates out on tour joined in the festivities and enjoyed the shooting, hunting and big dinners and the utmost cordiality and good fellowship prevailed. It was not an unusual sight on such occasions to see a score or more of guests to sit night after night at the hospitable table. Our father was in his element at these festivities and being a good raconteur he kept the party amused and lively with his anecdotes and humourous jokes. And music, singing and dancing was kept up to late hours. I still retain a distinct recollection of those gatherings and we children came in for a good share of the attention from the visitors and enjoyed the romps and petting bestowed on us. Those were days when the prestige of the Englishman stood high with the natives and the pledged word of the Sahib was as good as a bond. The planters then formed a link

that kept in touch the natives and rulers of the great 'Company
Bahadur'. The zemindars lived in cordial amity with the Planters,
as it was their mutual interest to do so, for large sums in advances
were disbursed through them to the villagers for the cultivation of
indigo. The people were contented and happy and loud in their
proclamation of gratitude to the 'Sircar Bahadur' for the Pax
Brittanica which had brought peace and security to the land where
for centuries tyranny and chaos had reigned.

This enchanting life came to an end when Gavin was twelve. JBJ was
doing well and was in a position to expand his interests. He was approached by a firm of Calcutta merchants, Fergusson Brothers, who
offered him a partnership in a sugar factory. Sugar was new to India,
but JBJ judged, rightly, that it had a promising future. With Fergusson Brothers he erected extensive sugar works at Ranjpur, imported
machinery from England and America, and sought the help of experts
on manufacture from the West Indies. The enterprise should have been
highly successful, but he was unlucky in his timing. All his money was
with the Union Bank of Calcutta, and in 1847 the bank failed.

> Every business man's face bore an anxious look, for no one knew
> when some big bill might be returned protested. Money could not
> be raised on the best security and business was at a standstill. . . On
> the sandy banks of the rivers to the north of Tirhoot immense
> masses of machinery are to be found strewn about, and high chim-
> ney stacks are the monuments of folly which represent the ruin of
> many a good man, and the spot where large amounts of capital
> were sunk.[47]

Fergusson Brothers went bankrupt. JBJ, faced with crippling debts,
sold his share in all the indigo estates and sold up the property in Calcutta that had stood in his wife's name '12 houses and lands besides'. He
cleared himself from debt but he never really recovered financially. He
took up other interests and made a living as editor of the *Benares Re-
corder*. In his free time he studied languages and wrote a history of Ranjit
Singh, the Lion of Lahore. But he soon quarrelled with the newspaper's
owners and left to join the Department of Public Works in Allahabad as
executive engineer. He died in Allahabad in 1851, only four years after
the failure of the bank.

After the financial crash and the death of her husband, Gavin's mother
took him and her other young children back to Calcutta to do what

was possible for their education. Two years later, however, she died of cholera. For Gavin the double blow of the loss of the family fortunes and the death of both his parents was a harsh test of character. He had enjoyed a sense of exploration and adventure with his father; later, supported and encouraged by his eldest brother, John Moore Jones, his own aggressive adventurous nature slowly asserted itself. He became aware of his ambition: to play a leading role in the new world of machinery and technology. He began disciplined study to succeed as an engineer and in 1857 joined his brother John Moore Jones on his indigo estate at Mendhi Ghat.

It was then that Gavin Jones was caught up in the events of the Mutiny and made his dramatic escape to Cawnpore. With John Moore Jones dead, Hugh Maxwell, married to Gavin's sister Charlotte, became his nearest kinsman. In 1861 at Cawnpore Gavin fell dangerously ill with smallpox and it was Hugh Maxwell who nursed him back to health, sent him to Mendhi Ghat to recover his strength and made plans for the young man's future.

With Hugh Maxwell's recommendation and the influence of his brother's friend Sam Weller, Gavin joined the Great Indian Peninsular Railway as part of the work force building the line between Jubbalpore and Hoshangabad.[48] The opening up of the country by the railways seemed to symbolise the possibilities for change and progress that Western ideas were now bringing to India. Gavin revelled in putting his engineering skills into practice, although it was a hard life – under canvas, miles from anywhere, surrounded by a huge camp of labourers, struggling to find ways to level the terrain, to build bridges and blast through rock. The climate, too, was formidable. In winter they shivered in the early morning dews and in summer the pitiless sun made the rocks too hot to touch. But it was the monsoon rains, washing away the work of months, that proved hardest of all. The rains brought cholera, dysentery, typhoid and mosquitoes. It was not long before Jones was seriously ill with malaria and the doctor, afraid for his life, ordered him back to England.

Very little is known of his life in England. When he had recovered his health he worked for a time as an engineer in the construction of the Great Eastern Railway. On his return to India he claimed expert knowledge of cotton manufacture so it is possible he worked for a while in an English cotton mill. But in 1865 in the London home of the future suffragette Charlotte Despard,[49] Jones met her younger sister, Margaret French, an unconventional young lady. She was one of a family of six –

five sisters and one brother (the future field-marshal and Earl of Ypres). Their Irish father, Captain John Tracy French, was a naval officer who had lost an eye at the Battle of Navarino and retired to his estates in Devon. He married a Scots heiress and while he ran his affairs with naval precision his wife withdrew from the world. She devoted herself to her prayers, leaving the children, virtually ignored, to run wild, defying their nurses and governesses. In due course the captain died and his wife became so odd that she was sent to an asylum where she also died. The children went to live with relations.

The girls grew up fiercely independent and rebellious, critical of a society in which women were virtually prisoners of marriage. Marriage was the one outlet and escape available to them, but they scorned having to be 'lady-like', gentle and submissive. Each had a modest but useful private income and before long they were living in London in a house run by the eldest sister, Charlotte. Here it was that Jones, in his new-found friendship with Maggie, was caught up in the animated discussions between the sisters on such subjects as Shelley's poems and his scandalous view that woman was an equal partner in marriage. They talked about Marx and social injustices in society and Jones described his vision of introducing new enterprise and change in India. He used Darwin's theories to rationalise his concept that Western ideas and technology would bring better conditions and material prosperity to the people of India. Maggie found him clever and unusual. India seemed most inviting.

Death of Charlotte Maxwell

The Maxwells gave a ball to the station on the night of 30 March 1865, when the company danced till dawn. Then Hugh Maxwell saw his wife and two little daughters, Lily and Nora, safely settled in Mussoorie with Fanny and Tom Tracy before making the voyage home for the sake of his health. Three girls were in England in the care of a governess, Miss Robertson, while the only son, Ralph, was preparing to return to India to join the family business at Cawnpore. Uncle Davie, Hugh Maxwell's younger brother, close to him in temperament and looks and even sharing the same day of birth, had settled in Bonn for the reason of his ailing wife's health, while Aunt Fanny, Fanny Tritton, Hugh Maxwell's only sister, was the cornerstone of the family in London.

Charlotte Maxwell and Lily, 1863.

Hugh Maxwell landed in London on 17 June, happy at the prospect of rest after a wearying voyage in the hot weather. He travelled to Paris to meet the three girls, Chattie, Maggie and Mabel; Miss Robertson had placed them at St Germain to study French and music. He was glad to find how well they were progressing. Next he and Ralph went to Ireland to stay with Tom Tracy's family at Bray and was able to report to Fanny that she would receive a warm welcome from them. A week in London and plans were made to accompany Aunt Fanny and her girls to

Boulogne, calling at Paris on the way to collect his overseas mail. Finally, the family party hoped to travel on to Bonn to visit Uncle Davie.

It had been a warm summer and Maxwell, his health improving, was enjoying it. Then, in the middle of August, news reached him in the South of France that his wife Charlotte had been taken ill at Mussoorie and had died on 22 June. His anguished reply to Fanny, written from Boulogne-sur-Mer on 18 August 1865, was marked 'via Marseilles and Bombay'.

> I can with difficulty summon calmness myself to acknowledge, and can well feel how painful a task it must have been to you to write the letter conveying the terrible intelligence that your beloved mother had been so suddenly taken from us by her Maker... It is evident that she must have suffered much and death must have been a blessed release to her, though a woeful affliction to us. [Dr] Bruce in the most feeling and kind manner assures me that change of climate would not have prolonged her dear life, and that she had the best medical advice... It would have been an unspeakable consolation to me to have shown her my boundless love for her to the last, and I am sure that my presence would have been no less to herself. Before receiving your letter I felt certain she must have thought of me, and it brings comfort to my heart to think that she is where she knows how deeply her loving words are cherished by me. God ordains all for the best, and humble resignation is due to His dispensations, but it is very very hard to bear the blow which has fallen upon me so suddenly and unexpectedly, and severed for ever the loving companionship of so many happy years of my life. In the ordinary course of Nature I thought it would have been my lot to have gone first, and that our precious children would still have had her fond motherly care and protection, but it has been willed otherwise, and with God's help I must now trust to be able to fulfil the duty left to me towards them.

The devastated Maxwell quickly made plans to return to India where his two youngest infants were in Mussoorie being cared for by Fanny and Tom Tracy. The Cotton Spinning and Weaving Co. had barely begun the construction of its buildings and, with the war in America coming to an end and a crash in cotton prices imminent, the mill's development would need skilful handling. On an impulse Maxwell invited Gavin Jones to return to India to oversee the mill.

It was the opening Jones had sensed must come. He proposed marriage

Major Tweedale, A. Ross, Captain Collins, Dr Bruce, Colonel Thatcher, 1865.

to Maggie French who at once accepted him.[50] In their official engagement photographs Maggie stands before an open piano wearing a silk
crinoline, the bodice and cuffs encrusted with jet beads. One hand rests
lightly on the sheet music allowing a glimpse of her handsome emerald
and diamond ring. Her expression is as composed and serene as it should
be for someone who would come to be called 'La Reine'. Jones, tall and
angular, stares intently in front, the soft growth of beard and moustache
partly hiding the effects of the smallpox.

Charlotte herself is a shadowy figure. Older than her brother Gavin by
thirteen years, she was the eldest daughter of Fanny and John Benjamin
Jones, 'JBJ', born in the days when he was still working for Palmer and
Co. in Calcutta. The choice of the planter Henry Hill of Tirhoot as one of
the sponsors at her baptism is appropriate; she was to spend many years of
her life as a planter's wife. In looks she took after her grandmother who
was half Portuguese and had dark handsome features.

A particular experience Charlotte enjoyed, before Gavin was born, was
being taken to London by her parents. This was JBJ's first visit to England
and they lived for two years in Lambeth. He took lessons in painting and
playing the flute and his artistic temperament blossomed. It was at this
time the portrait of Charlotte was painted, a little girl with large solemn

eyes, her cropped dark hair almost boyish. She wears a yellow taffeta dress and holds a thick cord of pearls as big as grapes said to have belonged to her Portuguese great-grandmother. She and the older children remained in England to complete their education when the rest of the family returned to India and up-country life at Babcha. Charlotte saw Gavin for the first time when she returned to Babcha as a fifteen-year-old and found him a little boy of three and a half.

Hugh Maxwell married her in 1839 and they went to live on his nearby indigo estate at Palee. It was a happy first home for her but later it came to hold grim associations for the family. It was on the same verandah where she loved to sit and wait for her husband to return for a late breakfast after riding to inspect the indigo crops that her brother Edmond and young nephew Clinton Kemp were murdered while they breakfasted with the Collector of Mirzapore in 1857.[51]

Her first child, Fanny, was born within the first year of marriage. In a succession of pregnancies Ralph was the only son to survive. There were three girls and several miscarriages and stillbirths. One infant, stillborn, was buried in the garden of the lovely old bungalow at Khamaria, near Mirzapore, under the peepul tree. There garlands are still placed in dim memory of a dead baby 'with a head like a snake'.[52]

After the Mutiny there were two more little girls born to Charlotte in Cawnpore. The last photograph taken of her shows her anxious look; the relentless childbearing routine was getting too much for her. She was often unwell, with what she called a 'tic' to the head, but her husband was too busy to notice and Charlotte in her diffident way kept silent. Millie Stewart was in no doubt about the problem: 'You will be surprised to hear that Mrs Maxwell has had a Daughter. . . owing to her not being very young now she had a most tedious time of it but now I am glad to say she is getting on, I went to see her yesterday and thought her looking very ill and weak, but she said she was better.'

Cawnpore *burra bebees* might find the Maxwell's style of living very grand but in Fanny's 1861 letters Charlotte comes across as being prudent and economical in all domestic matters. She impresses upon Fanny the need to save her *good* dresses and there are other little clues, such as refusing to buy a bow and arrow for archery even at a bargain price because it was the end of the season, that suggest that hers was a far from extravagant nature.

Hill stations, many of them first developed as convalescent homes for the soldiers, quickly became extremely popular with the nineteenth-century Europeans. The natural beauty of the setting, the delight of

Fanny Tracy, née Maxwell.

escaping from the hot weather in the plains, the wooded hillsides a reminder of England, all contributed to the annual exodus to the hills and an atmosphere of holiday charm. Houses were established on every beauty spot. Mussoorie was the Maxwells' favourite hill station, reached after an overnight train journey and then being carried up footpaths in dandies to a height of over 6,000 feet. For several years they rented Belvedere, a large house with views to the north as far as the Himalayas, and to the south on a fine night, down to the twinkling lights of the Dhoon. The air was scented with pine and deodars and the smell of burnt oak from the fires of the charcoal burners. It was cool and invigorating. Children enjoyed the freedom of activities never possible in the plains, while for the grown-ups there was a perpetual round of picnics.

This summer of 1865 the weather had been most unusual. First there were severe dust storms, 'crinolines were blown to the dickens, likewise bonnets'.[53] The dust storms were followed by terrific thunderstorms accompanied by torrents of rain and heavy hail: 'such lumps of ice fell on Sunday the 21st May that at Mussoorie Church the hail made so much noise the voice of the clergyman could not be heard.'

The first private amusement of the season was the ball in honour of the Queen's birthday on 24 May. It was subscribed by eighty people and went off very well, the General proposing the Sovereign's health. The Mussoorie correspondent of the *Mofussilite* reported on 12 June that the fourth picnic within a week had taken place that day and a ball given by the members of the Club would take place on the 16th, amateur theatricals on the 19th and tiffin parties daily. Meanwhile the station was crowded with visitors, with every hotel full and families sharing three and four in comparatively small houses, all anxious to escape the heat of the plains. The place was so crowded that many people could not even procure a place in church.

Charlotte's last letter to her husband was dated 17 June. There had been a great storm that day and she reported that the 'roof of the large upper-storied house, Charleville, was completely taken off but its forty [*sic*] inmates not harmed'. Hail 'of immense size' had fallen. Now she was taken ill. After anxious consultations, it was decided to take her down to Dehra Dun where the family friend Dr Bruce could attend her. It was the birth of the last of her seven children that had exhausted her. Worn out with child-bearing and a kidney complaint she suffered a heart attack and died on 22 June. She was buried not far from the main gate in what is now the old part of the cemetery.

Along the Mall, Mussoorie, 1866. Photograph by Rust.

5
Significant Events, 1865

─────

The *Pioneer* Newspaper

The year of the first Annual General Meeting of the Elgin Cotton Spinning and Weaving Company, 1865, also marked three other significant events for emerging Cawnpore. On 2 January the first number of the *Pioneer* newspaper was printed at Allahabad; on 23 February W. S. Halsey was appointed collector, and magistrate at Cawnpore and on 15 August the railway bridge over the Jumna at Allahabad was declared safe for traffic and goods trains were able to proceed for the first time non-stop from Cawnpore to Calcutta.

Up-country readers had been accustomed to the meagre pages of the *Mofussilite* with its cramped print. The *Pioneer* declared at a glance by its size and improvement of type and layout that a new era had arrived. About the size of *The Times*, it reflected the style and showmanship of its proprietor George Allen. He seemed to have a gift for knowing the people who mattered and being ahead with the news. His first editor was the Revd Julian Robinson, a man well informed on a wide range of subjects who was not afraid to express his opinion and be frank to admit if he was in any doubt. The paper came out three days a week until 1870 when it became a daily. Out of its twelve pages, six were devoted to advertisements. They were studied eagerly and convey a rich picture of life at that period.

> I must explain that the *Pioneer* is the leading newspaper of India. It is a sheet of abounding interest to all Government servants, because it publishes a list of promotions, sailings and everything that is important to the Anglo Indian exile to know. There are Reuters telegrams covering the news of the world, English letters by noted correspondents, local items, which, with its dignified literary style, combine to make its daily appearance an event.[1]

The front page carried Reuter's telegraphic news from London and the latest events abroad. The assassination of Abraham Lincoln reached readers of the '*Pi*' on 10 May and caused a sensation.

When the opening of the Suez Canal, attended by royalty, was reported on 29 November 1869, a fleet of vessels carried distinguished visitors including the Empress Eugénie of Russia, the Emperor of Austria, and Dutch and Prussian princes who travelled from Port Said to Ismalia to declare the Canal open. This was the sort of social detail that delighted readers of the *Pioneer*. So did a reference to the Oxford and Cambridge boat race, won in 1867 by Oxford in 22 minutes 40 seconds, over a 4 2/3 mile course. The new cult of the velocipede bicycle, which in London and Paris seemed a frivolous folly, but could spin along on *kunkar* roads, requiring no gram and no syce, caught the public imagination. 'By the time the P and O and the EIR Companies are superseded by balloon companies the bicycle may be found a very useful machine by slow and aged persons who still retain a preference for terrestrial travelling.'

Local events, articles on topical issues, scandals, social gossip and readers' letters all enlivened the paper. The libel case brought by Captain Jervis against H.E. Sir William Mansfield dragged on and on.[2] 'Without these military scandals society would have nothing to talk about, nothing with which to wile away the long dreary hours of an Indian summer.'[3] A sensation was caused when Headmaster Stobart of La Martinière boys' school at Lucknow was found to have marked an orphan, Cummins, with a branding iron;[4] and there was much mirth over an advertisement for a wife – 'must possess Rs. 40,000, dark blood no objection, strictest secrecy relied on.'[5]

Letters from readers were often entertaining and controversial, invariably signed with a pseudonym that stirred the curiosity of the local community. 'A Traveller' wrote complaining that the 'hills and ditches' of the road between Cawnpore and Fatehgarh were so disgraceful that pilgrims would not need peas in their shoes to ensure martyrdom. This was taken up by 'Nipper' who with glee poked fun at the contractors who it would seem were filling their pockets rather than the holes in the road. A third writer calling himself 'Lion's Den' wrote in disgust that he had been so alarmed by these descriptions of the Cawnpore road that he had tried to avoid using it, only to find the report greatly exaggerated. In his opinion the correspondence was the work of a disgruntled ex-employee of the contractor and the road had never been in better condition.[6]

The advertisements ranged from dates of sailing of ships, rates of postage or charges on the railway to full-page advertisements such as Bourne & Shepherd's photographic views or goods from the Great Eastern Hotel. In the very first issue Charles Nephew and Company took an entire page to proclaim their wares at the Lucknow Exhibition. These included clocks and watches with the comment that 'until recently natives of India took no notice of time. . .'

Many household names are still familiar. Dinneford's[7] Pure Fluid Magnesia, 'the best remedy for acidity of the stomach, heartburn and headache, gout and indigestion, especially adapted for Ladies and Children and Infants and for regular use in Warm Climates. NB Ask for Dinneford's Magnesia'; Lea and Perrins 'celebrated Worcestershire Sauce declared by Connoisseurs to be the Only Good Sauce. Caution against fraud. Ask to see that their names are upon the wrapper, label stopper and bottle.' 'Rowland's Macassar Oil' was featured,- 'This elegant and Fragrant Oil possesses extraordinary properties for promoting the growth, restoring, preserving and beautifying the Human Hair' (the villain of the piece presumably in the Victorian preoccupation with 'antimacassars', designed to protect furnishings from oily hair). Swaine and Adeney advertised whips 'as supplied under Royal Warrant (Prize Medal 1862)'; Heal & Sons advertised 'Iron and Brass Bedsteads for all parts of the world, Solid Mahogany Bed Room Furniture, entirely free from Veneer, very suitable for extreme climates, Horsehair and spring mattresses and every description of bedding for India and the colonies'.

Dinneford's Fluid Magnesia

THE BEST REMEDY FOR

ACIDITY of the STOMACH, HEARTBURN, HEADACHE, GOUT, and INDIGESTION and the best mild aperient, for delicate constitutions, especially adapted for Ladies, Children and Infants, and for regular use in Warm Climates.
DINNEFORD & Co., Chemists, London, and of Druggists and Storekeepers throughout the world.

N.B.—Ask for DINNEFORD'S MAGNESIA.

(1)

Advertisements from the Pioneer.

Remittance must be made payable in London.'[8] Savory and Moore advertised their toiletries through their Calcutta agents Bathgate and Co. Crosse and Blackwell their famous pickles, sauces and jams so sought after that they were constantly vigilant to prosecute fraudulent copiers.[9]

Cawnpore readers could send for 'an entire Suit of milled flannel Rs. 19.8, the suit – especially adapted for the rains'; or one of Thomson's 'Prize Crinolines, awarded the prize at the Paris Exhibition of 1867, available in three lengths and widths of 2, 2 and 2 yards, carriage free by Packet post'. Machine-made ice was available from Allahabad at two annas a seer, and pure tasteless block ice at three annas a seer from the Punjab Trading Co. Ltd at Lucknow. Murray and Co., also at Lucknow, supplied fresh salmon and oysters and white kid gloves. The confidence of these traders seemed to be summed up by a heading in capital letters inserted by Smyth and Co. 'Competition Benefits the Public and Nil Desperandum.'

Among the early Cawnpore advertisements was one in August 1865 announcing that Kellners Refreshment Rooms were now open at the EIR station. W. Dalziel and Co., where Tom Tracy did his purchasing, was now owned by the Upper India Commercial Association Ltd. They advertised a long list of imported stores including Bass and Tennent's London Bottled Ales, Guinness' Dublin Stout and Tennent's Porter, spirits of all the most approved brands, wines of the choicest vintages, oilman's stores from Crosse and Blackwell, French pâtés and hermetically sealed provisions. 'NB We receive Bi-monthly supplies of Overland Cheese, and a fresh cut is always obtainable, Castell's Jams and Jellies, Tart Fruits etc, French and English Dessert Fruits, Huntley and Palmer's Reading Biscuits, Assam Hill and China Teas, Manilla Cheroots and Tobacco of sorts.'

Small private hotels to provide accommodation for railway travellers were soon established. The United Service Hotel Cawnpore, 'Proprietor J.M. Inglis', offered 'Billiards, Conveyances on hire and Daks supplied'; Duncan's Staging Bungalow, established 15 March 1866, proclaimed it was under European management; while among the first Indians in Cawnpore to advertise was Baboo Ram, 'Saddle and Harness maker, Cawnpore. Workmanship in the European style, orders executed promptly',[10] and Sheopershad, 'Banker. Army Half Mountings and General Contractor, Tent Manufacturer and General Commission Agent. Established in 1858'.[11]

Touring companies regularly played at Cawnpore. Among the most popular were the Dave Carson Minstrels who guaranteed to make the audience experience the 'True and Genuine Laugh'. The repertoire included the hilarious 'Scenes in the Allahabad Police Court' in which Carson impersonated 'An Irishman, A Scotchman, A Frenchman, A Chinaman, An unprotected Female, The Mild Hindoo and John Exshaw No 1', ending his performance with his popular song 'The Dak Gharrie'.

When the Australian Acrobatic Gymnastic Troupe played at Cawnpore they were voted a huge success. A whole column in the *Pioneer* was devoted to their wonderful acrobatic performance, the beautiful symmetry of their figures and the amusement and diversion they had given with feats of daring never seen before.[12]

Indian Correspondence.

MY *PIONEER*.

Who tells me what I long to hear,
Price of XX. and Foster's Beer,
From which Bank's shares I should steer clear ?—
                 My Pioneer.

Who tells me who are born and dead,
And who of my old friends are wed.
Where to buy bonnets for my head ?—
                 My Pioneer.

Who tells me when the steamer's come,
Freighted I hope with letters from
The loved one in a colder home ?—
                 My Pioneer.

Who tells me where it rains or hails,
Or where the rubbee harvest fails,
And horrible hot wind prevails ?—
                 My Pioneer.

Who makes me Ps. and Qs. to mind
And never write a word unkind.
If in his columns space I'd find ?—
                 My Pioneer.

Halsey, Collector at Cawnpore

Ever since the East India Company had taken over the administration of that district in 1801, Cawnpore had known many dedicated and hard-working collectors. But not for fifty years, since the time of the ill-starred George Ravenscroft, had there been another so passionately devoted to the ideals of agriculture and the welfare of the common man as W.S. Halsey.

William Stirling Halsey was born on 27 July 1831, the elder son of R.H.W. Halsey Esq. of Henley Park, Ash, Surrey. Destined for the Civil Service in the days before it had been thrown open to competition, he was educated at the East India College at Haileybury. A glance at the syllabus gives an idea of the standard to which the young men were prepared for their duties in India. Sanscrit in the first term, Persian in the second, Hindustani in the third and 'Bengalese' and Arabic in the fourth, all against a background of classics, law, history, politics and economics.[13] Thus prepared and fired with the ideals, typical of Victorian England, of the benefits the Western world could confer on India, he joined the Bengal Civil Service on 15 March 1853.

Twelve years later, on 23 February 1865, Halsey was appointed magistrate and collector at Cawnpore. He was thirty-four years old and brought with him the deeply held conviction that in India there were opportunities to improve the lives of thousands with the introduction of better methods of animal husbandry and agriculture. He threw himself into his task at Cawnpore. Unlike Ravenscroft, to whom the dream was also a personal destiny, Halsey concentrated on the work itself. Few now recall his efforts but Halsey Road remains a memorial to honour him.

Within months of taking office as magistrate and collector Halsey was accepted into the community. By chance his younger brother Francis was also in Cawnpore, agent to the Bank of Bengal, and both brothers were keen horsemen and members of the newly formed Cawnpore Tent Club. Halsey's youthful good looks and enthusiasm made him popular with both Indians and Europeans. His first task was to tackle the horrendous problem of sanitation. Shallow open drains lay alongside the close packed houses in the congested filthy labyrinth of lanes within the city and bazaar. Human excreta was tipped into these drains attracting flies and encouraging disease. Halsey, believing in 'ozone', had roads widened, a spacious market place created and a canal built. The old cess pits were cleaned out and the contents taken to manure the Memorial Well Gardens where it would do some good. Night soil carts were introduced: starting at 10.30 each night, they would traverse all roads in the city, collecting the contents of iron buckets which were to be left outside by the inmates of the houses. The well-to-do were expected to put out one bucket for the household and another for the servants' compound. It was also required to provide a *puckka* 'necessary' for the servants. It speaks well for Halsey that the *Pioneer* was able to write on 25 August 1865:

> Native prejudice [against good hygiene] is dying under the good sense of the Magistrate, and of this no small proof is the willingness with which the Hindoos have allowed their Brahminee bulls to be trained to harness in the sewage carts, for I understand that the Municipal Committee which unanimously adopted this measure comprised a majority of Hindoos. The carts are light and strong, and built for single harness on an improved English pattern. You would hardly recognise your old friend or enemy, the shackled Brahminee bull, in leather trappings between two shafts.

Halsey's reputation for animal husbandry had preceded him so that when the idea for an agricultural exhibition at Allahabad[14] was mooted he naturally played a leading role. 'His thorough knowledge of all subjects connected with agriculture enabled him to assist greatly, both in arranging the Exhibition and in adjudicating the prizes for cattle.' Ali Hussein, the *tehseeldar* of Benares who registered, arranged and classified everything sent for the exhibition, had been trained earlier by Halsey.

The idea behind the exhibition was to bring together a large assembly of Europeans and Indians to see examples of modern machinery being made in India for cultivation and irrigation and to compare 'the splendid cattle of intelligent Native gentry with the primitive implements and miserable neglected animals indigenous to their Districts'. In the confident belief that agriculture was the basis for all prosperity in India, a talk was given to the audience 'impressing upon their minds that advancement is within the reach of even the most humble, if they will but apply with intelligence what they have had the opportunity of learning in this place'.

The project most dear to Halsey's heart, however, was the Agri-Horticultural Society's model farm. Almost within days of arriving at Cawnpore, Halsey persuaded the Municipal Committee to take over the old public gardens at Nawabganj (where Fanny and Tom Tracy used to drive to listen to the band) and form a society to set up a model experimental farm, with a grant of Rs. 100 a month for a superintendent.

The society invested in half-bred Leicester sheep, a fine Bhawulpore buffalo bull, imported pigs and an Arab stallion. The people were freely encouraged to bring their own animals to be crossed with them.

> As this was all new, it was impossible to levy any charge for the services of these animals: indeed we looked forward to the result of so satisfying the people that they would of themselves hereafter come forward and propose to pay for the services afforded: and I have no doubt the commencement we have made in this respect will bear its fruit in time. None can appreciate better than a native the practical results of an experiment, but no native in the world has less desire to experimentalize.

In order to help the farm pay its way, some of the livestock was kept for slaughter. Unfortunately the Khansamahs preferred to buy their meat in the bazaar and this experiment failed after four years.

Eleven *beegahs* of land – a *beegah* was five-eights of an acre – were cultivated with imported varieties of cotton, seed, tobacco and Indian corn but the problems of climate caused many difficulties. Only the immense nurseries of fruit and forest trees were really successful.

> The Society is proud to have it to say, that owing to its exertions, the Cawnpore station, instead of being the bare, sandy plain it was, is rapidly becomming green from the innumerable trees which have been planted during the past three years. So also the district roads, and the zamindars have been supplied with many thousands of trees of sorts. Of course many of these die from neglect or injuries done by cattle: still, however, the result has been on the whole satisfactory, and there are many roads along the sides of which trees are firmly established.[15]

Halsey's interest and involvement with the growing of cotton was to prove invaluable to Cawnpore and the Elgin Mills:

> In the course of a pleasantly written Report on the operations of the Agri-Horticultural Society of Cawnpore, the Magistrate speaks very hopefully indeed of the results which may be expected from the use of Hingunghat cotton seed in that neighbourhood. 'This year I got five maunds of it for a native gentleman in the district.

He had the advantage of the canal, and cultivated the Hingunghat exactly as he would have done the indigenous. The result was a most successful crop – so successful that he had the greatest difficulty in preserving any of it, all the people in the neighbourhood stealing it for the sake of the seed.' This reminds us, as an Irishman might say, of a story we can't remember. This, however, may do instead. Southey (or Walter Savage Landor) tells us of a very holy saint indeed, who used to traverse the wildest parts of Spain on a kind of bare-footed visitation, exhorting and charming the people. He wore hardly anything and ate almost nothing, and consequently worked the most surprising cures. Naturally the inhabitants came nearly to worship him where he passed. Indeed, the people of one district more pious than the rest actually murdered him at last in order to possess his relics, which it is well known were accustomed, until lately, to work miracles. The Cawnpore manner of appreciating a benefactor seems somewhat similar.

The Jumna Bridge, Allahabad

Hugh Maxwell, accompanied by Ralph and Chattie and the two Misses Bell, arrived back in India on 20 October 1865, passengers on the SS *Candia* from Southampton to Calcutta. A few days after their return to Cawnpore the *Pioneer* carried a detailed account of the opening of the Jumna bridge at Allahabad to rail traffic, a matter of considerable importance to Cawnpore and to the Maxwell interests.

The report on the completion and testing of the bridge conveys the extreme care and exactitude of the trials. A train made up of one goods engine, ten waggons loaded with ballast and a break-van was run over at a speed of 10 mph and the deflection and oscillation found to be negligible. Greater loads and faster speeds were tried out testing the effect on the upper and the lower, passenger, bridge, and at each main pier standing in the river. The results were declared to be most satisfactory and a credit to the designer, the late Mr Rendal (one of the passengers who had travelled with Carrington). Work could only take place during six or seven months of the year. The great damage was always from flooding when the river would rise all of fifty feet.

The bridge had fourteen spans. Progress was severely held up by problems with pier No 11. 'This unfortunate pier has become almost a household word – even small boys in the street may be heard making

Lucknow Bridge, with train approaching.

some remark about *lumber igarah*. The difficulties and risk against which the work on pier No 11 has had to contend for the last six months, have been not few nor trifling.'[16] Much of the trouble was that the engines which were used for pumping out were old and almost worn out.[17] They were finally got into tolerable working order and the water in the foundations was kept sufficiently low 'to enable the 52 feet arch to be sprung from the up and down steam wells at a point 9 feet below the lowest water level and 12 feet below the water level as it stood at the time'. The governor of the province sent his congratulations 'on the completion of this the middle link in the long chain of unbroken communication established by the East Indian Railway Company, for the first time in the history of India, between the right bank of the Hooghly at Calcutta and the left bank of the Jumna at Delhi'.

Dramatic accounts of railway accidents frequently filled the columns of the *Pioneer*. Statistics[18] indicated that most passengers who died on the railway were killed or injured from jumping out of trains in motion, while the majority of railway servants killed were found to have been careless in 'taking liberties'. These statistics overlook the fearful conditions endured by engine drivers and guards working out of doors during the hot weather. 'The shunting and making-up of trains at large stations like Allahabad and Cawnpore is a serious matter at present.' The driver of a goods train left Allahabad at three on Monday afternoon and died the following morning near Sirsoul station of heat apoplexy. The stress of the work tempted many men to heavy drinking. A number of deaths among the railway servants were due to heat apoplexy aggravated by excessive drink.

Passengers, too, suffered from the heat, becoming dehydrated in a train running into a hot wind. One exceptionally hot June the *Pioneer* readers were started by a letter from Dr Planck, the Sanitary Commissioner NWP, reporting 'on good authority' that five Europeans had died from heat apoplexy on one train journey and that such sudden deaths were occurring so frequently that the railway authorities were providing special accommodation at stations for the dead. Dr Planck added that the only way to avoid almost certain death while travelling great distances by train between mid April and mid June was to keep a wet handkerchief over the head so that the surplus water trickled down the back of the neck, or held in front of the face. In a few minutes it would need to be re-wetted and re-adjusted. Sips of very cold water were beneficial. A continuous journey of over fifteen hours should on no account be undertaken. If by chance a traveller was found insensible from heat exhaustion on a train he was to be taken out as quickly as possible, laid on a *charpoy,* his shirt removed, and water poured from a height of three or four feet in a steady stream over his head, neck and chest. Dr Planck cited the case of a man who only recovered after five hours of such water treatment.[19]

Not all references to the railways were so sensational. There were advertisements asking for tenders to be submitted for 'supplying two lakhs cubic feet of firewood for making 9,000,000 pucka bricks or 250,000 cubic feet kunkur for the Cawnpore Junction Railway'; notices announced freight rates or special concessions to tourists travelling at Christmas or the Doorga Poojah. Readers wrote in complaining of the lateness of trains or the inconvenience of the timetable. The problem was discussed of how to prevent the goods clerks accepting bribes from *mahajuns* anxious to get their cotton waggons sent off quickly. At this time all railway servants were European, but there were Indian guards and firemen by 1871. There was also talk of introducing separate carriages for Indian ladies.

The forgetfulness of the public in leaving personal possessions in the

'*Railway travelling in India*'.

carriages was, as ever, remarkable. Long lists of articles, 'Unclaimed Refusals', with the owner's name and address when known, were regularly published and made amusing reading: 'Mrs Lines, patterns of cloth, Cawnpore'; 'Col. Drummond, 9 pills from Charles and Co.'; 'P. Caffry, Esq, samples of plastering for houses, Cawnpore'; 'District Superintendent of Police, a musket bayonet, Cawnpore.'[20]

A story that went the rounds, considered good enough for the recently established *Punch* was that the guards had been briefed to take special note of obese passengers for fear they might die of heat exhaustion. This resulted in a number of stout persons being knocked up during a night journey by the guard inquiring if they were still alive!

In the *Pioneer* of 15 July 1867 there was a report on a series of documents published by order of the House of Commons on the East Indian Railway. The following passage is worth quoting:[21]

For a time, wherever the works were in progress, the whole rural economy of the district was turned upside down. Classes changed places. The long-despised labouring man found himself better paid and more sought after than the well-to-do cultivator. In one district the railway brought to light a system of praedial slavery as firmly rooted as when the English had entered the country ninety years before. It had continued safer for the poor man to be the slave of the rich man than to be his hired workman. Bondage was profitable to the people: our laws did not interfere directly with the institution; and so during the long years that Exeter Hall was declaiming on the African, slavery flourished unmolested under the sanction of the British Government in Bengal. It was reserved for the railway to do naturally for the hill people of the Santhal country what English philanthropists had done spasmodically for the blacks of Jamaica. Coolie recruiters were let loose on the country; the value of labour rose; every able-bodied man and woman could earn an ample livelihood by the work of their hands, and freedom became an object of ambition. But in proportion as the labour of the serfs became valuable to themselves, so also did it become profitable to their masters. Complications arose, the local officials bungled, the Calcutta statesmen could not make out what was wrong, and during a year of unexampled prosperity a peaceable tribe rose in revolt. Then came enquiry and explanation, remedial measures followed, and the nation which the railway found slaves it left free men.

6
Pioneering Days
1865 – 1872

═══

The Elgin Cotton Mills

Shareholders of the Elgin Spinning and Weaving Co. Ltd watched the progress of the infant company in eager anticipation of good returns on their investment. They were reassured to hear that Hugh Maxwell was back from leave and that he had arranged for his brother David to come out to India so that in future one or other of the two brothers would be in Cawnpore to look after Elgin interests. They were also delighted to welcome back to Cawnpore their young Mutiny hero Gavin Jones and to hear he had joined the Elgin enterprise.

There was much to accomplish: the construction of the factory complex, the installation of imported machinery, instructing the workforce in the production of cloth and yarn (which involved teaching the Indian workmen how to adapt their natural skills of weaving to the technicalities of machinery), and finally the marketing of the mill's products.

It was soon after the third AGM that it became clear all was not well. Matters came to a head; the board and Gavin Jones resigned. From an account Jones wrote many years later and from reports in the *Pioneer* it is possible to piece together something of the events. The misdirected zeal of the Commissariat officers unbalanced the strategy of the board and this dual control prejudiced the interests of the Company. But undeterred by the resignation of the experienced businessmen on the board,

> Nothing daunted, as befitting soldiers, and confident in their own ability to manage the business, they promptly organised amongst themselves a Managing Committee – the rules of the service prohibiting them from serving as directors – and assumed all the prerogatives and powers of a legally constituted board. – An

engineer of the D.P.W.[Department of Public Works] replaced the
expert engineers; the result was, as anticipated, a complete break-
down. The Managing Committee, trained in the traditions of the
Commissariat, being impatient and dissatisfied with the progress of
the building, arbitrarily removed the contractor for breach of
contract for having exceeded the stipulated limit of time. The
contractors sued the company for wrongful dismissal and proved to
the satisfaction of the court that the delay was owing to the neglect
of the Company's engineer who failed to supply them with working drawings in terms of the contract; and they were consequently
mulct in damages to the tune of 40,000. This, coupled with
extravagant waste of the company's funds, speedily dissipated the
working capital and before six months had expired under the new
regime the D.P.W. engineer retired and reverted to his legitimate
duties (having taken a year's leave to enable him to take up the
management of the company) leaving the mills hopelessly impoverished in liquidation.[1]

Hugh Maxwell's main concern was with the financial side of the
business. A brief glimpse from one of his letters suggests this. It is written
from Cawnpore on 1 September 1866, as he was about to leave for
England. 'I shall be glad to get away for I have been almost crazy with
accounts since I came down [from Mussoorie], and I was almost useless
all yesterday from sitting up till 12 the previous night with a small party
at home. . .[2] I gave in and went to bed at midnight, but Uncle Davie had
the benefit of whist up til 2 am. . .'
  During the struggle to set up the mill the Maxwells were fortunate in
having their own family business to fall back on – Begg Maxwell and
Co., merchants dealing in indigo and indigo seed. The Maxwell family
had been landlords and indigo planters in the Cawnpore district ever
since their father John Maxwell settled there in 1806. Before the Mutiny
their produce had been handled by John Kirk and Co. but with that
family wiped out in the uprising they had joined forces with Dr Begg to
set up Begg Maxwell and Co., combining work on the estates with
agency work.[3]
  Work on an indigo estate was tantalisingly capricious. While holding
out the prospect of wonderful profit the seasons were unpredictable and
could often prove disastrous. The heavy work took place at the time of
harvesting, leaving the rest of the year freer for other interests. This
gave Hugh Maxwell time to devote to the Elgin company and Ralph

Maxwell time to indulge his love of sport. However, the growing of indigo seed for commercial purposes came at the wrong time of the year, so that Hugh Maxwell was often on call during the worst of the hot weather followed by leave in England during winter when the cold and November fogs undermined his health. In fact 1869 was a good year:

> The Indigo Season has fortunately been a good one for us both at Bilsee and Ruar and Ralph, J. Dunbar and J. Maxwell will have good earnings from the latter. Our anxieties and troubles of the Seed Season are just commencing, but there is nothing very alarming in the prospects at present, the crop having like all others unexpectedly taken a favourable turn, when all hope of such an event was almost despaired of.[4]

While the Commissariat officers ran the mill the Maxwells could afford to watch and wait from the sidelines. Gavin Jones also looked to his own resources and set himself up as a construction engineer running a small company supplying sawn timber. Since the end of the disturbances there had been a bustle of activity to rebuild Cawnpore. With the coming of the railway and the boom in cotton, new businesses, screw houses, factories and offices were coming up fast. Many overreached themselves, failed and were bought up by others who tried again.[5] It all generated work for the construction companies.

It is not known where Gavin Jones's timber mill was situated but in all likelihood it was on the river bank, possibly at Byramghat where timber floated down river could be landed and which would be conveniently close to the work in progress on the new railway lines that would link Cawnpore to Lucknow. It suited Jones's temperament to work for himself; his timber mill prospered, soon to be advertised as a steam saw mill, and he took on an assistant, G. H. C. Wood. His engineering sheds probably included a double cylinder condensing steam engine, various lathes, drilling and shaping machines, a circular saw table and vertical log cutters.

Cotton continued to flood into Cawnpore. On the Fatehgarh road 'hundreds of hackeries in long lines daily traverse it'. At the station the platforms were piled high with bales awaiting despatch by train. The great accumulation of goods and the frequent delay in forwarding them caused constant comment. There never seemed to be sufficient waggons, and disputes frequently occurred over distribution, charges of bribery and corruption were everyday occurrences. A circular was issued to all station masters instructing them that a daily register should be kept of all goods deposited for despatch on the railway premises, but priority of receipt should insure priority of despatch and that all waggons be divided proportionately to the numbers of bales in each merchant's consignment.

The Commissariat officers at Elgin were thankful that in spite of all their difficulties in production they were no longer trading in raw cotton. In spite of what Jones writes, by the end of the engineer's sabbatical year from the PWD the Committee of Management succeeded in getting the first samples of manufactured cotton onto the market. Two advertisements appeared early in 1868, 'by order of the Committee of Management', offering yarns and a basic plain cloth in several widths. The yarn was in bundles suitable for dyeing and for the Indian weavers to use on their traditional handlooms.

In a glass case at Elgin head office today are framed a few pages dated 1868 referring to early samples sent by the company to Murray and Co., Lucknow, for them to dispose of at the best price available. 'I sent you 100 pieces of double warp cloth of which a large quantity has lately been bought here for Jharans – dusters – and 9 pieces of Drill. The former you may dispose of for any offer you can get over 4 annas per piece.' The amounts are so small it is a reminder of the humble start of the venture. There was at that time no local market for manufactured goods. Country dealers held back, hesitant to commit themselves to such an unknown product. Bundles of cloth fabric were distributed among the dealers as free samples to try to overcome their conservative reluctance. Once they saw the value of the goods and tested the market they came back to buy. But it all took too long. Too much money was locked away

List of Prices of Yarn and Cloth at the Elgin Cotton Mills, Cawnpore, for the week ending 15th February 1868.

DESCRIPTION.		PRICE.		REMARKS.				
YARN.—In bundles No. 20s.	Mule	@ 6·4	per Bl.	Each Bundle weighs 10 lbs.				
Ditto „	20s. Throstle	@ 6·14	„ „	ditto.				
Cops, „	20s.	@ 45	„ Md.					
CLOTH.--Double Warp,		@ 5	per piece.	Full piece weighs				
					8lb. meang.	24 yds.	by	32″
Plain Cloth		@ 4·12	„	ditto	7½lb. „	25	„ by	36″
Markin,		@ 5·8	„	ditto	7½lb. „	24	„ by	32″
Ditto,		@ 8·4	„	ditto	11lb. „	38	„ by	36″
Ditto,		@ 6·0	„	ditto	8lb. „	25	„ by	40″

W. B. THOMPSON,

Secretary.

CAWKP RK,
12th February 1868.

(243)

in stock and the Committee of Management could see no way to save themselves.

Jones believed that even at this crisis 'had the late members of the Board been invited to resume the reins, they would have financed and pulled the company through their difficulties and assured its success.'[6] But the Committee of Management were intent on closing it down. Their nominee, W. B. Thompson, returned to his duties as PWD engineer and announcements that the company would be voluntarily wound up appeared in all the papers.

The names of W. S. Halsey, the collector,[7] and Hingunghat cotton keep recurring in the early accounts of manufactured cotton in Cawnpore. The association was more than a coincidence. Hingunghat cotton, grown in the Central Provinces and famous for its long staple, was considered one of the finest cottons grown in India. When the Cawnpore Cotton Committee was first set up, one of the original promoters was Babu Nana Mal, 'an employee of A. Warwick from Hingunghat'.

Collectors in no less than twenty-five districts had been urged to experiment with the growing of various types of cotton, although in practically every case it proved to be a costly failure. But it is not surprising that Halsey with his natural interest in agri-horticulture grew trial sowings of Hingunghat cotton on the Model Farm.

Hingunghat lies some fifty miles beyond Nagpore. The Viceroy, Lord Mayo, made the long and tedious journey to it in 1870:[8]

Early in the afternoon they all went out to visit the cotton yard, and the Viceroy seemed much interested in what he saw there. The Hingunghat cotton yard is a hollow square with matting houses on the four sides. In these houses are ranged the simple wooden cotton gins (*churkas*) with which the Hingunghat cotton is so effectively cleaned. Each house falls inwards: in its front is a small yard where are piled pyramids of snow-white cotton. In each yard there are usually three pyramids, one of uncleaned cotton and one of cotton seed. In the centre of the square is a shingled platform where all the cotton weighments are made. The platform was heaped some twelve feet high with cotton bales. A large trophy of full pressed bales was at the archway of the square; and there was a very pretty arch of raw cotton inside the square. On the platform were arranged cotton workers of many kinds. First there were the women of the country working their little gins after their own fashion; then there was the cotton wool carder with his peculiar twanging implement. After him came the *dher* of the period with his little stock for rolling off the cotton into skeins; and by his side were cotton spinners with their ordinary spindles. Several specimens of Hingunghat cotton cloths were laid out in an adjoining shed, and one or two of the country looms were at work below.

Beyond the cotton yard was the factory of Messrs Warwick and Co., where screw presses turned out full-pressed bales, secured with iron, at the rate of about five bales an hour.

Warwick and Co. had a branch office at Cawnpore and when the Committee of Management decided to go into voluntary closure it was Warwick and Co. they brought in as agents and secretaries. A chance reference in a disgruntled reader's letter to the *Pioneer*, protesting at the unfairness, lack of proper competition and nepotism in the sanitary contract for Cawnpore going to Warwick and Co., discloses that W. S. Halsey and members of the Warwick family were related.[9] This family link and their common interest in the production of cotton played a significant part in the fate of the Elgin Cotton Spinning and Weaving Company, with ripples that reach Kanpur today.

The announcement that Messrs Warwick and Co. of Cawnpore and Mirzapore had been appointed agents and secretaries went out on the same day that a notice to the shareholders declared that the voluntary winding up of the company had been stopped as from 7 September 1868. The liquidator had discovered he was legally entitled to work the mill. An attempt was made to continue with the production while more sophisticated advertisements were directed at commanding officers and their requirements of regimental clothing or at police officers and yarn for manufacture in the jails.[10] But the timing was inappropriate. It was a poor season for cotton and prices of manufactured cotton fell dramatically.

Two factions now developed among the shareholders – those who wanted to carry on and those who wanted to see the mill closed down. These rumours reached the *Pioneer*, which carried an editorial to the effect that dissension in the camp of the Elgin Cotton Spinning and Weaving Company was to be regretted and that success could only come from the united action of the shareholders. This had been prompted by two letters. A shareholder called J. H. Walker complained that there was no board of direction and he, holding a large number of proxies, proposed to put forward a resolution at the next meeting to close the company down. Another letter, placed directly beneath Walker's in the same column, to ensure no reader could overlook it, was signed 'A Shareholder' and urged shareholders personally to attend the General Meeting. Walker's letter did not contain a fair and true account of the company's affairs.

A long and interesting letter written to the *Pioneer* by one of the shareholders who is closely identified with this pioneering adventure throws light on the problems at the mill. It is all the more interesting for including details that do not appear in Jones's account.

> Dear Sir, Will you kindly allow me a place in your paper to make some remarks anent the 'Elgin Cotton Spinning and Weaving Co.', which has been figuring before the public, in the shape of advertisements *pro* and *con* and sensational circulars from the pen of Mr. Walker, for some weeks past. It will not be amiss to give a *résumé* of the past and present state of the Company and its future prospects.
>
> Some five years ago the 'Elgin Mills Company' was first projected, and the capital, six and a half lakhs, was rapidly subscribed for, and the shares rose to a premium before the walls were built. Our first manager was an ex-traffic manager on the East Indian Railway; his career, however, was short, and it was during his tenure of office that a most extraordinary blunder was made in the drawing up of a deed of contract with the builders, who undertook to complete the building within a certain period, failing which they were to be mulcted in a penal sum fixed by the Company.
>
> It will scarcely be credited that this important document was written out on an undervalue stamp, which made it worthless for all legal purposes. The contractors did not fulfil their agreement, the bond was filed in Court and decree given to enforce the penalty, when, lo! and behold the Clerk of the Court discovered the mistake, and the contractors, instead of having to pay the Company, presented a nice little bill of thirty thousand rupees, which we had to pay them, and no measures were taken to recover from the party whose gross stupidity caused us this loss. The next waste of capital was caused by the extraordinary amount expended on the buildings, and which, like the former loss, can never be recovered.
>
> In due time our mills, &c., arrived from England and, to do Messrs. Platt and Co. credit, they are the very best of their kind, but like everything else we paid too highly for them. With the

machinery some Europeans were sent out to assist in putting it up and to superintend the working. The terrible time consumed in fitting up this machinery is known to all the shareholders, but many do not know that, had not Mr. Maxwell assisted, they might have been fitting them up to this day.

After a great deal of anxiety and patience our magnificent steam engine was placed *in situ* and commenced driving the mills for spinning yarn, though I forget the almost fabulous time that elapsed before the first yard of cloth was woven. I remember asking the cause of delay and being told that it was for want of a steam pipe, which might have been supplied from Roorkee in a few days, but no, it was somewhere in Calcutta, and as redtapeism was rampant, nothing but that identical steam pipe would do. This pipe cost us about ten thousand rupees! We were now fairly launched on the sea of prosperity, and justly looked on this magnificent property as our *El Dorado* which was to yield inexhaustable wealth to us fortunate shareholders; but somehow or other, notwithstanding the mills were in full work, labour cheap, and all under European superintendence, we could not turn the corner – there was some under-current drifting us backwards. We were getting into debt – ten, fifteen, fifty, a hundred thousand, which finally reached the astounding sum of one lakh and a half of rupees. At the first announcement of this alarming deficit we were all aghast. What was the cause? Simple enough. Someone was making his fortune, and that someone must have thrown a sop to Cerberus to aid him for these things cannot be done single-handed. The Augean stable has now been cleared, our expenses reduced one-half, our efficiency increased, and the management placed in the hands of Messrs. Warwick and Co.

We have now appointed professional accountants to examine the books. Amateur auditors for such extensive works is simple nonsense. Books like these at the mills ought to be examined critically and not superficially.

Major Aitken, one of our shareholders, deserves our thanks for his energy in our behalf; and although he cannot hold office in consequence of a stupid Government order, which should only refer to civilians, nevertheless takes great interest in the concern, and I only hope he will not allow his good nature to be taken advantage of by interested parties.

We are now only nine thousand rupees in debt beyond our own

circle, and this we could pay off tomorrow; and now we are quit of the firebrand, we may hope to get along smoothly and at no distant date to declare dividend. To allow the Elgin Mills to go into liquidation would be almost a national calamity for India, and after the statements made at the meeting it cannot be necessary.

The cloths made at the mills are inferior to none, the only object still unrealized being the manufacture of coarser qualities for native wear – an important desideratum which our Directors do not seem to understand.

There are many natives among the shareholders, and one holds an eighth of the entire number.

Government should give every assistance to an undertaking that tends to promote the commercial prosperity of the country.

With many apologies for overstepping the bounds of an ordinary letter,

I am, dear Sir, yours obediently,

VERITAS

Mr Walker and his proxies were driven off for the time being and the mill limped on. Extraordinary general meetings were called for from time to time. A passing traveller commented:

We appreciate cotton, either in the unmanufactured or the worked-up state; and although many hard or soft headed people (quite according to one's opinion though) are crying down the local mill, namely the Elgin Spinning one, I have been at some pains to enquire how far severe critiques upon the management and working are really justifiable; and I now beg to state that if shareholders will only 'wait a little longer', it is pretty assured that a return upon capital will come about.

His advice seems to have been heeded. If anything, interest flagged. At two meetings called there were insufficient shareholders present to form a quorum and so no business could be transacted. This unhappy state of affairs could not continue much longer. A petition to wind up the company appeared before the courts on 22 March 1870. It was signed by Hugh Maxwell, David Maxwell, Gavin S. Jones, Joseph Strong, Major Tovey, Lala Moolchund, Gooropersaud Sookul and Gyadeen Tewaree, all shareholders in the company, and Ralph Maxwell, Joseph Strong, Gooropersaud Sookul and Gyadeen Tewaree, creditors of the company.

Chattie (standing right) in theatricals at Mussoorie, 1869.

Creditors were asked to submit their claims within ten weeks to the court of the civil judge, Cawnpore, who would adjudicate on 5 November 1870. Notices of the sale of this valuable concern appeared in the *Pioneer*. At first the sale was to be held on 15 November, but this was postponed and eventually took place on Thursday, 22 December. Hardly anyone took the trouble to attend. Perhaps it was too close to Christmas, or perhaps people were more concerned making plans to go to the Dave Carson theatricals, billed for the 23rd and 24th and promising a 'Royal Programme as recently played before HRH The Duke of Edinburgh'.

Jones gives a graphic account of how the Elgin Cotton Spinning and Weaving Company was bought by Hugh Maxwell:

Notices of the sale appeared in all the leading newspapers for weeks in advance of the date appointed for the auction but so little was known of the value of the industry that the event produced no interest in commercial circles and on the day of the sale not a single buyer attended save the solitary purchaser to compete for the prize.

Local interest was also indifferently evinced as evidenced in the sparse attendance, a few were attracted by curiosity others who happened to be in Court on their own business looked vacantly the rest of the audience consisted of the late Chairman of the board of the Company and his personal friends who was the sole buyer. Punctually at the hour appointed the fiat went forth from the Judge and the Court Chaprasie advanced to the front of the railings that fenced the Judge from the people, and with no more ceremony than the bare announcement that the Mills were offered for sale to the highest bidder, above the upset price of two lakhs, in a loud voice called for bids. The late Chairman rose from his seat and responded with 'two lakhs and two thousand' the auctioneer sang out the bid repeating it for a considerable time, when the Judge broke the silence 'will no one give a higher bid' and looked around the audience for a response, but none came. Reluctantly he turned to the auctioneer and gave the order to 'knock it down', the hammer fell with a gentle tap on the rails and the solitary bidder became the fortunate owner of the Mill, 10,000 spindles and 100 Looms at one third the cost.[11]

The mill was knocked down in the name of Begg Dunlop and Co. of Cawnpore, but they withdrew and Begg Maxwell took up the shares. The partners in Begg Maxwell were Hugh Maxwell, David Maxwell, J. MacDonald Dunbar, Ralph Maxwell and Colonel Weller. It was Jones who had persuaded Hugh Maxwell of the huge potential of the mill and he was immediately reinstated, not as secretary but as manager. Within twelve months he had turned the ailing company into a flourishing concern and laid the foundations for decades of success. At the turn of the century its products had become household names throughout India. 'If it's Elgin it's good!'

Almost overnight things improved. Within three weeks a dividend of sixty rupees per share had been announced. Advertisements directed at indigo planters and commanding officers appeared in the *Pioneer* over the signature of Jones and convey his directness and enthusiasm.

By the end of the year a lengthy advertisement stated that new machinery had been imported and listed the goods the Elgin Mills were manufacturing for the information of 'Commanding Officers, Superintendents of Police and Jails, Indigo and Lac Manufacturers, Contractors, Tent-makers, and the Public in general'. Significantly they offered American drills for summer uniforms and *dhotis* plain or with fancy

NOTICE

To Indigo Planters.

THE ELGIN MILLS COMPANY are prepared to supply superior Press and Sheeting Cloth. For samples and particulars apply to

GAVIN JONES,
Manager.

CAWNPORE,
12th July 1871.

(1268)

NOTICE

To Officers Commanding Regiments and Police.

THE ELGIN MILLS COMPANY are prepared to execute orders for " American Drills," Double Warp and T Cloth, suitable for the clothing of Troops. For samples and particulars apply to

GAVIN JONES,
Manager.

CAWNPORE,
12th July 1871.

(1269)

borders. This was followed two months later with news of the setting up of a tent department, manufacturing tents of superior strength and durability at competitive prices. Even in this short time Elgin goods had gained a high reputation.

Since 1867 there had been a Government clothing department at Cawnpore run by Captain Chapman where white drill for summer clothing had regularly been imported 'similar to that worn by Regiments of British Infantry. Price 6 annas the yard'. Hugh Maxwell, realising how valuable Chapman's experience and contacts were, made approaches to him. The situation was resolved diplomatically by Captain Chapman's stepson, A. S. B. Chapman, leaving the Government Clothing Agency to become a partner in the Elgin Mills. Young Chapman's introductions secured valuable contracts to supply summer clothing for the army and police uniforms, something that ensured success.[12]

Circumstances improved. Lower counts of yarn were now being made using locally grown cotton, *dhotis* and cloth suitable for the Indian market were on offer and soon became popular. The workers at the mill were at last familiar with the machinery, credit and finance was once again obtainable on the confidence in the Maxwell name. Shareholders congratulated each other on having held on for so long.

An official entry in *Thacker's Bengal Directory* for the Government Clothing Agency appears in 1867, an entry that gave Captain Chapman as manager. By 1871 the Clothing Agency seems to have become well established with Captain Chapman as agent, and manager, assistant and accountant all employed under him. The entry in 1872, the last entry before A. S. B. Chapman joined forces with the Elgin Mills, lists Captain F. C. Chapman agent, A. S. B. Chapman manager, W. G. Bevis assistant and two Indian accountants and a moonshee.

It seems possible that the 'poaching' of Chapman to join Elgin was made possible by Captain Chapman remaining at the Clothing Agency while his stepson, A. S. B. Chapman, and the assistant, W. G. Bevis, left to join Elgin – ASB as a partner and shareholder, WGB as a hard-working assistant who had to wait until 1900 before being invited to become a partner.

ASB was born Arthur Stanley Betts, the son of an indigo planter in Bihar, in 1850. When his mother, soon widowed, married her young brother-in-law, Frederick Charles Chapman, ASB took the name Chapman. He was only twenty-two years old when he began managing the Clothing Agency. He was also a brilliant rider, which brought him into Ralph Maxwell's company. With a boyhood spent in the saddle on an indigo estate, he was always at ease on horseback and became a keen member of the Cawnpore Tent Club, with a reputation for being 'one of the best pig stickers in India'. He lived in a large bungalow known as the Red Lion; it stood on the river bank next to the DM's bungalow.

Little is known of him as a young man. He does not appear to have married and on his retirement he lived in London in North Audley Street. Judging by the collection of modern English painters whose work he collected, William Russell, Steer, Tonks, Enslie and Stacy, he was a man of substance and artistic taste. In his will he lists each painting, aware of its value, and leaves them to a lady who lives in Mayfair. He seems to have been a popular and generous godfather and a wealthy man with shares in the Elgin Mills amounting to over 1,250 Preference shares and about 3,000 ordinary shares.

The young assistant W. G. Bevis listed at the Clothing Agency was Walter Bevis, son of a hard-working but ill-paid schoolmaster in England who was often in debt. Young Bevis was plucked from Pitman's secretarial college in London as a likely candidate to succeed in the East

and on his arrival at Cawnpore lived as a paying guest at the Chapmans'
bungalow. His board and lodging were provided, his salary was Rs. 20
per month and 'the run of his teeth', on which he was expected to
provide himself with a pony and syce and feed the horse.[13] Determined
never to fall into debt like his father, even on this salary he managed to
save a little each month.

A letter WG wrote to his father soon after he arrived in Cawnpore has
survived. It includes some interesting sidelights on the contract for police
uniforms.[14]

> Now notwithstanding that C'pore possesses a police force of about
> a thousand strong, unless the Govnr Genl, with the liberal use of
> his pruning knife has reduced the number lately by a couple of
> hundred or so the Agency has to keep four of these which at 8-s
> per mensem makes the round sum of £24.0.0 per year, but you
> naturally say, why should I give £24.0.0 when I live within a
> stone's throw of the Police Office – many have asked themselves
> that question and resolved not to be imposed upon by the blackmail
> of these fellows, but in almost all cases they have had their dogs
> poisoned, and all their goods and chattels, even to the very sheets
> from under them, stolen in less than a week. The fact is this – there
> is a caste of people called Boriyas, who are thieves by open profes-
> sion, and always have been and always will be thieves – but the best
> of the fun is that the Police is composed chiefly of these miscreants
> and unless you want to be operated upon you *must support* one [of]
> the tribe by keeping him as your watchman. . .
>
> I don't think Capt C [Chapman] will stop long in England,
> he may come out immediately. The fact is that one of Capt C's
> enemies a Col Davis, who has long owed Capt C a grudge, no
> sooner he sees him off to England, than he uses his influence to
> wrest the Agency from CC and get himself installed, he for a time
> seemed as if he would succeed, but somehow or other luckily the
> Inspr Genl of Police has changed his mind – this of itself is enough
> to bring him out, but another thing is that CC recd orders to make
> some 25000 suits, these were made and passed by a Committee,
> now it seems that the Gov Genl in Council, (in consequence of the
> deficit of 4 millions which you know all about, no doubt) has
> ordered immense reductions in the Police. The Inspr Genl of Police
> consequently says he only requires some 16 or 17 thousand suits,
> and refuses to receive the full quantity for which he gave orders for

the making up – the consequence is that Clothing to the value of Rs 60,069.11.0 lies on Capt Chapman's hands. I lay anything he will be out in the twinkling of a bedpost so please lose no time in concluding arrangements about me.

Walter George Bevis married into an old-established Cawnpore family when in 1878 he married Eleanor Cline. His younger brother, F. J. Bevis, followed him to Cawnpore and joined the firm of Schroder Smith and Co. and married the younger Miss Cline, Evelyn, in 1884.

The contact between ASB and Bevis continued all their lives. Many years later there was a twist to the story. When ASB retired his nephew Jimmy Reeves joined Elgin and lived at the Red Lion bungalow. A keen rivalry developed between Jimmy Reeves and Bevis's son Harry who was running the Elgin Tent department the year of the Delhi Durbar. After Jimmy Reeves's sudden death from a brain tumour, Harry Bevis went to live at Chapman's bungalow and found in a drawer in Jimmy Reeves's desk bundles of love letters and messages of assignations written by the wife of the collector living next door at the DM's house. She had been a sergeant-major's daughter whose bold and handsome looks took the fancy of the collector. Unwisely he married her, sent her to England to be taught how to behave and conduct herself, but she did not care to change her manners and behaved very badly on her return. All that was coarse and rude in her behaviour seemed to have fascinated Jimmy Reeves and they met regularly and secretly at a small gate between the two compounds where a trellis of roses concealed them from view. Gossip had it that she died at Jimmy Reeves's feet, probably from an attempted abortion. Another version of the story gives the collector, McCallum Wright, and his wife both dying of DTs in different bedrooms within one week.[15] Servants at the collector's bungalow still speak of her ghost.

A Time of Fulfilment

Millie Stewart wrote on 7 August 1870:

> Hugh Maxwell's two younger daughters have got engaged to be married since they went to Mussoorie, the elder of them to a Mr Dunbar, a partner with Maxwell, and the other to a Dr Cherry of the 14th, the latter a very pretty girl. Mrs Tracy is with her father and sisters at Mussoorie. They went there in May and don't return

until October when the marriages will take place. So we are losing
all our young ladies.

A month before the prize of the Elgin Mills fell to him Hugh Maxwell
stood at the altar rails at Christ Church to give away his daughter Charlotte in marriage to his partner James MacDonald Dunbar. Two months
later there followed the marriage of his daughter Maggie to Dr Cherry.
The year ended with a grand family reunion.[16]

The weddings that took place for Chattie and Maggie were very
different from Fanny's scratch affair when she married Tom Tracy.
Everything was to be of the best and a large number of guests invited.
Aunt Fanny Tritton in London was called upon to carry out many
commissions, including ordering the wedding gowns and the trousseau,
chosing wedding presents and arranging their despatch, all at the shortest
possible notice. Her letters makes delightful reading.

Aunt Fanny Tritton, Hugh Maxwell's sister, like so many of the India
hands was an indefatigable letter writer. The habit was deeply ingrained:
it was partly the need to communicate and cherish family ties across
great distances and partly having the leisure time available. Over the
years she kept up a lively correspondence with her goddaughter Fanny
Tracy and now she described her part in the preparations for the two
Cawnpore weddings, writing from 14 Queensborough Terrace, Bayswater, on 6 December 1870 'on a cold winter morning with snow on the
ground and just struck 7 o'c am and a *bad* Pen'.[17]

> You have run us hard with your commissions that you wish to be
> sent in Maggie's Box – some of it can't be done as her box goes
> tomorrow night. We went to Mrs Beeton's yesterday to see how
> she was progressing in the order. She has only had a week to pre-
> pare *the Wedding* & other Dresses. She thinks she will have all ready
> packed to start on Thursday morng., the 8th, and whatever we
> have to put in the Box must be there tomorrow. In this weather
> dear Fanny it is impossible to run about shopping. It is fortunate we
> have the Carriage, but it can't be waiting about all day. We were at
> Mrs Beeton's Edward's & Marshall's yesterday while snow was
> falling fast.

'Maggie's Box' more or less duplicated the one sent off for Charlotte's
November wedding. Mrs Beeton was anxious to know whether Charlotte's finery had given satisfaction or if there were any likelihood of
alterations for Maggie's order, but no news had come from Cawnpore.

Aunt Fanny Tritton.

I thought Charlotte's Wedding Dress was *too fussy*, but that is Mrs Beeton's style, and a matter of taste. I think she overtrims for *young* girls, & of their height. I don't know how, or where, we are to get your Tulle Bonnet required for the Wedding, as it must be made, & that too by tomorrow! for they never have Tulle Bonnets in Stock in Winter, as you must know. About *the Presents* – we have to *think* & choose. I sent Maggie out a visiting book & Envelope Case, so we shall get a set for Charlotte as you wish & for Maggie something else must be thought of.

After breaking off to dress for breakfast and reading a portion of *The Times*, 'my usual occupation between Breakfast and lunch', Aunt Fanny continued her writing. She wondered where Chattie, Mrs James Dunbar, had gone for her honeymoon and commented that it was a pity 'Mehendee Ghat' had passed out of the family, 'that would have been a quiet Retreat' with many exclamation marks as if 'Mendhee Ghat' held special romantic memories of her own girlhood and possibly her own honeymoon when she had married a dashing Dragoon officer at Cawnpore. Then back to the business of the commissions:

> ...Fanny & Amy are just off to see if they can get a Bonnet made for you in time & a good many things at Marshalls still required for Maggie, such as Collars, handks., Ribbons &c, and to see if they can get some of the Organdie Muslins for you, but their summer Stock must have been cleared out long ago. Maggie has countermanded those she ordered, but when she or Charlotte wrote for them it was in Augt. & the Sales were on; but it is just possible they may be able to hunt out some, if so, they will be sent; they will get your narrow Lace Edging. I have asked Tom Maxwell to get your Tom's 'Necktie' – the most fashionable used for Weddings! & your green Batiste, & visit to Marshalls entails an hour or two, or the Girls are going to get some refreshment in Town & I will call for them at Marshall's or Mrs Beeton's at past 2 o'c.

Everything was completed on 7 December and included a bonnet, 'a pretty light new shape', two little inexpensive headdresses for Fanny, 'pretty and stylish' and a cloud as a gift from her. A regular carriage load of parcels from Glenny and Thresher, Edwards, and Marshalls were delivered to the anxious Mrs Beeton who was fearful the box she had ordered might not be large enough to accommodate everything. The dresses were given a last inspection, 'only bows and little etcetera to be

Margaret and Charlotte Maxwell, 1870.

added'. Aunt Fanny approved. 'I like Maggie's dress better than Charlotte's. It is simpler and less fussily trimmed and with the Veil will be very pretty.' At the eleventh hour Tom's necktie and the music arrived and had to be rushed direct to Mrs Beeton. The box went off via Grindlay and Co. Aunt Fanny sighed with relief and complimented herself that all had been accomplished within only one week. At the end of her letter she includes a note of the expenses on Fanny's commissions.

Fanny Tracy's Account

White Tulle Bonnet	1. 1. -
2 Head Bows 6/11 & 2/11	-. 9.10
2 Pieces Patent Valencienne Lace	-. 6. 6
13 and 15 yds French Muslins @ 13 ½d.	1.11. 6
12 yds. Muslin @ 10½d.	-.10. 6
10 yds. " Batiste @ 8½d.	-. 7. 1
5 yds. Green Ribbon @ 21d.	-. 8. 9
Gentleman's Neck Tie	-. 6. -
A Cloud from Auntie	£5. 1. 2

Since returning to India Ralph Maxwell had played a steady and useful part in the family concerns. His father wrote on 20 October 1869: 'Ralph has established rather a good status for himself I am glad to say. He has become a capital office man too and I anticipate a good deal of relief from his and James Dunbar's assistance this year.' He went on over the next forty years to be actively involved as proprietor, senior partner and director of the Elgin Mills. But it was as a sportsman he excelled.

Born at Dohreeghaut in the Goruckpore district in 1843, where in the pre-Mutiny days Hugh Maxwell had been an indigo planter, he grew up in that open air life of horses and hunting, love of the Indian countryside, knowledge of the village people and awareness of the beauties of nature. Sent home to school to Uppingham in 1855 under the famous Dr Thring, he only stuck it for eighteen months, leaving to go to a crammer to try for the ICS examination, now open to competition. He failed to get in and returned to Cawnpore with his father to play his part in the family business.[18]

The only son among six daughters, Ralph was always called Boyse within the family circle. Small in build, extremely energetic and good-looking, he was a dapper, careful dresser; his sisters ragged him that he never took his shoes off without putting shoe trees into them and complained of his 'whiskery' kisses. But he was no ladies' man, remaining a bachelor until his fifties,[19] enjoying living rough and often preferring

William Dickson, Ralph Maxwell and James Dunbar, with Vic, Son, Topsy and Sandy.

to be under canvas to living indoors. He was said to have the very self-contained temperament of the Maxwells who 'slept in their beds at night'. In the field of sport, shooting, steeplechasing, cricket, rackets, rowing, pig-sticking, he carried off all the prizes. He had the reputation of being a hard rider and a deadly spear and in his lifetime came to be considered the best pig-sticker in the north of India.

Wild boar had always been hunted in Cawnpore. Ralph rode with the so-called Tent Club and in June 1868 the Club was put on a proper footing with regular and properly organised meets, funds raised, a Club house established and formal rules drawn up. It was in 1870 that Ralph Maxwell took over as Hon. Secretary and continued to organise the Tent Club for eighteen years.

The district abounded in pig. The deep ravines in the banks of the Ganges formed impregnable strongholds for them from which they issued forth to feed on the sugar cane and other crops. An old boar after a month or two of sugar diet became heavy and savage, more inclined to fight than run, providing dangerous sport. In March, April and May when the crops were cut the pigs took themselves to the *jhow* jungle or the swampy small streams that intersect the district. Here in the cover the best hunting was available. Meets were held each week on a Saturday, hunting round islands and through watery nullahs from Bithoor to

Cawnpore Tent Club, 1866.

Jajmau, across the river opposite Elgin or as far downstream as Nujjuf-ghur where an old abandoned bungalow, once the home of a rich indigo planter, formed an excellent refuge from the heat of the day.

The rules of the club were strictly enforced.[20] The member of the club who up to 1 July each year had obtained the greatest number of First Spears received from the Club a coveted silver-mounted spear. The Tent Club dinner was the highlight of the season, sixteen members gathered at the Club house, 'conviviality and harmony were the order of the night. Song followed song in rapid succession and the evening will dwell in the memories of all present as one of the pleasantest in their lives'. They toasted the 'noblest sport in a sporting land, a boar in front and a spear in hand'.[21]

The group photograph of sixteen Cawnpore Tent Club members, in RWM's album (see facing page[22]) is marked 1866, yet it seems to tie in with the first dinner recorded. Besides Ralph Maxwell and W. S. Halsey, a number were to make headlines in the *Pioneer*. Buck, the man who sang 'Down, down in the village', the song of the evening at the Club dinner, later became Sir Edward Buck. Francis Halsey was agent of the Bank of Bengal and a keen organiser of wrestling matches.[23] Coghill was the energetic brigade major often mentioned in Stewart letters, one of the original shareholders in Cawnpore Cotton. Farrell the vet suffered a nasty attack on the road from Unao.[24] Brind, as the executive engineer Canals, was a very useful man to have as a member as hunting along canal banks was popular. Goad the district superintendent of Police was involved in a case of *suttee* which resulted in severe punishment. Tovey as executive engineer was frequently under criticism for the bad state of the roads in Cawnpore. Grant went on to become ADC to Lord Mayo.

Soon after taking over as secretary, Ralph Maxwell made arrangements for a hunt[25] at Nujjufghur to mark the occasion of the Viceroy's visit to Cawnpore. It proved to be an unmitigated disaster. Members of the Tent Club camped out at Nujjufghur while Lord Mayo was met at the EIR station and escorted by senior Army officers the twelve miles out to camp. Everything went wrong. A '*ticca*' phaeton had been hired to drive the Viceroy out, horsed by the Field Battery. The horses thought they were harnessed to a gun, put their backs into the work and pulled the box seat and the two front seats off the conveyance. 'They had an awful job to find another.' None of this was recorded in the Tent Club Log but Ralph Maxwell gave his version of the story.

I wished the difficulty had further delayed him, for he arrived at

Nujjufghur at an unconscionably early hour as we lay on our beds
'scattered all around' enjoying our beauty sleep in the cool of the
morning. I was awakened by Grant (R.A.) an old friend of mine
(then ADC to the Viceroy) who had hunted with us before – who
found me out. I expostulated with him and asked him why he had
not told Lord Mayo that the pig at Nujjufghur never come down
to the 'Kuttri' before 7 a.m. I pleaded in vain for delay and the
camp had to be roused up, chota hazri swallowed and we rode
down to the cover. Lord Mayo was clad in white, and strange to
say, was mounted on a black Irish mare 'which died a few days later
of heat stroke', but when, on reaching the 'Kuttri', he unfurled a
white umbrella, it was 'the limit' and all hope of sport was gone.
We killed no pigs as far as I remember; they were no doubt view-
ing us from the heights, highly amused. On getting back to camp
'H.E.' was seen enjoying 'mussuck' outside seated on an empty box,
the bhistie deluging him with water, but no one had brought a
towel for him and search had to be made for one. All ours were
wet, but at last my bearer produced one full of holes, but fortunately clean, which he had brought with him wherein to wrap
my soiled garments after hunting and Lord Mayo had to be content
with this. Thus ended a blank day with amusing incidents.

Gavin Jones's Quarrel with Maxwell

The quarrel between Gavin Jones and Hugh Maxwell occurred early in
1872, barely a year after Jones had taken charge of the mill and put it on
its feet. Writing many years later in retirement, Jones glosses over the
incident saying only that 'circumstances transpired' that caused him to
sever his connections. Within his family some believed the quarrel was
over financial matters, others thought there was some sort of scandal; but
the personalities of the two men must also have played a part.

Very little factual material exists about Jones at this time. He and his
wife Maggie settled into Cawnpore life and domesticity. From the way
they lived later it is likely that the bungalow was plainly furnished.
Neither of them had a taste for the elegant – the only elegance was in a
few pieces of silver and fine linen from the French side of the family.[26]

Jones never spoke of the Mutiny but kept the faded pink handspun
country-cotton drawers in which he had swum for his life carefully put
away as a memento. On the wall hung the bullet-riddled portrait of his

father, JBJ, abandoned in a field by the rebels near Fatehgarh. He made
no attempt to have the damage repaired. His attitude to work was tempered by familiarity with death. His brothers John and Edmond were
killed in the Mutiny, his sisters Charlotte Maxwell and Alice Saunders
died in 1865 within a few weeks of each other, and two other brothers
George and Frank were carried off in the same year, 1869, by disease. In
his own family, a first daughter was born in June 1867, then a son twenty
months later who only lived two months. Ultimately they had five sons
and three daughters with six of them reaching adulthood. While the
grandchildren came to love this tall, gentle man, his youngest son never
forgot how, made to sleep in his father's workshop at the end of the
verandah, he was woken every morning regularly by having Jones's
dirty shaving water flung in his face.[27]

Neither Jones nor his wife were particularly cut out for parenthood. He
took no notice of his sons and not much notice of his daughters. A private
man, troubled and cut off by his deafness, he withdrew into his own world
of ideas and heroic visions. This was the picture within the family but in
the world outside he gave a very different impression. A contemporary
described him as possessing 'a cold serenity, a silent forcefulness, a superior
vitality which made people turn to him and follow his advice'.[28]

At home he leant on his wife, dependent on her for household matters
and money affairs. His name for her was 'Pettums'. He would join the
family at table for meals, saying no more than 'Yes, Pettums, no, Pettums'; and as soon as the meal was ended push back his chair, stand up
and leave the table to go back to his workshop at the corner of the
enclosed verandah and pick up his tools to work on his latest creation.[29]
His woodcarving skills were a joy and a solace to him.

His heads of saints in profile were framed and hung on the walls;
bunches of fruit, pomegranates and nuts carved in relief on panels[30] that
were probably teak, ingeniously contrived to be interchangeable doors
for the sideboard that stood in the dining room. Maggie treasured a
delicate bracelet of wooden links hung with a pulley which he carved for
her all from one single piece of Himalayan boxwood – an intricate and
unusual piece of work, combining his interest in engineering with a
gesture of tenderness to his wife.

Maggie's temperament was a natural foil to his. High-spirited and
practical, she dominated the household, ruling over the children almost
tyrannically, organising the family lives without fear or imagination, the
very embodiment of her sobriquet 'La Reine'. Not surprisingly Hugh
Maxwell writing about the upbringing of his daughter Chattie once

Margaret Gavin Jones, 'La Reine'.   *Head of a saint carved by Gavin Jones.*

mildly indicated that Maggie was not an ideal influence with her modern ways. 'I wish there were some nice people at Cawnpore more of her [Charlotte's] age, with whom she could form companionship and association. Maggie Jones is well enough, as Gavin's wife and a good girl, but not of a stamp to improve Charlotte in any way. . .'

On arriving in India her wild spirit had responded to the scale of India. She felt set free from London conventions when she went riding across country. Here her fearlessness stood her in good stead, she loved to compete in the tentpegging teams that galloped three abreast at full stretch. A cup she won for 'tilting' in 1888 when she was in her forties suggests she kept up her enthusiasm for many years. This love of riding and the open spaces of the Indian countryside she shared with Ralph Maxwell. In old age when they both lived in London, Ralph Maxwell was a regular weekly caller at her flat. Their enjoyment of each other's company was remarked upon; that La Reine had become almost a mother figure to Ralph Maxwell and the quarrel between the two families was resolved.[31]

Was Hugh Maxwell a hard man to work for? The letters exchanged within the family show him to be exceptionally kind and thoughtful, taking a paternal interest in the affairs of all his children and grandchildren, putting his hand discreetly in his pocket to help them when funds ran low, but avoiding any fuss or show himself. Once when the girls ordered a sumptuous armchair for him, he protested 'All my life I have been accustomed to rough. . . and make the best of things.' He worked hard and steadily at the family business, never retiring, but he was content with his way of life and did not share the heroic vision that drove Gavin Jones. If he was dismayed at the quarrel and its consequences he never put it on record. Among the Stewart papers there are references in a couple of letters to George Debnam chaffing unhappily at the Maxwells' handling of the indigo estate he ran for them.[32] But apart from that one can only surmise that the chemistry between the two men made Hugh Maxwell chary of giving Gavin Jones too much power, while Jones was impatient at working for another older man.

So what brought events to a head? Was it young A.S.B. Chapman, the same age as Ralph Maxwell and sharing his passion for horses, brought into the partnership over Gavin Jones's head that caused Jones to challenge Hugh Maxwell? It is possible of course that he was also offered a partnership but stood out for higher terms than Hugh Maxwell was prepared to offer. Or it may have been that when Jones demanded a greater share in the profits of the company Maxwell made it a condition that he give up his independently run timber business and Gavin Jones refused. The extraordinary thing was that the moment the split took place two adjacent advertisements appeared in the *Pioneer*, one announcing that the Elgin Mills had made a change in their management and the other advertising the Cawnpore Steam Saw Mills.

Cawnpore Steam Saw Mills.

FOR TEAK and SÂL TIMBER, in Logs and Scantlings,

Apply to GAVIN JONES, Proprietor.

CAWNPORE,
6th April 1872.   (863)

Elgin Mills Company

CONSEQUENT on changes in the Management, it is requested that all future communications be addressed to

THE AGENT,
ELGIN MILLS COMPANY,
CAWNPORE,

11th April 1872.   (904)

People in Cawnpore were agog to know what lay behind all this. Clearly Jones had done a magnificent job of expansion at Elgin. But had the time and energy he had put into the work caused him to lose a certain sense of balance, so that he became determined to risk everything by demanding his own terms? Many theories were put forward but the protagonists kept their secret to themselves. Several years later when Jones started the rival Muir Mills, an angry exchange between him and the up-and-coming assistant, Henry Ledgard, perhaps mirrors the situation that may well have taken place at Elgin.

The Maxwells might not have been ambitious to become millionaires but the quarrel that caused Jones to leave Elgin and start a rival mill was the first step to the opening up of Cawnpore to industrialisation on a grand scale. Gavin Jones had foreseen it all.

> This unexpected turn broke up a monopoly of inestimable value, much to the chagrin of his late employers. The manufacture of materials for the summer clothing of the army and police uniforms, the introduction of tent making and stuffs suitable for the populace, had opened up a field of unlimited and untold value, that would have in a brief space of time made multimillionaires of the partners, the mill enlarged to one hundred thousand spindles – two or three thousand looms which the Manager had foreshadowed and predicted, all vanished into thin air. The Muir Mills laid bare the secrets and Mills grew apace in Cawnpore and the contagion spread to Agra, Delhi, Mirzapur and other places, which would not have come into existence had the secrets been preserved, for an indefinite period. The hundred thousand spindles and three thousand looms that savoured of 'castles in the air' have multiplied ten fold. Kindred industries have sprung up, that have enriched Cawnpore and made it the busy hive of industry that it is in Northern India, so that what proved a loss to a few individuals has been the means of the expansion and development of Cawnpore and the country around.[33]

John Stewart at the Harness Depot

For seven years Captain John Stewart experimented with the tanning of leather at the harness depot at Cawnpore. He was convinced that with the modern improved methods used in England the quality of Indian hides would compare very favourably with imported leather.

Experiments were carried out to make harness and military equipment, testing them in the services to see if they would stand up to the climate. Senior Army officers made regular visits of inspection to report on the progress of these experiments. They were impressed. Stewart put up a scheme to Government and in 1867 they sanctioned a large tannery and manufactory under his superintendence.

While the buildings were being erected John Stewart had been granted a period of indefinite leave to enable him to visit the principal leather centres of England and Scotland with the view of acquiring full details of all the processes in all their branches. Government of India sent home a hundred hides to be experimented upon. These Stewart took to Messrs Oastler and Palmer of Bermondsey and to Messrs Boase in Edinburgh. With their help he received introductions to other tanneries throughout the country, visiting in all over a hundred firms.

The Stewarts enjoyed their home leave, staying with family and friends, with the Stewarts at Ardvorlich, the Websters in Edinburgh and with Tina in London, showing off the children and revelling in the Western climate. Wherever they happened to be, John Stewart investigated his tanneries. In April 1869 he was informed officially that his leave was up and he must return to Cawnpore for duty before the end of the month. He heard that his buildings at the factory were coming up nicely but that his house was likely to be demolished to make way for the new railway bridge. Millie was thrown into confusion by the news of the voyage out and all her fashion requirements.

> I shall want another piqué and also two alpacas, I think they will be so useful in India and will look better than always washed muslins. . . I have only got one print muslin dress in my possession, a coloured one, mauve and no prints at all, so you see I want a good many things. I have just received from Mama a very handsome black moir such a beauty, so I shall have it made up most fashionably. Do you advise me waiting to have it made in London or sending it to my own dressmakers in Edinburgh. I find my sewing machine so useful, I could run up a skirt in an hour. . . I shall make up some Garibaldies[34] to wear on board ship and I shall then have quite enough for the journey.

The Stewarts had come to the terrible moment of parting from their children, the dread decision that hung over the lives of all English families in India. Should a mother put her children first and risk losing the love of her husband, or stay with her husband and have her children grow up as strangers? Millie wrote to Tina: '. . .only fancy, in less than a month now I shall have to part with all my children. I daren't try to realise it as I become quite upset.' Millie and John decided to leave all five children in England with a suitable lady to care for their welfare and schooling. Their letters for the next ten years are constantly absorbed with the problems arising from this situation – the horrendous cost, the unsuitability of the lady in charge, individual problems among the children, especially Mabel with her paralysed hand. It was pitiful but a common experience.

John returned to India. Millie was to remain behind to see the children settled and follow three months later. For the first time he decided to try the journey to Bombay instead of to Calcutta. In 1869 the GIP Railway had made considerable progress but was still not completed – the break between Nagpore and Jubbalpore was a great 'bugbear'. Writing from Allahabad, where he broke the journey to stay with Tina's husband, William Roberts, Stewart described it: 'I left Bombay on 3rd [July], Nagpoor on 5th – the only bother is heavy luggage but there is Bullock Train from Nagpoor to Jubbalpore and my boxes (6 maunds) came in 70 hours. I took Horse Dak making 2 nights of it, and waiting at Jubbalpore till luggage arrived, and now all my boxes including the one weighing nearly 3 cwt have gone before me to Cawnpore.' He told Millie that he had travelled with a Dr Mansell and they had secured for themselves 50 lb of ice, fowls, a bunch of plantains and a lot of mangoes for the bullock cart journey. It had been an unprecedentedly hot year and very unhealthy, everyone was complaining. Heat apoplexy had carried off many Europeans.[35] Stewart was fortunate that the rains had broken the day before he arrived at Bombay. 'It was cool enough in Bombay. . . I thought Bombay most jungly – no punkahs! They don't understand comfort there. The natives and in fact the whole community are bent on money making and swindling arrivals from England! I lived at the Byculla Hotel – a sort of Barrack! Bombay railways are however advanced in comfort.'

When Stewart arrived back in Cawnpore and word got around of the new ideas he had brought back with him, the Indian leather workers flocked to his factory. For generations they had tanned hides using primitive methods but they had never heard of 'currying' – a process which greatly improved the quality of the finished leather. They were also eager to learn European sewing, particularly the double English stitch. Before long the production of leather equipment was revolutionised. In 1873 the factory took a bronze medal at the Leipzig

Exhibition. Meanwhile as many as 2,000 workers were employed, many bringing their children along with them to learn the trade. Even at home Stewart was seldom free from the factory work. 'There are 100 people waiting with chits and messages and I have to pay away Rs. 5,000 to my workmen this afternoon.' All the same, 'The more I do the more is required of me.' Government sent a young officer to be his assistant but he did not last long; it seemed he thought working with leather was beneath the dignity of an Artilleryman. A small European work force of conductors and non-commissioned officers was built up and Stewart found himself responsible for their welfare. He started a school for their children which in time was 'countenanced' by Government and Millie helped with sewing classes for the wives and Christmas parties and entertainments for the families. Stewart was always aware of the benefit to Government of his enterprise and disgusted with his low pay and their lack of appreciation: '. . .there is no talk of any increased pay for me – everything is so tight and we are cut 7p in the £ for income tax! Is it not too bad?' High-ranking officers were constant visitors, enjoying the Stewart hospitality and inspecting the factory. On one occasion Colonel Lewis complimented Stewart on the work being done at the factory but was not able to hold out any hope for better pay. 'These swells are frightened of Govt and the state of the finances and none dare suggest any increases anywhere. I may say that my prospects have suffered materially from the deficit in public funds – but this place cannot fail to become known and very important and they must recognise it sooner or later by higher pay.'

On his arrival at Bombay Stewart had heard the welcome news that the outcome of the loss of their old bungalow had been resolved. They were to move into Bruce's bungalow, that old fortified house in which Bruce had handed over authority for the city to Sherer while cannon-shot from the Gwaliors bombarded them overhead. It was a huge house, 'a palace,[36] at Rs. 50- a month but requiring a Sudder Judge's income to keep it up nicely'. Stewart was in his element with so much to be done to make the most of the house and garden. After an absence of two years he found things had become very expensive, 'gram sells at 13 seers for a rupee'.

I am trying to spend as little as I can out here, but it is a fearful trial. I have got into a magnificent house which requires everything done to it. It is a Govt house, so I am getting the DPW to do a good deal, but there are many things they will not do and I fear my bricks and mortar and doob grass shokes will run away with some rupees. The compound is a maidan with not a tree or a shrub – I have to do all the gardening! Under these circumstances what is to become of me? I must get Govt to assist. I have commenced to live with the greatest possible bundobast – I have the mutton club again – and have started a moorgeekhana [chicken run], goats etc, everything is bought in quantities and stored and there is great tokana about expenditure. Alas I have a croquet ground and fine rooms so we shall be tempted to have convivial meetings and gatherings but I shall manage on in my homely and limited scale. I think I see my way to living on Rs. 300 or Rs. 350 a month or so Rs. 400 at the outside including everything – you can't say that's lavish expenditure. . .

Millie came out in October. Alexandria was *en fête* for the visit of the Empress Eugénie and the opening of the Suez Canal. When Millie arrived in Cawnpore and saw the house that was to be her new home she could not hide her satisfaction. 'Our house is so beautiful, the envy of everybody. . . How I wish you could see our splendid house. I never saw its equal and John has had such nice furniture made – and Calcutta matting put down in the drawing room.' News, too, came of the possible introduction of a measure which would give Artillery captains the rank and pay of a major, worth Rs.300 a month. The thought of being adequately paid delighted Stewart. He wrote on 3 July 1872:

> There is also a very pleasant chance of my getting increase of pay for my appointment here, and if the double event comes off I shall be a rich man. The manufactory has increased very much and the work turned out is now so run after that I am indeed the Burra mochee and am getting no end of nam as a chamar. I like the work and the place, have a very fine house and compound, I don't dislike the country and my wife has health and happiness as much as can be got without the children – and with that description we have everything to be thankful for.

On New Year's Day Millie gave birth to a baby suffering from spina bifida, which lingered pitifully for nearly five months. Millie went on to have two more children to help fill the gap in her life. She wrote to Tina on 3 May 1871:

> I shall enjoy a little quiet chat with you tonight for I am all alone in my glory, John having gone to dine at the Artillery Mess where

there is to be whist and I do not expect he will be home until very late. He goes to the Mess every afternoon now for two or three hours as a whist party has been got up there for the hot season. He has been five or six times now, and you know how thoroughly he enjoys the game and I am very glad he does for it is nice to meet his friends after his day's work is done, and as he is such a steady player, neither making nor losing money, I do not object at all to the amusement. However I think night whist a mistake and he does also, but being an invited guest tonight he had to go.

He is very well in health. I never knew him better and our new meal hours seem to suit both of us. We get up at half past 5 o'clock have a cup of tea and bit of toast – breakfast at past 8 o'c which consists of dall and rice, fish and eggs and bread and butter. No meat or anything solid. At 2 exactly we have tiffin and this meal we both eat heartily, then in the evening a light dinner.

John goes to his work at 6 and returns just in time for breakfast then he is off again at 10 and returns to tiffin and away again to whist soon afterwards. I sometimes go out to drive before he is back, for there are croquet parties and it is pleasant to meet the ladies there, and nearly every night I drive out with some lady friend and John drives the dog cart to the club then I pick him up there and we return to dinner.

I have not been very well and am now suffering from boils. I had such a bad one on my third finger of my left hand that my wedding ring had to be cut and then the boil lanced which immediately relieved it and now it is getting well. However more are coming but I do not expect them to be very bad as the tonic I am taking seems to do me good the Doctor says they come from weakness and insists on me drinking port wine so I shall be all right now I hope.

Poor dear Baby remains in the same sad sad state and is now terribly disfigured from water on the brain and her eyes are almost hidden by it and I have not seen the black of her eyes for a very long time. She suffers little pain now and sleeps a great deal which is such a comfort for the first month of her life she hardly slept at all and I felt this even more than she did. It worried me to hear the dear little thing in pain. I know she can never be better although I can't help wishing that she might. I take her out to drive every morning the fresh air makes her look brighter and she sometimes sleeps.

The Great Indian Peninsular Railway

A year after Stewart made the tedious cross-country journey from Bombay to Cawnpore the Great Indian Peninsular Railway line was completed and formally opened. A banquet was held on 7 March 1870, graced by the presence of the Duke of Edinburgh, the first member of the royal family to visit India on behalf of Queen Victoria. Mr LeMesurier, the agent, opened the speeches and set the tone for the evening: all who had taken part in the colossal enterprise were imbued with a sense of the heroic.

The Viceroy, Lord Mayo, brought the house down by his remarks that railways 'facilitate those three great occupations of man, in which, from the days of Adam, he has been mainly employed – namely, making love, making war, or making money. I have no doubt that this railway, like all others, will ever be found conducive to those three great objects, and that we may expect to hear of Venus, Mars and Plutus being constant passengers by the GIP.'

All Souls Memorial Church

The completion of All Souls Memorial Church had taken many years longer than anticipated. The original proposal, to build a church as a memorial to 'commemorate the valour and endurance of the heroic band who held out so long against the Nana Sahib and were on capitulation barbarously massacred by him' and as a thanksgiving for the restoration of peace, was put forward soon after the restoration of order by the Committee of the SPG Mission. But this idea was not well received in India where people felt this was a matter for Government. An arrangement was made: Government handed over Christ Church in Civil Lines, to the Mission, on the understanding they would continue to provide at least one service every Sunday for Europeans living nearby, and they in their turn handed over the sum of £2,000 collected as donations towards the building of a Memorial Church.

A site was selected at the north-eastern corner of Wheeler's entrenchment and Walter Granville of the East Bengal Railway prepared a design in a Lombardo-Gothic style. Students at Roorkee College drew up plans, fund-raising continued. On 17 July 1862 at a simple service the foundation stone was laid by the brigadier in command of the station.

John and Millie Stewart had a houseful of guests who had come for the occasion. They took them along to witness the ceremony. They noticed how many people were much affected and 'observed one or two in tears all the time'. While students at Roorkee College wrestled with the plans for the church, arrangements at the Memorial Well Gardens went ahead more speedily. Not however without some drama. The white marble figure of the weeping Angel carved by the renowned sculptor Baron Carlo Marochetti and presented by Lord Canning arrived but was found to be so colossal it would, if placed over the well, stand head and shoulders above the Gothic screen.[37] For several months the Angel lay in its box while agitated debate went on.

The plans for the Garden itself were originally laid out by Mr Walter Ferrier but before he could complete his work he was removed due to some disagreement with Mr Lance the magistrate. It was Lance who completed the landscaping of the avenues each leading to the focal point of the Angel. It was whispered that where the grass was patchy and refused to grow it was caused by the blood that had been spilt there. The luxurious growth of the flowering shrubs was due to the fact that they were manured from the sweepings of the municipal streets.

The idea for the church was that it would be filled with handsome

All Souls Memorial Church.

Memorial Well Gardens: photograph Bourne, c. 1865.

tablets and monuments to the mutiny dead. Upstairs a stone gallery ran round the building on three sides, lit by narrow gothic windows filled with coloured glass, each one named after a particular hero of the siege. On either side of the altar were placed a series of white marble panels set in stone, listing in column after column the names of those who perished.[38] The ceiling above the altar was a high dome painted in an azure blue studded with stars. Regiments and families of many who died contributed plaques and epitaphs. Two in particular came to be especially noticed. One to the men of the East Indian Railway who died defending the entrenchment and the other a simple brass plaque commemorating Charles Mackillop who died fetching water from the well for the women and children.[39]

The pillars of the church, each capital ornamented with flowers and leaves, no two alike, are a special feature. A junior ICS officer,

Richardson Evans, was directed to assist the PWD in the building of the pillars and hit upon a novel idea.[40] The Memorial Gardens where the Angel of Forgiveness[41] stood with crossed palms over the fateful well, were planted with an infinite variety of flowering trees and shrubs. Evans knew the gardens well, he called them his 'solace and delight'. Now instructed to provide designs for the capitals of the pillars he selected branches and blooms from a number of trees and shrubs. These were pressed round a model of the capital in fuller's earth, a sort of plaster of paris, and the draughtsmen made exact copies, transforming them into solid stone.

In September 1871 the Stewarts attended a fund-raising concert for the organ. In 1872 the Viceroy on his way to Simla stopped off for two hours to be escorted to view the Angel at the Memorial Gardens and the progress being made on the Memorial Church. 'The design and progress of the building, the position of the intrenchment, and the localities made memorable by the catastrophe of Cawnpore, appeared to excite His Excellency's warm support.' The Maharajah of Jodhpur presented as a gift the white marble for the chancel steps. Bishop Milman consecrated the building in December 1875 and exactly a year later the first service was held. The church was designed to seat about 700 people and had cost around £15,000.

7
The Rise of Industrial Cawnpore
1872 – 1883

Gavin Jones Starts a Rival Mill

Almost exactly two years after Gavin Jones quarrelled with Hugh Maxwell and resigned from the Elgin Mills, a small group of men foregathered at the bungalow of Dr J. H. Condon.[1] The meeting was informal; none of those present had any experience of textiles except Gavin Jones, who had called them together to put into action a scheme to erect a cotton-spinning and weaving mill. Emery Churcher, a barrister from a family long established at Fatehgahr,[2] took the chair (it was his brother David who had escaped with Jones and shared his thrilling adventures). At that first meeting on 18 February 1874 Jones suggested that a suitable site for the mill would be the piece of land he could sell them 'opposite the wrestling grounds'. He was asked to prepare an estimate for the cost of building the mill and to apply to Platt Brothers for the proposed machinery. They would call it the Muir Mills, after the lieutenant-governor of the province. It was resolved to build the mill by contract; each member of the committee was asked to play his part by ascertaining the rates of various materials and the work required.

At the second meeting there was further cautious progress.[3] Mr Churcher was appointed managing director at Rs. 100 per month. The site they had hoped to acquire from a Mr Cuthbert Cooke had proved too expensive – he had held out for Rs. 3,000 – so it was agreed to acquire Jones's site. At Rs. 1,500 it was a 'liberal offer'. Jones reported he had written to Platt Brothers for designs of a mill of 10,000 spindles. For the rest of the meeting they addressed the problem of how to raise the money to pay for the mill and decided to advertise the shares in all the local papers.[4] Jones also put forward the suggestion that his brother-in-law, J. P. French, would pay £4,000 to Platt Brothers, the first instalment on the machinery, provided he was allowed the benefit of the exchange and interest at 9 per cent on the sums paid, in advance of the calls on his shares. Since it would take two months to get calls in, the meeting accepted this suggestion.

At this stage the directors were joined by H. B. McLeary, a banker,[5] who offered them much sound practical advice: that an office be hired at Rs. 20 per month, a *babu* engaged at Rs. 25 and a *chaprassie* at Rs. 5. They now noticed there was no regular contract with Jones for the building of the mill, so a letter was drafted for the record. He in turn brought to their notice that nothing had been settled about the carriage and delivery in the mills of the machinery and ironworks arriving at the railway station from Calcutta. They fixed a rate of Rs. 3 per ton for conveying and placing all machinery into the mills 'in such places which may be conveniently at hand for fixing in position'. The boiler being exceptionally heavy, it was agreed that a lump sum of Rs. 150 be paid to Jones for the carriage from the railway station and placing it in the boiler house.

On 30 April 1875 progress at the mill was sufficiently advanced for Dr Hinde to propose and Dr Fitzgerald to second that an engagement be entered into with Gavin Jones as manager and agent for the Muir Mills Co. Ltd, 'to take effect from the date when the Mill commences work, at a salary of Rs. 400 per month and a house, rent free, and also 10 per cent commission on all clear profits, as declared by the auditors'. It was carried immediately. In one or two clauses they sought to tie him down; in the light of the quarrel at Elgin they make interesting reading:

> 1 That Mr Jones devote his whole and undivided time to the busi- ness of the Company, and does all his present business within 12 months from the date of the signature of the agreement.
> 2 That he do not enter into any new engagement or accept any contract from the date of signing his engagement; that six months' notice on either side is required to terminate his engagement, and that all minor details of Mr Jones's engagement be left in the hands of the Directors and that the terms of Mr Jones's agreement in the Elgin Mills be adhered to as closely as possible. The draft of the agreement to be submitted for approval to the shareholders.

Jones did not take kindly to the proposed contract and submitted a draft of an agreement that he *was* prepared to sign. This was discussed at a meeting which Jones did not attend. The directors were not pleased and recorded the following statement: 'The Directors having perused the

Gavin Sibbald Jones.

draft of Mr Gavin S. Jones's agreement, as submitted by him, do not consider that the company can accept it, as the terms are unprecedented, one-sided and detrimental to the interest of the shareholders.' They left the matter open as they did not see the need for any immediate action until the mill building was finished and the machinery fixed.

The directors might huff and puff but they could not do without Jones. When Churcher resigned after what was possibly a difference of opinion with Jones, Dr Condon proposed Jones for managing director. McLeary objected that until there had been a settlement of accounts with Jones as contractor of the company, his appointment as managing director was illegal. Jones handed in his resignation of the contract in writing and guaranteed personally the completion of the weaving shed without loss to the company. The shareholders were prepared to wink at the Act – no other course seemed open to them. 'Owing to the paucity of non-official local shareholders who could have been nominated to the office' they felt the present arrangement was in the best interests of the company, adding: 'It is necessary that he [Jones] should be conducting the business of the Mill now that they arc about to begin manufacturing.'

Jones held his first meeting as chairman on 2 October 1875. They discussed what they would burn in the boiler – *babool, imli* and *maula* wood – and to ask contractors to tender for its supply. There was reference made to engaging a Mr Law as carding and spinning manager. Law had originally come out to work for Elgin and had been tempted away. The most important part of the meeting, however, was devoted to authorising the directors to enter into an agreement with a respectable native firm 'for the purpose of purchasing and disposing of the manufac-tured produce of the Mills, and to open a cash credit account for the transaction of all necessary business connected therewith'. The first agency was with Messrs Phoolchund and Makhunlall. They had also looked for a respectable native firm from whom to purchase raw cotton. The shareholders were informed that arrangements had been concluded with Hernandrai Roopram of Cawnpore for the conduct of the business and credit advances of Rs. 200,000 when required. The fee to Jones as managing director was Rs. 150 per month.

As he brought that first meeting to an end Jones must have looked round at the faces at the table with considerable satisfaction. He was thirty-eight, he had emerged as the sole controller of what had been built up as a joint venture. Moreover he had at last achieved what his inner vision had always led him to believe was possible.

Early Days at the Muir Mills

The early minutes of the meetings held at the Muir Mills give an interesting glimpse of the pioneering problems, the lack of experience of commercial law, the problems of engaging staff, the suspicion and distrust between the board and their employees over the safeguarding of the secrets of manufacturing that might make their fortunes.

The scale of the operation can be assessed from a comment that there was not sufficient work in the office for three persons. Office hours were from 7.30 a.m. to 11 a.m. and again from 1 p.m. till the mill closed in the evening and 'no absence can be tolerated'. Experiments in burning coal were carried out, revealing that the cost of burning wood was only Rs. 58 a day while coal was Rs. 81.50, but the coal gave much better results. Insurance was placed with many small companies and when one of the directors suggested it should be placed with the London and Lancashire, it was turned down. At the time of the Kabul expeditionary force in 1878 the Muir enjoyed considerable success in providing the Commissary General with waterproofs with a finish invented by one of the directors, Surgeon-Major J. B. Hamilton. While stationed at Cawnpore he had developed this treatment and now demanded Rs. 2,000 for his 'patent waterproof'.

The directors kept a nervous eye on Jones's restless energy. At first their only worry was that he might go on to start yet another cotton mill, but in 1876 he formed a small private company with his friend Dr Condon to manufacture wool. Because of the climate the manufacture of wool had not been contemplated before, but the idea appealed to Jones. He started a small mill with a single mule and two power looms on which blankets for the native market were woven from the coarse country wool. They were also suitable for policemen's greatcoats and horse-clothing. When William Cooper, a newcomer to Cawnpore, joined the board of Muir he at once brought up the fact that 'as Mr Jones's position with reference to his own business and his connection with the Company has not been properly defined since his election as Managing Director, resolved that it be done now, that he be restricted from undertaking any work which would require his presence out of Cawnpore or that would interfere with the efficient supervision of the Company's operations'. The proposal was seconded by Dr Condon and carried unanimously.

It was not until 4 March 1879 that the agreement was finally drawn up and accepted.

He must devote the whole of his time and attention to the conduct, superintendence and improvement of the business thereto whether carried on in Cawnpore or elsewhere in India. The said Gavin Jones shall not at any time during his connection with the said company as such Managing Director enter into or undertake any engagement with or accept any contract from Govt or any persons, company or companies whatsoever, save and except any contracts and engagements entered into on behalf of the said company without the written consent of the Directors at the time being of the said company. The said Gavin Jones shall and will be faithful and just in all his dealings on behalf of the said company, and do his utmost to promote the interest and extend the business thereof. He shall not divulge any of the secrets or dealings related to the said company or the business thereof. . . He shall have full powers over the engaging and dismissing of employees. . . He must keep proper books. . .

In consideration of the performance by him of all the covenants on his part, the said company shall pay the said Gavin Jones a salary of Rs. 400 p.m. and an allowance of 75 p.m. for house rent, and also a commission of 10% on the net profits and a further commission of 2½% on such profits when the same shall exceed 20% on the paid up capital of the company, and the said company shall also at their own costs provide the said Gavin Jones with medical attendance and medicines. . .

He shall not participate, directly or indirectly, with any cotton mill within 500 miles of the said city of Cawnpore. . . Should he so participate, directly or indirectly, in the promoting or otherwise, in any such mill, to pay to the company Rs. 25,000 by way of liquidated damages.

The company can dismiss him within 3 calendar months . . . if he be guilty of fraud, embezzlement, mismanagement or gross misconduct. Except as above mentioned the said company shall not be at liberty to determine the service of the said GSJ on any account whatsoever, and to avoid litigation, the question of mismanagement or default of contract would be determined by the individual opinions of 3/4 of the shareholders of the company.

Jones continued his independent stance, carrying on his own saw mill, never limiting himself to too close an association with any one enterprise. Even in 1880 he is officially listed as contractor and proprietor of Steam Cotton Mills.

William Cooper

In 1876 the name of a man who was destined to play an important role in Cawnpore appears in the minutes of the Muir Mills. William Cooper went on to become the first president of the Upper India Chamber of Commerce on its formation, the first member of Cawnpore society to be knighted and was reputed to be 'a double millionaire'.[6] When he died at his home, Castle Carey, in the Channel Islands, his desk was found to be full of gold and precious gems. In 1909 he became deeply influenced by the spiritualist movement and in particular by a medium called Percy Beard through whom spirits from the psychic world spoke and appeared to him. He was so impressed that he recorded these events, *Spiritual Manifestations, A Brief Record of My Own Experiences.*[7] It is from this that some details of Cooper's early life are available.

William Earnshaw Cooper, born in 1843, was the youngest son of a Lincolnshire farmer. His childhood had been clouded by this unsympathetic, harsh father who rarely spoke to his large family, took no interest in their welfare and was often drunk and violent to their mother. William was his mother's favourite child and with her active encouragement he set out at the age of eighteen to seek his fortune in India. She died shortly afterwards. The scene of his parting from her remained vividly in his memory.

In India his farming background led to his working on an indigo estate up-country at Chuppra, district Sarun. Always serious-minded, he had a warm heart too – in later life there were many incidents recalled by people he went out of his way to help or encourage. But while still a young man he got caught up in an unfortunate situation when he moved to the Ruar estate at Etah, one of the Maxwell properties. The estate manager was taken ill up in the hills and died and the widow, a woman considerably older than Cooper, with a teenage daughter, flung herself at him. The only honourable course open to him seemed to be marriage. He married Harriet Newcommen at Delhi in 1873 and soon after arrived in Cawnpore with his wife and her daughter as the managing partner of Begg Sutherland and Co. Henry Sutherland of Calcutta had taken over the Maxwell business involvement with Dr Begg and the firm continued to trade as produce merchants.

Mrs Cooper was a tall, handsome woman with a commanding presence, large clear blue-grey eyes, a straight nose and full rounded chin. Invariably her head was swathed in a fine white 'cloud' of tulle.[8] All their married life she was in poor health, continually suffering from fainting fits, pains to her heart or attacks of breathlessness. She suffered at least one imaginary pregnancy. Perhaps Cooper never forgave her for trapping him into marriage and she for her part was aggrieved by his lack of affection for her. She called up emotional reinforcements: her mother and sister came to live with them.

The distractions of his home life, however, did not interfere with Cooper's ambitions. While working for Begg Sutherland he played a part with the Muir Mills and in this connection, thanks to his psychic experiences, he left a description of Lala Madho Ram, the company's agent.[9] He claimed that the Lala, 'the principal member of a native firm which for years held the important position of sole agent for the disposal of the entire manufactured produce of the Muir Mills', manifested himself in order to thank him for a service rendered.

The Lala was a handsome man with clear cut, aquiline features and beautiful grey eyes. His hair was white beneath a tightly wound white turban, his moustache and beard also white. He wore a ring with a broad flat red stone, like a great seal. On entering or leaving the room he would always place his hand upon his brow and bow slightly in salutation. His voice, although he was a perfect Hindu scholar, had slight imperfections so that when he said 'Hamara Sahib', as he invariably did, he mouthed the vowel and it sounded like 'Homera Sahib'.

It was suggested at one time that the Lala's firm of Phoolchund and Makhunlall be invited to resign from their position as agents, but Cooper realised they were in financial difficulties and the loss of the Muir Mill business would have resulted in their collapse. In his position as chairman of the board, Cooper used his authority to oppose the scheme. The old Lala had died shortly after this and, according to Cooper's account, subsequently materialised to record his gratitude.

During his years in India William Cooper made a serious study of the philosophy and religion of the East. He became a vegetarian and surprised his European friends by keenly supporting the protests against the slaughter of cows. In his retirement he turned to spiritualism.[10]

George Allen

The commercial circles of Cawnpore were listed year by year in *Thacker's Bengal Directory* and it is evident how closely interdependent they were — for directors and agencies and commissions. It is not known how William

William Earnshaw Cooper.   *George William Allen.*

Cooper met George Allen, the well-known proprietor of the *Pioneer* newspaper, but by 1879 they had set up the company Cooper Allen and Co., trading in country produce. One of the first coups they effected was to persuade the Muir Mills management to entrust them with the buying of all their cotton.[11] They set up an office to look after this at Hingunghat.

This came at a time George Allen had planned to retire. He had been awarded the CIE in the New Year's Honours, he was nearly fifty. His idea had been to set up a possible succession for his two elder sons: George Berney Allen and Henry Deacon Allen were finishing their schooling in England at Clifton and were due to come out to Cawnpore to work for Cooper Allen. But now circumstances transpired to change his mind. It was Gavin Jones's idea that Cooper Allen should set up a Government boot factory manufacturing army boots; and it was this that decided George Allen to return to India for another twenty years.

Jones had always been friendly with John Stewart of the Harness and Saddlery Factory, admiring his practical knowledge and identifying with his entrepreneurial skill. Socially, too, the two families got on well.[12]

Jones was aware of the success of Stewart's work and the considerable saving to Government. He also knew Allen had the ear of many Army bigwigs at Simla and was close to the influential circle of the Viceroy's advisers. He proposed to Cooper and Allen that they should put up a factory to manufacture boots and shoes and appoint Stewart as inspector. If they could secure an Army contract Jones offered to build the factory for them. He was confident that fortune and honours would surely follow.

These four men, Allen, Stewart, Jones and Cooper, made an impressive group. Three were old *koi hais* who had known India before the Mutiny: only Cooper was one of the 'new men' and even he was a mature thirty-seven. Allen was the oldest, his hair and side-burns greying, his moustache worn full, a tall commanding figure with an aristocratic demeanour. A story was told by Clive Rattigan[13] of how George Allen, on home leave in London, met a member of the family in the West End and offered him a lift to Kensington in his hansom cab. He gave him directions: '13 Prince's Gardens.' 'Bayswater, sir?' the cabman inquired. 'Do I look like Bayswater?' Allen reproved him. 'Kensington, of course, my good man.'

Stewart, now a colonel, was a short burly figure with a huge untidy beard and twinkling eyes. Jones, balding, very tall, a big man in every way, had a coolness of manner that contrasted with the inner passion of his ideas. Cooper, from his bearing, you might have mistaken for a military man. He was sensible, serious and level-headed, with a beautiful speaking voice and a fierce directness in the way he looked at you.

George Allen's official residence was at Allahabad, a fine bungalow across the road from his newspaper office and the printing works of the *Pioneer,* where his love for the paper that his single genius and ability had largely created led him sometimes to give the boys a hand.[14] In the hot weather months he moved with his family to Simla where he lived at The Retreat at Mashobra, an hour's rickshaw ride out from Simla proper, an idyllic setting with magnificent views to the distant mountains. He does not seem ever to have lived at Cawnpore himself.[15] Once his sons were working at Cooper Allen and living at their bungalow, Fairlawn, he probably visited on occasions. But through the *Pioneer* he indirectly influenced the development of Cawnpore. It was Allen who linked it with the outside world, lifting its leading businessmen into distinguished levels of society and bringing to them an awareness of the coveted honours that could be won by men in public life.

As a young man Allen came out to India about 1850 and tried his hand at *zemindary* in Oude. Finding the opportunities in planting limited by lack of communications, he joined a family business, Peake Allen & Co.,

From the Pioneer *of 14 August 1876.*

established in 1851, and based at Umballa, Lahore and Simla. The firm prospered under his imaginative salesmanship. It was said that their fortunes had been made by tooth powder – there was one very old man at the London office of Allen Brothers who recalled the packets of tooth powder made up and sent out to India.[16]

Then came the Mutiny. Allen was present at Delhi as a volunteer, enduring all the trials and tribulations while maintaining a reputation for being the best-dressed man at the siege.[17] The story goes that he found an old printing press and started a daily broadsheet. From this he went on to organise and maintain a service of runners carrying information for the British authorities. Things had barely begun to return to normal when he married a young girl of seventeen, Charlotte Ludlam, at Meerut – her home town, where the male Ludlams had run the North Western *Dak* service and her mother had been a milliner. If, as seems probable, the family escaped to take refuge at Delhi and it was during the siege Charlotte met Allen, it may have been the Ludlams' experience that helped in organising the service of runners.[18]

Allen now decided to leave retailing and follow his natural gift for journalism, and in January 1865 the *Pioneer* was launched in Allahabad. The first number carried an advertisement for Allen Brothers (late Peake Allen and Co.) and for the first and only time George Allen's name appears as their agent. Further down the page an advertisement for the Punjab Trading Company (late Peake Allen and Co.) indicated that the family business had changed hands, but a witty letter written by Allen confirms that he was still the managing director.[19]

Two years later a prominent advertisement announced the sale of valuable land and property in Oude, 20,000 acres in all, including Allengunj, about eighty miles from Sitapur; and on the banks of the River Sardah 5,000 acres of the richest forest lands, free of Government revenue for ever. The *Pioneer* had originally been set up by a group of subscribers, so perhaps it was the sale of this *zemindari* land that gave George Allen the capital to buy out the other shareholders and become the sole proprietor of the paper.[20]

Much of the success of the *Pioneer* was due to Allen's gift of being able to assess a man's ability and fit him to his job, coupled with an exceptional charm of manner that coaxed the best out of people. As soon as the *Pioneer* was firmly established he was able to employ an expert staff while he concentrated on news and views from the headquarters of the Government of India. Before relinquishing that responsibility and appointing the paper's special correspondent at Government headquarters, he was himself present at numberless interesting functions and events and was actually standing by the side of Lord Mayo when the Viceroy was murdered by a fanatic while visiting the Andaman Islands.

The special correspondent at Simla was Howard Hensman. 'Simla was another world. Here the Hierarchy lived and playing whist with Great Ones who gave him special news was the correspondent Howard Hensman of the *Pioneer*.'[21] Princely contributors' fees were paid to highly placed officials in every Simla department, with the result that every impending official change was announced first in the *Pioneer*. It gained the reputation of being first with the news and was considered the most influential paper in India, occupying a position as unique as that of *The Times* in England. Hensman held the monopoly of official news throughout Allen's lifetime, a privilege deeply resented by rival newspapers. This monopoly continued until Lord Curzon threw it open by creating a Press Bureau in retaliation for the *Pioneer* daring to criticise him 'for his tongue and the first person singular'. Hensman was barred from all the Viceroy's functions.[22]

In 1876, some ten years after the death of his first wife, Allen married again. Maud Turner was the daughter of the Revd J. Fisher Turner of Winkleigh, Devon, and sister of Charles Turner, a High Court judge at Allahabad, and Montague Turner, shortly to join Mackinnon Mackenzie in Calcutta – both soon to be knighted and to have distinguished careers in India. Their wide circle of friends enjoyed the Allens' generous hospitality at Allahabad. In the same year Allen brought in James Walker and William Rattigan, the Punjabi financiers, as his partners on the *Pioneer* and in return joined them to organise their newspaper *The Civil and Military Gazette* in Lahore, 'the chief organ of Northern India European opinion' with which Rudyard Kipling was later to be associated.[23]

Turning from his newspapers to go more closely into the possibilities of a Government Boot Factory to be put up by Cooper Allen, Allen wrote a series of letters to John Stewart.[24] He needed vital information that only Stewart could give him. Having realised Stewart's obsession, late in his career, to have his work recognised and rewarded by Government, he plays upon this. It is an example of how Allen worked.

[*Allahabad, 12 December 1880*] I think I have heard that you once took the trouble to work out pretty carefully the cost of making ammunition boots. If such be the case might I trespass upon you kindly to tell me what you think a perfectly safe basis of cost to work upon, estimating leather, labour, work and everything at *quite outside* prices. Can they certainly be made in quantity for Rs. 2/8 a pair by people able to command plenty of capital and the best facilities of every description?

Some little time ago Major Newmarch tells me a man backed by some large Calcutta firm went up to Govt. on the subject of the Army Boot Supply but when he was informed that the Ammunition Boots cost him eleven shillings a pair he withdrew remarking that he could not work at the price. Unless Cooper is radically wrong in his figure that man was a duffer!

When I was in Calcutta the other day your locum tenens had not been appointed General Stewart said. He again spoke of the splendid work you had done for Govt and on my remarking 'The least you can do is to make him a CIE,' he answered 'Something must be done certainly.' A cautious man, General Stewart. But I cannot believe that such service as yours will go unrecognised.

[*Allahabad, 14 December 1880*] . . . Mr Cooper makes the *outside* cost of Ammunition Boots RS. 2/12 per pair and having the greatest faith in your judgement in the matter of the kind I have urged him to reconsider all his calculation, before we become irretrievably involved in a heavy speculation that will not pay reasonably well for a speculation of this kind.

The Viceroy is now decidedly better but the fever fluctuates a good deal and he is now so miserably weak that it is thought he will not move hence before the middle of January at the best.

As for your deserts as a public servant I *cannot* believe they will be overlooked. White the Military Secretary is a very nice fellow and a friend of mine – he is I think the right sort of man to put what is due to you and if General Stewart does not move in the matter, though I fully expect he will, I will watch my opportunity with White.

[*Calcutta, 10 January 1881*] . . . As you have taken such interest in the Boot question I write to tell you that we have concluded a contract with Government for 25,000 pairs of boots of sorts, for seven years from date of the first supply being ready to begin with – the quantity taken to be doubled if the Boots answer. Cooper will give you full particulars on his return a few days hence. We have been very fairly dealt with, the authorities one and all seeming most anxious to see the experiment properly tried and to give it every chance of succeeding.

I cannot forget how much we are indebted to your sympathy and assistance in bringing the project to this present stage.

Allen was the man who could pull strings. The man in Cawnpore who saw to the everyday running of affairs of Cooper Allen was William Cooper. A letter he wrote many years later describes the outcome of these negotiations.[25]

> In 1880 I made an offer to the Govt of India to start a factory for the manufacture of British Army boots. This resulted in the Contract of 1881. In 1885, I think it was, being pressed for funds, I asked the late Sir George Allen, who at the time was in Simla, to interview the later Sir Auckland Colvin – then Financial Secretary to the Govt of India – with the object of obtaining a loan of five lacs from the Govt. I was called to Simla. I saw Sir Auckland Colvin and explained matters. The loan was sanctioned after a short interval. In my gratitude for the financial assistance – without which our whole concern might have collapsed – I said incidentally 'You may examine our books if you like to see how we spend this loan; and you may also satisfy yourself that we do not make unduly large profits' – or words to that effect. This offer was taken advantage of as we know to our cost! The contract price of B/A boot was, at that time, Rs. 5/12 per pair.
>
> This, in effect, is the simple story of the origin of that objectionable 'examination' clause in the Contract which for so many years has worked so disastrously for CA and Co. *Is the Govt Contract worth retaining?*

'That Child the Factory'

War with Afghanistan and fear of Russia kept the Harness and Saddlery Factory at full steam. John Stewart called it 'that child the factory'.

> I have 1,500 men working away in the Factory and we can't keep ahead of the orders. I have not seen India so excited since the mutiny. All our troops are converging on the Frontier and the stations down below are denuded. Here we have only 250 Europeans of the Buffs and not a soldier Native or European besides. The Regiments are all blundering up to the Front – but delaying here and there for want of transport. The Commissariat

has failed – the country is impoverished, we are short of Horses, Bullocks, Camels, and even Elephants. For economical reasons Govt abolished its Stud Department, its Bullock breeding farms and several Elephant Keddahs and now here we are at a crisis without animals to go to war with. It is extraordinary how we are so unprepared for war, with all our expensive army and it shows how the cry of reduction made by you liberals should be combated. How about Gladstone now, you must admit that he was mistaken in his confidence in Russia![26]

All through 1880 the family letters refer to the extreme pressure of work. Millie wrote to Tina:

> John is particularly busy on account of the war, he gets telegrams all day long and has to be at his Factory before chota hazari as well as after 4 o'clock, so he is actually hardly ever in the house. . .
>
> The last fortnight [Stewart added as a postscript] and all through the Xmas week has been coming thick on my Factory. The last fighting at Cabul when Genl Roberts was driven into Sherpore by the Afghan Hordes, has determined Govt to push on reinforcements and I am overwhelmed with orders for all manner of equipment – my Factory is working overtime and even Sundays are not holidays. In the midst of all this we have to give the children's party and Xmas tree!

Tina, at Stewart's request, had sent out boxes of toys and gifts to be distributed to the seventy or eighty children, attended by as many grown ups, at the annual fête held for the senior staff. The festivities left Stewart with a severe bout of indigestion and constant headaches. '. . . Within the last 6 weeks I have equipped 3,000 mules with pack saddles and gear for the Transport Department. I have been making at the rate of 100 saddles a day and despatching by Rail to Jelum!'

Stewart's good name stood high, the factory had earned much credit over the past two years. News of the Afghanistan campaign appeared mixed, with Ayub Khan making a successful sortie against General Roberts, but it was only a matter of time before Millie could crow 'What a victory over Ayub Khan Roberts has had. 27 guns taken! He will be a Peer now. What a grand march he made and with John's *packsaddles,* I hope he will mention them.' Official letters arrived complimenting Stewart on the services he and his factory had rendered to the army during the operation in Afghanistan.

It was at this time that George Allen and William Cooper approached him for advice over their proposed boot factory. Early in 1883, when General Napier Campbell was staying with the Stewarts, on inspection duty, they went along together before breakfast one morning to see 'Cooper and Allen's Boot Factory'. The extra burden of work would be a labour of Hercules but Stewart was hopeful and anticipated additional pay for his double duties. He confided to Tina: 'There is a proposition to make me Govt adviser and arbiter between the new Boot Factory and the Govt Clothing Dept which has the supply of Army Boots. If the Govt appoint me to help them in this job they must give me more pay and I have a chance of netting more money . . . if only I can have health to take it up.'

The challenge suited him and Millie wrote joyfully to Tina: 'John is so much better and able for the extra work Government have given him to do, namely to superintend Cooper Allen's Factory of supplying boots and shoes to the whole of the Indian Army. You would be surprised to see John so full of spirit and so strong, nothing seems to fatigue him, only he must be careful of diet . . . an assistant is to come but he will not be much use at first. . .'

In April on a visit to Calcutta Stewart wrote from the Great Eastern Hotel:

> This Hotel is very full and not very comfortable but it is so centrally situated that I can get through business quickly. . . I have done business in Hides and have seen the authorities of the Military Dept about my new appointment as Head of the Boot Factory. I shall only have the general superintendence and shall be paid some Personal Allowance. I am in high favour with the authorities and master of the situation, my health is wonderfully good, the sweating down here does me good, I am in a bath all day.

By the end of the year all his high hopes had been dashed. 'The Govt have not been liberal in the allowance granted to me for the new duties connected with Boots. They have given only Rs. 100 a month, mean and shabby.'

The Ilbert Bill

Hugh Maxwell had never retired but spent six months of the year in England, leaving the running of the Elgin Mills to Ralph Maxwell and

Chattie's husband, James Dunbar. Ralph was still unmarried but young Willie Tracy, Fanny and Tom Tracy's eldest son, was coming on well and Hugh Maxwell derived considerable satisfaction in guiding and advising him – and getting him out of debt. Willie was destined for the Army, the 2nd Queen's Regiment, but there was always the possibility he would ultimately join the family business.

Taking a leaf out of Gavin Jones's book, the Maxwells were thinking of putting up a woollen mill. In July 1881 Hugh Maxwell tells Fanny that James Dunbar is returning from Manchester with 'a heap of plans and estimates'. In the event a separate woollen mill unit was incorporated in the existing premises and the Maxwells introduced new machinery, sent out via Calcutta since that was cheaper than via Bombay. They also brought out a weaving master in woollen serge.

In 1883 Hugh Maxwell wrote his last letter, a long letter to his son-in-law Tom Tracy, mostly about Willie's preparations for embarking on the troopship *Malabar* for India, and the Burma campaign. It describes the uniform and outfits he required to kit him out for the tropics. The letter ends, however, with a comment on the Ilbert Bill, a measure that was causing a considerable howl of protest from the non-officials in India. It is particularly illuminating for its reference to the fears of the business community in India of the 'Manchester interests'.

I suppose you have not escaped recording your opinion on the Ilbert Bill question. Whether right or wrong in principle, or the necessity of the measure, it is surely most unwise to provoke so much race animosity as has been excited by the course Lord Ripon's Government are pursuing in the matter. The native feeling shown through the native press ought to convince the Govt. how unfit the native mind is to appreciate and sympathize with European ideas of administering the government of a country and people. Baring will I fear be a loss to us manufacturers; there was some chance of his arguing out successfully his measures for promoting local industries.[27] Auckland Colvin is more likely to be a creature of the present ministry and so disapprove of such rapid progress in the development of the resources of India for the sake of Manchester interests. The latter are getting seriously cut into by foreign and colonial competition.

Genuine attempts had been made to honour the promises of the Queen's Proclamation. Indians were employed in fairly large numbers as magistrates, civil judges and as subordinate revenue officers, as well as in clerical work, but the opportunity for educated young men of good family to compete successfully for the Civil Service was very limited. The appointment of Lord Ripon as Viceroy brought a new spirit of liberalism. He believed passionately that 'it would always be the aim of the English Government in India to train the people over whom it rules more and more as time goes on to take an intelligent share in the administration of their own affairs'.[28] The Ilbert Bill, brought in on 2 February 1883, by Sir Courtney Ilbert, the newly appointed Law Member of the Viceroy's India Council, proposed an amendment to the law which would allow Indian district magistrates and session judges jurisdiction over European British subjects in a court of law.

British subjects since the days of the East India Company had enjoyed the privilege when living up-country of being tried by session judges and district magistrates who were European British subjects. For those accused of crimes punishable by death, trial was at one of the three Supreme High Courts. Now with the appointment of Indians to senior judicial posts this anomaly was racial discrimination and the Ilbert Bill was an attempt to put matters right. Lord Ripon held such a contemptuous opinion of the non-official community, or was so badly advised, that he was completely out of touch with their views. The people who were most likely to be affected by the new measures were never consulted.

The Government officials' attitude was broadly sympathetic to the needs and welfare of the Indian people and 'the harsh and aggressive treatment of Indians' by the non-officials, greedy and exploitative, thinking only of their own pockets. To the great majority of the non-officials this was grossly unfair. On occasion, certainly, shameful incidents made headline news in the press but they were little different from similar incidents elsewhere in the Western world at that time when the poor – and women in particular – were often discriminated against. Many of the criticisms against the non-officials in India were fostered by the 'Manchester crowd', anxious to protect their export market to India. Hence one read of 'the Nabob, yellow-faced, ordering round more curricles, with dark crimes on his conscience and a shirt for every day of the week'.[29] What Government circles in India so often overlooked was that if a businessman made a profit he also put his life's work into schemes which developed the native resources of the country, schemes in which he needed the collaboration of Indian capital and a labour force. Without these he could not succeed.

Government officials were so opposed to the business community that they could speak of repressing and ignoring them; the hostility towards the profit motive took all the persuasion of men like Cooper and McRobert (see pp. 281 ff) to correct. Sir Penderel Moon's account of the affair highlights their predicament: 'The disgruntled groups, the Bench, Bar and men in business and the planters, made an uproar of a protest, meetings were held at Calcutta, the press attacked the Viceroy and Ilbert unmercifully. A watered down version was eventually agreed upon but it was in effect a surrender by Lord Ripon to the organised pressure of the non-officials.'[30]

The non-officials had succeeded in defying Government and forcing an amendment to the Ilbert Bill. The effectiveness of organised political agitation was not lost on educated Indians. The Ilbert Bill was the turning point at which a sense of national identity was born and organised political activity began.

Death of Hugh Maxwell

In October 1883 Hugh Maxwell suffered a stroke. He lay in the little front room at the family house in Norwood, London, conscious but paralysed down the left side, and in considerable pain. The doctor attended every two hours and a nurse was engaged to take it in turns with their housekeeper to be constantly with him. Ralph and Uncle Davie were sent for and a message despatched to Maggie and Dr Willie Cherry. Mabel, the daughter who was never to marry and who had been his constant companion in spite of family fears for her frailty and instability, wrote to Fanny Tracy:

> It was scarcely an hour after I wrote to you last Friday when the Doctor came to us, & said he was sinking rapidly, without hope of rallying – even then we could not realise it, but all clustered round his bed with heartfelt prayers that he might yet be spared to us – but later on we began to pray that he might be released from more suffering, & be with his Maker.

Earlier he had been lying comparatively calmly and sleeping at times. The family took it in turns to tiptoe into the room to see if there was anything they could do for him.

> . . . About half past five Ralph was called up to assist the nurse in lifting him onto an easy chair whilst the bed was being moved so as

to be more accessible on both sides. He had such a longing to be taken out of the bed, & the Doctor said he might be moved gently. On his being replaced in bed, a soothing mixture was given to him, but by that time swallowing was difficult, & he could take nothing without choking. Then the heavy breathing commenced. Ralph was so tender & loving, & you could see how it cheered darling Papa to have him at hand, & tending him. The girls stood on each side holding his hands till the last – & Uncle Davie, Ralph & I were also close by his bed.

His breathing was very laboured, & distressing to listen to, but the Doctor assured me that all pain had ceased, he was perfectly conscious, & though articulation was so difficult, we felt his 'yes' was very heartfelt, when he replied to our many questions. I first told him of his approaching death by asking him if he felt at peace, & assured him that God was with us in that solemn hour. I also asked him if I should tell you & Charlotte & Maggie that he was then thinking of you, to which he replied 'yes' very fervently. Uncle Davie also reminded him of his treasures in Heaven, & the assurance we have of a blessed life hereafter, & the Doctor knelt by him repeating 'the Blood of Jesus cleanseth us from all sin' & other words of comfort – & saying we were all deeply distressed, but would be comforted by knowing that he was prepared for the great change. I sent for Mr Watson but as he was out Mr Brennan came in his stead – it was too late to take the Sacrament, but he gladly assented to the proposal of offering up a prayer, & Mr Brennan prayed very earnestly & touchingly for him & all of us – after which, a calm seemed to settle over our Darling & all present. He lingered on about a quarter of an hour after this when suddenly he opened his eyes & looked upwards, then his head fell & after a few soft sighs his spirit fled, just as the clock was pointing to nine. His last struggles lasted from about six o'clock in the afternoon till then. . .

The funeral took place on Wednesday, & his remains now rest in a sheltered corner of the Lower Norwood Cemetery. We hope to visit the spot next Sunday morning. Only the immediate connections & intimate friends were invited to attend.

8

The Stewarts: Family Life at Cawnpore
1874 - 1883

A Wedding

Life for John and Millie had taken on the usual pattern of families with
long associations with India. All five Stewart children were in England
for their schooling, with Tina keeping a careful eye on their development. Her own children, meanwhile, were old enough to return to India
to be launched in their careers out there. The two eldest and first to
return were Helen and Charlie Roberts. Helen came to live with John
and Millie; Charlie went up to Bilsee to work under George Debnam on
the indigo estate, but made regular visits to the Stewarts.

The presence of Helen in the house was a matter of both interest and
some anxiety to Millie. She was a young woman of independent views
and before long had given her heart to a most unsuitable Army officer,
Rowland Oakeley, who was incapable of passing his exams, could not
hold his liquor and was hopelessly in debt. John tried to reason with her
but she had set her heart obstinately on the match. As John reported
somewhat ruefully to her mother, she had a thing about the military:

> I can assure you Cawnpore is no more a military station than any
> other – and there are rather more civilians, merchants and un-
> covenanted men than at most other places – and what is more our
> House and our sympathies are both said to be more civil than Mily.
> It is at our house where all the civilians come to Badminton – we
> are quite of the Civil Faction. But Helen took a decided milt. turn
> from the day she came. We were obliged to change our church to
> please Helen! We thought the humdrum of our dear old Burrell
> was too slow for Helen and therefore we went to the Cant. Church
> after Helen had repeatedly sighed for the sight of the red coats and

the sound of the band. In all her proclivities she is downright mily. There are at least half a dozen well off civilians and merchants of the old Mirzapur type that Helen could have married here if she had smiled on them and attracted them.[1]

Far more worrying for John, however, was his wife's continuing depression. She had never recovered from the birth and loss of the spina bifida baby, she was sleeping badly and 'full of fancies'. John, alarmed for her health, packed her off to England in April 1875, hoping that the change of climate and being reunited with her children would restore her to her former happy self.

For John it was a lonely period – it was just as well that constant inspections from military bigwigs kept him busy. There were financial problems, too; the anxiety of finding £1,000 a year to send home for his family was bringing on headaches. But neither John's personal pressures or Millie's absence deflected Helen's wedding. It was fixed for 12 October 1875. John personally supervised the making of the wedding cake and the details of the wedding reception. The invitations were printed at a local press and as plainly as possible. The cake looked majestic, 'like a tower of Babel, adorned with ornaments and favours, quite equal to anything out of Gunter's shop and far superior both in look and in taste to anything from Calcutta or Allahabad'.

[John to Tina. *Cawnpore 15* and *16 October 1875*] I feel I must write you to tell you of your dear girl's departure from my home and from under my care after a wardship of 2 years 9 months nearly.

On Sunday morning after closing my last to you Helen wanted to take the Sacrament for the last time as a spinster and as she wanted Oakeley to go too I arranged to go with them. It was early in the morning but Oakeley sent out word to say he was not coming – I suppose he was lazy. Helen wrote him a note with orders to come after us but he did not appear. . .

Monday was employed in arrangements, putting out the presents, taking a photo of the cake and arranging for the group and also in signing the Settlement Deed. . . Oakeley, Helen and Antonio and I signing it and Uncle Geo and Charlie attesting the signatures. . .[2]

Mr Scobell had told me the whole choir were to be in church to sing the wedding hymn and he suggested that the men forming the choir should get cake and wine – so I had to make a small cake at the last moment and sent it down to him on Monday with some bottles of champagne to give to the men after the ceremony. On Tuesday morning we finished the arrangements of presents, putting Dick's illustrated labels on all the Home presents. Antonio wrote labels for all the Indian presents and we laid out more than 60 labels – all our drawing room ornaments were removed and Helen's presents put on all our tables. . . At 10 o'clock a Mrs Pauling, wife of one of my overseers, came to dress Helen – she had been quite lately lady's maid to Mrs Jones[3] and was well up in her work and of great use to Helen. At 11.15 the Joneses and Miss French drove up and then Miss Lushington drove off with them to be in waiting at the church door – Antonio, George and Charlie drove off afterwards and last of all Helen and I drove to church in our carriage and pair of white horses – I was in full dress uniform. Mrs Graham came a few minutes before Helen was dressed to see the final touches.

Helen was very nervous and excited and I did my best to calm her and her tenderness and gratitude expressed at the last moments of her spinsterhood were very gratifying. Arrived at the church the bridesmaids were in waiting and we walked slowly up the aisle with lots of people in uniform and in plain clothes on either side of us – the Wedding Hymn was being sung and the assemblage looked gay and happy. Helen was shaking on my arm as we stood before the altar and she was very pale and nervous while the clergyman addressed her and it was with difficulty she could get out the words after the clergyman. 12 o'clock struck, that is the gun fired soon after the knot was tied and while the Exhortation was being read. This part of the service was new and a much prettier exhortation than the old one. The sermon occupied nearly half an hour and then we entered the vestry while the bridesmaids handed out and presented the favours. Everything was signed and attested, then the bride and bridegroom came out and walked down the aisle to the Wedding March played by Mr Dale.

We arrived at home before 1 pm and fully half an hour or more was taken up in looking at the presents and admiring Dick's pictures. There were nearly 80 people, for many had come down from the Hills just in time and had had invitations after all the printed ones were finished. Everyone of the society of Cawnpore and two or three people just out of society but on our visiting list were asked and only a few stayed away – some of the ladies because they were interesting and a few because they had no dresses! . . .

While everyone was admiring the presents we slipped out and

Helen and Oakeley signed the Receipt for the £300 the Fund gives on marriage. I also got Oakeley to write his will the day before, a copy of my will – but he wrote it so badly that Charlie had to write it out and we got Oakeley to sign it after his marriage. . . After all the signing was over Helen went up with Oakeley's sword and cut the cake . . . the almond paste was perfect and everyone admired the cake wondering where it had come from and saying England. The Champagne was Giesler's A1 dry and it was very good and soon after it began to flow the spirits of the party got up.

George Debnam was primed up to propose the bride and bridegroom, I insisted on this as an honour to his age and to an honour of the old man at Kensington.[4] He did it nicely – Oakeley replied in rather a jerky nervous way, he is not much given to that sort of thing. Then came the photo group, this was an awkward part of the business which I had dreaded and it made the meeting hang fire. While we, that is the wedding officials, stood for the picture the other people did not know what to do and crowded round. The people included in the group were Helen, Oakeley, Miss Lushington, Miss French, Mr Moberley best man, Mr Dawes groomsman, Mr Scobell parson, George Debnam, Antonio, Charlie and self. We had to stand 3 times and there was an awkward pause in the festivity . . . after this Charlie made a speech which he had partly prepared, a very amusing one and said with much presence of mind and cheek. He proposed the bridesmaids being the youngest and happiest bachelor in the room. Mr Moberley returned thanks and proposed the Ladies. A young griff named Baker of the 73rd – a very ugly fellow – then spoke amusingly and returned thanks. Mr Churcher gave the parson and his wife and Mr Scobell returned thanks in an appropriate speech in which he eulogised Helen and told an amusing anecdote of how she had played patience for so long not only in this matter but at cards – she used to play the game called the Queen and Her Lad in which the Queen of Hearts waits for the Knave and they come together – she played this at the Club and Mr Scobell observed that at last the lad had come to his queen! Mr Sobell proposed my health and I returned thanks, then Helen was dressed and came out and went off under showers of shoes and slippers and rice.

It was rather early for the train, but the people were getting tired so I spoke to Mrs Stone my asst's wife to allow the pair to drive to her house and wait a quarter of an hour till the train went off. They did so and the party all left, but a few of us stood and saw the pair cross the bridge opposite our house to go into Oude – they went to Onao to spend the night at Mrs Maynard's house – and next morning they returned and went off to Agra straight. We saw them at the station for 5 minutes and gave them wedding cake and some things they had left behind and one or two boxes. It was very unfortunate the Oude train was late and they had to bundle out of one train and into the other in no time and had it not been for me asking the station master to stop the up train they would not have been able to go and must have had to come to this house again for the second night of their married life. After their train left we saw Miss Lushington off and she carried a bit of wedding cake to Mrs Lushington. George Debnam and I cut up the cake and distributed it to the ladies who had not been present and we cut about 6 lbs and put it into tin and soldered it and I despatched it two days ago by Parcel Post to you addressed 10 Minto Street. I hope you will get it all safe. I paid all freight and you should not be charged any custom duty. I also sent you by Parcel Post a musical pheasant which Helen packed and desired me to send you. . .

You will be caring for and tending my wife when this reaches, God bless you and God bless also your daughter who has entered upon grown life. God bless my darling Millie too.

Your very affectionate brother

J. STEWART

To everyone's amazement Millie's low spirits were cured by the surprise birth of a son, Jock, just about the time of Helen's marriage. John began to make plans to go home on leave and join her in England in April 1876. They returned together with the baby at the end of that year to begin what was to be for them a golden decade. Millie surmounted both terrible heat the following summer and her acute embarrassment at being again pregnant after twenty years of married life to bear another son, Augustus. These two little boys, their second family, gave them immense joy. Millie had become confident, capable and houseproud; the Stewarts' letters home are full of their pleasure at living in Cawnpore.

Charlie Roberts travelled twelve hours by *dak* to join their party for Christmas. He was just recovering from a broken jaw – he had been flung out of his carriage in an accident – and his beard concealed the scar. John took him off to play billiards at the club and on Christmas Eve

Millie drove him down to the English shops which were ablaze with lights and had various attractions on display like the Wheel of Fortune with cheap prizes to be won.

> *Xmas day* [*1877*]. Dearest Tina I don't see much chance of writing very much to you today, it is such a busy day always and we have only just returned from church where we went at 11 am. Charlie accompanied us and he was delighted with the Memorial Church which is really very beautiful. The service is always good but today the music was grander than ever as Mr Dale C.S. and Mr Wright, both highly accomplished musicians, led the choir and played the organ and this latter is a great beauty, one of the finest organs in India. It was 1 o'clock before the communion service was over and the amount of Natives and dalehies [baskets of fruit, nuts and sweet-meats traditionally presented at Christmas as a mark of respect] to look at took a long time and kept us in the verandah until tiffin time and after that I began to prepare for the party, filled ever so many vases full of flowers – the flowers are very beautiful just now especially roses.
>
> 26 *of Dec.* Dear Tina I had no time yesterday to write, we had a most successful party 10 in all and it was all over by 12 o'c. Charlie and a young fellow Cruickshank talked to one another a good deal during dinner. He is shy to ladies but seems to talk uncommonly well on various subjects. He is very contented and happy with his lot and in first rate health. He still smokes a good deal and he and John enjoy pipes together. Jock and Charlie have great fun, he is the Horse and runs about with Jock on his back, John running after and making the child laugh so loud and heartily. Baby lies on his back on the floor as Jock used to do in your dining room, he is very bright and happy and crows so prettily. Charlie drove down to the station to meet Henry Sanderson but he didn't come, is to be here tomorrow. He visited Jamsetjee, the Parsee merchant, on his return home and purchased a lot of things, amounting to Rs. 112. 6 dozen pints of Beer was amongst the items, toothbrushes at -/12/- each and a tiny sponge for 1/8/. I hope you spent a happy Xmas yesterday and I wish you a very happy New Year. We talk much of you all and wonder who formed your Xmas party. . . We have another dinner party tomorrow, 12 with guests and on Saturday we give a tremendous *tamasha* [show] to the children of the employees in the Factory – besides all the ladies and gentlemen are coming with their

children. A very long table is to be placed in the dining room and it is to be covered with cakes and sweets of all kinds which I have been superintending all the week, such boxes of cakes I have and won't the little things enjoy them. How Lilian, Ethel and Helen would enjoy them – dear children, I hope they have spent a happy Xmas. I expect a letter from them tomorrow! John and I are writing in the Dining Room near the fire, Charlie is reading a novel by the fire but has now gone to bed. I am very sleepy and must go too.

So with fond love my dearest Tina from John and self,

Believe me

Your very affect. sister

AMELIA STEWART

Proclamation and Famine

It was Disraeli's idea that Queen Victoria should assume the title Empress of India and in 1877 a great durbar was held in Delhi to honour the proclamation. Over 70,000 guests were invited, including 77 ruling princes in all their panoply and 300 other Indian nobles, government officials and military commanders, with envoys from several eastern states[5].

Although Cawnpore was not of sufficient importance to merit any place in the celebration, John Stewart managed to slip away and stayed with his friends the Pollocks to witness the event.

Victoria, Empress of India, medalet.

I left for Delhie [*sic*] on the 30th [December] to see the Tamasha. Pollock asked me to shake down in his tent, was 3 or 4 days away and saw the wonderful sight, the Proclamation... I was quite satisfied that it was the proudest thing of its kind that had ever been done in India. The sight, the company and the occasion were such as will never again combine to make a pageant that outshone the Field of the Cloth of Gold.

Certainly it outshone the misery and privations of that year's famine. The weather had conspired against the populace. All through April and May there had been light showers. June as usual was dry baking heat but by July there had been no sign of the rains. Only two showers had fallen and the country was dry. John Stewart recorded, 'Ploughing not half done – all over India it is the same and if it lasts another week there will be a general famine.'

His diary takes up the story:

22 August The weather continues without a drop of rain, but sultry and disgusting. I don't think I ever felt India so abominable as I feel it this year – it has broken my spirit. Getting on to the end of August and not a blade of grass to be seen – no crops – no vegetation – but hot west winds killing even garden shrubs and plants – all the rain we have had from Rainy season were two showers on 1st and 2nd July and also two slight showers on 2nd and 3rd August.

12 Sept No rain up to 12 September. Tatties[6] going in my writing room. Did you ever hear of such a season in the NWP? I never saw one like it. Fanmine is now almost certain.

24 September Even today our Tatties are acting as if it was May weather and we have not had a drop of rain all this month, only 3 inches have fallen the whole of this season, a terrible famine must follow if no rain comes within the next 15 days for the fields already sown are without any sign of a crop and it would be useless to re-sow on top. It is a sad sight to see the country so parched and barren and the distress amongst the poor is pitiable. We already pay famine prices for everything in the Bazaar and atta sells at 9 seers per rupee. The Magistrate is getting up relief work for the many who are now almost starving and about the corners of the road are to be found the maimed, halt and blind in the most pitiable conditions begging for food.

6 October Only fancy here we are without a drop of rain up to the 4th Oct, a total failure of the Khareef Crop and no moisture in which to sow for the Rubee.[7] The famine will be terrific. Already all servants and workmen on Rs. 4 a month are beginning to starve, so what must be the case of families and poor villagers who have not so much. I employ 1500 of the poorest class of Cawnpore Chamars and they have an average of 4/- or 5/- each per month and on that have to support their families. The consequence is that I am beset on all hands. They take a hold of my feet and I can't get along without kicking them, they wish me they say to kick them. I am obliged to help them by private charity for I like my work people and most of them have been with me for 15 or 20 years. Government will do nothing more than supply work in the districts – my people are all townspeople and have lived for years on their earnings in my Factory. They cannot avail themselves of Relief Works. With Rs. 4/- or 5/- they carried on all right in a time of plenty, but they are pinched and there is much misery now with gram at 10 seers and there is every likelihood of gram going to 6 seers or 5. My means for private charity are very limited, but a bright idea has struck me. . .

John wrote to his brother Jim in Scotland to put out an appeal among their friends and rich neighbours to raise money to help the workforce at the factory. Jim wasted no time. He had the letter printed as part of an appeal for the Cawnpore Famine Relief Fund and the response was such that there was sufficient to distribute among those who were unable to work as well as among those who could. Many of the poor wretches had not had a full meal for over six months. Stewart had earned for himself the title 'Ma-Bap'. From the factory's early days his enthusiasm and dedication to the improvement of leather had won him the workers' respect; but it was probably his concern for their welfare at the time of famine that really endeared him to them.

Under the wide verandah at the back of his bungalow Stewart would hold durbar with his workpeople around him. His was reputed to be the first works committee of any ordnance factory in India. The labour was employed, enrolled and paid by intermediary contractors, a system that worked well and continued until 1920 when the first strike took place.

Many stories were told of 'the grand old man'. Wearing a large topee, his face half hidden by an immense bushy beard, sometimes in the evenings he would ride round the homes of workers who lived near the factory. His pony was white, a sturdy beast capable of carrying his huge bulk. In the mornings he would be driven to the office in a phaeton, with a smartly dressed syce sitting on a high seat in the front. Once it was found that quite large pieces of leather were missing from stock each day.

> This caused his officers a great deal of worry until they decided what to do and with great fear in their hearts the sergeant at the gate was told to stop the old man going out and search his phaeton. The syce was found sitting on the top of a number of new pieces of leather neatly cut to size under his cushion. The Superintendent was very embarrassed and that was most probably the start of all vehicles being stopped for search in the interests of the owners.[8]

The Great Landslide at Naini Tal

In the hot weather of July 1878 Millie painted a most cheerful picture in a letter to Tina.

> We have got the rains at last and are all feeling the better. I am enjoying sitting in the verandah all day long and the boys play about beside me. Jock is in splendid condition never ailed once since those back teeth came. He runs at a great rate and chatters continually, he is very gentle and the servants are all so fond of him. His great delight is to be shown pictures and he walks about with a volume of *Punch* under his arm. Gus is a gem in the way of health . . . he stands up at a chair quite firmly and crawls very fast. His Dhai is a great success and he has had no food yet, sucks lumps of ice and crusts. . . I wish you could see the neat costume Jock wears in the hot weather. A miniature shirt with frills down the front, sailor collar frilled, pair of knickerbocker drawers frilled and a red belt. Everyone admires it and he is so cool. . .

For John Stewart pressure of work was considerable in what he called 'these stirring times'. He was constantly in demand – 'Everyone is wanting something and they can't fight without leather.' But it was telling on his health, so he decided that next year he would take his family up to 'Naynee Tal' during the hot weather. Naini Tal was a favourite hill station for people from Lucknow and Cawnpore. The first twelve houses were built in 1842 on the hillside overlooking a picturesque lake. Since then it had developed into a little town, becoming the summer headquarters for the governor of the North Western Provinces. There was a

Two of the Nightingale sisters boating at Naini Tal.

church, St John's in the Wilderness, several small hotels and guest houses, a popular club house with boating facilities, polo, cricket and tennis, and the usual complement of schools, shops and small cottages designed for summer visitors.[9]

John rented End Cliff for the season for Rs. 1,000. It was furnished but to make it really comfortable quite elaborate arrangements were made. He took ten days' leave to escort Millie up there, with three carts loaded with the piano, crockery, glass and furniture of all sorts going on ahead. The house was just above the cricket ground on Aya Path, on a ridge where there was sunshine up to 3 p.m.

The Stewarts were so delighted with the arrangement of the hill house that they took Prospect Lodge for the following year, sharing the house and the *bandobast* with Millie's sister-in-law and her family. Ominously, however, they commented on the heavy rain:

> This is a very extraordinary season at Naynee Tal. We have rain every other day through the month of May – it is pouring now. . .

The general view, Naini Tal. Photograph Gangi Sah.

It is raining terrifically now so that we can't hear ourselves speak, the noise upon the iron roof is beyond description, I have had to put cotton in my ears to deaden the sound, and the poor children were so frightened, poor Jock kept calling for his Bearer Urgoon to come to him. The thunder is deafening and the lightning so bright that I do not wonder at poor Jock. . .

On Thursday 14 September the rain began again. On Friday and Saturday there were thirty-three inches. The ground became sodden, like porridge, and on the Sunday, 19 September 1880, a slight earthquake started a landslide. An avalanche of rocks carried away the Victoria Hotel, sweeping it into the lake. 151 people were reported killed or missing, 43 Europeans and 108 Indians.[10] The same day Millie wrote to John describing the terrible experience.

My dearest John, A terrible calamity has befallen this place, fearful loss of life and property. I tried to describe to you yesterday's rain but I am afraid failed, as I was writing to you the storm increased if possible and at 2 o'c the hill behind the Victoria Hotel came bodily down completely burying the Victoria Hotel, Bell's Shop and the Assembly Rooms, landing in the Lake. Major and Mrs Murphy and Mrs Turnbull were reading in the Library at that moment, so went along with the building, there may have been many more, but these we know were there.

There had been a lesser landslip a few minutes or hour before which brought down part of the Victoria burying the inhabitants, it is supposed, in the ruin. So the Depot was called on for help to extricate the bodies, 50 men and also Balderston, Sullivan and a young fellow Hackett, also a doctor, but we don't know yet, they were busy looking for bodies when the final crash came and carried them and all the debris into the Lake. When the first landslip took place those who were safe in the Victoria took refuge in Bell's shop and must have perished when it gave way. Then a terrible panic took place amongst the people living near and each and all left the houses for refuge elsewhere. The Walkers rushed to the MacIntoshes, Col and Mrs Billy Barlow (whom we didn't know had come) to us, the other Barlows to the Attleys, the Miss Barlows to Mrs Turner, others to the Christisons until every house there was deserted. We were sitting quietly in the drawing room after lunch wondering if we should ever get out again when Kate and Edward said they would venture as far as the Library. The Jhanpanis stood aghast at the very idea saying it was no day for sahibs and memsahibs to go out. They sent for Beer and the man returned saying it was impossible to go along any of the roads. I didn't heed what he said thinking of last year, so Kate and I went but on getting to Nurcick's shop Kate couldn't pass, it was a perfect torrent, so turned back. Edward got off his Horse climbed the little parapet and got down, they then met the Barlows walking dripping wet and searching for us – Mrs B had to climb the parapet. I heard all I have related. Presently a Dandy appeared in the verandah full of bags, blankets etc. I rushed out to ask what it was for when the men told me the Barlows were on their way up and would I send my Dandy for the memsahib which I did. They came by the approach by the Kitchen, above the Club, and from them we learned that it was only too true all that the servants had been saying. They were frightened and such a sight as if just out of the lake.

Edgehill where they were had partly given way and all the servants' houses had vanished. Col Barlow had witnessed both landslips and describes them as something awfully grand and in a moment all was over, like two huge clouds of dust, a crash and all disappeared in the lake. Where the three buildings stood not a trace left of any of them, just a few bales of flannel and other goods strewn about where Bell's shop stood. Both men in Bell's shop were killed but the women were saved and it is also known that Capt Harrison, Hotel Proprietor is amongst the victims. The Goodriches and Mrs Taylor could not be found and it is supposed that they were in the Assembly Rooms preparing for the Ball to come off tomorrow. . .

I think the house is very safe but one can't help feeling nervous, there are reports that a lot of houses are down. I should say the Ponsonbys might be one of them but we don't know. It cleared a little and Kate went down to Church but the rain is on as bad as ever, only the light is strong as if the sun was attempting to shine – so we trust this may be the case as it is a good sign when the weather changes at this town. It has been such blackness and darkness ever since Thursday afternoon.

Col Barlow has come in command here and the report of loss of life in the Depot alone has just come to him. There were among the working party 15 men and non commissioned officers and 16 officers and it is supposed that Mr Taylor must have been amongst them. There was no Doctor mentioned but as both gentlemen heard there was one perhaps it was Dr Hannah. Poor Mrs Balderston, how terribly sad and she is alone, the Haywards having gone into Lake Cottage house, the one the Bazetts were once in and which many people told them was very unsafe. I hope when they knew this that they went at once to the Balderstons again.

A young Depot officer named Carmichael is another victim. He was one of the working party. When it cleared a little just now we all went into the verandah to see what remains of the Assembly Rooms, just one wall is standing of the dancing room, Bell's shop and the Hotel debris is all collected in a mess close to the water so the victims must be under it. How terrible that they can do nothing today, it is evidently not going to clear yet and natives prophesy a whole week of this weather. I am so thankful now that we didn't buy a house. I shall dislike the place more than ever. We do say now that nothing would induce us to return to Nynee Tal again. I ventured to the reading room on Friday night but felt so nervous while there that I only remained a little while. The wind howled and the lake looked so fierce that I was thankful to be home again. Mrs Murphy and Mrs Turnbull came in with Mrs Straight the lawyer's wife, they were full of merriment and fun, laughing, poor people, I couldn't help watching the three ladies, particularly Mrs Murphy, they were dancing at the party until 2 am of Saturday and dead by 2 pm. Is it not truly awful? What a bad name this place will have now for its unsafeness, there was the hill on which a boulder came down last year so none of it is safe. Mrs Proctor is very ill with inflammation of the lungs. I saw her on Thursday just as the rain began, she begged me to stay until it was over!

No dak of course yet – it is 12 o'c and I doubt of getting yours of Friday at all today. The Gwallor [cow-man] has been and says there is no rain now. I must send this off soon to enable it to be on time. Don't be alarmed about us. I think we are safe in the house. No carpenter will come. I sent the Molly [gardener] to try for one and they could get no coolies to work with the working parties. The Native Temple of course has gone into the lake.

I shall write home this week. Much love.

Ever,

A. STEWART

Family Reunion

After years of anguish over Willie's lack of academic prowess the Stewarts had sent him to a crammer's, wondering if he would ever pass his exams and get into the Army. Finally they begged Tina to take him under her wing and have him live with her. They hoped that her example would inspire him and the plan seems to have worked. John was on his way to the club when the telegram was handed to him. Willy passed! He sent for a bottle of champagne to celebrate the result with his friends. The club was out of it; but there was fizz enough anyway in the content of the telegram.

Willy was to join his regiment, the 65th, in India. He had been only five years old when he left Cawnpore but he was the 'burra baba' and the servants were thrilled to hear he was back in India and due to spend ten days' leave in Cawnpore at Christmas. 'All the old servants are anxiously looking out for him, preparing the Lawn Tennis court with great nicety as they say the burra Sahib is to come and in making the Cake yesterday I heard the old cook say it must be extra good this year. . .'

Willie and Charlie Roberts made up the party for Christmas, living in tents in the garden and having romps and sham fights in the swimming bath John had built. Millie and some of the other ladies also swam but only when they had the bath to themselves. Christmas festivities as usual were the highlight of the year – 'I don't know', wrote Millie, 'when we had such a festive week.'

In March 1881 Lord Ripon the Viceroy visited Cawnpore and John Stewart, now a full colonel, had to escort him round the factory. Millie told Tina all about it.

> John had to go to the Station to meet them so we all went. . .
> I with John and the children. The latter were much excited to
> know which was the Lord Sahib. Jockey thought the officer in the
> Cocked Hat must be him and when I pointed out a very little
> insignificant-looking individual his face fell and he said 'Where is
> the Lord Sahib?' Gussie was only taken by the golden gates of the
> railway carriage and danced when the band began to play, looking
> so comical at the time but Lady Ripon laughed and turned round
> to look at him. He imitates the native style of dancing and is full of
> fun and merriment. . .

Only a week later the Stewarts were on their way to England on furlough. The time had come for the second family to be left behind for schooling. When John and Millie returned a year later they brought with them their two eldest daughters, Lilian and Ethel, grown up young ladies, but almost strangers to them. Mindful of all they had learnt from Helen Roberts's unfortunate romance they watched the launching of their daughters on Cawnpore society – mostly with pride but just occasionally with a touch of anxiety. Their letters to Tina, meanwhile, concluded, as a collection, at the end of 1883.

9

The Technicians: That Second Circle

═══════

John Harwood

The 1880s brought an influx of technicians and their families to Cawnpore, as well as a tremendous flurry of building work that included the construction of the mill premises themselves and the numerous bungalows required to house the new staff. Weaving masters, spinning masters, carding masters, engineers, fitters, dyers, were all in demand; some were already working in India and were attracted by better terms up-country, others were engaged from England.

Three men who came to the Elgin Mills as technicians went on to establish their own mills: John Harwood, Atherton West and Frank Horsman. John Harwood joined the Elgin Mills in 1880 as a weaving master, having already had ten years at a cotton mill at Bombay. Within a very short time he had organised the finance to build and launch the Cawnpore Cotton Mills. Mrs Harwood started up the first engine on 4 July 1885, just over two years after John had resigned from Elgin.

The Harwoods were typical Lancashire folk. John Harwood was born near Darwen of working-class parents and started work at an early age in a cotton mill where he became a taper. He and his wife went to live at Accrington, then emigrated to the United States and from there accepted an offer to work at a Bombay mill. In Cawnpore John Harwood was for many years vice-chairman of the Cawnpore municipality and on his retirement in 1898, handing over the mill to his son, he was given an illuminated address in native handiwork testifying to his work in the interests of Cawnpore. It was a treasured possession.[1]

Back in Accrington in retirement, John Harwood continued his civic interests and served three years in succession as mayor. But it was for his part in raising the Accrington Pals during the early days of the First World War that he is still remembered. The Accrington Pals, the 11th

Battalion East Lancashire Regiment, the cream of Accrington's young men, went into action on the first day of the Battle of the Somme, 1 July 1916. Within twenty minutes 585 men of the battalion of 700 were killed or wounded. It was a day Accrington never forgot.[2]

Alfred Butterworth

By 1882 Gavin jones had decided to launch the Cawnpore Woollen Mills, Army Cloth Manufacturing Company Ltd, as a limited liability company. In response to their advertisement for a weaving master, Alfred Butterworth, my grandfather, went out to India.

For three generations the Butterworths had been woollen manufacturers. During a period of depression in the industry Alfred Butterworth's father had left Hinchcliffe Mill at Cartworth in Yorkshire and moved south to Chipping Norton, in the Cotswolds, where he brought up a large family and worked at Bliss's Tweed Mill. Alfred followed his father into Bliss's Mill and met and wooed a mill lass called Polly Cotton. Family legend has it that he went up to London for interviews for two possible jobs, one in South America, the other in India. He was more impressed by the man from India (perhaps it was Gavin Jones himself), and decided to take his offer. Technicians, it seems, were so much in demand that they could pick and choose. Alfred and Polly were married in London on 16 October 1882 and sailed a few days later on one of the P & O ships that made the run to Calcutta every fortnight. The ship was steam but carried sail for emergencies and livestock for the voyage. The Suez Canal had only recently been opened and the Butterworths followed all the sights as listed in the *Illustrated Route Chart, Travellers' Handbook to Egypt and India; with coloured views of the Chief Harbours and objects of interest visible from the Deck of the Steamer on the route*.

In Cawnpore they lived in a red brick bungalow called The Palms in the shadow of the high walls of the mill. The plot of land next to the bungalow was the site of an old pre-Mutiny bungalow where Lord Roberts had been born in 1832. Here the Lalimli Club was built, the centre for social events for the senior staff at the Woollen Mills and named after the tamarind tree near the main entrance in the mill compound, the only one in the district to bear red flowers – the 'lal [red] imli' and chosen as the company trade mark.

Within a year Alfred had been appointed mill manager, a post he held

Polly and Alfred Butterworth, with ayah and children Bee, Lu and Alf.

for over thirty years. While identifying with the success of the mill, he had no ambitions to start a mill of his own. He took a keen interest in the practical and construction side, but his forte was in his dealings with the labour force. Very strict, very fair, he came to be almost a father figure to the men. He was also something of an amateur physician and workers often came to see him when they needed medicine. On one occasion, when a new chain saw was installed, the workforce was assembled to watch how it worked and to be made aware of the dangers. One old man walked up to it inquiring, 'Will it really cut off my finger?' and put his hand to the blade. The tip of his finger was cut off instantly. Alfred Butterworth called for a bowl of warm water and hurried the man back to The Palms. There he stuck the top joint back on, bandaging it with tiny splints but not attempting to stitch it. The finger healed and rejoined, even though it was left slightly crooked. Alfred's reputation was made.[3]

It was Alfred's habit to carry a short stout swagger-cane under his arm, rather like a sergeant-major. Sometimes he would use it for correction, when, for instance, workers broke the rules by bathing or washing their clothes in the water channels in the mill compound. Hot water from the boilers ran round these bricked channels until it had cooled off

Two of the Woollen Mills staff, the day the first train (below) came to Cawnpore Woollen Mills, 1888.

and was returned to the tank. The punishment for not leaving it well alone was either a fine or a summons back to The Palms in the evening for a sharp cut from Alfred's swagger-cane. Invariably the culprits chose remedial treatment at The Palms, which they took in very genial part.

Atherton West

When John Harwood left to start Cawnpore Cotton Mills, the Elgin agent wrote asking Platt Brothers, from whom they bought most of their machinery, to select and engage a suitable weaving master. Atherton West, a Darwen man who had served his apprenticeship at nearby Burnley, and a man called Stott were engaged for Elgin.[4]

West and his wife Martha (*née* Fitton) sailed for India in 1882. Mrs Fitton, West's mother-in-law, had presented him with a small pocket Bible which he used for the first time at the service the following Sunday. He had it appropriately inscribed: 'Presented to Atherton West on his leaving Ashton Monday the 13th November 1882 for Cawnpore India by Mrs Fitton. First used at Service on board P and O Steam Ship *Thames*. Sunday the 19th November 1882.'[5] They docked at Bombay on 11 December.

Elgin's new weaving master was a bluff, no-nonsense professional, physically imposing, with a beard closely trimmed to his broad face. He really knew his job and delighted in the quality of the fabric he could conjure from the loom, the checks and stripes that could be woven into borders, the variety of textures – shirtings, drills, desooties and tent cloth. He kept a punctilious record of all the fabrics he produced with notes of how the loom was set up, the quantities of cotton used, the widths of the looms, the costs of production. There was an ulterior motive in all this. He was convinced that, given financial backing, he would have the knowledge to start a mill of his own. His small pocketbooks are filled with details of his daily observations, the working and running costs at Elgin, at Muir, even at mills as far afield as those being put up by wealthy Parsees at Bombay. He had little respect for the Maxwells and the Dunbars: they might be the agents but the know-how was with him and the other technicians. At a time when both Elgin and Muir were competing with their tents and both winning silver medals and first-class diplomas at the Melbourne Exhibitions of 1880/81,[6] the weaving department at Elgin was still on a modest scale, no more than 275 looms, many of those dating from the first looms sent out by Platt

Atherton West and Martha, his first wife, Alwyn and Bert, 1889.

Brothers. These were managed by no more than five *mistris* with names like Moogorally and Aladeen, Doorga Pershad and Dhurnjeet, each in charge of forty or fifty weavers, and with one senior *mistri* in overall responsibility.

Inside the weaving shed the noise was deafening, too loud to make yourself heard; West had to make sign language to his *mistris*. Overhead ran the shafts and belts connected with the engine, which was driven by the steam boiler. On either side of each loom were picker sticks. As the lever pulled the overhead belt into place, each machine started up, the picker sticks whipping the shuttle back and forth with a loud crack. The bar or arm of wood before the reeds slammed forward and back, shunting, kicking. Cotton fluff clung to everything, everywhere there was the warm nutty smell of the cotton itself, contrasted with the pervasive reek of oily rags.

Atherton West's notes (in which he drops his 'h's and scatters Hindi words as he did in everyday speech) are a testament to his professionalism and his determination to get on. Once he considered going to work in Russia, another time joining his brother William in Bombay. But in the end it was at Cawnpore that he saw his future. He had none of John Harwood's ambition to play a part in local affairs. His wife died in childbirth in 1890 and is buried at the Cantonment cemetery. He was left with two small sons, Alwyn and Bert, of whom it came to be said that Atherton West trained 'one t'ae Mill and t'other to office'.[7] A deeply homeloving man, he had an English kitchen range sent out from Lancashire and built into his house so that he could relax with his feet up in front of it and a cup of tea in his hands and not feel so cut off from his roots. He was immensely proud of his second wife Kate, a widow with a young daughter, and often said 'I'm only a common working man but my wife is a lady born.' They had two daughters, Mary and Elizabeth.

The following extracts from West's pocketbooks give a picture of the man and his work:

August 1883 Got 5 lbs of Cotton called Nankeen Khakie. Grown at the Government Model Farm Cawnpore, to make into a sample piece for an officer of the lines, made in a 52 Reed, 16 x 16s 36 Pinion. Drill.

Take the price of raw cotton it costs about one anna per pound, to card and spin pay all wages and deliver the same to me, then one anna per pound will pay for making it into cloth, paying all wages etc. A rough calculation, but on the right lines.

Oct 83 This month engine very slow, out turn very little. Large can of Bombay Varnish, opened Aug 22 and finished Nov 6th two months and 12 days. A.W.

Nov Mina is boate crab for weaving everything appears to be terribly dried up after the monsoons. A.W.

Dec 4 83 For the last few days every kinds of yarns is doing horrible; 30s I am obliged to stop, the weavers can't work it. Engine running slow loosing [*sic*] from 2,000 to 5,000 rev.tions per day.

Dec 12th 83 Mr Maxwell took charge. All years very bad. Mr Baron we have charged with taking tips from the cotton agents and putting bad cotton through.

Dec 17 83 Mr Stott changed his mules and throstles draft; put them one tooth closer, which we think is doing much better. Mr Baron changed the weaving mixing from 2 3/4 hank roving to 3 hank; but the yarn is doing much worse. We think he made his change in the roving frame *only*, this he denied to Mr Maxwell. New friction warping machine, Singleton's patent.

Jan 21st 84 Mr Maxwell urgently wants 80,000 yards of No 2 and 3 Drill by the end of Feby. March 15th, not later.

March 17th 84 Order for Mr Maxwell's drill completed. The double warp 50″. A complaint was sent, along with a piece of Doosooty cloth made in 1882. Saying the double warp of 8 and 9 '84 was not equal to former orders. Mr Maxwell wanted an explanation he not having found out that the order was Doosooty and *not* double warp as my order. Made a check trousers piece for Stott Baron and myself, on check loom, red, and blue check 2″ apart, with blue weft 10s and a 36 wheel. The Agent put the price at -/6/ per yard. 26.4.84.

June 4 Sent sample of Khaki twill as officers cloth for approval. Today the Agent said he would stop all looms the stock was getting too large, all godowns full up. We are making a 50 yard red side Saleeta and selling in Bazaar at -/3/1 per yard and still our firm will keep same kinds of cloth in godown, before sell them at less than -/4/- per yard (made out of same yarn, counts etc; the 50 yard ones cost a little more in making with having English Turkey red yard for edges). 24/6/84.

July 4th 84 A report gives: to the Agent . . . we ought to have over the usual calculations on account of the irregularity in attendance of hands. They are never sure of coming two days together.

July 6th This week the Agent wanted a report of all working expenses in every department (Mr Baron was paying Rs 100/- more than the corresponding month of May last year. The Agent sent for Mr Ormston and wanted an explanation over the extra men he now had in his department and for his few men he is paying Rs 80/- per month more than our late man Mr Porreto. But said Mr O they are not my men, so the Agent gave orders to our baboo to discharge all the extra hands, the baboo said I dare not.) The Spinning Dept is a few decimals more per lb of yarn than it was in 1883. But taking all the Mill, through or to the Spinning Dept it is costing 6 pic per lb to work it to yarn. This is a terrible great thing and would be if the Mill was mine, expenses would have to come down.

Mr Dunbar took charge Dec 12/84 is going to make great alterations.[8] Today Dec 19 Mr Ormston having made a drawing for new chimney, for Perumsook's estimation, he also told engineer and Baron there is no system in things, everything must be weighed before going out at the Gates and we in the Bungalows are using too much fire wood, he does not want us to be without fire but be careful and only have a little at night etc.

New chimney commenced to build Monday Dec 22nd 1884 contractor Perumsook probable cost 26 to 2700 Rupees. Perdahs for Mr Maxwell and Mr Bevis. 5 feet 4″ wide, 7 feet 8″ long, 3 prs Mr Maxwell, 2 prs & 1 long one Mr Bevis, 6 prs sent to godown. Started working from 6 a.m. till 6.15 p.m. order given to work as long as possible. *March 3/86* Through the war in Egypt and the little Scare, with the Russians marching on Herat, we are having a little splendid trade, tents wanted in all directions.

3/1/85 A very large tent finished for a nawab, a beautiful thing, cost 7,000/- Rs. 10 looms working on Baron's patterns of check cloths . . . and orders coming in every day from all parts of India for them.

Feb month Raised Alishere, rate of wages from -/10/- per 1000 lbs of cloth to -12/-.

From March '85 Started my own Joinery, before could not keep up with my joiner's work and was told it kept about 6 men for my Dept but can keep comfortably going with 2 men under my care.

March 18th Paid to Mr Butterworth Rs 200 borrowed at 8%.

March 22/85 This morning the new chimney was completed, also the old boiler plated and commenced burning wood instead of coal, which we have been doing for some time back. Coal is very expensive in Cawnpore. The draft in all boilers this a.m. something splendid, the Engineer thinks we shall have no more slow running.

March 23 1885 Started all looms. The Engineer having finished the boiler (plating) also the new chimney, since then we have had some splendid running, never any cause to send a chit to say the engine is slow. Chimney 90 feet. The Agent is trying if it will do the needful before putting any more on.

Sunday April 5th Went 5 feet higher with the chimney. Since it started there has been a saving of Rs 18/- per day between working with coal and wood, and the steam can now be kept going easy with wood.

Sunday April 26th Mr Ellis late of Scotland working at the Jute Mill, was thrown out of his trap while riding along with other 3, and dyde, near Dr Rennie's Bungalow. Interred Monday morning 27th by Mr Maxwell.

May 29th Wheel flew in pieces, breaking 3 Mules, 2 halfs was carried outside and the 3rd Mr Stott is repairing being only slightly broke, it knocked a pillar down and singular to say, everybody was at work, and nobody not even scratched.

June month was very bad month. Engine terribly slow. Mr Ormston put the fault on *wet* wood as *usual* the insufficient boiler power but now he must find a new *hole* having got a new boiler working. A great contrast between this and *his heavy* report about *dirty machinery*.

June 8th Sadharic, Drawer in, got three fingers caught in the finishing machine. I reported the matter to the Agent. The difference between burning *wood* and coal reaches Rs 3000 per month.

June 24th Rains broke and as not been known to be so much rain fallen in a fortnight's time before for the last 24 years. Mr Dunbar was enquiring from a Native if West and Stott took any liquors. He gave orders to stop Maiter and Bheestie from Bungalow. Can't be satisfied without bullying something or body.

During the hot and rainy season of '84, I was fearfully troubled with *fever*, and *ague,* and started again during the hot season of '85. (April 27th) Dr Deane gave me the receipt and every time he meets me he say, I made a good cure of you, you are looking so well.

Hands employed in my Dept from August 1st Total 185.

Dr Deane's perscription [*sic*] *against cholera.* Dr Deane on visiting Mr Mellor came into our house and told us all to be *very very*

careful, what we eat etc and by all means not to take any purga-
tives, and go at once to *Charles Chemist* and get a mixture, he had
ordered Charles how to make it, spirits of Camphor, 15 drops on a
piece of sugar, and after that wash it down with a few, 20 drops of
chlorodine. Take this if we are relaxed and pain in bowels, this
being the way cholera starts, for about 2 days. *15.10.85.* Engine
same as usual. Mr Sherwood from Middleton Junction arrived on
Saturday Oct 31st.

Monday November 2nd 1885 Mr Dunbar lost his temper in discussing the term for a new agreement, so under the *present* circumstances we agreed to part, he pressing me very much to accept
bounty which lies at his *word* whether he pays it or runs his pen
through, same as he did with Parkinson and others after being on
bounty, if they got too much, Oh, I think half of this is sufficient
for bounty.

   November 2nd Mr Dunbar and me not coming to terms, I have
agreed to leave and accept the situation of Weaving Master at
Manockjee Pettit's Bombay. Later. Maxwell wanted me to stay
and have given good terms. Engine during November was run
rather better than the same month's previously, Mr Sherwood
having been rather more strict on the men than our late man was,
Mr Ormston.

   On the *Jany 12* I drew my wages and having heard outside that
he, 'Mr Dunbar', was about to take part of my bounty, that being
94/4/- he considering that sum detrimental to the Company's interests. I said nothing but took my wages came home and the
following day sent in my resignation from date till the end of
March. In reply he sent a long letter of explanation, I simply
replied that I having made up my mind to leave, I could not alter
my decision.

   Soon after the Maxwells acquired the Elgin Mills they needed more
finance to extend and improve the mill. In view of his knowledge of
cotton and his association with Warwick and Co. of Hingunghat, Collector Halsey was the obvious person to consult. He put them in touch
with a wealthy Marwari from Faruckhabad[9] called Lala Baldeo Dass.
Since the first British traders had become established at Cawnpore they
had largely depended in their various enterprises on Indian financial
support from bankers and moneylenders. Baldeo Dass agreed to make
the loan and in order to control his interests established the family firm

Lala Juggilal.

of bankers Ramnath Baijnath in Cawnpore and sent his sixth son, Juggilal, to act as cashier to the Elgin Mills. There Juggilal advanced money and paid the salaries of the staff. It was not long before Juggilal and Atherton West were good friends.

West waited four years for his opportunity and then attempted a small mill of twenty looms with shares held in the names of his own family and those of A.F. Horsman, a fellow technician at Elgin. When it failed West turned to Juggilal and entered into a contract with him, for 5 lakhs. The Victoria Mills was launched in 1886 and Atherton West moved into an imposing two-storey house nearby.

Two delightful stories are told of Juggilal. The first took place when he was a very young man at Elgin. The money he was in charge of was kept in the office safe and one day there was a theft from it. The previous evening Juggilal had got ready the cash for the payments next day, only to find Rs. 500 missing next morning. He reported the loss to West who after thinking it over said that Juggilal would have to make good the loss himself. Young Juggilal was very indignant; the safe was in the custody of the mill and he felt in no way responsible. He accordingly informed

West he had no intention of making up the loss and packed his boxes to return to Farukhabad. Rather then lose Juggilal, West capitulated and the mill paid. The friendship between West and Juggilal dated from then.

Many years later, when West was managing the Cawnpore Cotton Mills, Juggilal was acting as cotton supplier to the mill and had made a contract for some thousands of bales at a certain price. Not long after he had entered into this contract the price of raw cotton rose considerably and he was faced with a loss of at least Rs. 25-30,000. West and the directors, realising the situation and appreciating the great financial help Juggilal had given the mills from time to time, decided either to raise Juggilal's price or allow him to cancel the contract. When Juggilal was informed of this he was indignant. He thanked West and the directors for their consideration but said it meant more to him to fulfil a contract than the loss of money. 'Kindly put it in the minute book that Juggilal refused the Company's offer and will fulfil his contract.'[10]

From Juggilal's contract and relationship with the technicians at Elgin – men like West, Horsman and Duckworth – and his own exceptional instinct to know whom to trust, a mutual regard and respect built up that was to have far-reaching consequences. Juggilal's son Kamlapat was given a sound training by West and Horsman, the basis ultimately of the present-day Juggilal Kamlapat industrial empire.

A. F. Horsman

A. F. Horsman, who joined Elgin as a fitter putting up machinery, was a Yorkshireman from the little town of Gargrave. Known as Frank (his real names were Albert Francis), he was one of a long line – there had been a Francis Horsman at Gargrave for generations. This one was born in a small stone cottage not far from the old church. The front door entered directly into the parlour and the table standing in the window was covered by newspaper to keep the sunshine from fading the polished surface. Two upholstered chairs stood on either side of the big ugly grate where his mother baked vatbread and muffins.

On the death of his mother he decided to chance his luck in India. With his wife Alice, née Fielding, a Yorkshire mill girl from near Halifax whom he had married in 1882, he went first to Bombay and then Indore, to Holkar's Cotton Spinning and Weaving Mill. There he saw a notice pinned up from the Elgin Mill advertising the position of a man who had

died from plague. Frank took the job and in 1886 the family settled at
Cawnpore where in time the Horsmans would have their own mill and
his sons become millionaires.

A short thick-set figure, Horsman was extremely powerful and liked
to boast that he had been able to stretch the rubber lining round the
porthole window in the cabin on the voyage out.[11] He avoided the
limelight, however, and any publicity. He was one of the old school of
hardworking, practical men whose work came first; indeed he was interested in very little else. There was almost nothing about cotton he had
still to learn and his knowledge was rated second to none in those parts.
West quickly persuaded him to join the Victoria Mills where together
they worked for many years. Like West, Horsman saved his money,
watched and waited, planning for the time when his two sons would
be able to join him to start a mill of their own. His wife shared his
aspirations. Alice Horsman was the custodian of the family fortune, very
shrewd, very careful and very thrifty, and not ashamed to demonstrate
her knowledge of working practices and the fallibility of human nature.
It is said that Mrs Horsman would go down to the cotton market in
Couperganj on a country cart and there she would buy a quantity of the
raw cotton, known as *capasse* – the cotton that still had the seed in it. She
took this cotton to be ginned, opened up, have the seed taken out of it,
combed and cleaned, all the time keeping her eye on the operation. The
ginned cotton was packed not into sacks but *gudas,* huge bundles, and
when it was done up a bullock cart was called for and the bundles were
piled up on it. Mrs Horsman would then be driven in the bullock cart to
the mill with her precious cargo of carefully selected cotton. The reason
she sat and watched her cotton being ginned was to ensure the good
quality cotton she had selected was not switched for something inferior.
At the mill it was her habit to sit at the end of the mules and take the
weight of the yarn in her hand as it came off the line. At the end of the
day she would go to her husband and tell him the weight of yarn for that
day.

On Horsman's office desk he kept a cylindrical slide rule, fat and
yellow, like a rolling pin with one wooden handle and a tachometer in a
blue velvet box, a rev counter for testing the speed of shaft and a box
of Speaker's cashews, very strong, very pungent tablets to sweeten the
breath; also several copies of tiny books (priced at Rs. 2 each) - *Hindustani Made Easy, How to Speak Hindustani Fluently in a Fortnight.* He never
learned to speak a word of Hindustani but he would hand every Lancashire man he engaged one of these little booklets and say: 'I expect you

Mr and Mrs Horsman, with Harry, Albert, Alice and Ethel.

to speak the language, lad, if not in a fortnight, then in a month.' Made into the desk was a cupboard in which he kept hidden a bottle of whisky. He was partial to a quick swig of whisky at the end of the day, but he knew his wife would be coming in to report on the weight of the yarn and would kiss him. If she smelt whisky on his breath there would be a spot of bother. So with one eye on the door and his ears cocked for the sound of Mrs Horsman's footsteps, he would fiddle away with his key to unlock the cupboard and get the whisky out. All round the keyhole were scratch marks. Once he had had his evening whisky he sucked his Speaker's cashews.[12]

Liquor was the subject of the long-standing feud between them. Mrs Horsman was determined to prevent her husband from enjoying the demon drink. Once a month Horsman drove in a hired *tikka ghari* along the Mall to Jamsetjee's to buy their stores and requirements. Jamsetjee was a Parsee merchant who sold groceries, jewellery and liquor. At the back of the shop was a sort of cubby hole where passing customers would stop to enjoy a drink and a chat. It was quite an institution and Frank had on occasion enjoyed a glass or two of red wine there. Unfortunately Mrs Horsman discovered his secret vice and on the next occasion he set off she cut the buttons off his trousers to prevent his getting out of the *ghari*. When the lads inside the shop heard that Horsman Sahib was outside, they came to see why he had not joined them. He told them the reason and they pulled him out, tied up his trousers with string and insisted he should join them in his usual tipple. The poor man had to face his wife's wrath on his return home.[13]

Alice Horsman was a remarkable woman. When many years later she retired, a widow, to live out her last years at her home town, Elland in Yorkshire, she was visited by her elder son, Harry, a proud young millionaire who had just bought a Rolls-Royce. He drove up to her cottage – she could have lived in a manor house but insisted on a modest establishment – and offered to take his mother for a drive across the moors. She said that would be 'champion' and went to put on her bonnet and cape. Harry was fond of telling the story: 'I opened the back door. I helped Mother in and was just putting the rug round her when she looked round the car and she said, "This is a lovely motor car, Harry, how much did it cost?" "Well, I paid two thousand five hundred for it, Mother." "Eeh," she said, and she got out of the car exclaiming, "I'd rather walk." She could never be persuaded to go out in the car.'[14] Harry had the last word, however, when he and his brother Albert built and endowed the Alice Horsman and Dufferin Hospital in Cawnpore in her memory.

Mr Chadwick

Not all the mill staff fared as successfully as West and Horsman. There was the case of the unfortunate Mr Chadwick at Muir. He had been engaged as spinning master on the death of John Davis, 'who fell victim to cholera'. Before long, disturbing reports of inefficency and careless mistakes reached the ears of the board. The charges against Mr Chadwick were listed in the minutes for 26 October 1886.

The Manager in September last called upon Mr Chadwick for an estimate of the roller skins used in the Mill, the estimate being called for for the purpose of indenting in England for a further supply. He apparently gave them an incorrect answer, with the result they spent 2,500/- more than they wanted.

The second matter was the way large out-turn was broken and bad cops produced for several months up to October, showing in the opinion of the management that quality had been sacrificed to quantity. That yarn had been turned out without any regard for its fitness either for the market or for the weaving department, consequently large quantities of cops were to be rejected and ultimately sold out as waste yarn.

The third matter was the receipt of bobbins, the majority of which were too large for the spindles but the same were put on the spindles and used for a considerable period before being accidentally discovered.

The Directors view with extreme displeasure several matters connected with the spinning department, which have come to view, and cannot allow them to pass un-noticed. The spinning master of the Company in common with the other Masters draws emoluments such as are given by no other Mill in India and the Directors expect at least thorough efficiency in return. It is clear Mr Chadwick has neglected the work of his department and that the Company's interests have suffered in consequence. The Directors are disposed to deal severely with these cases, but in view of the report by the Management, that matters improved and their recommendation that these cases should be allowed to drop, the Directors decide that on this occasion Mr Chadwick be informed that the Directors have had the work of the Department under scrutiny and consider that it has been not only unsatisfactory but that gross negligence has been displayed. Should there be any cause to complain of Mr Chadwick again it will be necessary to take the severest notice of it that is in their power to do.

Three days later Mr Chadwick was sacked, as was reported in the minutes for 29 November.

The Meeting was convened by the Manager to consider his report that Mr Chadwick the Spinning Master had shown such gross insubordination and insolence in the office on Saturday the 27th that the Manager was compelled after reading to Mr Chadwick the minutes of the Meeting held on the 26th to inform him that he must consider himself dismissed from the Company's service from that afternoon. That he would be paid up to that date but that no passage money or any other payment whatever would be made to him and that the Manager's action would be placed before the Directors for confirmation. Details of Mr Chadwick's conduct were stated and the Manager's action approved and confirmed. It was then resolved that Allen Bros be written to about another Spinning Master.

The Cawnpore Volunteers

The new generation who came out to India with an awareness of the Mutiny were eager to form and train a body of men who in any emergency could be called upon to support the police or the regular military. The Cawnpore Volunteers were one of the products of that enthusiasm. Mills vied with each other to be represented by as many men as possible, mill owners rubbed shoulders with their mill hands in the clubhouse. Atherton West, John Harwood and Alfred Butterworth took the parades and manoeuvres very seriously, rising to become majors and colonels. They wore their Volunteer decorations and continued to use their ranks in civilian life. But there were, inevitably, a good many more maladroit volunteers, overweight or unfit, comic figures in 'helmets so fashioned that it was impossible to fire a rifle without turning them back to front; tunics so tight that a visiting card in the breast pocket caused a bulge; and a steed cluttered up with a bit which weighed many pounds and a saddle which only a strong man could lift'.[15]

The first parade took place at Green Park, watched by the whole town. The men were totally unfamiliar with mounted drill while the visiting Volunteer adjutant revealed himself unaware of the proper words of command. Sergeant Garnett, fresh from his dragoon regiment and newly arrived at Stewart's Harness and Saddlery Factory, was hurriedly sent for. He put them through movement after movement until every man was stiff and sore and the horses flecked with foam; but honour was restored. The occasion was voted a huge success.

The next parade marched to the Station Theatre. Mr Sterndale of the

Sereant William Garnett.

Badge with the 'Angel'.

Bank of Bengal was elected commandant, young Mr G. B. Allen adjutant. For their uniform they decided on blue with white facings. Sergeant Garnett[16] was asked to become paid instructor but for the time being this was blocked by Government.

The idea for the Volunteers' Club was accredited to John Harwood. It was very much a centre of social life, with reading and smoking rooms, a music room, a ballroom and a bar, 'and is the resort of most of the Englishmen of the place, for in Cawnpore most of the English are volunteers'.[17] Twice a week the regimental band played in the grounds. The walls of the club were hung with trophies and shields won by the local companies. Shooting matches and sports were regularly held and there was fierce competition for the cups. Millie, writing to Tina in February 1883, describes the combination of military training and social diversion that surrounded them. Only the previous week the Volunteers had given a fancy dress ball to the Station.

> This morning before 8. . . I drove to see a sham fight, the enemy were supposed to be on the other side of the river which were represented by mud gurrahs [earthenware water pots] and on this side all the troops, cavalry, Artillery, Native Infantry, British Infantry and Volunteers were lining the Banks extending for at least

Officers of the Cawnpore Volunteer Rifle Corps. Seated, middle row from left, Colonel Begbie, Sir William Cooper, ?, Alexander McRobert; front, Dr C. A. Fuller and Alfred Butterworth.

¼ of a mile and kept firing across and blowing up mines and sinking *gurrahs* floating down the river, supposed to be the enemy escaping. Officers and men were flying about on horseback giving orders in all directions and the ladies and gentlemen of the place who rode were galloping after them. . .

There were sports this afternoon to which we all went – tent pegging, cutting oranges with the sword etc were the order of the evening. A great concourse of people were there.

The Volunteer movement was eligible only to Europeans and Anglo-Indians. Now, with the threat of a possible third Afghan war, its importance as a reserve took on a political significance. Educated Indians requested permission to become Volunteers and their petition was supported by Indian editors: 'We are living in different times . . . our ancient civilisation by coming in contact with the modern civilisation of the West has been impregnated with a new vitality . . . the Indian people are being fast saturated with a new set of ideas; their feelings and aspirations are undergoing a thorough change; they are becoming a new nation altogether.'[18] But Government, nervous of a repetition of the hostility that had been whipped up by the Ilbert Bill, was cautious of a 'hazardous experiment', aware that the agitation might be an attempt to make political capital out of an awkward demand. In making allowance for Anglo-Indian prejudice and mindful perhaps of the Bihar Volunteers' near mutiny, they turned their back on the champions of Young India who clamoured for 'unflinching impartiality, equal justice to all parties, and sympathy with legitimate aspirations'.[19]

These political stirrings went largely unnoticed in Cawnpore. The Volunteer Corps consisted of the Cawnpore Light Horse, for many years commanded by Ralph Maxwell, and the Cawnpore Volunteer Rifles, whose commandant was William Cooper. Their mottoes were, respectively, 'Defence not Defiance' and 'Forewarned, Forearmed'. Before long a group from the East Indian Railway joined the troop and by the turn of the century five sections had been formed: Cooper Allen, Civil Lines; Woollen, Victoria and Muir Mills; NW Tannery, Elgin Mills and Water Works; H and S Factory; and Cantonments. The importance of the corps was epitomised by the knighthood awarded to William Cooper, the first such honour in Cawnpore – although his work at Cooper Allen might have been more deserving than his efforts with the Volunteers.

Many mock battles took place out at Jajmau where the last remaining bastion of the ruined fort stood high above the Ganges. This was where in 1765 General Carnac had received the Nawab of Oude, Sujah Dowlah, coming in defeat to place his allegiance with the East India Company. It was an ideal place for military manoeuvres. Alfred Butterworth never tired of recounting the stories of battles his Volunteer Corps had won. Once he outwitted the enemy by dressing his men as women in *burkhas* and sailing in flat-bottomed boats past the enemy defence. Another time the enemy were tricked by a funeral party in disguise complete with corpse bound for the burning *ghat*.

Intense rivalry existed between teams from as far afield as Jhansi, Saugor, Etawah and nearer home, Lucknow, for the annual shooting trophy. On one occasion at Lucknow the home team fired with Martinis while Cawnpore mustered one Lee-Enfield and the rest Lee-Metfords –

'at least three of which had passed through the rigours of the Tirah Campaign'. The team had travelled to the match by rail, being shunted into a siding at night where the men sat up late playing cards. When the match was over and everyone's health heartily drunk and responded to, the teams were treated to a day out in Lucknow, returning late to their carriage which was attached to a goods train and trundled back to Cawnpore. A story went the round that 'one of the team fired in his dancing pumps and went to the races and to dinner in the same appendages'.[20] But they had won the trophy by sixty-two points with the grand average of over ninety points per man.

Cawnpore Volunteers: Alfred Butterworth centre, Henry Thomson left.

Retirement

═══════

John Stewart, the Sad Parting

John and Millie Stewart left India for good on 27 May 1887. The month
before he had been given a farewell dinner at the Cawnpore Club.

On Tuesday the 19th instant some members of the Cawnpore Club
gave a farewell dinner to Colonel Stewart, R.A., C.I.E., and Mr
H.B. Sterndale, both of whom are leaving the station shortly. Some
thirty members sat down to dinner. Colonel Worsley, C.B., in
proposing Colonel Stewart's health, referred to the latter's long
thirty-years' residence in Cawnpore, and asked all present to join
him in wishing Colonel Stewart a prosperous journey to the home
of his forefathers in Ardvorlich. After the toast had been drunk
with three cheers for the Stewart Family, Colonel Stewart told his
hearers how he arrived at Cawnpore, 29 years ago, by the first train
that ever entered the station, and long before the Club or any of the
present large mills and factories of Cawnpore had been built or
thought of. Indeed, it may be said that Colonel Stewart has been
resident in Cawnpore long enough to have outlived his old friends
and the many others who know of all he has done for the station in
former years.

The health of the other guest of the evening, Mr Sterndale, was
proposed by Mr Moule, the Collector, and was drunk with musical honours. Mr Sterndale has been Agent of the Bank of Bengal
here for eleven years, and although his connection with Cawnpore
has not been nearly as long as Colonel Stewart's, he has always
shown a lively interest in all that concerned the welfare of the
station. As Commandant of the local Volunteers, Mr Sterndale at
one time nursed that body, by dint of labour and expense, through
a very precarious stage of its moribund existence; and the valuable

John Stewart's farewell.

experience which he had acquired when in charge of the Queen's Gardens at Delhi was very useful to the Memorial Gardens at a time when they would otherwise have been left solely to the care of the Sergeant who is their official custodian. The evening's festivity closed with a hearty rendering of 'Auld Lang Syne', and the two guests were carried in triumph round the room on chairs elevated on the shoulders of the more energetic of the company.[1]

It was the year of the Queen's Golden Jubilee and in the Honours List Stewart was awarded the CIE. This was the only recognition he received for his life's work. Their son Willie noted in his diary: 'The Guv saying goodbye to our dear old Cawnpore home. He left Calcutta on the 27th. I sent a farewell telegram. Such sad letters from them both at the idea of parting and the very shameful way Government have treated them.'

Gavin Jones, whose own heroic work had also gone unrecognised officially, understood very well what Stewart must be feeling:

We are tempted here again to touch upon the extraordinary idiosyncrasies of Government in neglecting to bestow some mark of appreciation and recognition of the great and invaluable service rendered by the founder of this great industry. The success he achieved paved the way to vast economies and untold benefit to Government and the Country. Yet he was allowed to retire in his old age after a lengthened period of strenuous and invaluable service, with nothing more than his bare pension. It is no exaggeration to say that he saved the Government and the Country hundreds of lakhs and built up works that provide the army with an indispensable equipment, whilst it has been of enormous benefit to the people and the Country. Men he had helped to develop the sister factory, that has earned for them princely fortunes, have been recipients of the coveted honour of Knighthood, whilst the maker of these and the real benefactor of the Government and Country left its shores a poor Scotch Laird, with no more than the slender pension of his rank, which under any circumstance would have been his for his long service, unrecognised and unrewarded.[2]

LEFT *Millie Stewart with her eldest son Willie and his dog – the effigy at Bhagwatdas Temple.*
RIGHT *Effigy of Colonel John Stewart.*

Stewart was convinced his health was broken and that he had only a very short time to live – he even refused to buy himself a new kilt. In fact as laird of the old family estate at Ardvorlich he and Millie continued to live happily for many years, while in Cawnpore there remains a remarkable memorial to them both. The Bhagwatdas Temple, alongside the factory, has on one facet of the dome, alongside Hindu deities, an effigy of Colonel John Stewart riding his pony. On another facet Millie is depicted with their eldest son Willie beside her and his little dog. The idea of associating Europeans with the temple dated back to the time of the Mutiny when it was said Havelock had given orders that saved the temple from being blown up in clearing the area to protect the bridge of boats. The figures of Havelock and Neill stood side by side.[3] John Stewart's intervention was less dramatic but sufficient for the owner of the temple to express his gratitude by commemorating him and his family in effigy. When, probably in the 1880s, the canal was to be dIverted, badly affecting the bathing *ghat* at the temple, it was Stewart who put in a word with the authorities and had the canal's route altered. The effigies remain today, a happy reminder of the Burra Mochee, and at one time, according to an article in *The Sphere* in 1921, were kept smartly painted.

Gavin Jones's Row with Ledgard

The year that Stewart made his sad farewells was also to be the year in which Gavin Jones announced his intention to retire. In 1887 Jones was a man of fifty, still vigorous and loath to hand over all he had created. His resentment and suspicions of Henry Ledgard, a younger colleague ambitious to run the Muir Mills, were crystallised in a bitter row.

Ten years earlier William Cooper had proposed that steps be taken to secure the service of a competent young man to be trained for the management of the company. In response to an advertisement for a management secretary two applications from London were received. Henry Ledgard of 36 Gutter Lane, Cheapside, EC, was deemed to be the more suitable candidate and the managing director was authorised to write to him for testimonials. If these proved satisfactory, he was to be engaged on a salary of Rs. 250 per month and his passage paid to India.[4]

For Gavin Jones, who disliked any challenge to his authority, Henry Ledgard was a little too enterprising and energetic.[5] Very soon there was a clash of personalities, small misunderstandings arose. Over the purchase of materials for an extension of the mill Jones took exception to the tone of Ledgard's letter. Ledgard gave the apology demanded and said he had intended no offence.

To a boardroom where the guarding of trade secrets had become almost an obsession, it was a shock to hear in 1885 that some of the company's mill masters held shares in rival cotton mills. The directors decided 'that it should be a special condition of the Company's service that no employees shall be permitted to hold shares in any other company carrying on business similar to ours. Infringements of this rule will necessitate the removal of the offender from the Company's service.' In this mood, they were not pleased with rumours that Ledgard was planning to put up a rival mill, and the extent of their anxiety is revealed in a series of letters between Jones and Ledgard at the time his contract came up for renewal. Ledgard had been away from Cawnpore on six months' home leave and on his return from England his contract had only four months to run. To some extent the situation mirrored that which had taken place between Hugh Maxwell and Gavin Jones. As soon as Ledgard was back in Cawnpore Jones tackled him.

November 7th 1885

My dear Ledgard,

As I hear you have arrived, I write these few lines with reference to a point which I think should be cleared up before you resume your duties at the Mill. The Directors and I have come to the knowledge that whilst you were in England on leave, you identified yourself with a scheme to start a mill, in opposition, and that you have come out prepared to put the matter in train, should you fail to obtain from the Directors better terms for service when your present agreement expires. I shall be glad if you will let me know, per bearer, or at least before you resume work at the Mill, whether such information as above cited is correct or not.

I hope you had a pleasant voyage out.

Yours sincerely,
GAVIN S. JONES, Managing Director

November 8th 1885

My dear Mr Jones,

I received your letter last evening, and in reply beg to inform you that the information you and the Directors have learned is totally incorrect. Further I may mention for your satisfaction and

My father saw a girl of 17 with size 1 feet standing on the piano . . . . he fell in love with her.

Henry Ledgard as a young man and his bride. Reproduced from Some Memories of a Great-Grandmother *by Lady E. M. Smith (privately published).*

that of the Directors, that I have not opened negotiations of any firm or any persons whatever, either verbally or by correspondence on the subject of starting a mill, of any kind. I have not come out to put such a scheme in work, whether I obtain better terms of service or not from the Muir Mills, at the expiration of my present agreement.

Yours sincerely,

H. LEDGARD

A few months later, encouraged by reports from Walter Butler, Ledgard took up the cudgels once more in a letter to the directors.

February 22nd 1886

Dear Sirs,

As requested by you in meeting held on Friday last, I beg to submit the subject matter and individual expressions as nearly as I can remember of the conversation I had with Mr Butler,[6] at the Oriental Club [in London], about October 1st last year, respecting my agreement with the company.

I mentioned to Mr Butler that before leaving India in April last, I had spoken to Messrs Cooper and Beer[7] about the renewal of my agreement, which expires in March. But that they had both considered my application somewhat premature as there was then nearly a year unexpired. I informed them that my object in bringing the matter up, so long beforehand, rose from the fact that when I should return from leave, there would only be about four months unexpired, and should it not be renewed, it might be inconvenient both to the Company and myself to make other arrangements, at the last moment. I explained to Mr Butler the further remuneration I should ask from the Company in a renewal agreement. He remarked that he hoped I would come to terms with the Directors, and said 'Supposing they don't give you what you want? What action will you take?' I told him I was not in a position to say what I would do, but I hoped for a renewal of my agreement and both Mr Cooper and Mr Beer thought favourably of my application, though they were not in a position to record their views so long beforehand, but that if it came to the worst I could start another Mill as some friends in England had offered me money and I should therefore have no difficulty in that respect. This remark was made, not from having any idea of starting a Mill, as I did not for one moment contemplate doing so, and would here mention most emphatically that I did not tell Mr Butler that if the Directors did not give me the terms I wanted that I should start another Mill, nor that I should return to India with all preparations made for doing so. I further told Mr Butler that I had when visiting some Mills and machine makers noticed several improvements which I shall suggest when I reach Cawnpore, and also that I had expended besides, other sums, about £20, getting a new set of blocks for an improved tent catalogue, but that before I offered them to the Muir Mills I should like to be satisfied that there was a probability of my remaining with the Company. I then represented to Mr Butler that I was of the opinion that better terms than those offered were to be obtained from the machine makers for the supply of the extension machinery. Considering the very depressed state of the industry in England and the extreme efforts being used by makers to obtain orders I am pleased to see that the letters he wrote to one of the Directors has led to representations being made by the Company which has resulted in very substantial extra discounts being obtained.

Yours faithfully,

H. LEDGARD, Management Secretary

Memorandum by Managing Director referring to Mr Ledgard's statement dated 22nd Feb. 1886

1 The Directors will observe that in the first instance Mr Ledgard gave an unqualified denial of all complicity in maturing plans for starting an opposition mill, or to coerce the Directors to give him better terms on expiry of his agreement on the 19th or 20th, by threatening to leave and start a new mill if his demands were not satisfied. Mr Ledgard now submits a modified statement which, as the Managing Director reads it, contradicts his first denial.

2 The Directors are aware that rumours were rife in Cawnpore during Mr Ledgard's absence on leave in England, that he intended demanding better terms for re-engagement, failing which he intended to start a new mill, which Mr Butler's warning to the Directors confirmed.

3 The Managing Director forwarded Mr Ledgard's denial of November 8th last to Mr Butler for confirmation. In his reply dated 18 December Mr Butler says 'I was glad of a chance of showing the Directors Ledgard's real character, and now they can't trust him. If I were a Director I would sack Ledgard now. Of

course he is lying. I can assure you that letter of his astonished me, no man could have spoken more plainly than he did, he told me that everything was arranged, money and all, and I believe he did try and hope to succeed. However, we all know the gentleman now.'

The Directors will note that Mr Butler's statement is diametrically at variance with Mr Ledgard's first unqualified denial, and subsequently modified statement. If Mr Ledgard's statement is carefully read the Directors will find internal evidence in it to prove beyond doubt that Mr Ledgard was engaged in a scheme to start an opposition Mill. Mr Ledgard states that he said to Mr Butler that 'if it comes to the worst he would start another Mill as some friends in England had offered me money and I should have no difficulty in this respect'. Now it is clear that for Mr Ledgard's friends to offer him money he must have introduced the subject and what is more, gone deeply into the matter, to enlist their confidence and support. It is not likely otherwise that people in England would have offered money for investments abroad without being satisfied of its safety and the possibility of the investment proving a success. The statement bears out Mr Butler's reports and more positive proof could hardly be forthcoming of Mr Ledgard's intentions. Further, Mr Ledgard proceeds in the coolest manner possible, to inform the Directors that he had made an entirely new set of blocks for an improved tent catalogue, but that before he offered this to the Muir Mills 'I should like to be satisfied of the possibility of my remaining with the Company'. To the Managing Director's mind this adds confirmation to the evidence already deduced that Mr Ledgard was engaged in a scheme to start a rival mill for he had not the shadow of reason to doubt his engagement would be renewed. He himself tells us that 'both Cooper and Beer thought favourably of my application'. Wherefore then did he with-hold the blocks? The conclusion is that Mr Ledgard made good use of his knowledge of the Company's business and the Company's Tent Catalogue to improve upon it, and his retaining the possession of the material which properly should be the property of the Company is contrary to the terms of his agreement and a direct violation of his contract.

Mr Ledgard's presumption reaches its climax in the concluding paragraph of his statement, wherein he insinuated that the Company obtained better terms than those offered by the machine makers through his instrumentality and expresses himself pleased at the results of his representation. Mr Ledgard assumes the mantle of mentor and guide of the Directors and Management and but for his forethought and considerate help the important matter would have been neglected. The Directors are aware that Mr Ledgard for obvious reasons makes a practice of deprecating the Managing Director's services in the eyes of the shareholders and efforts have not been wanting on his part to prejudice him in those of the Directors, singularly Mr Butler's letter from which the Managing Director has quoted above, contains evidence of this fact. Mr Butler says to him, 'His, Mr Ledgard's, interest was to find fault with your management and he no doubt made the most of the commission business and it was apparent from some remarks he made that I gave you a hint about writing to Hicks and Platts.' It is needless to remind the Directors that long prior to any communication through Mr Ledgard's instigation the Managing Director had urged the London Agents of the Company to take advantage of the existing depression and secure better terms for our machinery etc. The Agents invariably answered that the makers were prepared to discuss the question when they were in a position to place the orders. With these facts before the Board there can be but two interpretations to Mr Ledgard's proceeding and conduct: that by his insidious manoeuvres Mr Ledgard was seeking either to work the Directors to make better terms, or he was preparing to start a new Mill in opposition while still in the service of the Company. Mr Ledgard has tried this plan before, and succeeded, owing to his intimacy with the late Mr Petman, then one of the Directors, who brought the fact that Mr Ledgard had threatened to leave the Company unless his terms were accorded to, to bear on the Board, using all his influence in Mr Ledgard's favour, with the result of Mr Ledgard obtaining concessions which the exigencies of the Company at the time forced them to grant, and which no company would have given an assistant manager except he were in sole charge. In this instance, he is again using the same means but has employed methods which in the mind of the Managing Director renders his belng retained in the Company's service a real danger to the interests of the shareholders. He has seriously compromised himself and as the Managing Director reads it, brought himself under the penal clause of his agreement and is evidently aiming at being able in future to dictate his own terms, whatever they might be, and the Managing Director foresees that the Directors will be forced to grant these demands else they will have to face the certainty of his joining an opposition with the entire knowledge of the Company's business and constituency.

The question before the Board is this in reality: is Mr Ledgard a fit person to succeed the Managing Director in full control of the Mills? The Directors have often answered this in the negative and with the facts now before them they cannot possibly re-engage him. The Managing Director cannot conscientiously recommend it, for his presence on the Mills would be a constant source of uncertainty and danger. The Managing Director therefore advises that Mr Ledgard be invited to put his own plan into operation, now. It would do no harm to the Company now, but might compromise its position hereafter. The matter is undoubtedly a serious and unpleasant one, but the Managing Director would be failing in his duty were he to act otherwise than place the grave question thus prominently before the Board for their consideration and decision.

The matter was earnestly discussed by the board. At one time they were prepared to offer to raise Ledgard's salary to Rs. 700 per month with 1% commission on profits and in the event of his succeeding to the full control of the mill Rs. 800 and 2% commission. But ultimately, when they came to accept Ledgard had compromised himself, they agreed he had gone too far to be re-engaged. Ledgard wrote saying the terms offered to him were not sufficiently liberal and the board let the agreement terminate at its expiry date. However, they could not resist breathing fire and brimstone. They let him know they believed they had grounds to convict him of breach of contract and that he was liable to a penalty of Rs. 15,000 but 'they have no desire to be vindictive, in fact have evinced a disposition to condone it'. They warned him that if within three years he attempted to put his scheme into operation the directors would adopt such measures as they might think proper to enforce the penalty.

Samuel Johnson, a less controversial personality, with a background in the railways, was appointed the next managing director at Muir. Henry Ledgard joined Cooper Allen. He never attempted to set up another mill but devoted his energies to running the boot factory where he had a distinguished career, earning a knighthood and becoming a respected figure in Cawnpore society.

Gavin Jones announced that he intended to retire in April 1888. Right up to the last minute he was busy with plans for an extension to the mill, with 600 more weaving looms. The directors agreed a bonus and pension but they were still wary of Jones and inserted a clause that these were subject to his not returning to India or being connected directly or indirectly with the cotton industry. Like Stewart, Jones left Cawnpore unrecognised and unrewarded by government. But in his own mind and in the estimation of his contemporaries Gavin Sibbald Jones was indeed the 'father of the cotton industry in Cawnpore' – the phrase came to be used over and over again. 'There was hardly a factory that was not, directly or indirectly, an off-spring of his brain.' He had succeeded in his vision of teaching the Indian labourers how to utilise their work on Western lines and he had turned a town of sad memories into a valuable asset to government. Ten years later he was back in Cawnpore with a further valuable scheme.

Alexander McRobert: The New Man

McRobert Arrives

George Allen took pride in claiming that he had been personally responsible for Rudyard Kipling going to the *Pioneer* at Allahabad and for a Scotsman called Alexander McRobert going out to Cawnpore as a chemist.[1] Travelling from Bombay to Cawnpore in 1885 with his young bride Georgina, McRobert* broke his journey to stay with the Allens in their splendid bungalow at Allahabad.

One might suppose, because of his long association with the Cawnpore Woollen Mills, that McRobert was engaged to go out as manager. In fact, as his close friends knew, he was engaged as a chemist for the Muir Mills. There was then a confusion: someone in Cawnpore took on a chemist while McRobert was travelling out and by the time he arrived the post had been filled. The somewhat sheepish directors inquired if he knew anything about wool; to which he replied 'No, but I can learn.' So in a matter of weeks of arriving in Cawnpore McRobert found himself in charge of the Cawnpore Woollen Mills and his talents moving in an entirely new direction.[2] The Cawnpore Woollen Mills were the base on which he built his empire, lifting Cawnpore to undreamed of heights and bringing Gavin Jones's work to fruition. Gavin Jones was the Father of Cawnpore, McRobert was to become its uncrowned king.

Unlike the majority of men who came to India at this time, Alexander McRobert was already thirty when he arrived. He was a man who knew his own mind. Stories abound about his extraordinary attention to detail, his abundant energy, his fierce determination that money was not to be wasted; while his 'abrupt, alert manner' was cause for considerable merriment behind his back.[3]

---

*Throughout his life McRobert kept the spelling of his name to McRobert, but after his death Lady MacRobert preferred to use the other version of MacRobert.

A slight, stooping figure, with very little presence, plain features and a short clipped moustache, he wore his hair cropped close to his head. When he was thinking he had a habit of smoothing the top of his head with the palm of his hand. He spoke quietly, but on occasions, very sharply, with a touch of Scottish accent. If you asked him a question he would sometimes pretend not to have heard, to give him time to consider his reply.[4]

He paid little attention to his appearance, buying clothes to last. His topee, he was proud to say, was thirty-seven years old at a time when they could be bought for less than two rupees. People noticed his clothes were often patched and mended, it was said, by the Lalimli tailor. His day started at 7 a.m. when he went over to the mill. The bearer would come over later to tell him breakfast was ready and he would go back to the bungalow and eat it in fifteen minutes. The porridge was set out in typical Scots fashion, one bowl of thick porridge and another of milk, and he would take a spoonful first from one and then the other. He never left the Mill before six or seven in the evening when the *Pioneer* arrived.[5]

There was a joke that went the rounds: 'What is the definition of rigid economy? Answer: A dead Aberdonian.' McRobert was certainly a super economist. Every rupee had to be wisely spent and produce value for money and it was a serious crime for anything to be wasted in the mill. He went right through all departments of the factory every morning and if there was the slightest indication of waste or carelessness the department overseer was severely lectured and warned.

Even in small matters he was just as insistent. To post a business letter to Calcutta on Fridays was strictly taboo. The letter was unlikely to be delivered until the Monday morning, so the instructions were to wait until Saturday as there might be another letter or receipt to go to the same party and then all could go in one envelope, thus saving one envelope and its separate postage! This was not a mean streak but an intense application to matters of business. Walking through the office he once pounced on a young assistant. 'Did I see you tear up an envelope?' Then followed a harangue on the cost of stationery and the wickedness of waste. After that, whenever he passed that particular young man he would inquire, 'How many envelopes have you torn up today?'

He never drew his pay but reached on the cashier to give him whatever cash he needed. Every penny had to be accounted for. 'Money was his god, he never spent ½d when ¼d would do.' Staff were asked to save any sovereigns in their pay packet which he bought to use as tips on the voyage home. When the accounts were sent out to shareholders he would write notes on them rather than spend extra postage.[6] Once towards the

The staff of the Cawnpore Woollen Mills.[7]

end of his life his doctor found him working busily at his desk and asked him what he was doing. 'I am fascinated by figures. In 1884 during the Afghan campaigns we charged the wrong amount for the blankets we supplied. They should have been 2 pice more per blanket and that would have brought us an extra 2 lakhs.'[8]

One young assistant, dissatisfied with his pay, asked for an interview. He went in to the office of the Burra Sahib, who indicated a chair and told him to sit down. McRobert counted on his fingers all the advantages the young man enjoyed – wages, medical, free house, passage home, etc. 'You're a millionaire,' he concluded. The young man bolted.

The doctor McRobert engaged for the mill fared better. 'Now,' he said, 'you are going to get a big salary. You'll live very cheap.' 'I'm not interested in the salary,' the doctor rejoined, 'I'm not interested in living cheap. What I'm interested in is how much I'll save per year.' 'Now,' McRobert said, 'that's the very best question you could have asked. On that question alone you get the job.'

There was only one occasion when McRobert was said to have been at a loss. The overseer of the spinning department was a heavily built Yorkshireman named Sanderson who had rather a gruff voice and stood

6 foot 4 inches tall. On his round of the mill that day, as McRobert entered the spinning department, the power was switched on to start the spinning mules. It was noted that one of the Indian workers gave his mule a push to set it going. The Burra Sahib was aghast at this procedure and immediately began to lecture the overseer, pointing out that the machine would be pushed out of alignment, would damage the yarn and so on and so on. Sanderson said nothing and after several minutes McRobert asked, 'Haven't you anything to say for yourself?' Then Sanderson gruffly replied, 'Mr McRobert, sir, when you get as old as those mules somebody will have to give you a push to start your morning.' McRobert walked out without a word. But the story was repeated with glee.[9]

McRobert's Background

McRobert came from an unexceptional background. He was born in a 'but and ben',[10] a two-roomed cottage, one of a family of eight children; two sons and six daughters of a humble, hard-working, respectable family. The baptism entry reads: 'John McRobert, labourer, Ann Street, Aberdeen, and his spouse, Helen Collie, had a son born 21st May 1854, named Alexander, baptised 28th May by the Rev Charles Skene, Witnesses Peter Wright and J. Kerrie in the parish of Old Machar.' Two weeks after he was born the family moved to Newhills, four miles out of Aberdeen, where he lived for the first eighteen years of his life. His father was employed as a dairyman.

Newhills was dominated by the Stoneywood Paper Works, owned by A. Pirie and Son (later Wiggins Teape and Co. Ltd). Stoneywood had a name for the heavy quality paper they produced for ledgers as well as for fine writing paper and high-grade printing paper. The works provided many local jobs; a horn sounding out across the fields would call the workers to the two shifts. The firm set up the village day school and it was there under the tutelage of Mr W. A. Williamson that Sandy McRobert's imagination was fired to learn all he could about the wider world.[11] Boys at the school went barefoot in the summer to save shoe leather – on 1 June their boots were oiled and placed on a shelf until 1 September. The Piries used to ride to hounds and play polo and it was during the summer months that the children on their way to school dreaded meeting the hounds out exercising. The hounds would sniff and lick their bare feet and the children took to running and sitting in a ditch, hiding their feet until the hounds had passed.[12]

At the age of eleven Sandy McRobert and his schoolfriend William Cormack left school to work at Stoneywood Paper Works as scavengers. Their hours were 6-9 a.m., 10-2 p.m., 4-5.30 p.m., stopping on Saturday at 2 p.m. – a 56-hour week. Both boys were quick and mentally sharp and were duly moved up into the office. Determined to better themselves and rise above the drudgery of office clerks, they both attended evening classes in Aberdeen, taking a horse bus to cover the four miles and returning home after 9.30 in good spirits, discussing what they had studied and learnt.[13]

When Sandy McRobert was eighteen, his father, like many other Scotsmen at the time of the 'clearings' took his wife and family to Canada in an attempt to better themselves. The McRobert family were among 400 passengers to make the voyage in 1873, leaving Sandy McRobert on his own. The company moved him to their Union Works in Aberdeen as a bookkeeper and he took lodgings nearby.[14] With no family ties or demands on his time he devoted every spare minute he had to his studies. There was a time when he studied seventeen subjects simultaneously and passed in them all. He was already acquiring a reputation for prodigious industry; word went round that a companion looking him up at a late hour found him with a wet towel round his head absorbing the dictionary. He read widely to improve his command of written English, attended debating societies and was a regular churchgoer. In his room he surrounded himself with maxims:

> *Note 5* Many fail, not from want of ability or opportunity, but from want of *Resolution*. [Underlined. McRobert had no intention of failing.]
> *Note 6* Keep the demon indolence at bay!
> *Note 8* Don't act like a weathercock. Fix on some desirable end and keep your eyes on that end till attained. Otherwise you will fritter away time, and are non-effective.

The notes are an indication of the standards he lived by.[15]

In 1880 McRobert made a trip to Canada to visit his parents. It is not clear how he was able to be away from his job for two months. He and another man from Stoneywood had recently applied for the job of cashier at Culter's Paper Mills, Aberdeen. McRobert failed to get it. Perhaps this spurred him on to consider his future carefully. It is believed he went to Canada to assess his chances there, but what he saw of the life decided him against emigrating to join the McRobert family.

He sailed from Glasgow on the *Manitoban*. He was not a good sailor

Every day Notes

Note 1

To acquire a good literary Style to copy out re peatedly long passages from a model Author.

Note 2.

" Self-reverence, self-knowledge, self control,

These three alone lead life to sovereign power."

Tennyson.

Alexander McRobert as a young man.   From his 'Everyday Notes', 1878.

and resented vomiting up the dinner he had paid to eat. The notes in his small pocket diary reveal his insatiable interest in everything going on, especially any natural phenomenon with a sense of wonder, like the phosphorescent gleam on the ocean at night and the halo of prismatic colours when the sun pierced the fog. Meals were meticulously noted, he had a keen sense of time. When the sea became calmer he became bored with the monotony of shipboard life. St John's, Newfoundland, he dismissed as 'shabbily built, mostly of wood with only the churches and the cathedral handsome buildings'. They sailed up the St Lawrence to Quebec. He commented that the people were very civil but many of them could only speak French. After a rail journey of forty-eight hours he reached New Brunswick and Hopeville, the farm his father had worked hard to establish, clearing the land, cutting down the forest (occasionally bothered by bears), putting up his own house and barns and surviving the Canadian winters. Every member of the family was employed, the youngest children put to watch the cattle, listening to the bells round the cows' necks as they grazed in the forest.

To while away the tedious journey McRobert made notes of anything unusual he saw.

Fences around fields. No nails used. Fellow passengers jabbering French. Engines scream. Oxen two wheeled cart with hay. No fences. Snow tunnels. Pigs go in the fields. Device to prevent cattle, pigs and horses leaping fences. Water for engine raised by windmills along the track. Clay ovens, log huts. Annoyance from retailer of apples, cigars, nuts etc. Annoyance from smoking carriage. Jolted dreadfully. Cup of tea 25 pence. 'All aboard'.

Old John Mcrobert, accompanied by two of his children, Helen and John, brought a waggon to the rail depot. 'On the way to Hopeville there was a dreadful jolting and our luggage suffered much, portions being pitched out occasionally. Found everything at home better than I had expected.' However, he did not stay long: a week later he made his goodbyes and left to visit Boston. This he found much more to his liking, the streets 'quite as stirring as London'. He was fortunate to be there at the time of the 250th anniversary celebration of the city's founding and witness the two processions. The place was so crowded with visitors that he had to share a room with three other men - it cost him one dollar. He was impressed with the telephone lines, street bars, restaurant checks and the magnificent public library. He was also pleased to have his boots blacked for 10 cents. But he confided to his diary that he found in many ways 'that the Yankees are not to be trusted to keep firm. Their motto seems to be "First Chance".'

Back in Aberdeen McRobert augmented his meagre salary of 30/- per week by taking a part-time job as lecturer in physics and chemistry in two of the city colleges. Every holiday was devoted to furthering his studies. An ex-pupil recalled his great enthusiasm for knowledge of all kinds. 'On his own account he started an Evening Class in Woodside School, when such were not very common. The class consisted of men and women of different ages and I was one of four of one family and we thoroughly enjoyed it.' His subject then was animal physiology.

In 1881 he made a visit to London, travelling by train and staying in Kensington to attend a course of study at the Science Institute.

Left Aberdeen at 4.30 p.m. Weather showery with bright gleams of uncertain sunshine.

Disagreeable headache. I am in a compartment with another gentleman. The carriage is very comfortable. We have not spoken to each other yet. Princes Street 10. Got out and stretched my legs for 15 minutes in the station. After arranging with the guard to keep the compartment inviolate resumed occupation at 10.18. and we pulled the blinds closed from prying eyes until 10.20 when the train set off. Having now a seat each we prepared to spend a conformable night at full length.

Dunbar at 11.10 tickets checked.

Berwick 11.50

A splendid night and the comet in full view.[16]

Newcastle 1.30 and the comet still in view but dimmer by reason of the increased daylight. Newcastle has a fine station. etc.

King's Cross at 8.15. Hired hansom to Walton Street and was presently obstructed by a Sunday School Treat procession. Got to Walton St at 8.45 and was in attendance at South Kensington Museum at 9.45 a.m.

29 June. Slept soundly till 6.30 got up at 7.30 dressed and had breakfast before 9.

30th June visit to the House of Commons. We found the house discussing the Land Bill in Committee. We had not been many minutes in when I was delighted to see Mr Gladstone get on his legs. I had never heard him speak before. His enunciation was very distinct and his manner earnest. Mr Marr (of Union Works) left at 6.30 but I stayed on until 8. Mr Gladstone spoke several times as well as did Sir Stafford Northcote, Mr Forster, Lords John Manners, R. Churchill etc.[17]

Service at St Paul's.

Visit to Bromley.

Work at Museum finished at 5 p.m.

Suffocating heat 94 in the shade.

I witnessed the most furious thunderstorm I can remember.

Working all day at compound pendulum apparatus.

Apparel in Hyde Park.

Dark coat. Dark or light vest. Light or blue trousers.

Boots always light and not infrequently patent leather. Tie and collar may be anything, but the headgear must be chimney pot. Very few exceptions to this. The hat may be white and the gloves shades of yellow brown slate or even black. Good tweed suits seem permissible in which case other particulars remain unaltered . . .

Inspired by his working holiday in London he returned to Aberdeen with renewed zeal. It was then he met his future wife, Georgina Porter, who was also working at the Union Works until she left to become a manageress in a nearby laundry. When the offer was made of a

£400-a-year job as chemist at the Muir Mills, McRobert proposed and on 31 December 1883 he and Georgina were quietly married. Sandy is given as 'clerk (envelopes)'. Shortly afterwards McRobert sailed for India and Georgina joined him the following year.

McRobert at Work

Many people have wondered what took McRobert to Cawnpore. The answer is found in the obituary written by Dawson of Allen Bros. It was in response to Allens' advertisement for a chemist for the Muir Mills, probably in the *Mercantile Guardian,* that George Allen selected Alexander McRobert. On his arrival at Cawnpore he was met at the railway station by William Cooper.[18] The directors and partners of the Muir Mills, Cooper Allen and the Cawnpore Woollen Mills were so closely inter-linked – Cooper Allen being the managing agents of the Cawnpore Woollen Mills – that the mix-up over the job of chemist was not difficult to resolve and McRobert was appointed managing agent's representative. The Cawnpore Woollen Mills, for all their boast of being Army Cloth Manufacturing Co Ltd, were still a modest enterprise, struggling to avoid bankruptcy. *Thacker's Bengal Directory* lists an accountant, a mill manager (my grandfather, Alfred Butterworth, promoted from weaving master), a dyer and finisher and an engineer.

In our family there is a story that McRobert found the situation so desperate that he appealed to all members of staff to lend him every penny they could spare of their savings to help him get the mill going. This they did, which speaks well for his persuasive powers, and in time the money was returned in full, though with no interest to reward their risk.

Luck was on McRobert's side. Affairs on the North West Frontier were very unsettled. The fear of Russia invading Afghanistan and thereby threatening India caused the government to increase the army by 11,000 British and 12,000 Indian troops.[19] In the bitter cold of the mountains they all needed blankets and warm uniforms and McRobert seized the opportunity. The mill worked night and day; McRobert himself put in eighteen hours a day. The New Egerton Woollen Mills in Dhariwal, Punjab, were acquired to eliminate competition and increase production, and additional staff were engaged. At the height of the struggle the foreman struck for more money and was promptly fired. McRobert's expertise as a chemist assisted him in the practical running of the mill. From that time the Woollen Mills never looked back.[20]

McRobert was a born salesman with a natural talent for knowing what would attract the public. It was he who recognised the potential in the rare specimen of red-flowering tamarind growing within the mill compound and made Lalimli the trade mark. He set in hand a vigorous advertising campaign. 'Do You Know the Secret of Good Health? It lies solely in the clothing you wear . . . pure wool clothing is the one and only safe clothing for India . . . but it must be Pure Wool and you can rely upon getting this if you buy LALIMLI.' Within a year he had achieved incredible results. Some notes he made while on a visit to Rawalpindi in 1885 give an insight into the first contracts. Lord Dufferin had been recently appointed Viceroy of India and a meeting had been arranged with the Amir of Afghanistan, Abdur Raman, at a large standing camp. At the very time of that meeting news of the Russian attack on Penjdeh was received.[21]

At 8 a.m. Colonel Parker sent in his card and he drove me to the Govt Godown with my package of samples. Saw the sets of followers' clothing sent on from Quetta and Madras, the others hadn't reached Pindi; settled that the followers' blanket, for all India, would in future be the present followers' blanket, with a white stripe down either side – i.e. longitudinally. Colonel Parker wanted the stripe at the end, but I persuaded him to have it at the sides. The distinguishing feature is designed to prevent the natives exchanging the blanket in the bazaar for an inferior. Booked an order for 10,000 certain, additional 10,000 to 15,000 promised.

Warm coats. Madras is quilted khaki drill outside cotton wadding, cotton inside khaki buttons. Quetta sample is too dear. Khaki drill, blue serge soldiers' flannel, three layers. After discussing the matter I managed to make him believe that the cotton wadding was ridiculous and the Quetta coat too dear and that the drill exterior and followers' blanketing inside was the very thing. Agreed.

Pyjamas, madras wide condemned. Quetta narrow. Approved. (Khaki substituted for blue) (We can't dye blue).

Bazaar price of blanket, two rupees four annas. Afternoon – went to Viceroy's camp with Rust[22] who managed to photo Duke and Duchess of Connaught, both went off riding immediately after with a small party. There was a bright scene at the camp which is laid out in walks, fountains etc. Duke of Connaught, Sir Frederick Roberts, Sir James Lyle, Lord Downe, Lord William Beresford etc. had tents. On our return we found the band and pipes of the Seaforth Highlanders discoursing music in front of the club opposite my hotel run by Rawbury. Snake charmers. The scene is like a bit of Hyde Park. There were a great many pedestrians out and a great number of carriages and traps, fetching costumes everywhere. No wonder the dressmakers and milliners thrive. And as this was going on the Amir drove past with his retinue to the Viceroy's camp. The Afghans are ferocious-looking fellows.

This was a man who eighteen months earlier had been a mere envelope clerk earning 30/- a week. That he was now working and mixing in such society is almost unbelievable. It might have turned the head of a lesser man but McRobert never wavered from his modest manner. The workforce knew they had an outstanding manager, a hard-working taskmaster who drove them as hard as he drove himself, but straightforward and plain-spoken. Cawnpore society recognised the energy and ability of this new man and acccpted him as a leader among the captains of industry. His 'Lalimli Maxims' are illuminating:

LALIMLI MAXIMS *Revised 10-12-14*

1 Never try to put a customer in the wrong. Rather endeavour to make the path of retreat easy for him.

2 Averments made by customers must be accepted even when they are incredible.

3 A customer is always right, and must be satisfied every time – especially if a lady.

4 Never try to score off a customer. Disarm him with unwavering, dignified civility.

5 Never guess at what an obscure statement means. Ask the author to make his meaning clear.

6 When sentences threaten to become involved cut them up into shorter ones.

7 Aim at a terse style, and direct mode of expression. Above all, avoid diffuseness and vain repetition.

8 Be sparing in the use of adjectives, and more frugal still in the display of superlatives. Reserve emphatle language for critical occasions.

9 Never say anything likely to irritate merely for the pleasure of saying it. No matter what the provocation. Aim at politeness always.

FIVE REASONS WHY

the celebrated " LALIMLI " pure wool fabrics are unsurpassed.

No. 1. Because they are pure wool throughout, and pure wool clothing is the ideal of health.

No. 2. Because they are honestly made, without sophistication of any kind.

No. 3. Because they last longer than the shoddy imitations usually imported.

No. 4. Because they are cheaper than imported woollens—we are manufacturers, not merchants.

No. 5. Because they are specially designed to meet the exigencies of climate.

Write for our booklet **D**—the information it contains will be useful to you, **and it costs nothing.**

Address:

Cawnpore Woollen Mills Co., Ld.,

CAWNPORE.

 Published at The Edinburgh Press, 300, Bowbazar Street, Calcutta, by the Board of Management of the St. Andrew's Colonial Homes, Kalimpong, Bengal

10 Spelling is a delicate subject, and no opening should be given for criticizing it. When in doubt consult Chambers. It is quite safe.

11 Never submit a draft you would be ashamed to sign as a letter.

McRobert and Georgina

In McRobert's success at the Cawnpore Woollen Mills he was tremendously supported by the character and personality of his wife Georgina. There was a quality about her of sincerity, an almost childlike trust in goodness, a genuine wish to smooth the lives of those about her and to help in any way that was possible. Georgina Porter was born in Aberdeen in 1851, a youngest daughter though she never knew her father. He was a steamboat stoker, often away from home, and at the time of the Gold Rush jumped ship to join the scramble to find gold on the Fraser River in British Columbia and was never heard of again. Perhaps it was the hardship her mother endured, trying to bring up her daughters and son in the little house in Gaelic Lane, that moulded Georgina's deep faith and trust in the goodness of God's will. She struggled to live by these standards all her life but it left her with a sort of sadness.

In October 1885 she sailed from Liverpool with a lady companion to join her husband in India. McRobert came to Bombay to meet her and they posed at Bourne and Shepherd's studios to have their photograph taken together. They were never to be parted for any length of time again. Georgina, two years older than McRobert, was a big, heavily built woman with a plumpness that for all her efforts she was unable to control. Her complexion was delicate, a foil for her dark hair and blue eyes. But it was the sweetness of her expression that conveyed the harmony she brought to those around her.

The entries in her diary written at the time of her arrival at Cawnpore convey her dismay at the first impression of their house, a bungalow within the mill compound, still in the process of being completed. Raw, red brick, it had none of the graciousness of the old company-style house she had stayed at in Allahabad with the Allens. She lived in it for twenty years but was never able to bring herself to think of it as 'home'. It was called Sheiling House.

The entry on 2 December hints at the cruel disappointment when she found she was not pregnant. Georgina and Alexander McRobert had no children. This was to be a recurring disappointment and great sadness between them. When my mother was born, the youngest of seven

The McRoberts on Georgina's arrival in Bombay.

ABOVE *Interior of Sheiling House.*   BELOW *Tea in the garden: the McRoberts with Mr Gilmour (right).*

Butterworth children, Georgina pleaded to be allowed to adopt her but that was not to be. My mother's second name, Georgina, was in deference to Georgina McRobert.

23 Nov 1885 Reached Allahabad about 7 a.m. met Mr Allen at the station and was invited to his bungalow to breakfast. Drove to the Fort and through Alfred Park. Then went and had breakfast. Mrs Allen is a good-looking young woman. She is the second wife. Miss Allen was there also Dolly. A lovely house they have and were most kind to us. Left Allahabad at 11.30 and reached C'pore at 5 p.m. Alec's trap and horse was at the station and he took me to the Memorial Gardens on the way home, reached the bungalow at 6 o'clock and found Mr Gilmour awaiting us. He is a fine young fellow and I think I shall like him much. Had tea and then we were left alone for the evening. My first impression of the house was anything but pleasant,[23] as trades people were working on it and the rooms had a bare cold look. Still I felt glad at having a shelter and being with my darling husband again, neath a roof I could call home. Had dinner and then turned out the contents of 3 boxes I had with me after whleh we retired to rest.

24 Nov Alec went to the mills after 9 o'clock and I looked out soiled clothes for the dhobi and after tea had a drive until dinner. It was dark and I could not see the sights but the trees seemed lovely. Wrote letters.

Thursday 26 Nov Alec took me to call for Mrs Butterworth found them very nice people. Saw over the mill in the afternoon most interesting to see the looms at work and the wool being spun.

Friday 27 Nov Mrs Butterworth took me a drive in the morning. Enjoyed it very much.

1 Dec An uneventful day walked in the garden. I don't seem to do any work at all now, neither do I read much. Am awfully bitten by mosquitoes.

2 Dec Wrote letters to mother and to Mr Damton. Saw silver etc cleaned. Hope to get things arranged bye and bye. Am much deprcssed this morning in consequence of a keen disappointment. Had bright hopes which God has seen best to dispel for the present at least. May he keep me from being fretful over it. He knows what is best and although it is very hard still I do wish and pray that He may make my will subservient to His and order all my steps for the best. May God hear my prayers in His own time and way.

7th Dec Received calls from Mr Gavin Jones Manager of Muir Mills, Dr Condon Civil Surgeon and Mr H. Allen. Alec shot a fine large pariah dog bull species this evening poor beast. I saw it in its death struggles and felt sorry.

8th Dec Dined with the Allens and found them very nice the eldest son George was there also Mr Bock. Mr Gilmour had tea with us this afternoon. I like him.

9th Dec Mr Gilmour dined with us this evening he brought me a pretty set of purdahs from Lahore. We had a fine drive before dinner.

10th Dec Mrs Maxwell called for me, promised to help sing at the choral festival Christmas Eve. Went to their practising in the chapel this evening. Enjoyed it very well.

11th Dec Mrs Gavin Jones called for me today. She is a gentle-woman. Got a kind invitation to call on her.

12th Dec Went to sale at Noronhas. Alec bought a chair and some pretty vases. Mr Gilmour dined with us in the evening.

24th Dec Got a lovely white cashmere from Alec for my Christmas gift. Played chess with Mr Gilmour who again had dinner with us. Had a parting 'peg' song etc. He goes to Agra tomorrow.

For Georgina the new life called for considerable adjustment – the lack of privacy in an Indian household, the host of silently-moving servants who might appear at any moment, requiring supervision and direction, not to mention the labourers whitewashing and painting the rooms. The language, too, was a problem to her. She apparently never made any serious attempt to speak or understand it; even such simple words as 'chota hazri' she continued to refer to as 'little breakfast'. It was for Alec that she tried her best to make the house comfortable and relaxing after his arduous day in the mill. Personally she found the servants very difficult to handle and the climate extremely trying. Sometimes she could not resist longing for her old home and her family in Scotland.

McRobert provided her with a carriage and horse and also encouraged her to learn to ride, sometimes running behind her horse in an attempt to give her confidence. He was not a demonstrative man but years later when Georgina's favourite horse died, he had a hoof mounted in silver. Perhaps those early, more carefree days together in Cawnpore meant much to him.

Among the wives of the mill staff and the young men in the mill there were many ways in which Georgina was able to give motherly advice,

The Lalimli Club.

particularly in times of sickness. On one occasion when a visitor to Cawnpore on business from America fell ill with smallpox, she took him in and nursed him back to health; all done so quietly that only those in her close circle knew about it.

Every New Year's Eve, the anniversary of their wedding day, the McRoberts gave a big dinner and dance at the Lalimli Club. Both the Elgin Mills and Cooper Allen had their staff club and it is likely McRobert set up the Lalimli Club soon after taking over as manager.[24] With his sure touch he chose a site near the mill where once stood the bungalow in which Lord Roberts had been born, thus creating a further link between the Lalimli Mills and the new Commander in Chief.

Recognising the important role McRobert was to play in Cawnpore, one of the senior ladies, Mrs Kirkman, sometimes called 'Mardi', or 'Kirkie', or 'Little Nell', wife of a partner of Ford and Macdonald construction engineers, took Georgina under her wing and groomed her in how to dress and entertain and about what would be required of her as a social hostess. But Georgina's true interest lay in caring for others in quiet unostentatious ways.

Extracts from Georgina's Letters

1st Sept 1888

My dear Mother,

    The rain ceased yesterday and today is fine. If you saw our

house, rain marks everywhere. All our dykes [walls] are down. The poor natives' mud houses are a sad sight to see, roofs off and walls down.

19 Sept 1888

My dear Mother,

They are so busy at the Mill fitting out an Expedition for the Black Mountains that they are at work night and day meantime . . . this placc is not home but we have been well and very happy here so we must be content to bear its ills too.

20 Nov 1888

My dear Mother,

We have charming weather now, it would delight you to enjoy our cool nights and mornings, especially after the hot days we have passed through, the change is most grateful. Our new vegetables are coming up well, we have turnips, carrots, beetroot, tomatocs, radish, celery, lettuce, cress and a few other well known seeds, also a fine crop of peas. Salads are greatly used here and are I have no doubt good for the blood.

I have just bought from the butcher a leg and loin of mutton for 12 annas that is 3/4 of a rupee. The joint weighed 8lbs. I often wish we could share the good meat to be got here for a little money with you all at home. Beef and mutton in the cold weather is very good. Some butchers feed their animals well, but many do not give them good grain consequently the meat is tough and poor. I often wish for the plain home fare, for the cooks are often careless and one is in a measure entirely in their hands. I try to get the men to be cleanly in their habits and to use the towels, dusters etc. I give them daily only for the purposes I name, still you will find them occasionally using one duster for all and it does annoy one so. Then they lie so much, it is really impossible to find out the truth about anything, and the poor cat is invariably taxed with all the breakages.

This is a great bathing day at Bithoor 12 Miles from here . . . we went out riding this morning and met thousands of people all wending their way to the festival, men, women and pretty little children all so quiet and nice, no drinking and bad language going on like what you would see and hear from a lot of holiday people at home. I often think these poor things set a good example to us in many ways.

Camp Naubasta
27th Feb 1889

My dear Mother,

I am still a prisoner with my foot which is swollen and painful if moved in any way. I am taking good care of it and only moving to give out food etc. This I must do, or else we would have everything stolen, if I gave the keys to the servants. I have something like 60 fowls of one sort or another just now, yet I only get a few eggs occasionally, the sweeper steals them as soon as they are laid, then sells them to the cook, who in turn sells them to me, as if he had brought them for cooking purposes from the Bazaar. Do what you will you will always in cases like these be outwitted by the mild Hindoo who will steal and lie about it, in the most barefaced manner. One must just grin and bear it and make the best of them, for they have some good qualities after all.

It is cold in C'pore but it is *colder* in camp, and that is why we come out to the jungle for a change. It is the most delightful life you can imagine, you have no idea how we shake and shiver on getting up in the morning and jump into our warmest clothing in double quick time and long for the sun to shine to thaw us a little. It fits one for the warm weather which will be soon upon us.

I have got a dress and hat from home for going home with, the dress will have to be laid aside until October, as it is woollen and the thinnest material only can be worn during the summer and part of the rains. With our united love,

'GEORGIE' MCROBERT

Cawnpore
30 April 1889

My dear Mother,

We are in the middle of the hot season. Today I have 23 chickens hatched. About 2 o'clock I ran over to the hen house to see them the air felt stifling and the sun was burning hot and shining just overhead. In the house with the doors all shut up and the punkahs going it is most comfortable but the poor Sahibs, Alec for instance, that must go thro' the Mills and pass out and in, in the sun it is trying. We try and look after ourselves all we can and we keep well despite a high temperature. We get up about 5 a.m. and have a sleep in the middle of the day. I have other 7 hens sitting on eggs, many of the chicks will die, the heat kills them off. I suppose they can be kept alive but it takes one some time to find out how to treat sick cats, dogs, horses and fowls in this country. I spend lots of time seeing the horses groomed, animals fed etc. it is always something to do and the beasts get to love one so.

Cawnpore
9 June 1889

My dear Mother,

We are having very trying weather just now, so hot and stifling today the sun is obscured and a yellow glare seems over all the air. It is weather in which one can hardly do anything. A great many deaths have occurred within the past ten days, deaths from heat sunstroke and apoplexy etc not in C'pore especially, but all over India. The past two nights it has been impossible to sleep more than 2 or 3 hours and this even with our beds out in the open and a punkah over our heads. It is just now in the bungalow 98° and this is early morning. We hope for the rains soon, they are due on the 15th but will likely be a little later. We are both well however I am glad to say. Alec lies down for a rest in the hottest part of the day so we do our best to keep going with ice drinks etc. The thing is to 'keep cool', a maxim my husband used to do his best to induce my good mother to adopt in the old days.

The chickens are dying off daily. I think 20 or so must have died this past week – poor mites they feel the heat so much.

I left this spacc for Alec to add a line, he is so lazy he positively declines to write. I after a little persuasion got him to make a cross.

X

3 August 1889

My dear Mother,

We have had some rain but not nearly enough, the dry hot days are very trying. I had a bad attack of bile and sickness, when Alec was away. I sent for the doctor and I was then his 24th patient – suffering from the same complaint. He says it is just the hot damp weather, the liver won't act and all the body gets full of bile etc. I am all right again - Alec is suffering something the same. We had a long ride this morning, and both feel better of it, although we came back dripping with sweat, and tired enough to go to bed again. This is the time when one thinks of home and its climate. It will soon pass however, and in October the fine cold days begin again when we all pick up and put some colour in our faded cheeks . . .

LEFT *Albert Priestley, the sculptor, with his wife.* RIGHT *Mrs Priestley's tombstone.*

We have so much to be thankful for, for we always have such good health. Two friends we used to know well, a Mrs Eastaway and a Mrs Priestley, have both died and their two children within the past 10 weeks or so. It is sad to go into their houses and see these two poor fellows sitting sad and all alone, wife and child gone.[25]

The Upper India Chamber of Commeree

By 1889 the scene in Cawnpore had shifted. Gavin Jones and John Stewart had left; Gavin Jones's place at Muir had been taken by Sammy Johnson, the man who more than any other was to bring out the worst in McRobert; Henry Ledgard had moved to Cooper Allen. The Elgin Mills was coasting along under the management of Ralph Maxwell, James Dunbar and A.S.B. Chapman, John Harwood was extending his base at the Cawnpore Cotton Mills, and Atherton West had been joined by A.F. Horsman at the Victoria Mills. At Cooper Allen the dominant force was William Cooper.

The list of commercial companies in *Thacker's Bengal Directory* in-cludes many new names and cites the expansion of existing ones. In the previous September a group of men had met together at the Assembly

Rooms for a preliminary meeting to discuss the formation of a chamber of commerce to represent their interests - Calcutta, Bombay, Karachi and Madras already had their chambers. The needs up-country were different from those of a seaport and the virtue of a chamber was seen not as a narrow base to protect Cawnpore interests solely but to protect the general commercial interests of the North Westem Provinces and the Punjab. Twenty-two firms representing a capital employing over a crore of rupees opted to become subscribers.

In the past Govemment had never taken the trouble to consult the various manufacturers, bankers and merchants in Upper India about proposed legislation that would affect their interests, but now businesses in Upper India would have a say. The chambers of commerce proved also to be an avenue to official recognition and public honours. With William Cooper in the chair and W. B. Wishart taking notes, thirteen men sat round the table discussing the proposals and queries raised, and drafted the rules and procedures. Subscriptions of firms, associations and individuals in Cawnpore were to be Rs. 200 per annum with out-station members paying Rs. 100. The business was to be managed by a committee of not less than five and not more than seven, the president, vice-president and committee were to be elected each year by ballot and only one representative of a company or bank was to be allowed at any one time on the committee. Only one Indian name appears. At the end of the meeting office holders for the year were balloted for. George Allen did not attend the meeting but significantly the chamber reports were printed at the Pioneer Press, Allahabad.

MINUTES of the Proceedings of the first General Meeting of the Members of THE UPPER INDIA CHAMBER OF COMMERCE, *held at the Masonic Hall, Cawnpore, on Thursday, the 17th January, 1889, at 5 P. M.*

THE following gentlemen were present, *viz.—*

W. E. COOPER, ESQ. ... *Cooper, Allen & Co.*	W. G. BEVIS, ESQ.... *Elgin Mills Co.*
A. S. B. CHAPMAN, ESQ., *Elgin Mills Co.*	M. SARGON, ESQ. ... *Breul & Co.*
G. B. ALLEN, ESQ. ... *Cooper, Allen & Co.*	J. HARWOOD, ESQ. ... *Cawnpore Cotton Mills*
W. HAUPT, ESQ. ... *Ernsthausen & Co.*	*Co., Ld.*
E. C. BALL, ESQ. ... *W. Vale King & Co.*	S. M. JOHNSON, ESQ., *Muir Mills Co., Ld.*
A. McROBERT, ESQ. ... *Cawnpore Woollen Mills Co., Ld.*	W. B. WISHART, ESQ., *Begg, Sutherland & Co.*
A. WEST, ESQ. ... *Victoria Mills Co.,Ld.*	W. SHINN, ESQ. ... *Agent, Alliance Bank of Simla, Ld.*

By Proxy, viz.—

G. W. ALLEN, ESQ. ... *Pioneer Press.*	J. WALKER, ESQ. ... *Alliance Bank of Simla, Ld.*
H. C. REINHOLD, ESQ.... *Agra.*	
S. WHYMPER, ESQ. ... *Naini-Tal Brewery Co., Ld.*	JOGGEE LALL ... *Babu Lal, Behari Lal.*
	E. A. WEST, ESQ.... *West's Patent Press Co. Ld.*
A. ROGERS, ESQ. ... *Saharanpur.*	
A. E. SHORTER, ESQ. ... *N.-W. P. Soap Co., Ld.*	J. TATE, ESQ. ... *Allahabad Bank, Ld.*

The different firms who had expressed their willingness to become Members of the Chamber were then ballotted for, with the result that the following firms were unanimously elected, *viz.*—

The Allahabad Bank, " Ld.,"   Cawnpore.

The Alliance Bank of Simla, " Ld.," „

Messrs. Babu Lal Behary Lal,   „

Messrs. Begg, Sutherland & Co.,   „

Messrs. Breul & Co., Cawnpore.

The Cawnpore Flour Mills.

The Cawnpore Cotton Mills Co., " Ld."

Messrs. Cooper, Allen & Co., Cawnpore.

The Elgin Mills Company,   „

Messrs. Ernsthausen & Co.,   „

The Muir Mills Co., " Ld.,"   „

The Naini-Tal Brewery Co., " Ld."

The N.-W. P. Jute Mills Co.,   " Ld.," Cawnpore.

The N.-W. P. Soap Co., " Ld.," Meerut.

The " *Pioneer* " Press, Allahabad.

Arthur Rogers, Esq., Saharanpur.

H. C. Reinhold, Esq., Agra.

Messrs. W. Vale King & Co., Cawnpore.

The Victoria Mills Co., " Ld.,"   „

West's Patent Press Co., " Ld.," Etawah.

The Cawnpore Woollen Mills Co., " Ld."

Office-holders for the year were then ballotted for, and the following gentlemen were elected :—

W. E. Cooper, Esq.	...	...	...	*President.*
A. S. B. Chapman, Esq.	...	...	...	*Vice-President.*
J. Harwood, Esq.	...	...	...	*Member of Committee.*
A. McRobert, Esq.	...	...	...	„ „
J. Tate, Esq.	...	...	...	„ „
E. C. Ball, Esq.	...	...	...	„ „
W. B. Wishart, Esq.	...	...	...	„ „

On the Chairman representing that funds might be required during the first year, in excess of those which are likely to be immediately available, the following firms agreed to deposit in advance, rateably, from time to time as necessary, sums not to exceed in the aggregate the three years' subscriptions of each, to the Chamber, *viz.*—

Messrs. Vale King & Co., Cawnpore.

„   Cooper, Allen & Co.,   „

The Elgin Mills Co.,   „

The Cawnpore Cotton Mills Co., " Ld."

The Muir Mills Co., " Ld.," Cawnpore.

The Cawnpore Woollen Mills Co., " Ld."

The proceedings closed with a vote of thanks to the Provisional Committee, coupled with the name of their Secretary Mr. W. B. Wishart, on behalf of the new Chamber for the work done.

W. E. COOPER,

Chairman.

During the year the Chamber dealt with a variety of matters. In June, for example, Government put forward a proposal that all women employees in factories should be allowed four days' holiday per month. The members made their comments. Cooper Allen and Cawnpore Woollen Mills were of the opinion that there was no difficulty in meeting this proposal. Cawnpore Cotton Mills, Cawnpore Flour Mills and the Jute Mills suggested Sundays should be the natural and fixed holiday for the women. Atherton West went along with that provided no two or three holidays occurred simultaneously and added 'In our opinion the matter should be left to the employer.' The Elgin Mills expressed their views more fully in a note:

> In my opinion any hard-and-fast rules regarding holidays (under the peculiar conditions of labour in this country) are to be deprecated. A native does not appreciate the regular Sunday holidays, but prefers to get a holiday when he wants one, which is usually when some caste or religious function demands his presence. If he cannot be allowed these, he stops away without leave, and supposing that this happens twice a month, he gets 6 holidays instead of 4.
>
> I think, therefore, that all possible latitude should be allowed to employers to fix, from time to time, the four statutory monthly holidays to be observed in their particular factory. It may so happen that in one and the same month there may be four Mahomedan and four Hindu festivals. In such a case (an exceptional one certainly), I can see no reason why the Hindus should not have their holidays on their own festival days, and the Mahomedans on theirs, and then all the Sundays in that month would be working days.
>
> Regarding women, I see no reason why they should not work under the same rules as men, – if handicapped in any way by vexatious conditions they will cease to be employed in cotton mills.[26]

Mr Amold Beer of Beer Bros, dealers in country produce and proprietors of Cawnpore Jute Mills, brought up in December the problem of deterioration of cotton grown in Cawnpore district due to the fraudulent wetting of cotton. It was recognised by all the members that this abuse must be stopped but how to go about it? Some argued it was a matter for a test case in the courts, others that if it was brought to the notice of the Collector he would take action. The committee decided to ask Government to take steps to put a stop to this form of cheating.

Perhaps the most interesting item for discussion was a matter arising from contracts for police uniforms. Government had in 1881, and from time to time, passed resolutions stating that it was their policy to 'give utmost encouragement to every effort to substitute for articles now obtained from Europe, articles of *bona fide* local manufacture or of indigenous origin'. Provided quality and price were right, the Indian-made goods of local materials should be purchased rather than imported goods. However, a notification in the NWP *Police Gazette* of 7 January 1889 advised that the Inspector-General had appointed Lala Kanhiya Lal as contractor for the supply of uniforms.

> The Inspector-General has been pleased to appoint Lala Kanhiya Lal to be the contractor for the supply of uniform for municipal, cantonment and town chowkidars for three years, at the following rates:–
>
> One drill suit consisting of knickerbockers, turban, drill coat and pattles at Rs. 3-8; one serge coat at Rs. 4-8. All District Superintendents of Police are directed to obtain the clothing for municipal, cantonment and town chowkidars from Lala Kanhiya Lal, paying him at the above rates.
>
> As the amount allowed for the clothing of each chowkidar is Rs. 6 per annum only, the serge coat cannot of course be supplied to the whole of the men in a single year. District Superintendents of Police must obtain these coats gradually from saving after the drill clothing has been paid for; a margin must also be left for the supply of a few great-coats each year.
>
> Accoutrements must not be obtained from Lala Kanhiya Lal, but from Cooper, Allen and Company.[27]

Not surprisingly the Elgin Mills, Cooper Allen and Muir Mills were up in arms. (The uniform being made by Kanhiya Lal was from imported American drill.) They had no quarrel with the contract going to Kanhiya Lal but they protested vigorously at 'the anomaly of Government, on the one hand professing encouragement to local enterprise, and yet sanctioning a large contract (extending over 3 years) for clothes for the use of their own Police, to be made up of a material manufactured in a foreign country, and this too in a city where cloth of equally good quality is made of indigenous material and by the natives themselves'. They pressed that the contractor's contract should be altered to ensure he used locally manufactured cloth.

Within weeks of the first general meeting of the Chamber of Commerce another important meeting took place at the Cawnpore Woollen

Mills. McRobert had steered the affairs of the company so well that he was able to insist that there was no longer any need for Cooper Allen to act as managing agents. Tactfully, William Cooper was asked to continue as a director of the company but effective power was now in McRobert's hands.[28]

A dividend of 10 per cent, free of income tax, was announced for the year on the paid up capital and a bonus of Rs. 1,600 granted to the European staff. McRobert had a bonus platform in the office. There he would sit, in raised-up splendour, with a huge pile of coins on the table in front of him. Everyone was divided into either first, second or third class and under each category each got a bonus of one or two or three months' pay. It was quite a ritual.[29]

Later in 1889 the Cawnpore Woollen Mills negotiated to buy out from the Elgin Mills the woollen business they had set up, along with the machinery and goodwill. Shortly before Hugh Maxwell died he had decided to extend the Elgin Mills to include the manufacture of woollen serge (an extension officially listed from 1883 under Mr J. Mellor, weaving master). Ralph Maxwell, however, decided to concentrate on cotton and McRobert was glad to acquire the additional machinery and at the same time nobble a competitor so close at hand. The transaction was carried out in a cordial manner. Ralph Maxwell, accompanied by A. S. B. Chapman and Mr Bevis, attended the meeting and Ralph Maxwell was appointed a director. The meeting put on record their high appreciation of the services of Mr A. McRobert, 'to whose exertion the highly satisfactory state of the Company is mainly due'.[30]

McRobert and the Douneside Connection

McRobert was a very private person. No letters have survived between him and Georgina but the acrimonious correspondence between him and his parents over the acquisition of Douneside – now the seat of the MacRobert Trusts – gives a glimpse of another side of his personality.

For some time Alec and Georgina had received pessimistic reports from the McRobert parents on the problems they faced as pioneer farmers in New Brunswick, Canada. Perhaps Georgina longed for a home in Scotland and in three years Alec had saved enough money to be able to invest in a property. He therefore decided to buy a house and farm near Aberdeen and persuade his parents to return to Scotland to live in it. The house would be a base for him and Georgina when they went to Scotland on leave and the farm would provide his parents with a home and a livelihood. The property too would be a sound investment.

McRobert got in touch as early as September 1887 with a land agent, Mr Paul, who found them a suitable property, valued at £2,500.

> In the Land Valuator's report it was described as follows:- 'The small Estate of Douneside – held as a single farm containing 115 acres arable and 7 acres of fir wood and hardwood belts. It is favourably situated within one mile of the village of Tarland, with a sheltered and sunny aspect to the South and South-East and commands a pretty view of the valley of Cromar and the Deeside hills beyond.'
>
> The Dwelling House is rather a superior double Cottage with back Kitchen wing, with out-houses well finished, and surrounded by a moderate sized and well stocked garden. This Possession would have considerable attractions to a retired person fond of farming and country life. There is a good Dwelling House, and the place is near the village for supplies and where Church, School, Market, Doctor and Bank are available.[31]

The parents, Helen and John McRobert, sold their farm and stock at Hopeville and, accompanied by their younger son, John, sailed for Scotland. The experiment was not a happy one. McRobert wrote demanding to know every detail, convinced he was doing a good turn to his parents. He was unable to appreciate that a father might not like to be dictated to or patronised by his son, particularly a father who had beaten his son every night when a boy for no good reason except that he *must* have misbehaved.[32]

Old Mr McRobert, slow and suspicious, found it difficult to write letters or to understand them and resented having to take orders and feel indebted to his successful son. Georgina wrote lovingly to her in-laws, calling them 'Mother' and 'Father', meanwhile trying to smooth things over with her husband. McRobert came close to selling Douneside and 'shaking the dust thereof from my feet for all time'. However, in 1890 Georgina and Alec went back on their first home leave to make Douneside their home in every sense of the word.

A letter detailing how his mother was to supervise the laying of the new linoleum and carpeting at Douneside makes daunting reading. Not surprisingly the awkwardness between father and son continued, McRobert bitterly complaining it had overshadowed their home leave.

McRobert's parents.

The hurtful letters continued for another two years, by which time McRobert refused to mention the subject any further.

Cawnpore 8 July 1888

My dear Mother,
    Your letters of 29th May are to hand and I am risking one more line to Hopeville on the chance that you may be detained rather longer than you expected. We are very glad you are to get clear so soon, and that you think you will be able to get good prices for both farms and the stock thereon. We believe you will like Douneside. The parish minister Mr Skinner is a great friend of Mr Pauls and he has been taking some interest in the place. I expect the manse is quite near. Mr Paul has engaged a grieve and two or three

servants who are putting in the neeps etc. The grieve is a son of John Spark the ground officer at Muchells. When you arrive and take possession of Douneside I should like my Father to see that all accounts have been paid and get the stamped receipts for them. When writing last I sent you copies of all the bills I knew of. Two horses have been bought and are now in use but I think four horses will be required as the station is so far away. The implements that have been purchased are of the latest improved designs and I quite agree with you in thinking everything should be of the very best. The full cost is not very much greater than for lower class articles. I think you win be able to make a good thing of the farm and I trust you will find life there much pleasanter than at Hopeville. We are sorry to hear you are not yet as well in health as could be wished. Ina has written to Mrs Porter [her mother] and she will expect you. . . You should come over *intermediate* and not steerage. The difference in cost is small, and the difference in comfort great. You will know yourselves best whether to ship from Halifax or Boston to Liverpool or Glasgow. . . You will be very sorry to leave all your old friends in the colony I am sure ...

26 Aug 1888

My dear Father,

We should like to know all about your Arrangements before leaving Hopeville, your journey to Boston, what you thought of it and your voyage to Liverpool and journey to Douneside. I hope you have found everything satisfactory. Give us all the news please as we are longing to know *fully* how things are. Mill continues to increase trade 10% for ½ year dividend.[33]

Cawnpore 1st Sept 1888

My dear Father,

We were very glad to get your and Mother's letters by last mail. We were pleased to know you had arrived safely at Douneside and all well.

I will take up in detail the points of your letter, but before doing so I want to tell you that the Indian Mail leaves Aberdeen every *Thursday* afternoon. If therefore you post your letters on Wednesday morning they will be in ample time. Your letter is dated 4th August a Saturday, but it bears the Aboyne postmark of 6th – Monday. Had you posted it at Tarland on Wednesday 8th it would have reached us just as soon and you might have had time to give us more news. Georgina suggests that you might manage for some time at least to make a practice of writing to us every Sunday. There must be a great deal to tell and explain, and I am sure none of you will grudge the trouble. You must always keep in view that out here in India we have an extraordinary longing for our English letters. There is no day looked forward to with as much interest as that on which the home letters arrive. If you saw the crowds who go to the Post Office and wait the sorting of the letters you would I am sure resolve to keep us free from the disappointment of 'no letters'.

Everybody is the same. There is nothing about you or Douneside too trivial to be valued by us and the fullest particulars about *everything* will be most welcome.

All you have said about the farm we have carefully noted. I gather that you are somewhat disappointed with the soil etc but that the house is quite as good as you expected. Can you get the house photographed and yourselves also? Please arrange to do so and send us copies.

You do not seem to realise that you are the *master* at the farm, and that what you say is all. Nothing that Mr Paul has done or arranged binds you, and I did not expect that all dispositions made by him would be perfect. I depend upon you to look after my interests as well as your own. You are altogether mistaken in supposing that I wish Mr Paul to manage or act as factor for the estate, and I am surprised you should have imagined such an idea could enter into my head. Now that you are in possession, and in charge, Mr Paul has no authority to do a *single* thing, and he understands that quite well. I wish you to act upon this distinct understanding. . .

Now as regards Douneside, we do not see why the men should make a bothy of your kitchen. Have them sent at once to the croft house spoken of by Mr Walker. Are these not habitable? If they are not they must be repaired. Get the house *comfortably* furnished at your own convenience, tidy up the garden and make the whole establishment a model. Do not let the question of rent annoy you. That can be arranged on a sound basis after you have tried the place and its capabilities. For the present I expect I must be content if you can make enough or spare enough to pay the mortgage interest, and public burdens. . .

Anything you buy you will of course pay for and keep an

account of, but nothing else. Let me know how you stand for money and if you will require an advance to enable you to carry on the farm satisfactorily. If so when and about how much? I wish to know as accurately as possible what demands there are likely to be upon me so that I may have time to make arrangements.

C'pore 14 Novr 1888

My dear Mother,

I am sorry the weather has been so unsuitable for harvest but you write about it so much like you used to do about the Hopeville harvest that I am tempted to believe affairs have not been quite so bad as you paint them. Perhaps you have got into the habit of exaggerating a little – of course without meaning to do anything of the kind . . .

I do not quite understand what my father means when he says he has been trying to get Mr Paul's affairs settled ever since I gave him authority to do so. You must both of you have understood that you represent me in every way from the first moment you set foot in Douneside or I must have expressed myself very badly. If anything has been done that should not have been done since you arrived I shall hold Father entirely responsible. . .

I understand you to say that the whole of the soil is very light. Is this so? Are the fences in good order? and are the fields well laid out? Are they well sheltered? What are the belts of trees like? Thriving? Is there a mill dam? If so is it suitable? If the thrashing mill is useless it must be put right, or replaced. All the implements and appliances should be of the highest class. . . Am glad you are pleased with the horses, but I suppose you will want another pair. Get as many cows and other stock as you may consider necessary or convenient. You cannot make bricks without straw. . .

We want to know all about *your voyage* and full particulars of your landing in Liverpool, what you did in Liverpool, how you got to the train there and how you all stood the railway journey from Liverpool to Aberdeen. . . I want to know exactly about all your movements. What kind of a dog have you got? . . .

Let me have a full report about the state of all the buildings and if these are worth putting into proper order. Describe them fully please. I am sorry no vegetables had been put in for you and I hope you will have enough potatoes and a good crop of fine quality. I fear you will miss your early rose. Are there trout in the brook?

What are the sizes of the fields? Are they well drained? . . . Are the servants good? You will want a servant girl also. How did you leave all the Boston people? You don't say anything about them. Did you hear from Agnes and Mary [his sisters].

Yours affectionately,
A. MCROBERT

39, Dee Street
Aberdeen
6 June 1890

My dear Mother,

You will know that we were in good time for the train yesterday morning. We got to town allright and found the weather splendid. Today it is raining and very cold. Next week Anderson the carrier will bring out for Douneside:

Linoleum for lobbies

Carpet for stair

Staples and pins for stair carpet

Linoleum for Dining Room

Linoleum for Sitting Room

Carpet Square for Drawing Room

Rug for Drawing Room and tacks for fixing the linoleum to the floor

Linoleum for Stair Landing

The Linoleum for both Sitting Room and Drawing Room will be 12 feet wide and the exact length of the two rooms. The pattern for the Dining Room is in squares, that for the Sitting Room small circles. The linoleum for the Hall and Lobbies will be in four pieces the exact lengths required. In the case of both the Sitting Room and the Dining Room there will be 3 to 4 inches of the floor left uncovered at each side. In fixing the Linoleum use as few tacks as possible if you decide to lay it before we return as it stretches slightly. You should at any rate get the male members of the household to cover the Sitting Room Floor and the Lobbies, if they are frightened the Dining Room may await our return. Anything cut out from the fireplace may come in for the window or may even be enough to make up the width if cut into strips. In this case you had better place the Linoleum close to the wall at one side leaving 9 inches uncovered at the other. *Cut the Linoleum with a strong sharp knife*.

Cawnpore
6 Novr 1890

My dear Mother,

I have received from my Father - a letter dated 13th October – the like of which I suppose was never written by a human being. It is the production of a madman or worse, and if it is the style he wishes to adopt towards me it will be far better to stop all communications. As he is evidently incapable of understanding the plainest and simplest business matter, I think it would be well if, before putting pen to paper again, he would take the opinion – of a despised lawyer for example – or any other person of common sense, as to the meaning of the documents he chooses to be so offensive about. He says the lease does not guard against his being put out without warning. It is a lease for 19 years! He says Messrs Collie have sent him a Factory or Commission binding him to perform all sorts of things, and refers to previous employers not requiring security for his honesty; and he has certainly made himself a first rate laughing stock for Messrs Collle's office. The document he is so frightened about, as if it were the plague, is simply a power of attorney giving him authority to act for me. I am very glad he has not seen his way to accept it, as a man who could write such a letter as that of 13th October is not to be trusted with such powers. It may be worth while to state however that it does not *bind him* to do anything at all. It only binds me.

I have had quite enough worry already about Douneside, and I will not submit to any more. My Father has chosen deliberately and wilfully to misrepresent and misunderstand my action. This is a matter about which it should have been unnecessary for me to offer any explanations. God knows I have done my best to make you both comfortable and I have spent very nearly one thousand pounds (in addition to the purchase price of Douneside) with that end in view, and it is hard to receive in return the blackest ingratitude. I now know what to expect and therefore cannot be disappointed again. I have quite enough work here, and if I am subjected to any more vexation about Douneside, I will instruct Messrs Collie to sell the place at what it will bring, and endeavour to forget that I was ever such a fool as to expect that what was intended for unselfish kindness would be appreciated, or that I would get credit for wishing to do good not evil. . .

Cawnpore, 19 Novr 1891

My Dear Father,

I am sorry to hear of your poor crops the past season. I remember however you did not expect much as the shift was poor. I don't think I ever heard the result of your operation in 1890.

I duly received your letter written in July and perhaps I ought to apologize for neglecting it so long. The fact is I have been unwilling to continue what it appears can only be a painful discussion. Until you can frankly get rid of the idea that seems to possess you that I am a swindler whose every action has to be carefully watched and counteracted, then there is little chance of our having anything pleasant to say to each other. You appear to have some grudge against me, the cause of which you will not explain.

I went home last year expecting nothing but what would inspire me with feelings of the liveliest satisfaction, and it was only when I got home that I began to find you had a grievance that embittered my whole visit. I then began to understand that there was some hidden meaning in certain mysterious remarks in previous letters from you, but what is at the bottom of it all I don't know.

I never thought it would have neen necessary to explain that I bought Douneside solely that it might be a home to my mother and you in your old age. It is of no possible use to me – in addition to the £1,800 still due I have paid £600 and charges for the property, and some £700 for plenishings and furnishings. All this I am ready to sacrifice if that would rid me of your reproaches. You are apparently not satisfied with your position. I have told you to leave the place if you are so minded and I will arrange for the sale of the property. You can go at any time you like, and on any term you like, but I am determined to be rid of the constant worry the possession of the place has given me. I have no desire to see it again. You demanded a lease, with what object I could not fathom. I instructed a firm of respectable lawyers to prepare a lease with the usual provisions, and you declined to have it in the most objectionable manner. You said it was purposely prepared so that you could not accept it, and to this day you have deigned to give no other explanation. And yet after treating me in this way you expect me to adopt an attitude that you would consider proper in a father to a son. God knows you seem to be bent on extinguishing every spark of filial affection that was ever in my heart. I only want you to tell me in what respect I have injured you and you decline to do so.

I have quite enough to do with my work in India without being constantly vexed and annoyed from home.

I note you have paid 1/6 and costs for repairing a Gladstone bag and an account of £7.3.6 (for £4.0.6.) for valuing Douneside. If you mean that you paid these for me I am sorry I cannot agree to the proceeding. You are very foolish to pay anyone that asks you for money. I have left no debts for you to attend to and it would surely have been right to apply for my sanction before making the payments you mention. I have no idea on what ground you made them. You also paid a wage to Mr R. Murray, Dundee, £3.7.3. but he has refunded the amount.

I hope you will now see your way to come to a friendly understanding with me. You cannot be happy any more than I am by this unseemly squabbling and recrimination, and I am not going to have my life made miserable by continuing this miserable dispute. I cannot plead with you any more. I feel nothing but good will to you, as I know you are only deceiving yourself

Yours affectionately,

A. MCROBERT

Cawnpore, 31 March 1892

My dear Father,

I duly received your letter of 22nd December last and would remark that you still have an altogether mistaken idea in thinking that you came to Douneside 'for my good'. 'For my good' is not in it at all – the real truth being that you occupy the farm for your good and it is not necessary to consider me in the matter at all. . . I myself believe that I have done as much and even more for my relatives than most people think it their duty to do. However I will let that pass. I do not feel that I have anything to reproach myself with in this respect and my conscience is not uneasy. I am sorry you should have such a poor opinion of me, but I cannot help it. I have done what I could to remove the misunderstanding and I will not refer to the subject again.

I hope you are well and prospering.

Yours affectionately,

A. MCROBERT

George Allen: The Emergence
of New India

Indian National Congress

Allen Octavian Hume, the 'Father of Congress', and George Allen, the
proprietor of the influential *Pioneer,* were implacable opponents. They
held very different views on the role of the British in India. Both had
experienced the horrors of the Mutiny, Hume as a district officer at
Etawah, George Allen at the siege of Delhi. Hume, in the restoration of
law and order, had been faced with hanging mutineers. Typically, he
insisted on giving each man a fair trial and designed a patent drop to be
as merciful as possible. Men prayed – 'first that they might be tried
by Mr Hume, and next that, if found guilty, they might be hanged
by him'.[1] Hume was a Scot, brought up with radical views that he
learnt from his father, Joseph Hume, MP. For twenty years he served as
a district officer, indulging his passion for ornithology and dreaming
dreams of the future of India. Perhaps his repugnance for his Mutiny
duties weighed heavily on his conscience.

George Allen on the other hand believed – along with many others of
that period – that the government was founded on conquest and that
India was such a vast country with such enormous diversity of languages,
castes and customs that it would be many years before the idea of Indian
nationality could take shape and any sense of national identity take hold.
He argued that it was unrealistic to press Western political ideas upon
the Indian people before they were ready to adapt to them. The *Pioneer*
had the ear of the most influential men in government and the level of
patronage it received alienated the other newspaper proprietors. Allen
himself had a trenchant style. He thundered at the philanthropists of England for encouraging ideas that were 'beyond the powers of an India in the
long clothes of civilisation and only just learning to mimic the language of

European politics without much attention to its meaning'.[2] Such statements in non-official circles won him admirers but made an enemy of Hume and of educated Indians. Whether Allen actually advocated holding back the emergence of New India or was merely pragmatic in pressing a policy that allowed time for change is for the reader to judge.

After nine years as secretary to the government in the Department of Revenue and Agriculture, where he did important work on the reform of the salt taxes, Hume fell foul of his senior officer and was dismissed, relegated to the Board of Revenue at Allahabad. Three years later, in 1882, he resigned the service to devote the rest of his life to organising a national movement in India sharing his ideas with other liberal sympathisers. In particular he had high hopes of the new editor of the *Pioneer,* A. P. Sinnett, who had been appointed in 1872. Sinnett, like Hume, had become a fervent theosophist, under the influence of Madame Blavatsky, and propagated the doctrine in the *Pioneer*.[3] This was too much for Allen: Sinnett was replaced by a more middle-of-the road literary man, George Chesney.

The appointment of the new Viceroy, Lord Ripon, whose avowed objective, which he approached with missionary zeal, was to further India's political advancement, coincided with Hume's leaving the service and devoting his whole energy to organising an Indian national movement. Hume had the ear of Lord Ripon; the two men had many ideals in common. Hume was always aware of the power of the press and when Sinnett was replaced as editor of the *Pioneer* and anti-Government feeling over the introduction of the Ilbert Bill was running high, Hume wrote in dismay to Ripon: 'I much fear that we shall have the *Pioneer* against us. Allen is of the worst type of educated Englishman, sneering at all things native and natives generally, always much guided by the opinions of a clique of civilians who were despots who wanted and want to keep the people for ever in the cradle. . .'[4]

The first Indian National Congress was held in Bombay in 1885 under the presidency of W. C. Bonnerjee. Delegates came from all over India. Seventy in all attended, mostly lawyers, schoolmasters and newspaper editors, having been 'pressed and entreated to come'. Hume became general secretary, a post he held until 1908. In a cordial and moderate atmosphere the president set out the objects of the organisation, 'the fuller consolidation and development of those sentiments of national unity that had their origin in our beloved Lord Ripon's ever memorable reign'.[5] Of all the newspapers in India only the *Bombay Gazette* reported the first Congress meeting.[6]

Lord Ripon was replaced by Lord Dufferin, also a liberal sympathetic to the political aspirations of educated Indians. Hume continued to consult with the Viceroy but found events were not moving swiftly enough. He became more and more of an agitator. England was always a decade ahead of India in social attitudes and Hume only had to look to England for examples of how to stir up trouble.[7] He held meetings and circulated pamphlets which declared forcefully against the government. Even those senior officials who sympathised with his views became alarmed at the dangerous methods he was using to further his ends. In particular they were afraid that Congress, being predominantly Hindu, would antagonise the Muslims and thereby cause friction between the two communities. Congress tried hard to make Muslims welcome, to give proper considera-tion to their views and allow an opportunity to hold office. The majority, however, held back to follow their own leader, Sir Syed Ahmed Khan. 'The Muhammadans, as a body, will not adopt a movement initiated by Hindus, and they detest the claim of the Hindu, whom they dispossessed centuries ago, to return, in whatever guise, to power.'[8] Meanwhile Duf-ferin began to see Hume more and more in the role of a troublemaker, a man with a bee in his bonnet – 'a mischievous busybody . . . cleverish, a little cracked, vain, unscrupulous, and I am told, very careless of truth.'[9]

Congress ultimately played so important a part in India's political history that it is necessary in thinking of the subcontinent in the last decade of the nineteenth century to get into perspective its modest begin-nings. It was 'a microscopic minority', according to Dufferin, to which no reasonable man could expect the British government to entrust the control of the Indian Empire 'for whose safety and welfare they are responsible in the eyes of God and before the face of civilisation'. He concluded that 'some loyal, patriotic and well-meaning men' desired to take 'a very big jump into the unknown by the application of democratic methods of government, and the adoption of a Parliamentary system, which England herself has only reached by slow degrees and through the discipline of many centuries of preparation'. Congress remained for thirty years a small organisation of moderates, content to cooperate with the British.

George Allen and the Wreck of the *Tasmania*

The personality and style of George Allen was never better demonstrated to his reading public in India than by the shipwreck he and his family

Wreck of the Tasmania, *from the sketch by G. E. Hale, surgeon, medical staff. From the* Illustrated London News *of 30 April 1887.*

experienced in 1887 when the P & O liner *Tasmania*,[10] on which they were travelling was wreckcd off the coast of Corsica with the loss of thirty-four lives.

The proud name of P & O, synonymous with the carrying of mails, that precious link, and the longed for and delighted in voyages on home leave, was familiar to all English people in India. It had been founded in 1837 when three men won a contract to carry mail on their handful of paddle-steamers to Spain and Portugal – hence the 'Peninsular' in the name. When the contract was extended to include Egypt, the world 'Oriental' was added. 'The Company acted as postman for British interests east of Suez for a hundred years.' Using the famous overland route, services were extended to India in 1842, to Singapore and Hong Kong in 1845, Australia in 1852 and Japan in 1859. By the time the *Tasmania* came into service, the P & O ran a fleet of forty-eight large, fast and comfortable ships.

The *Pioneer* of 4 April 1887 carried a list of passengers sailing on the *Tasmania*. Among those travelling from Calcutta to Marseilles were 'Mr and Mrs G. W. Allen and child'. On 20 April the shocking news of the catastrophe was briefly reported. After navigating the Straits of Bonifacio between Sardinia and Corsica the *Tasmania* had run onto rocks. Numbers of the *Pioneer* over the next four weeks were filled with letters and reports from the sufferers giving their version of events and with replies from the P & O defending their reputation for the care and safety of passengers. True to form it was George Allen's graphic account that filled a whole page and caused the greatest sensation.

PASSENGER'S NARRATIVE

The wreck of the *Tasmania* appears to have created a very considerable sensation in London, and in the *Standard* of 26th ultimo appears an account of it, bearing the well-known signature of Mr G. W. Allen, which we republish in full:

The *Tasmania,* a nearly new screw steamer of over five thousand tons, built of steel, left Port Said for Marseilles on the evening of Tuesday the 12th of April, with about three hundred souls on board. She was well found and ventilated, the fare excellent, the arrangements of every kind displaying a studious desire on the part of the great Company which owned her to secure the comfort and contentment of her passengers. The dinner hour of the following Saturday saw a jovial company gathered in the brilliantly-lighted saloon, for we were within twenty-four hours of our voyage's end, our programmes for the journey across the Continent were in our pockets, and every heart beat high with glad expectancy. Captain Perrin, having seen the ship safe through the Straits of Bonifacio, had retired to his cabin about an hour, leaving the second officer (Mr Curtis) in charge. The chief officer (Mr Watkins) was called for his watch at four a.m., and due on the bridge seven or eight minutes later. At four minutes after four the sleeping ship was rudely awakened by a sudden crash, which made her shiver from stem to stern, and roused every soul of us to terrible consciousness. The steady pulse of the screw stopped instantly, making the dead silence of the next few seconds, broken only by the tramp of hurrying feet on the deck above, more appalling. Another deafening crash, and soon three or four crashes in quick succession, the ship staggering with each concussion. Then, from every cabin, men, women, and children rushed in their nightclothes out of the darkness into the dim saloon and towards the companion stairs, filling the air with their piteous cries and agonised inquiries: whilst the rush of water and the confused tumult of voices above increased the horror. There was – there could be – no doubt of what had happened; and if there were, the ominous command for all the passengers to dress as quickly as possible and come upon deck soon dispelled it.

Once there, the nature of the disaster was but too clear to every one. Day had just broken. From the after bridge, close to the captain's cabin, where a group of ladies and children, and some two or three husbands, were huddled together, half-dressed, exposed to the bitter north wind, the whole ghastly picture was before us. The ship had run straight upon a reef; her bows were setting down upon the bottom some thirty feet, her keel churning up the sand from below and discolouring the sea all around us, whilst her stern was impaled high upon a rock. She was lying over to leeward, so that her windward side opposed a barrier to the waves, but for which none could have been saved. In our rear, less than a stone's throw distant, was a substantial beacon of masonry, on the wrong side of which our course had been taken, over which the waters perpetually broke, sweeping all the fore part of the half-submerged vessel; beyond, the open sea. In front and to our left an eager group of men, with the chief officer in command, were struggling to lower the two starboard boats – two out of the three which, so early, alone remained of the eight there were originally. They had been removed within the davits from which they were suspended the day previously, which greatly increased the difficulty of releasing them, and from the ship listing over had become jammed. There was a crowd of passengers at the gangway ladder, eager to be taken off; some aft, standing by their life-buoys, others already in the rigging, in preparation for the worst. Lying off the wreck, a hundred yards away, was the gig, with the doctor (Powell) and carpenter, both of whom had swum off to it, in charge. The long line of coast, with a lighthouse at the point, lay before us, with here and there a village nestling in the hills, a tower, or a patch of cultivation, the mid-distance broken by a line of jagged reef. At last the doctor's boat got away with some six or eight ladies and children, and at last – for it seemed an eternity, though only an hour or two – the two other boats were launched. The second boat, in charge of the boatswain, was 'rushed' by the second-class passengers, some thirty people, all of whom, with two honourable exceptions – men, women, and children – got away, the men who had jumped into the boat in the course of lowering it refusing the captain's peremptory order to them to leave it. The third – the life-boat

– was in charge of Mr Andrews, an officer in the Company's service on leave, the second, third, and fourth officers of the ship accompanying him. She bore away some fifty or sixty ladies and children, all save two of the former – Mrs Walker and Mrs Pigott – who elected to remain with their husbands. The work of getting the forlorn fugitives lowered was one of great difficulty and danger, for the boats rose and fell on the heavy ground swell a height of from twelve to fifteen feet, and whilst the children were thrown on board, their mothers had to be lifted in at the critical moment when the boat was poised on the rising wave. To write of the mute agony of what seemed those last farewells would be profanity. Suffice it that the women behaved with the calmness and courage of martyrs.

We saw them safely off with a sense of infinite relief, and for the time our spirits rose almost to cheerfulness as we counted the chances that the wreck would hold together and rescue come. Yet our plight was pitiable enough. It was now about ten a.m. A small sup of whiskey and a few fragments of biscuit, more or less soddened with salt water, recovered from the passengers' cabins by the stewards, was our fare. As the day wore on the wind strengthened, and the waves, breaking over the wreck with increasing violence, not only deluged our scanty clothing and half paralysed us with cold, but obliged us to cling to the bulwarks for dear life. By degrees the captain's cabin and the companion went, and one after another our frail shields from the force of the enemy were carried away. The captain himself was among the earliest victims. Whilst endeavouring to reach the chart room on the forward bridge, as is believed, with the object of rescuing the ship's papers, a part of the sky-light of the engine-room, which had become unshipped, knocked him off his feet and pinned him by the chest, and though the chief officer, one of the stewards, and a passenger made desperate efforts to release him, a violent sea breaking over at that moment carried him away. He was seen no more. Most of us then sought refuge at the stern end of the poop, in the lee of the smoking saloon, and joined the group which was still in comparative safety there. Meantime, the chief officer, almost deserted by his crew, but aided loyally by some of the passengers, the Earl of Buckinghamshire, Major Cooper, of Lord Dufferin's Staff, among them, had contrived to rig up a couple of rafts, each of which might have carried fifteen or twenty people at a push. One of these rafts was washed overboard with a solitary lascar when just ready for launching, and with it the Earl, who, however, keeping his head, managed to save himself by almost a miracle; the other, when already floated, was taken possession of by eight of the Seedi boys, who calmly cut the rope before our eyes; but they paid dearly for their treachery, as, being unable to steer their craft, they were borne away into the broken waters near the reef, and only one man reached the shore. At about four p.m. the look-out announced that a craft of some sort was approaching, and, after a long and weary wait, we made out that it was the life-boat. Once again our spirits rose, the precautions necessary to stop the native crew from rushing it, the need of giving prior deliverance to the injured and invalid of our company – for one, Sir Bradford Leslie, had been almost crippled by a fall – were eagerly discussed. But alas! the boat, evidently undermanned, was making little or no way, and by dusk she went about and made once more for land. So much we could conjecture, that her living freight was safe; but what of the remaining boats? What could we conclude from their also making no sign? As we learned eventually, however, their passengers had all reached the shore safely, at distances varying from four to thirteen miles, and it may suffice to add here that, whatever the simple peasants of the rude coast could do to lighten the sufferings of the shipwrecked people, was done with such self-denying thoroughness and generous sympathy as entitles them to the gratitude of every Englishman. The officials at the little town of Sartene and Propriana, through whose agency and that of the British Consul at Ajaccio the sufferers were able eventually to rejoin their husbands and friends, vied with their humbler neighbours in the performance of these ennobling offices. Mr Curtis hurried across country between 8 and 10 miles to the nearest telegraph station the instant he landed, and flashed to Ajaccio an urgent appeal for help to the passengers on the wreck; to this we owe it that succour came. For not a sail of any sort was sighted all the day.

As dusk began to set in the wind still increased, and we were evidently in for a bad night. By night, beyond two or three of our number who remained outside from first to last, and some of the crew who still either clung to the rigging or perforce sought precarious shelter on the deck, we had all squeezed into the smoking saloon – a low room, strongly built of steel, about sixteen feet by fourteen and nine feet high, with a pent-roof of thick glass, and barred windows with Venetian shutters all round. No words of mine could quite picture to another the horrors of that terrible night. There were seventy or eighty human beings – passengers and stewards, and sailors, black and white – huddled into that cage, the sea breaking with stupendous force upon it, dashing through and over the roof and windows, drenching its occupants, swamping the floor. As each succeeding wave struck it the wreck shuddered and shook; the metal keel grated on the bottom with a scrooping sound; the receding wave left us with a swirl and a sullen roar, and we held our breath in suspense whilst for an instant it seemed as though the weight of the blow had dislodged us from the rock on which we were mercifully pinned. Then there was the pitiful cry of the lascar or Seedi who would force himself desperately into the doorway, only to add to the number of helpless and paralysed of his kind already cumbering the ground, and who was, in mercy to the rest, ejected, only to die of exposure in the open; the frequent warning to be careful of our one poor lamp; the weary inquiry as to the hour of a man who had a watch; the false alarms from without and within of people whose fevered fancies conjured up a rocket or a light. Worst of all, perhaps, our own reflections, for we were face to face with death. All this till about eleven p.m., when the wind changed and slackened, the sea gradually fell, and we felt relieved of the certainty that but for this, in a few hours at the most, the end must have come. With the first glimpse of daylight the look-out reported a sail on the horizon, and in the right quarter, but, already the prey of several false alarms, we refused for an instant to be beguiled. A quarter of an hour later and all doubt was removed. It was not only a sail but a steamer, and making for us in a bee-line. What our feelings were only wrecked men can realise. We were saved. In less than an hour a trim little yacht, the *Norseman,* belong to Mr Platt, of Oldham, was at anchor a few boats' lengths from what remained of the *Tasmania:* we hailed her with wild cheers, and within another hour or so she had sailed with us for Ajaccio, from which port she had started for our rescue at one a.m., and we bid adieu to our gallant saviours with a feeling of gratitude that can never be effaced.

There are legally appointed tribunals which will lose no time in making a competent inquiry into the cause of the above terrible calamity, and I will not presume even to hint at the due apportionment of blame. But that a ship should be lost in fair weather, on a moonlight night, on a well-lighted coast – that this is a matter requiring searching investigation is evident. It may be trusted, also, that the Court will pronounce some opinion on the question both of age and the test of fitness for command in the persons of the captains of these large passenger ships, upon whom such an enormous responsibility in respect of human life devolves. We all liked and respected Captain Perrin, a kind and courteous gentleman, full of solicitude for the comfort of his passengers; but he had been more than twenty years in many trying latitudes, was obviously in bad health, and when the blow fell was utterly dazed and almost helpless, and quite incapable of taking his proper place. The Company must pay men more and retire them in their prime. But if poor Captain Perrin was physically unfit to face a great disaster, what shall I say of the crew? It was almost wholly a lascar crew. About such crews in general I offer no opinion; but about the utter and lamentable collapse of this particular one there is absolutely no doubt. When the ship struck a number of these men rushed to the two port boats on the poop, and let them down in a panic, with the ports open, only to capsize. From that moment the native crew became impervious alike to order, remonstrance, or threat. They were so many logs, and worse. Again, several of the stewards began looting those cabins which were accessible at an early date, and it will be necessary to inquire why, if No. 2 boat could be trusted in charge of one petty officer, it required that a special officer should take command of the life-boat, with the second, third, and fourth officers to help him. Had these no possible duties still on board? I say with regret, but with the utmost deliberation, that there was something seriously at fault in the discipline of the ship's company. It was a fair-weather organization, but the moment a strain was put on it, it broke up.

May I crave a few more lines more or your space to publish the names of those of the ship's officers who by general consent did well. Mr Watkins, the chief officer, behaved nobly, the passengers presenting him with a purse and a handsome written testimonial before they parted; Mr Leslie, the chief engineer; Mr Baigent, the chief steward; Mr Salter, one of the cabin stewards; the storekeeper; and Mrs Arnold, one of the stewardesses, deserve our warm thanks. Among the second-class passengers, Messrs Stormont and Cufflin, who refused to save their skins at the price of their manliness, earn honourable mention. Of the passengers, Major Cooper, brave, cheerful, full of resource under difficulties, did admirably. Indeed, I may say, on the authority of the chief officer, who had every opportunity of judging, that the coolness and discipline shown by the large body of passengers was extraordinary; in only one instance did I see the white feather, and that not in the case of an Englishman.

The total loss of life was thirty-four, including the captain, fifth officer (drowned whilst lowering the boats), and Quartermaster Hall, washed from the rigging. The deaths were almost wholly among the Seedis and lascars from cold and exposure.

The Hearsey Case against the *Pioneer*

The year that saw the launch of the Upper India Chamber of Commerce at Cawnpore was also the year that an extraordinary incident took place at the *Pioneer* offices at Allahabad, involving the good name of George Allen.

Early in January 1890, at a meeting of Congress at Allahabad, a number of legislative proposals were discussed and one of the speakers, a keen Congressman opposing the Contagious Diseases Act, was Andrew Hearsey. He was a son of the distinguished General Hearsey of the 'Damn his musket' incident and had been riding beside his father when Mungal Pandy, inciting the sepoys to mutiny, was arrested on parade and the regiment disarmed.[11] The inherited fighting spirit of the Hearseys had turned to brawling and law suits, which had brought him up against the authorities and persuaded him to throw in his lot with the supporters of New India.

The *Pioneer* reported the Congress meeting briefly. Then Kipling, who had been transferred from Lahore to the *Pioneer* office at Allahabad,[12] asked George Allen if he might describe the affair of the Congress meeting from his own point of view. George Allen concurred but reminded Kipling to be good-tempered since he had only recently dined some of the Congress leaders, including Bonnerjee and Norton. Kipling's sketch in which he used the words 'the brown Captain and a half-caste' slipped past the editor and duly appeared in the *Pioneer*. When Andrew Hearsey, the 'notorious Captain Hearsey', a man of quick and furious temper, read the piece he felt so insulted he went round straight away to the *Pioneer* building, pushed past startled *chaprassis* and peons, confronted the editor, George Chesney, in his office and proceeded to horsewhip him. He was arrested, fined and sentenced to one month's imprisonment. The *Pioneer* did not leave it at that and George Allen on 26 January printed an attack on Andrew Hearsey.

> ... One Andrew Hearsey, notorious in these Provinces as 'Captain Hearsey', was yesterday sentenced by Captain Hewett, Cantonment Magistrate of Allahabad, to one month's imprisonment, and in

default of his finding sureties to keep the peace for twelve months, to a further term until sureties are found, for an assault committed under circumstances briefly reported in our local columns. Mr Hearsey, originally a Lieutenant in the 107th Foot, closed his career in the Army under pressure from the then Commander-in-Chief. In 1864 he was fined Rs. 100 for an assault. During the ten years ending in 1884, he was convicted seven times for various offences against the Penal Code; in four of these instances for breaches of the peace. It may be hoped, on public grounds, that Mr Hearsey's ruffianly propensities will be effectually discouraged by the salutary action of the Cantonment Magistrate. To the honour of the Native Bar it should be added that more than one of its leading members refused to hold a brief in Mr Hearsey's defence.[13]

As soon as Hearsey was released he brought a case against the *Pioneer* and Chesney and Dare, the editor and the printer, were brought to trial. The case against Dare was dismissed and when George Allen cabled from London that he had written the offending article and the responsibility was his, judgement was given clearing Chesney.

George Allen returned to India to find himself facing ten charges in the Calcutta High Court for defamation of character in a third prosecution brought by Hearsey. He lost no time in contacting the Governor of the North Westem Provinces (A.P. MacDonnell) with an appeal to bring the matter to the attention of the Viceroy. It was all done with great tact and discretion, with the object of getting the trial transferred from Calcutta to Allahabad. At Allahabad the prestige of the *Pioneer* would almost certainly succeed in squashing the case.

Several arguments were put forward against Calcutta. Hearsey, 'the warmest of Congressmen', was backed by semi-seditious Bengalis, 'who have a wild notion that in striking at the *Pioneer* they are striking at the Government of India'. Allen believed that no Bengali jury would be impartial. Furthermore he had reservations about the judge appointed to hear the case, Justice Norris, a man 'infirm of temper' and, according to Alien, unfavourably disposed to the *Pioneer,* as was evident from his attitude to it during his handling of the recent case against Chesney and Dare. Allen pleaded for the appointment of a new judge.

Also to be considered was the influence of the hostile Calcutta papers, their trade jealousies fanned by the fact that only a few months earlier the *Pioneer* had walked off with the prize of the contract for printing government orders from under their noses. While the *Pioneer* was unable to comment on the case *sub judice,* the other papers, English and Indian, felt under no such restraint. Allen was convinced he would not get a fair trial at Calcutta.

Hearsey on the other hand had fought official high-handedness for years and become 'a sincere friend of the people and a worker in their cause'. He launched an appeal for funds to fight his case, linking his personal battle with political issues, referring to the fight as being No Congress versus Congress and inciting opinion against 'our common enemy the *Pioneer'.* He made the mistake, however, of promoting his cause by using Bonnerjee's name to head the subscription list. Allen was actually at Lahore with Bonnerjee when this was brought to his notice and Bonnerjee angrily denied his involvement, calling it 'a damn lie'.

Government stood back cautiously, commenting that both Hearsey and Allen were in 'the same box'. If Allen could not get a fair trial at Calcutta it was equally likely that Hearsey would not get a fair hearing at Allahabad. Government, anxious not to appear to identify with the *Pioneer* 'before the eyes of every native of India', came to the conclusion that to transfer the case would smack of partiality. Although they went so far as to consider bringing in a fresh judge and, should it become ncecssary, a change of jury, Calcutta it must be: 'Refuse the prayer.'

The London Office: Allen Brothers & Company

George Allen was seldom in Cawnpore but his influence and reputation touched many emerging industries through his London-based company Allen Bros and Co. It had started as Peake Allen and Co. of Albion Place, London Wall in 1859, a family concern (the Peakes were related to the Allens) but in 1865 it was listed as Allen Brothers at the same address. The firm originally made its money exporting tooth-cleaning powder to India, then expanded into general trading, becoming East India merchants and acting as agents for many Indian companies and charging commission on orders placed through them by these companies. Allen organised an efficient network of outlets that catered for the market's every need. Head Office was in London; this was where staff for overseas were contacted and engaged and their passages arranged. The Manchester office took care of shipping and the Bradford office wool samples and the orders for machinery. In India there were offices at Calcutta and an interest in the Caledonian Printing Press, a shipping office at Bombay, and in Cawnpore ultimately three offices to maintain contact with the mills.

No order was too small to be arranged by Allen Brothers, from expensive silver canteen sets – presentation presents to retiring staff – to a wonderful selection of toys for the annual Lalimli Club Christmas party, or shirts for Indian maharajahs ordered from the royal shirtmakers. It was a two-way trade and in return came bristles and bone meal and sisal exported from India and bundles of copies of the *Pioneer* and *Civil and Military Gazette* to be distributed to old India hands in England. In the 1880s the directors were Mr Cockell whose office was decorated with huge glass tanks of stuffed fish, and the stout and jolly Mr Dawson who was careful with money and often travelled abroad on business for the company. Office boys were recruited from a nearby school, starting on 10/- or 12/6 a week, aged fourteen. It was a time when even office workers wore top hats and sat at high stools. The day started with a prayer in the office. Hours were 9.30 a.m. to 6 p.m. but no clerk thought of going home before 7 p.m. and the directors worked long and late hours.[14] Apart from running errands and keeping the stamp desk, where accounts were closely scrutinised, an important duty for the office boys was to fill the directors' inkwells, one with ordinary and the other with copying ink. Directors' letters were handwritten in copying ink, with copies made by inserting the letters in a book bound with tissue paper, covered with a wet rag and put in a big screwdown iron press. If the rag was too wet the original writing would completely disappear. Woe betide the boy who filled the inkwell with the wrong ink, for then the letter could not be copied at all.

The great day of the week was mail day. With the Victorian obsession with time and punctuality, every Thursday was devoted to ensuring the post caught the P & O boat train to Marseilles for the weekly steamer.

On Thursdays most of the staff were expected to stay until 9 o'clock. It was a terrible rush all day as the shipping documents had to catch the weekly steamer, otherwise goods would have arrived in India without the necessary papers to clear them from Customs so we simply had to catch the last post at the GPO in St Martin's le Grand, EC. We had to grab a cab and if we had no time to put the sealing wax on in the office we used to take matches and a candle to do it in the cab. There was only one mail a week and on arriving at the GPO there was always a crowd of messengers from the Chartered Bank of India and the National Bank of India etc all doing the same thing. The office allowed no reps or callers on mail day and it was an understood thing in the City that no travellers could be seen on Thursday in Indian merchants' offices.[15]

Everyone rolled up their sleeves, put invoices into envelopes, burnt their fingers with sealing wax, tied up bundles of letters and dashed for the 8 p.m. post.[16]

In Cawnpore Allen Brothers had one office at the Cawnpore Cotton Mills, open from 7 a.m. to 12 noon, where cloth and yarn were sold and contact maintained with the mill manager. Old Mr Horsman, even at the time when he was building his own mill made a practice of calling in every morning. The story is told that Horsman came in one day accompanied by a new hand, one Mr Durie, who boasted that after six months' study of the mill he thought he had complete knowledge of the art of cotton spinning and use of Indian cotton. Horsman put him in his place by replying drily: 'Do ye say so now, Mr Durie. Ah well, after 40 years man and boy I am pleased to say I learn some little thing new nearly every day of ma life.' The second office was strategically placed in the bazaar, on a narrow street looking into the Juggilal Kamlapat Temple;[17] it was open from 3 p.m. to 6 p.m. attending to imports, mainly textiles from the United Kingdom and the Continent. The third office was in Civil Lines, a much more gentlemanly affair, staffed by two senior Europeans who manned the export of bristles and sisal from the nearby plantation. (One assistant confessed it was while visiting the plantation and sleeping out in the open that one midnight he shot the meteorological gauge to bits in mistake for a panther!)

To any new arrival at Allen Brothers the Cawnpore Burra Sahibs were gods in the business and social firmament, to whom they spoke only with genuflection. So great was McRobert's stern reputation that they were taught to make the sign of the cross on their chests when passing Cawnpore Woollen Mills or even writing its name.[18]

The legend persisted. Even in recent times when I wrote to a contemporary of his asking for information I was sternly rebuked for calling him McRobert and not, as was proper, Sir Alexander McRobert.

13

The Westcott Brothers

'Quit Ye Like Men'

The last decade of the nineteenth century was the noblest chapter in Cawnpore's history. In terms of material success the mills had a further twenty years of expansion ahead before they reached their peak, but from the standpoint of the harmonious cooperation between all strata of society, the last years of the century were remarkable. This was almost entirely due to the influence and example of two brothers, George and Foss Westcott. Their personalities, dedication and Christian vision had an impact on the whole community of Cawnpore that was both unifying and uplifting.

The SPG, Society for the Propagation of the Gospel,[1] had been established in Cawnpore as early as 1820 and had set up the Cawnpore Free School and after the Mutiny had taken over the running of Christ Church. Now in the summer of 1889 the secretary of the SPG in London received a letter from the Bishop of Calcutta appealing for helpers at the Cawnpore Mission. That very day the secretary received a letter from Dr Westcott, then Canon of Westminster, saying that his two sons were eager to work in the mission field in India. As a result the two brothers found themselves in Cawnpore, now an industrial city and so an appropriate place to put their theories to work.[2] Their father, later to become Bishop of Durham, was a constant source of encouragement and practical support. In particular he stressed the need for holiness in all things, however mundane – Christ required holiness in industry, commerce and all social life as well as in the individual.[3] The Westcott brothers faced a special challenge in the legacy of the terrible events of the Mutiny in Cawnpore; they longed to heal the wounds between the communities. Their father's admiration for India as a great *thinking* nation made them eager to learn from their Indian contemporaries.

First they set themselves to acquire a knowledge of Urdu, Hindu beliefs and customs and the Mohammedan religion. They also found time to call on the English residents. The response was remarkable. The residents were charmed by their youthful enthusiasm and their eagerness to include pastoral duties with their missionary work. Their congregation steadily increased in number. Ladies offered to set up working groups to raise money and the St Andrew's Guild was formed.[4] Others volunteered to sing in the choir, look after the church, or organise fancy fairs to raise money. Three years after their arrival the Bishop of Calcutta formally confirmed that the mission clergy in Cawnpore should also be responsible for all 'pastoral charges in civil lines'.

This attitude of the Westcotts, that they were there to serve the whole community, not just preach the Gospel to non-Christians, went a long way towards breaking down the old prejudice against missionaries.

> Ordinarily missionaries are so fully occupied with their own work that they seldom meet with their fellow-countrymen, and frequently complain that they take no interest in Mission work. Meanwhile the English come to feel that the missionary regards them as un-Christian for not taking a more active interest in work about which they practically know nothing. They complain of unjust treatment and unjustifiable neglect, asking whether they too have not spiritual needs which the Mission clergy might attend to. In such complaints we may see one of the reasons why Mission work is sometimes criticised by English Christians.[5]

They were emphatic that the time spent among the English congregation was not misspent. They relied on personal example as their most persuasive asset; and in this they succeeded wonderfully.

The brothers, through consulting together at all times, divided the work into two different areas of responsibility. George devoted his energies to raising the standard of work in the High School, the old Free School, so that the gift of education should be as widely available as possible. Foss was in charge of the evangelical work and of creating industrial workshops for the mission boys.

George Westcott started an energetic rebuilding and enlargement of the school and by 1894 was able to claim that the two classes, each of twenty-two students, were 'a very respectable beginning for College classes in these Provinces where education is a comparative novelty'.[6] Educational facilities in the province were meagre, 15 colleges and 2,000 students in all. In Cawnpore itself in 1891 there were only 600 people literate in English. Local residents were involved from the beginning.

Canon George H. Westcott (seated), with Foss Westcott, the Bishop of Chota Nagpur.

Evening classes were started, Mr McRobert from the Woollen Mills taught book-keeping, Mr Sanders from the German firm of Schroder Smith took turns with Mr H.D. Allen and Mr Logie Watson of Cooper Allen to teach correspondence; the Revd Arthur Crosthwaite, newly arrived from Cambridge, taught shorthand. There were regular debates and lectures on religion, but these were conducted in a spirit that encouraged students to try to find the truth for themselves.[7]

The word spread about the excellence of the teaching and the arrival of Arthur Crosthwaite to the SPG Mission made it possible for a hostel for non-Christian students to be set up, the first of its kind. The college journal describes Crosthwaite's own picture of it.

> It is built, like most native houses of any size, round a small court-yard and has three storeys. On the ground floor are the rooms used for cooking, which necessarily take up a good deal of space; as a native eats his food in the room in which it is cooked. Here is also a well and two small living rooms. The majority of students, of whom there were eleven, live in four rooms on the first floor. My room, used both as a study and a bedroom, is also on this floor and looks out upon the street, so that I am in the very middle of my family.
>
> On the roof there are two rooms, one of which is a common room, where I and most of the students sit and read in the evening. It is also used by the Hostel Debating Society, and for games and so on. It is a pleasant room and has on its walls a number of photos of College classes, football and cricket groups, etc. [Q.P., July, 1898.]

Characteristically he does not mention that he had no fans and no separate bathroom and latrine for himself, and only water from the well.[8]

The standard of teaching was excellent, covering English, philosophy or history, the classics, Sanskrit or Persian, mathematics and science. Later a law class was introduced. The titles of the textbooks make impressive reading. Sports were also encouraged, football, cricket, athletics, and later on, hockey. Burra Sahib played full back and Chota Sahib forward, in a gesture of cohesion between students and staff.

In 1892 the High School became affiliated to the University of Allahabad (then ten years old) and was renamed Christ Church Collegiate School. George Westcott was its principal. As numbers grew it became clear that more staff were necessary. On his first home leave George Westcott proposed to the SPG Standing Committee that the English staff

of the mission should be strengthened and converted into a brotherhood and that more funds should be made available to enlarge the class-
rooms and living quarters to bring the school up to college status. The
suggestion was sympathetically received. Two Oxford graduates were
engaged[9] and in 1896 the brotherhood of five members came into existence. It was understood that all who joined the brotherhood should be
unmarried and remain at least five years. Salary was Rs. 200 per month,
Rs. 90-100 for messing, the balance to cover everything else.[10] Thereafter events moved swiftly. In August 1897, in a terrific downpour of
rain, the opening ceremony of Christ Church College took place. 'Quit
ye like men' was chosen as the College motto.

On top of his many college duties George Westcott somehow also
found time for leisure pursuits. He wrote *Guide to Cawnpore,* published
in 1892, and later contributed several important chapters to *The Story of
the Cawnpore Mission* (1909). He also began his detailed research into
Kabir and the Kabir Panth. He enjoyed watching wrestling and he was a
keen amateur photographer, constantly photographing the Indian people
at work or at their religious devotions. In particular he was interested in
the fakirs, the religious ascetics who often lived naked, their bodies and
matted hair covered in ash, artists of the punishing posture. But perhaps his greatest delight was growing roses, for which the climate in
Cawnpore was ideal. His garden was landscaped with nine rose gardens,
elaborately set out round a sundial, and he kept the house sweetly scented
with huge bowls of cut blooms.

His students were attracted to his gentle genial looks, although his
manner was often very cool. A story is told that he was once walking
round the rose garden with a lady who poured out her heart about the
death of her husband. Someone who had accompanied them remarked
afterwards that Westcott had been rather unreceptive to her distress.
'Heard it all before,' Westcott tersely explained.[11]

India has always suffered from famines. If the monsoon rains fail, the
human harvest in February/March produces little or nothing and the
people die. Children left orphans in these famines were often rescued by
the mission and given shelter in the mission homes. In the famine of
1896-7 the mission found itself called upon to provide for close on 300
orphans, 80 of them boys. Many had suffered acute privations and died
young, especially of consumption. These orphans became Christian converts. From the beginning it had been policy to teach them a manual
trade, such as tailoring or carpentry.[12]

When the Westcott brothers arrived in Cawnpore they found an

ABOVE *Foss Westcott's printing workshop.* BELOW *Some of the women Mission workers at Cawnpore; Deaconess Annie Scott seated second from right.*

experiment had been made over the previous few years to place orphans in the mills as apprentices. Eight or ten boys had been sent from Benares and Goruckpore to learn mill work in Cawnpore. It had not been a success. The boys had been selected as the most troublesome and in Cawnpore they had no regular home or supervision out of hours. In the mills they were faced with a virtual trade union of caste against an outsider. Mill managers had enough difficulty with Hindu and Muslim workers and were reluctant to add a third difficulty. Foss Westcott assessed the problems and opportunities and decided the solution was for the mission to have its own workshops and teach the orphans to the highest standards itself. In this way Foss became responsible not only for the evangelical work but for the introduction and development of industrial workshops.[13]

A proper home was built with a missionary in charge as a housefather.[14] In 1892 the Mission Press was started and quickly became established as Christ Church Mission Press and self-supporting. It printed church magazines, college periodicals, the local weekly newspaper, the Indian Church Directory and several books, one of which was George Westcott's *Guide to Cawnpore*. The press was followed by a carpentry shop making good-quality furniture. In 1902 at an industrial exhibition they won a gold medal for the best carpentry exhibit. Later a brass foundry was added which turned out fine ecclesiastical brasswork for many churches in India and Burma. Foss Westcott took home leave the year after his brother and raised funds to extend the workshops and to bring out English managers to supervise the workshops.[15] In time the mills set up their own foundries and took away many of the mission workers to mend their own machinery.

The orphanage for girls was administered by English lady teachers and missionaries – not an easy assignment since the girls often proved even more difficult to look after than the boys. Soon after they arrived in Cawnpore the Westcott brothers appealed to their father, the Bishop of Durham, and two of the Durham diocese lady workers, the first of several, volunteered for work in the Cawnpore mission. The Epiphany Girls Orphanage gave a home to girls until at sixteen they left to get married or went to train as nurses. The Zenana Mission, on the other hand, concentrated on visiting Indian women in the seclusion of their zenanas, to talk to them and stir their imagination about the outside world they were not permitted to enter.

In 1898 the dream of a mission hospital came true when the foundation stone of St Catherine's Hospital was laid.[16] It was a two-storey building with wards shaded by wide verandahs and living quarters for the nurses upstairs. The staff consisted of two doctors, an evangelist and two nursing sisters, all English, an Anglo-Indian matron and about twelve Indian nurses receiving training. The evangelist taught the patients hygiene and Bible stories and hymns, visited the patients when they returned home and acted as house mother at the hospital. The matron was in charge of food and hospital servants. Among the Indian nurses the more experienced acted as dispensers, in charge of out patients and night duty, while at least half were probationers. Most of the nursing fell on the English sisters.

There was endless frustration in trying to overcome caste prejudice and ignorance of causes of illness among the Indian women and persuading them to brave the displeasure of their families and come to the hospital for treatment. A lady of high caste sent her servants to purify the room she was to occupy. It was washed down with Ganges water and then carefully rubbed over with cow dung. One little boy, brought in dangerously ill with pneumonia, survived the crisis and a few days later was on the road to recovery. The relatives, however, alarmed at the sudden ceasing of the fever, insisted on taking him away to bathe him in the Ganges as a last hope. It was done and the boy died the same evening.[17]

Many infants were brought to the out patients' clinic *in extremis* from repeated doses of opium. The mothers were determined that the greatest harm that could befall a child was to let it cry, so in spite of severe warnings they continued to give the child opium. When patients could be persuaded to be admitted to hospital many would leave before the treatment was complete, or take fright at the last minute and return home only to come back when the disease was too far advanced to cure.

But it was the home visits that were the most heart-rending. One case was reported where the hospital doctor was called to a young woman of twenty who was found to be bleeding to death. It was a form of haemorrhage that could be stopped in a few minutes by a minor surgical procedure. The old grandmother, suspicious of all new forms of treatment, insisted that medicine could be given but the doctor must on no account touch the patient. The doctor pleaded with her; at first he had the grandfather's support but this petered out when the hostility of all the relatives became apparent. They quietly encircled the bed and crowded the doctor out of the house. The patient's husband followed her outside weeping bitterly. He did not dare go against his parents' wishes. In two hours the young woman was dead.

At the College students won scholarships and degrees. Plays were so well produced they were often repeated at the Station Theatre for the public to enjoy. In sport the College teams beat élite visiting teams. New buildings were put up, including the library and, ultimately, the science blocks. Many of the future leaders of Cawnpore, in politics or business or on the municipality, men such as Munshi Jwala Prasad, Lala Bishambhar Nath, Brigendra Swaroop, Fazlul Rahman, Narain Pundit Arora and Pundit Prithi Nath, sat at the feet of Burra Sahib and Chota Sahib.[18]

In every sphere of Cawnpore life the Westcott brothers played their part. Foss Westcott was officially nominated as chaplain to the Volunteers; he also organised meetings of the Literary Society at the Chamber of Commerce. At a time when their father the Bishop of Durham was settling a three-month-old strike of the Durham coal miners by calling a conference at his own home,[19] the Westcott brothers were meeting and discussing labour problems and labour relations with Alexander McRobert and William Cooper. The Bishop's influence went deep.[20] Through a family connection several young men went out to the mission from Pembroke College, Cambridge, and even C.F. Andrews, the great admirer and follower of Mahatma Gandhi, was said to have been influenced by the Bishop of Durham.

The Westcott brothers in their turn became mediators between East and West. There may not have been many converts to Christianity in their time but their practical work and personal inspiration, the dedication of their lives to share their vision that all men and women should be able to come to the knowledge of the truth and live free from oppression, injustice, poverty, fear and ignorance was an example to all. In tribute to the brothers it was said: 'The coming of the Westcotts to Cawnpore transformed the whole character of the city.'[21]

ABOVE *George Nightingale with his daughters Violet and Lilian and a friend (left).*
BELOW *Cawnpore tennis party – Butterworth second from right.*

Bicycle picnic at Cawnpore, c. 1900.

ABOVE *Ralph and Florence Maxwell with guests, at the Maxwell bungalow.*
BELOW *Drawing room of the Dunbars' bungalow at Elgin.*

ABOVE *Picnic at Jajmau, c. 1900.*
BELOW *A river picnic, from the Butterworth album.*

14

Last Decade of the Nineteenth Century

―――

The Return of Gavin Jones

John Stewart was enjoying his retirement in Scotland as laird of Ardvor-lich with Millie beside him running the household. It was ten years since he left Cawnpore. He kept in touch with events there through his friends and in particular through his daughter Helen, married to R. H. Skrine of the ICS.[1] Then, with surprise and some misgiving, he received a letter from Gavin Jones asking him all sorts of questions.

16th July 1896

My dear Stewart,

A friend has asked me to get him the following information. It's all about leather and especially Cawnpore leather and as there is no better authority than yourself I could not do better than appeal to you and hope it will not be giving you too much trouble.

1 Compared with English made harness and saddlery how did the leather made at the H and S Fry stand the climate and the heavy wear and tear of India? I believe the articles you turned out stood the test better than English.

2 Do the boots and shoes made at the Govt Boot Factory (C.A. and Co) wear as well as the English manufacture? There used to be great complaints when the boots were first made and I remember that the rejections were heavy but I fancy now that they have got well into the work they have got over this difficulty.

3 Could you kindly give me an idea what used to be the relative cost of the raw hides, tanned hides, and manufactured leather – as far as I can remember I think the average cost of the raw hides was about 4 annas a lb. I don't know exactly what you reckoned cost of conversion into leather nor am I sure what you passed the manufacturers' articles in your books at about 8 annas per lb – which covered cost of

raw materials, tanning and currying and manufacturing. If you have scruples about the source of my information I will treat it as confidential – there is nothing sinister in my enquiry.[2]

Two weeks later Jones confided to Stewart that he was planning a trip out to India, spending the winter months out there. He aroused Stewart's curiosity by his remarks on Cawnpore and the rich prizes in the leather trade.

> From all accounts Cawnpore has changed immensely since we left, both the Woollen and Muir have extended their works and premises and the Rly runs right into the mill compound. CA and Co are coining gold faster than they know what to do with it. I hear C is going to buy a property near Brighton for £10,000. A trip to the old place will be very interesting.

C of course was William Cooper, though it was at Bournemouth, not Brighton, that he bought a handsome property.[3]

Stewart's replies were sufficiently encouraging for Jones to come clean in a letter dated 4 August and marked 'Strictly Confidential'. A powerful syndicate in London had planned to establish a tanning and leather manufacturer in Cawnpore, floating the company in London with £100,000 capital, or, if necessary, in Calcutta. They hoped to have Stewart as chairman, Jones as secretary, with a local board in Cawnpore working through managing agents.

> If you agree to help us I think it can be arranged that both of us should be allotted sufficient numbers of paid up shares to qualify for office in remuneration of our services, for we can both claim to be experts, you in tanning and manufacturing whilst I as Engineer in the erection of the buildings, machinery and workshops, the others concerned being purely men of business with no special experience in these specialities.

In a postscript next day he urges Stewart to try to obtain information through his friends at the India Office on the aggregate value of harness, saddlery, accoutrements and boots supplied by the Indian factories to the Army in 1895. He ends with the tempting thought that 'neither of us need engage to arrive out there except in the cold weather, it will be a nice holiday trip for three years particularly when the expenses are paid and our services are substantially recognised. *Don't let the cat out of the bag whatever you do.*'

Cawnpore had always been a centre for the leather trade and since Stewart introduced modern tanning methods to the Harness and Saddlery Factory and Cooper Allen won the Army boot contract, many small operators set up leather works in Cawnpore. In 1896 the official *Bengal Directory* lists thirty-one firms in Cawnpore either making leather goods or dealing in hides; some were Germans, a number were Indian. The amount of trade was colossal: Jones quotes exports from India in 1895 as being 3,499,165 and says that London alone imported 4,400,885 hides that year. The figures that Stewart duly extracted from the India Office revealed that Cooper Allen had supplied 86,700 boots in 1893. No quantities could be given for 1895 except that 5,803 pairs of Highland shoes had been ordered the previous year.

Among the smaller firms was Foy Bros, established in 1872 as country produce agents, who since 1881 had manufactured good-quality footwear by hand and light machinery in their works close to Murray and Co. on the Mall Road. Edward Foy entered into an ambitious scheme in partnership with T.T. Bond, the engineer in charge of the Government Flour Mill, to build the North West Tannery Company, to rival Cooper Allen. When the partners found themselves hampered by lack of capital, they turned to Wishart, secretary of the Chamber of Commerce, for help and advice. Ironically, they were not the only ones: the Stewart Tannery in Agra, too, sought his assistance. John Stewart had unwisely dabbled in a factory of his own in his last years in India and, finding it too much for him, had sold out and cut his losses.[4]

Wishart had been the representative of Begg Sutherland since 1876. He was quiet and self-effacing, short, thick-set, with an ugly face in a huge head; he had the look of a seedy lion. He devoted initially all his time and energy to developing local business – there was something about the emerging Cawnpore that fired his imagination.[5] Only with the greatest difficulty could he ever be persuaded by his wife to take a holiday.

Gavin Jones thought very highly of Wishart:

We could not have a better man than Wishart, he is a very able man and as you know is the life and soul of the NWP Chamber of Commerce of which he is the Secretary. Cooper owes to him being a member of council, he writes out all his speeches for him and guides him in all the business of the Chamber and if he wished would be the leading man in the NWP. I know him well as he was on the Board in the Muir Mills, as soon as all matters are arranged we three will meet privately in London to give the finishing touches to the scheme. Wishart is a great friend of Sir E. Buck[6] and is sanguine that he will get him to join and he further hopes to induce Rutherford Deares of the Allahabad Bank to take part, so that on the whole there will be no lack of good Anglo Indian names to represent the Board either in London or Cawnpore. C.A. and Co would not have the wisdom to join us and I doubt whether it would be good policy on our part to ask them; apart from the opposition such a course would arouse I do not think the Govt will care for a concern to deal with who would be all-powerful, whereas they would be pleased with competition and help a new rival. I would on no account ask C.A. and Co nor even hint to them that a competitive scheme is on foot. A[7] as master of the '*Pi*' could do us a lot of harm, it is therefore on this account that we are so careful to keep the thing quiet, at present Wishart you and I are the only custodians of the secret.

The NWP Tannery Coy were started at Cawnpore a few years ago, they have a well planned and laid out Tan yard and Factory but lack funds to make head. The Stewart Tannery Coy at Agra are in a similar plight and quite in Wishart's power and he believes that we could get both concerns into our hands on very easy terms so that we could make a good start and be in a strong position to compete for a portion of the Boot Contract when it expires;[8] but as I said before, apart from this there is a tremendous field for operations as we could beat the English manufacturers if we desired to operate in Gt Britain.

The scheme that Gavin Jones and Wishart 'together hatched' was under the auspices of Begg Dunlop and Co., London, a sister firm of Begg Sutherland and Co., Cawnpore – 'very wealthy and has a high standing reputation both in London and India'. Five names had been proposed for the London board: John Stewart as chairman, Sir Edward Buck (due to retire shortly from India), Walter Butler, a member of Begg Dunlop and the man who had stirred up the trouble with Henry Ledgard, and Gavin Jones. In Cawnpore Begg Sutherland were to be the managing agents with Wishart to represent them and a local board of three or four directors. Walter Butler, who regularly spent the winter in Cawnpore, was to be one of them.

There are several there who will readily join when they come to see that we are in earnest and have a good base to start.

As soon as the Coy is floated and the capital assured we intend to get the NWT Coy to amalgamate, they occupy that splendid site between the Elgin Mills and the old magazine, the property once owned by old Mrs Shearin – they have got up a well laid out tan yard and workshops and there is room enough to erect larger works than CA and Co's. Wishart believes that they will join if for no other reason than self defence, as they have spent all their capital on works and have nothing left to carry on with, so that if they stand aloof they will be sure to perish and lose their all; whereas by amalgamating they will obtain shares in value that in the course of five years will be worth more than their outlay, which at present under any circumstances is in jeopardy – this acquisition would save the Coy two years in building and organising and by the time the boot contract expires we will be in position to tender. If the NWT Cy decline we have other ideas to go upon and at worst would build new works and be ready in time to compete. But apart from these boots there is a vast field for our operations which you with your experience must see.

If there was any difficulty in floating the scheme in London, Jones was confident there would be none whatever in India, where their names were well known and where 'the public are fully aware that there is money in leather. Cooper Allen's rise you may be sure is not hid under a bushel and Cooper's ostentatious living must be enough advertisement for us apart from other considerations in our favour.' He believed that 'native bankers' would take up the idea with enthusiasm, as they had with every scheme he had launched previously; and, with John Stewart involved, the entire capital could be subscribed within a fortnight of the prospectus's publication.

Jones sat up late drawing up notes and details for a prospectus, based on the figures Wishart had sent him of likely costs. He relished the prospect of a tight fight ahead. 'Cooper has bought a fine Estate in Bournemouth where he intends to settle down, he will return to Cawnpore for the winter and come home for good in summer – old Allen is going out too for a few months so we will have a good meeting when the bomb explodes.' He worked on plans for pits and workshops, considering the arrangements for the construction of machinery and the fitting out of the factory. He sent off the prospectus next day when it had been copied, adding 'Cooper will be very wroth but I cannot help that, I must do something for my sons so must disregard such obstacles.'

As October approached, the month when passages were booked to return to India for the cold weather season, Jones invited Stewart to travel down from Scotland, stay with them in London and attend a meeting with Begg Dunlop's partners. At Begg Dunlop there was a flurry of activity as they discussed with their brokers the state of the money market in London. Suddenly, however, a cloud appeared on the horizon. Jones knew that for his scheme to succeed McRobert must be persuaded to join them. But McRobert was a wily old fox. While Jones and Wishart had been hatching their scheme he had summed up NWT's predicament and promised to help them.

> *26 Sept 1896* Our interview with McRobert after a great fight resulted in his consent to join our scheme on the understanding of the Coy giving them a liberal percentage for good will. The position of the NWT Cy has altered greatly in their favour since McRobert joined them, putting in 1½ lakhs himself, they have closed their share list with six lakhs subscribed against 1½ lakhs eight months ago. McRobert has great faith in leather for when we offered to pay the NWT Cy in cash to simplify matters, he volunteered that they would prefer taking part in cash and the rest in shares.

The meeting to launch the Imperial Tanning and Leather Manufacturing Company Ltd on the London stock market took place at Leadenhall Street at 11.30 a.m. on 14 October between Cruickshank and Sutherland, two of the Begg Dunlop partners, and their broker, and Gavin Jones and Wishart. Jones described the meeting as 'long and satisfactory' but had to prepare Stewart for a disappointment and a change of plan. The broker advised that the state of the market precluded any chance of a successful launch. It was therefore decided that Cruickshank and Wishart should leave for India shortly to form a syndicate to raise 5 or 6 lakhs in Calcutta and for Wishart to buy up the Stewart Tannery and the North West Tannery on the best terms possible. 'We all anticipate some difficulty with McRobert.' The intention was to work the two factories and then organise a company to take over the businesses as going concerns. Begg Sutherland were to finance the syndicate; 'if no hitch occurs with McR the matter will be plain sailing and the object will be sooner accomplished.' This adversely affected the financial inducements on offer to both Jones and Stewart but Jones nevertheless booked a passage for 3 November with his wife and their daughter Eva. He hoped Stewart would be happy with the new terms and come out to be in Cawnpore before Christmas. 'I consider your presence at Cawnpore of great importance so hope you will accept the proposal. This arrangement is to be kept perfectly secret as the fact of the Coy not having been floated leaking out will prejudice negotiations with the NWT Cy as McRobert is certain to take advantage of it, therefore please keep it very quiet.'

Luck was not with the syndicate. The year had been one of severe famine, the monsoon had failed with disastrous results, and money was scarce. Jones arrived just before Christmas and asked Wishart to wire Stewart to the effect that in spite of all their high hopes the scheme must be put in abeyance until more favourable conditions prevailed on the Calcutta market. 'Bank of Bengal rates are 10%, quite unprecedented and 14% has to be paid for loans on good security, you will understand from this how difficult it is to raise the wind. I am working the matter quietly with Wishart and now that good rains have fallen in those parts hope that matters will soon be easier.'

For Jones the disappointment in the hold-up of the scheme was to some extent mitigated by his delight in being back in Cawnpore. He was astonished and excited by the progress that had taken place in the last ten years. He wrote to Stewart:

> Cawnpore is greatly changed, the mills and factories are developing enormously and new schemes are on foot to start large cotton mills, tanneries and iron works on an extensive scale. It will interest you immensely to see the old place.
>
> The divi divi[9] around the H and S Fry has grown and the entire surroundings are most beautiful, some fine houses have sprung up on the civil side all showing great progress and prosperity of the community, land has advanced in value several hundred percent and sites for houses and works are extremely scarce, houses with large compounds are being divided and dwelling houses created on them, the Simla Bank is building a house that will rival the Bank of Bengal and the old Bungalow with its familiar thatched roof is a thing of the past, pucka houses have displaced them throughout, whilst the cantonments look the same dilapidated forsaken place as of old, the contrast is quite remarkable.
>
> I hope you will be able to see the old place, to those who knew it in the fifties the change is very interesting.

His letter ends on a personal note. 'My wife and Eva are both very well, thoroughly enjoying the change. We have taken half this house, old Noor Mahomed's Hotel, we are very comfortable.' It was

Mahomed's Hotel in which the Nana Sahib made his headquarters in 1857 and later that same year it was to Mahomed's Hotel that Jones, Edwards and Probyn were led when they arrived wretched and emaciated after three months in hiding from the mutineers. William Russell, the *Times* correspondent in 1858, had also stayed there. Stewart would not need to be reminded of the association with the name and place.

On 21 January 1897 Jones wrote to Stewart in what was to be the last letter in this particular correspondence. Not only did he have to admit there were difficulties on the Calcutta market but he had also misjudged the response from Cawnpore itself. Since he had last been in Cawnpore Hindu attitudes against handling the leather trade had hardened. Resourceful as ever, Jones turned his hand to another area of development, a foundry and engineering works so that mill repairs could be handled in Cawnpore and not have to rely on Great Britain and Calcutta.

The tightness of the money market has been too much for BD and Co in Calcutta and BS and Co in Cawnpore and there is no prospect of improvement till the next monsoons set in. The winter rains have been good in general and as I write there is every appearance of more in those provinces, so that the famine apprehensions are over but as the last rains failed at the end of the season the poor man's food was insufficient, hence the scarcity which will continue till the next Kharif crops are assured, the rabbi will turn out well throughout the country with the moisture ample now to develop the flourishing crops.

I have been very disappointed with my native friends whose prejudices prevent giving support to our scheme, they were very ready in '87 to put in lakhs into my scheme but shy off now – old Tulshiram was as eager then as can be, now he too pleads the objection of his 'bhai-bands'. They offer me not ten but twenty lakhs to go into cotton spinning or *any other* industry but leather they cannot touch! I have not given up the matter and as there is not so much prejudice against manufactured leather work, I proposed to them to separate the two and have a Leather Factory in which the Hindus may join without doing violence to their religious feelings, they are inclined to listen to this and if I can get one or two big men to come in the others will follow like sheep. There is no hitch with the NWT Cy but no progress has been made towards an amalgamation owing chiefly to want of success on our part to get the capital, they however do not know this and things are kept in profound darkness not to show our hand. CA and Co are extending their works very largely and although they know that the Imperial is looming they are very nervous about the future of their own monopoly.

You will hardly believe it that travellers have appeared from Austria and other parts offering to purchase hundreds of thousands of pairs of boots for the continental markets but no one has time to accept the orders. I fully anticipated that Cawnpore would become a great leather manufactory and would probably rival Northampton, it makes me impatient when I think of my inability to seize the opportunity and those wretched Hindus with their prejudices holding back.

In the mean time I am starting a foundry and Engineering works with a small capital, there is a very good opening for it now and I hope to lay the foundation for a good rising concern in the near future but I will not rest till the Imperial is floated, I am working the Mahomedans, unfortunately they are not wealthy nor are they so enterprising as the Hindus.

I don't think you need bottle up the secret of the Imperial project, it is everybody's property now only no one knows what the projectors are doing.

He called the new enterprise The Empire Engineering Co. Ltd.[10]

To his surprise and dismay, with one exception, he received no encouragement or support from the firms in Cawnpore. It was not until several years later that this mystery was explained. So great was Jones's reputation as a pioneer that rumours had circulated that this new enterprise was just a means of raising finance to start a new cotton mill or leather works. Jones found himself combating a boycott that crippled the development of his new scheme. The ensuing heavy losses nearly wrecked the enterprise. It was only his faith in himself and his determination to persevere, even if without support, that staved off catastrophe.

He was joined by his son Tracy Gavin Jones, the only one of the boys to go into business. As a child Tracy had such poor physique and limited sight that the family feared for his future. When he left Clifton, however, he set out in 1895 for what was then Rhodesia with a bag of carpenter's tools and £10 in his pocket. This was the time when Cecil Rhodes was extending the railway in Africa and Tracy trained as a mining engineer. During the Matabele war he served with the Rhodesia

Cawnpore wedding, Gavin Jones seated left.

Horse and narrowly escaped with his life. Thereafter he returned to Cawnpore which was to be his home for the next fifty years.

Father and son built up the Empire Engineering Works, extending the foundry and sawmills with the most modern machinery until it was hailed as the largest and most progressive engineering shop in Upper India. 'They were capable of building a bridge or making a railway waggon down to the shaping of a bolt.'[11] The contract for the supply of keys to the railways was one of their small successes.[12] In all they did they were keen exponents of the real Swadeshi cult, that India must be self-supporting.

Gavin Jones finally left Cawnpore in 1907. The Imperial never came to be floated and John Stewart did not return to Cawnpore. The North West Tannery continued an independent existence, the Stewart Tannery in Agra was sold to a German, G. von der Wense, an Agra merchant, who brought the entire factory to Cawnpore and built a modern plant at Juhi. He tempted W. B. Shewan, the highly experienced tanner from NWT, to join him, and *Shewan Sahib ka chumra* became a household name for the best leather. But no one was able to knock

Cooper Allen from the secure position they had established for themselves in the leather industry.

The Cawnpore Tent Club

There is a photograph (opposite) in the Maxwell family album of a group posed under the spreading branches of a peepul tree out at Gungaganj.[13] It was taken on Christmas Day 1896 when the members of the Cawnpore Tent Club, having completed their pigsticking activities, had been joined by the ladies. Possibly La Reine and Eva were among the bystanders. Jones had confided to Stewart that 'my wife is quite herself, as active and animated as in her youth! She and Eva have gone off to see a pig-sticking meet. . .'

Ralph Maxwell had been secretary of the Cawnpore Tent Club since 1870 and his name was linked with its reputation for excellent sport. Meets were attended by men from as far afield as Lucknow and the variety of the sport had been further enhanced when canal officers joined the field and made canal bungalows and towpaths available. These 'Reminiscences of a Secretary' appeared in the *Hog Hunter's Annual*.

> Hunting on the canal was different to that in the Kadir and one had to be educated to it. Parties on either side of the canal riding abreast at one and the same time, but having a few Spears on either side to force the pig to break into the open country by entering the plantations and heading him, where fencing in and out of baghs gave us a change from the monotony of the lie of 'Kuttri' on the banks of the Ganges. Moreover, the canal imparted a pleasant coolness and shade on the tow path and the walk home of an evening after hunting – it might be two or three miles – to camp was delightful. The bridges were three miles apart and one pair of young sportsmen, new to the game, rode a pig three miles from one bridge to the next, and then brought him back again to the line of Spears who had not started in pursuit as the pig was a small one. Though disappointed at losing their quarry they had thoroughly enjoyed the gallop.
>
> So far as I was personally concerned, arriving at the camp, I was much interested in the dusk of the evening watching from one of the bridges pig emerging from the plantations on either side, stand listening for a moment, and then trot off to their night's feeding ground in the open. In this way one could pretty well tell what

Christmas Day meet at Gungaganj, 1896.

prospect there was of sport on the morrow. It was also interesting to watch, during the day, bird life of more or less brilliant plumage and butterflies of every hue. Canal hunting was capital sport and exciting, and anybody's pig when he crossed and recrossed the canal.

The canal did not always run full, and on one occasion, on a dry day when three Spears only turned up at the meet, it was agreed to ride independently of each other. The pig were to be driven from some high grass growing on a high ridge adjacent to the canal and towards the canal. When the beat began it was noticed that a difference of opinion existed between John Watson (13th Hussars) and his mount, and he was presently shot out of the saddle. Cruickshank (ICS author of *Over the Valley, Over the Level*, etc) on the right meanwhile went after a pig early, then my chance came and I accounted for one before he reached the canal. Changing horses I was again riding, this time after a pig down the dry bed of the canal, which, in a short while, he left and sought shelter in a dhak jungle close by. Being alone, I was puzzled how to act, but feeling certain he would break and retrace his steps, I got under cover and waited patiently for some time; presently he showed himself, pausing for a moment, and made straight back for the dry bed of the canal. I let him get out of sight and then went in hot pursuit. We were not long in the canal before we were out again as the sluices above had been opened and a big body of water came rushing down. I think the pig must have sensed it as, until I saw him nip up the bank, I wasn't aware of what threatened. I killed him shortly after.

An amusing incident occurred at a meet at Patrarah on the Hamirpore Road. For some time it seemed as if we were going to have a blank morning, sounders were seen but no warrantable boar, and at last all, seemingly, returned to camp weary of doing nothing. I remained behind to confer with Prag and some of the Natives

Sketch from The Hoghunter's Annual, *vol. 2, 1929.*

about, when suddenly a distant view halloa fell on our ears. I galloped to it and found 'Bara' Payne (2nd Queen's and afterwards on the Staff of General Sir George Richardson in Ireland) gazing intently at a bush beneath which lay a huge boar. We pricked him out and soon were alongside of him. On receiving the spear he began to dodge about among the corinda bushes and I lost sight of him for a moment. Presently I heard a voice shouting 'Maxwell, Maxwell, where are you? I've been tossed into a "gooseberry" bush and the pig is trying to get at me.' And in this predicament I found him on turning the bush. I couldn't help laughing at the sight – there was Payne right in the middle of a 'wait-a-bit' thorn bush kicking all he knew to ward off the pig. The pig, spotting me as I came round the bush, left Payne and charged straight at me and got his quietus at once. I released Payne from his couch on the thorny 'gooseberry' bush and he was well pleased it was all over. When we got back to camp great surprise was expressed and Jennings twitted me for what he termed my 'pocket boar'; but the laugh was on our side.[14]

Not all the incidents out hunting were so innocuous. Pigsticking was a violent sport. If the pig jinked and a horseman was unseated he could be most savagely gored. In 1865 the *Pioneer* reported the district superintendent of police was very nearly killed when his spear broke and stuck in the pig leaving him defenceless. Favourite horses fell or were gored and had to be shot. On one occasion a boar was hunted and killed in the Memorial Well Gardens; another time the cry went up that a boar had been seen in the city and the secretary was sent for at 5 a.m. It charged through the narrow lanes chased by the crowd and was finally killed at Sarrafa Bazaar.

Maggie Maxwell, Hugh Maxwell's second daughter, lost a son at the sport. She had followed Chattie to the altar and married Dr William Cherry in February 1871. In 1898 the camp was held at Hajipur Bagh. Bertie Cherry had recently joined the Elgin Mills as an assistant, proud to join the family concern. Like all the Maxwells he was a keen horseman. On the Saturday, while beating the *jheel* and high grass, the first spear went to Bertie Cherry. A short distance further on another pig appeared and after a long run through grass Cherry was again first spear. A tall, slender young man, with tight blond curls, he was a hero at the camp fire that evening. Next day, Sunday, a boar broke cover near the tents. Cherry chased it, the boar jinked to the left across the pony, bringing it

The Cherry family, Bertie in centre.[15]

down violently. The boar was killed and Cherry was picked up unconscious and carried back to Cawnpore. He never regained consciousness,
the base of his skull was fractured.

Such was the fame of the Cawnpore Tent Club that visiting bigwigs
were often entertained to sport, although those occasions were not always included in the Log Books. The story of Lord Mayo's disastrous
meet in 1870 was only disclosed later and Ralph Maxwell was prevailed
upon to describe two others – 'which were communicated to me by
General Sir George Richardson, to whom I wrote for dates':

Richardson (6th B.C.), after showing him some sport at Allahabad,
sent on to me Count Tisza. We dubbed him 'Count' for brevity,
though his brother, the Prime Minister of Austro-Hungary, was
really the Count – a Magyar and a *homo ad unguem* ['a man to his
fingertips']. He had provided himself with a couple of Arabs in
Bombay, and rode as all Austrians do. We gave him two days'
pigsticking at Bardhunna and got six pig. On getting a first spear
he jumped off his horse and embraced us all round. On the last

evening on adjournment to camp, complimentary speeches were exchanged over glasses of 'Pommery' as a pick me up before dinner. Before leaving, the Count asked me to look him up at Budha-Pesth on my way home, which I did, but he was engaged in his Parliamentary duties and we only saw him in the House making a speech.[16]

The third was a pigsticking meet at Pariell, given by the Chief Commissioner of Oudh to the Prince of Wales [later King Edward VII]. Barrow (Deputy Commissioner of Oudh) and I were engaged for several days having the dry ditches – the ground was intersected by them – shaved, but in spite of those precautions several saddles were emptied and Lord Carrington had the misfortune to break his collar bone. General Sam Browne controlled the line of beaters from an elephant. At lunch (Kellners' E.I.R.) waiters failed to turn up with the champagne, but fortunately Mrs Maynard, wife of the District Superintendent of Police, produced a couple of bottles, brought in case of accidents, from her howdah, so all went well for the Prince; but outsiders had to be content with the modest whisky and soda. On return to camp a small

'Death of the Pig': *from series by E. Hobday, 1907.*

repast was indulged in, and the ten pig, the day's sport, were displayed on a mound turfed with green sods and with a fountain playing in the centre – Barrow's idea – and very refreshing it looked.

But the star turn of the Club was Prag, the Tent Club *shikari*. He was a great standby at both canal and *kuttri* meets and really Ralph Maxwell's private servant.

He was my garden coolie in 1865 when quite a youngster. Perceiving that he was an intelligent youth I took him on as my *Shikari* and a keener one I have never come across. He accompanied me as such on many a shooting expedition, and for marking snipe and quail I have never met his equal. He was a goatherd by caste. On the Jumna Ravines, when out ravine deer shooting, he milked many a goat for my bottle of cold tea. I taught him to ride early, and when I became Secretary of the C.T.C., I put him into pink. John Watson provided him with a hunting cap which was discarded later for the puggri as being unsuitable for the climate. He could ride and kill a pig if required, but it was very seldom that he was allowed to use the spear. I never sent him out for khabar as the Club had Chuprassis for the purpose, but he was good at sifting khabar and never let us down.

An excellent caricature of him was painted by Shand, D.P.W. One hangs in the Station Club at Cawnpore and another, a duplicate, was presented to me by the C.T.C. and now hangs in my study in London, the centre of a group of pigsticking pictures by Captain Hobday. When I took it to be framed, the shop attendant asked me if it was usual for natives to ride pigs.

This picture and his story, written by Alex Shakespear,[17] appeared in the *Hog Hunter's Annual*, 1929, vol. 2.

Let me tell you something about Prag, who I imagine held a record for service with any Tent Club in India. I believe he is first mentioned in the Log of the Cawnpore Tent Club in 1863 [in fact the Logs date only from 1869] and he was with the Club when I rode my last pig in 1907.

When I use the words 'service with any Tent Club', I should explain that he was really in the service of Mr R.W. Maxwell, the Grand Old Man of the Cawnpore Tent Club, although he was permitted by his master to act as Club shikari. He died only a few

Prag.

years ago and I think his years must have numbered more than three score and ten, although, when I used to question him about his age, his only answer was that he was as old as 'Maxwell Sahib'.

For knowledge of pig craft, I have never met his equal, and when he was younger and his eyesight was good, his ability to detect the size and sex of pig at long distances was nothing short of marvellous. I never used to hesitate if I heard Prag give a 'View Holloa' and I seldom found he was at fault. He was always extraordinarily keen and often riding back with him to camp in the evening, I have been mightily entertained with his tales of the hunting of bygone days. He was a beautiful horseman, with perfect hands and a very deadly spear – often I have known him assist very materially in accounting for some pig when a party, much reduced in numbers by misadventures of kinds, had lost their pig.

Prag was possessed of an almost uncanny instinct in picking up the line of a pig, just as some huntsmen have with a fox, when hounds are at fault. I recounted one incident in which Prag played a valiant part; the late Alec Cunningham, of the Gordons, was hunting with us and, after being alone with the pig for some distance and separated from the rest of the party, he took a bad toss which laid him and his horse out. Prag had seen him coming down and managed to get up just in time to divert the attention of the boar and induce it to charge him as it was on the point of attacking Cunningham who was on the ground and helpless. He was an enthusiastic advocate of the overhand spear, which was compulsory with the Cawnpore Tent Club till recent years and when the under hand grip was made admissible, I am sure he thought that pigsticking was going to the dogs.

He always accompanied Mr Maxwell on his shooting expeditions and I have never met his equal for finding a snipe, however difficult the ground. Even in his old age, his power of endurance was nothing short of wonderful and often after a long day after snipe, I have known Prag to walk fifteen miles home and think nothing of it.

It is a good many years ago now, but I still remember a boar that Prag and I accounted for under most exciting circumstances. We were riding home in the twilight, only three of us and two of those novices, after having got four pig, and Prag and I were a good distance in advance of the others. When passing a thick clump of grass, we almost stepped on a large pig – I was sitting loosely in the saddle and the pony I was riding performed various acrobatic feats which very nearly brought me off. We could just see the pig make off and he took a line across a series of nullahs, which would have been difficult to negotiate in broad daylight, but which it was madness to attempt in the failing light; however, Prag shouted to me to come on and we both set to it. How we got across those nullahs and on to level ground beyond, I could not tell you – I was riding a very clever Arab pony who always seemed to have a leg to spare and well! we achieved the apparently impossible, picked up the pig on the other side of the nullahs and eventually despatched him. I remember we then very solemnly shook hands. We had to leave the pig where he lay, as the beaters were far away and the shades of night were falling fast.

'The Immortal Joe Lee'

In all probability the travellers from Austria offering to purchase thousands of pairs of shoes for the Continental market stayed at the Railway Hotel run by 'the immortal Joe Lee'. Shrewdly he had kept a visitor's book in which travellers were encouraged to enter remarks. They found the hotel 'snug', 'clean and comfortable', 'conveniently close to the railway station', 'the service good'. But most of all they came to visit the one where the worst horrors of the Mutiny took place. Joe Lee, as a Mutiny veteran with first-hand knowledge, was able to satisfy their morbid curiosity.

It was an extraordinary story. Joe Lee was a Welshman, born in 1829, one of twenty-two children of a farmer with a smallholding near Shrewsbury. He claimed he had joined the 53rd Regiment of Foot, the Shropshires, and arrived in Calcutta in 1844. He served in several campaigns, being wounded at Sobraon, and in particular the Mutiny campaign where he won the Mutiny Medal with clasps for the Relief of Lucknow and the Relief of Cawnpore. He left the Army in 1865 to better himself in civilian life. After some years on the railway and on a tea garden in Darjeeling, he decided to retire to England. But while at Allahabad arranging his passage home he saw the Railway Hotel, Cawnpore, advertised for sale in the *Pioneer*. He bought it and for the next thirty years he and his wife made a nice little business running it.

Joe Lee published a little booklet[18] that visitors could use as a guide to Mutiny sites and events. Over a game of billiards people would attempt to draw him out and question him more. It did not take much persuasion to arrange for Joe to take them on a guided tour. The Revd H. D. Williamson, travelling with his daughter, made a typical entry in the visitor's book: 'Quite satisfied. Mr Lee most attentive in showing us the sights of Cawnpore. He gives thrilling details as an eye witness such as can be obtained from no book or pamphlet. Everyone who wishes to see Cawnpore well [no pun!], should obtain the services of Mr Lee as chaperon. 26 Oct 1881.'

As time went on it became apparent that Joe Lee was on to a good thing with his Mutiny tours. Some Cawnpore residents, however, began a whispering campaign that he was a bit of a fraud and could not possibly have been present at all the events he claimed. When a *bona fide* Mutiny veteran, William Forbes-Mitchell,[19] who had served as a sergeant in the 93th Sutherland Highlanders, visited Cawnpore and put up at Lee's Railway Hotel, they asked him to check up on Joe and, if possible, catch him out.

An article duly appeared in *The Statesman*. First, Forbes-Mitchell described his impressions of Cawnpore thirty-five years after the Mutiny events when as part of Sir Colin Campbell's advance he had crossed the Canal under a blistering fire from thirty-six well-served heavy guns of the Gwaliors.

> On the 19th August 1892 I stood on the top of the Cawnpore Woollen Mills, and counted *thirty-six* chimneys of sizes belching out smoke from more than three times that number of steam boilers; and in my perambulations through Cawnpore I paused at each of the Mills, and I dare say many of the Managing Directors and Managers must have considered me a most inquisitive globetrotter (rather early in the season), when I invariably asked them the number of natives employed in each Mill, and the amount of wages paid, monthly, for only *native* labour. But as a rule I got a straight answer to a straight question, and when I got back to my room in Lee's Railway Hotel, and totalled up the figures, I found that the European industries of Cawnpore are paying, *monthly,* an average of Rs. 1,36,000 for *native* labour alone!!! Month after month, throughout the year, this amount of money is being expended by the European industries and European enterprise of Cawnpore, and, without a single exception, every one of those industries has been built up by independent European enterprise, and that within only the past quarter of a century.

William Forbes-Mitchell had been entertained by Mrs McRobert and Mrs Johnson, wife of the Muir Mills director, and was impressed by what he called the 'Captains of Industry, the Field Marshals, Generals and Brigadiers'. Mr Ledgard, the same man with whom Gavin Jones had quarrelled, was now with William Cooper on the point of retirement, virtually running Cooper Allen with 'a Division of nearly twice the numerical strength of the force with which Sir John Campbell retook Cawnpore from the grasp of the Gwalior Contingent'. Ralph Maxwell was eager to take Forbes-Mitchell to the top of the mill chimney at Elgin but McRobert had forestalled him and already shown the visitor the view from the terrace of the third storey at Cawnpore Woollen Mills. But it was Joe Lee who really caught Forbes-Mitchell's eye.

> In this notice of my friends in Cawnpore, there is one individual who deserves a whole chapter to himself: that is, the immortal Joe Lee, and I must devote the rest of this chapter to informing the readers of the *Statesman*

HOW I DISCOVERED JOE LEE
—MY OLD FRIEND 'DOBBIN', OF 1857

I had never seen Joe Lee, nor heard of him to the best of my belief. When I revisited Cawnpore on the 19th August, 1892, I then heard of him from several gentlemen resident there, and, I may as well say at once, that the general opinion was, that Joe Lee was addicted to expanding the truth with regard to what he had seen of the events of the Mutiny of 1857. Some enemy had spread a report, that Joe had not actually seen anything of Cawnpore and the scenes which he so graphically described. . . I was inclined to believe it more than likely, that I would find Joe Lee more or less a humbug. I, accordingly, returned through Cawnpore *via* Jhansi, arriving by the mail train, I. M. Railway, from Bombay and allowed myself to be annexed by Joe Lee's man at the Railway Station. I soon after found myself in a comfortable room in Lee's Hotel, and, after a bath and chota hazree, I requested an interview with mine host. I introduced myself as a commercial traveller from New York, who had been with General Lee in Virginia. He asked me all about New York, which he had himself lately visited on a pleasure trip to America. I was, however, not prepared for this, and was in danger of falling into the pit I had dug for Joe Lee, for I knew nothing whatever about 'Brooklyn Bridge', 'Manhattan Island' &c, &c, so I had to plead that I was very tired, and gladly accepted a copy of Joe's book, *The Indian Mutiny and Events at Cawnpore during* 1857, to read, before starting to visit, with my host as my guide, the scenes described.

From the first interview I was convinced I had seen Joe Lee in 1857, although 35 years had considerably altered him; but I remembered his voice more than his features. So we had barely started on our round, when I asked him if he ever heard of a man, a Sergeant, I believed, in the 53rd, by the name of Dobbin, who had called to Sir Colin Campbell, the Commander-in-Chief, on the 16th November

'57, in front of the Secundrabagh, 'Let the two thirds at 'em, Sir Colin, and we'll soon make short work of those murdering villains.' When I asked this, Joe drew himself together in his buggy, and, looking me straight in the face, replied, 'By Jove, how do you know about that? I am Sergeant Dobbin; it was I who called to Sir Colin. How came you to know about it?' I replied, 'I read it in America in a history of the Indian Mutiny', to which Joe replied, 'I have never seen that mentioned in any history I have read.' I replied by asking how it happened that 'Sergeant Dobbin' of 1857 could become 'Joe Lee' of 1893? 'Oh! that is easily explained,' said Joe, "Dobbin" was a nick-name given to me from a character which I used to represent on the stage, and all the officers and men knew me better by the name of "Dobbin" than they did by my real name.' I need not take up the time of my readers with all my conversation with Joe Lee. Let it suffice to say that it was most amusing. I made him take me all over the route by which the 42nd, 53rd and 93rd advanced against the Gwalior Contingent on the 6th December 1857, all through the city, past the Memorial Gardens and Well, &c., &c., past where the Fort stood (now Government Harness Factory), and every now and again Joe would draw up the horse, stare at me, and exclaim, 'By Jove you have read history to some purpose. I have shown many visitors over Cawnpore, but I have never before met one who remembered details like you.' This went on, till we finally got to the Memorial Church on our way back from Suttee Choura Ghat, where Wheeler's force was destroyed by the treachery of the Nana, and at every detail of history which I remembered, Joe began to question me the more closely on his side. At length when we got to the church, Joe became so excited, when describing all about the massacre and pointing out names on the tablets, that he actually commenced to cry, and the tears ran down his cheeks; and it was almost as bad with myself, but my emotion was caused more through suppressing laughter, because, all this time, I firmly believed that Joe was describing what he had not seen, that is, I believed he had seen just as much as I had done myself, and nothing more, and all his descriptions about gathering the bodies of the murdered women and children, putting them into the well, and so forth, I believed to be an expansion of fact. However, when we got to the church I brought out another incident connected with my former acquaintance 'Dobbin', which I had kept in reserve. I may as well explain that on a campaign every soldier carries his own tin-pot, in which he receives his grog, &c., and Sergeant Dobbin had a famous tin-pot, made of double block-tin, ornamented with drawings of the regimental colours and with all the honours engraved on it, also the 'Retreat from Lucknow' and the 'Relief of Cawnpore'. I saw a cook-boy of the 53rd with this highly ornamented tin-pot, and I annexed it for my own use. But when we were encamped at Cawnpore, Sergeant Dobbin sent a notice through the camp, offering a reward for the recovery of his tin-pot, which, his cookboy had reported, was annexed by a corporal of the 93rd, and the reward offered was a quart bottle of grog; so I took back the tin-pot to Sergeant Dobbin, and in return he filled my water flask with rum, and pretended that he valued the tin-pot because of the beautiful manner in which it was engraved. But I had found out the real reason. The tin-pot was what old soldiers called a Bagdader tin-pot. It had a false bottom to it, and two drams of rum could be so cleverly concealed, in the bottom, that the pot might pass inspection as empty. This was the reason Joe Lee, *alias* 'Dobbin', was so anxious for its recovery. However, when I returned the tin-pot, I did not tell him that I had discovered its secret compartment, and Sergeant Dobbin was careful enough not to enlighten me. Well, when we were in the church, and Joe had described most of the tablets and wept with excitement, I suddenly asked him if he remembered the incident of Dobbin's tin-pot being lost on the 'Retreat from Lucknow'. Joe Lee at once dried his tears, and, looking me straight in the face, said, 'You have seen Cawnpore before, and you know more about the Mutiny that you pretend to do. In what history did you find an account of my tin-pot? I have had my suspicions of you for some time. You know too much. I believe you are the corporal who brought back my tin-pot!' Then I was obliged to own up, for being in the church, I could not bring myself to carry the deception further.

On returning to the Hotel, Joe Lee brought me his old regimental records, in which I found the following duly attested entries: 'Corporal Joseph Lee, Regimental Number, 3167; served in the 53rd Regiment, Shropshire Light Infantry, under Sir Colin Campbell, in the Peshawar Valley, 1851 and 1852; served throughout the Mutiny campaigns, 1857, 1858 and 1859; Relief of Lucknow from 10th to 24th November; Relief of Cawnpore, 1st to 6th December 1857; Serai Ghat, 9th December 1857; Kali Nadi

Bridge, 2nd January 1858; Shumshabad, 28th January 1858; Storming and Capture of Miangunge, 23rd February 1855; Siege of Lucknow, from 2nd to 19th March 1858; Kursi, 24th March 1858; Passage of the Gogra, 25th March 1858; Action at Bungaon, 3rd December 1858; Tulsipore, 23rd December 1858. Mutiny Medal with two clasps. Wounded in left arm at Cawnpore on the 5th December 1857.

So much for my interview with Joe Lee. Of course, I will not guarantee that Joe does not occasionally expand the truth by mixing up what has been told to him with what he has seen, but, taking him all round, there are but few Europeans, now alive, who know, from personal knowledge, more about Cawnpore in 1857, than Joe Lee does, and I cannot close this account of my revisit without stating my belief that Cawnpore without Joe Lee would be equal to an edition of Shakespeare with Hamlet expurgated, or Robbie Burns without Tam o'Shanter, or with Holy Willie's Prayer, all cut out. Joe Lee is an institution in himself that Cawnpore cannot afford to lose, and I advise the good people of Cawnpore to cherish him as one of the ornaments of their station, and adopt the advice of the poet towards him – 'Be to his faults a little blind, Be to his virtues very kind'. . .

Joe Lee *was* with the 53rd at the Secundrabagh on the 16th November '57 – I stole his tin-pot at Bunnec Bridge on the 28th November – I returned it to him at Cawnpore about the 3rd December – so I *am positive* that Joe Lee saw as much of the Mutiny as I saw myself. So much for my direct evidence; and here I will end this chapter.

(Sd.) WILLIAM FORBES-MITCHELL
Late 93rd Highlanders

Great-Aunt Emma's Visit

Great-Aunt Emma was one of the many tourists to visit Cawnpore. She set off alone for a two-year trip, staying with relations in America, Australia and now India. She arrived ten days before Christmas 1887 and stayed three months with her brother, Alfred Butterworth, and his wife Polly, who lived at The Palms, in the shadow of the Cawnpore Woollen Mills, next door to the Lahmli Club and opposite the Christ Church school and mission for orphan girls.[20]

The McRoberts driving out from Sheiling House.

That first evening at a small dinner party Great-Aunt Emma was introduced to Mr and Mrs Shewan of the North West Tannery and Mr Anderson of Cooper Allen and learnt that the Butterworths were part of a well-knit group of friends that included Mr and Mrs Bond of NWT and Mr Priestley, the sculptor, and his second wife.[21] They met every Wednesday at the Shewans for a musical evening and took it in turns to play host each Saturday and Sunday, returning home on Sundays from church service for dinner and whist. At the musical evenings Alfred sometimes played the harmonium, his favourite piece being 'The Lost Chord'. No lady would think of going out to dinner without her music and a good singing voice was greatly admired. Apart from Alfred and Polly, Great-Aunt Emma addressed everyone formally, never by a Christian name. The hours set aside for making and receiving calls were 12 noon to 2 p.m. and 4.30 to 6 p.m.[22] Next day the serious matter of making 'calls' began. The first was to Mrs McRobert, who returned the call the following day. 'It is the strange custom here for strangers to call on the residents – except in the case of a bride arriving – so have fulfilled the requirements though do not admire it.' Great-Aunt Emma was also startled at social events to hear the speaker address his audience 'Gentlemen and Ladies'.

She was taken to all the Mutiny sites, not once but several times. On the very day she arrived, as soon as she had unpacked she was driven to the Memorial Well Gardens for her to pay respects to Cawnpore's place in history, although they did not stay long as it was already getting dark. Twice she drove out to Suttee Chowra Ghat, the scene of the massacre at the boats, and stood 'in sad thoughtfulness gazing at the sacred Ganges'. Twice she visited the Memorial Church, examining all the inscriptions and admiring the memorials in the church windows. She explored Wheeler's Entrenchment, following the map and tracing the foundations of the ruined buildings, picturing how it must have looked during the siege. Another day she drove the long distance out to the Savada Kothi where nothing but a flight of steps remained of the building that had housed the Nana Sahib's prisoners. She was also lent books about the whole sad episode and copied chunks of the story into her diary.

While the average tourist only came to Cawnpore to see the Mutiny sites, Great-Aunt Emma could get a sense of what it was really like for a European to live in Cawnpore. One of the first priorities was a visit to the Lalimli Mills where Alfred Butterworth was manager.

View of Suttee Chowra Ghat.

Cawnpore Woollen Mills.

This morning Alfred took me through the Woollen Mill, which is an extensive one, employing over 2,000 hands. They make a great variety of goods, blankets for use in hospital – army – & otherwise. Serges for military use, European & native, with firmer serges for gentlemen's clothing. Shawl wraps used so much by the natives, socks, gloves & cardigan jackets. Tussa silk is spun & woven, Tussa silk & worsted braids are manufactured. Thick felting for saddle linings & putties – a band about 4½ inches wide for wrapping round & round the legs of natives – more particularly servants; in fawn, scarlet, & other colours. There is also a tailoring department, where amongst other garments greatcoats for army wear are largely made. Was conveyed by 'Lift' to top storey, from there walking up a steep flight of steps to the roof of one portion of the mill, which is of course flat, & used for drying purposes; & where I obtained an extensive view of Cawnpore,[23] looking from this eminence like a huge wood, with the scattered buildings nestling amongst the trees, with here & there Mill chimneys towering above; the white buildings dotted about & peeping through the thick & extensive foliage: extending about 7 miles from outside point of Cantonments, to ditto Civil lines, & from this point I realised more fully the distances we so often drive in an evening when visiting various friends.

At the bungalow all was bustle and excitement over the preparations for Christmas. Four of the Butterworth children were at school in England, with only Cyril and Kitty at Cawnpore, but there was still a stream of friends from the mills driving up to deliver colourfully wrapped parcels for the children's pillow cases. Cyril and Kitty were beside themselves with anticipation. Polly Butterworth's Christmas cake and Christmas pudding recipes have been handed down in the family: hours of work went into the cleaning and preparation of the dried fruit, arms ached over the beating of the mixture. On Christmas Eve the treat was a visit to Noronha's on the Mall.

Just before dinner this evening drove down for a little shopping and to see 'Noronha's'[24] illuminated display, very brilliant on Xmas and New Year even, he is a large auctioneer also a proprietor, his grounds on these occasions are a blaze of light from thousands of little lamps, consisting of small earthenware saucers filled with oil, a wick resting on one edge, very primitive, but certainly effective, both gateways were arched and illuminated, & on the roof of one building, lamps formed large letters – into – A Happy Xmas – The Volunteers band played in the enclosure, swings and hobby horses were erected for the amusement of children. A jugglery performance going on in one building, where preparations were going on to form 3 lucky turn tables, filling them with tempting prizes for the evening competitors who were inclined to chance their luck at them.

On Christmas Day everyone was woken by a group of Indian Christian singers singing 'Once in Royal David's City', followed by several companies of natives with drum and cornet, 'and as the latter performer constantly fell short of wind, the former predominated; the tune of course indescribable, recalling the Chinese and Japanese style...' All through the morning a succession of Indian visitors called to pay their respects and bring baskets of sweets, fruit and vegetables and small toys for the children. The day ended with a party at the Shewans. Great-Aunt Emma suggested pinning on the donkey's tail and Mr Priestley sketched a donkey and cut it out. The blindfolded players enjoyed the fun.

For Boxing Day Alfred had arranged a special treat.

This morning Alfred accompanied me to the bazaar taking with us his *baboo* – office clerk or writer [used in a broader sense in the present day: i.e. any native who can read and write English is a *baboo*] – to show us about, and take us to a special Hindu Temple; our chief object. No leather is allowed inside these buildings, as belonging to the sacred animal the cow, & as I did not care to walk about in my stockinged feet, provided myself with my bedroom slippers of cork soles, & as we had to leave the carriage at the bottom of a steep, narrow lane, put those on before leaving it. This is a private temple, now belonging to two brothers, wealthy native bankers; it was their father's before them and since coming into their hands, has been, and still is, undergoing renovation, the work has now been going on for 3 years, and will take as long again, and has cost 10,000 rupees so far (and expected to cost as much again). It is a marvellous place, utterly beyond description, a blaze of shimmering glass, in all the colours of the rainbow, & in the most lovely designs imaginable, archways divide the centre square from the outer one, and every arch is different in design; formed by myriads of tiny pieces of glass, into flowers, birds, animals, & set designs of all kinds, tinsel braids, beaded ditto, & even brooches placed under glass, assisting; bevelled pier glass forming some of the centre pieces, strips of it in other places; this glass, & all the plain coloured pieces had come from England, but all the painted glass was Indian work. Rich and most elaborate chandeliers abounded, and the doors closing up the Gods in separate, and minor, temples were composed of massive German silver. We were introduced to both brothers, who were delighted to show and explain everything to us; also appearing much gratified at the pleasure it gave me, especially when Alfred told them I had been nearly round the world, had seen beautiful things, but never anything to equal that, and that I should tell all my friends in England about it on my return. We shook hands on taking leave; one of the brothers was greatly disfigured with the ravages of smallpox; it is a favourable opportunity to state that the natives consider that a great honour, and will seek smallpox in order to be pitted by it. There certainly is no accounting for taste.

The pleasure of Christmas week was marred by the death on 29 December of Mrs Mettam, one of the ladies in the Butterworths' circle of friends. She had been lying between life and death all week after the birth of her little son. The story of the Mettams' romance had quite caught the imagination of Cawnpore. Fourteen years earlier Mr Mettam, an accountant at Cooper Allen, had lost his heart to a young woman in England. She was so devoted to her ailing mother, however, that she felt unable to accept Mr Mettam's proposal. He returned alone to India, they ceased to correspond, but she remained very much on his mind. When eventually the mother died the young woman, anxious to try to trace Mr Mettam, came out to India and took a job as a music mistress at a school in Lucknow. Fate was kind – they met again and married almost immediately. Now after only two years of married life, she was dead. Great-Aunt Emma attended the funeral and noted that the corpse was carried from the hearse and lowered into the grave by personal friends. 'It was heart-rending to see the pale stony visage of the widower supported by Mr Anderson[25] and Mr Fraser whose wives had done so much for his wife. Tears came unbidden to the eyes of many.'

New Year's Eve was traditionally a big night of celebration in Cawnpore. For the McRoberts it also marked their wedding anniversary which they celebrated each year by giving a party at the Lalimli Club. Invitations for a dance had gone out to about fifty people but because of the gloom cast by Mrs Mettam's death the dance was postponed and a dinner party held instead. Toast after toast was drunk in champagne and the ladies did not rise from the table till ten o'clock. Music and games followed and on the stroke of midnight all gathered in a circle, arms crossed, to sing 'Auld Lang Syne'. Birthdays, anniversaries, welcome to a new bride (Mary Duckworth and Albert Silver had just returned from their honeymoon), welcome and farewell to visitors, all were meticulously observed. It is difficult to know if this was the natural coming together of expatriates far from their mother country, or whether in part they had absorbed the importance attached to ritual observations among the Indian people. But it was a distinct feature of life in India.

Except on mail day, when everything came to a halt for the precious letter to be written home, there was a non-stop round of social activities: a fête at the High School, prizegiving at the American Episcopal Mission where Mrs McRobert gave away the prizes, 'mostly dolls', a drive to the Cawnpore Club to hear the band of the Madras Infantry, a children's picnic organised by Mrs Shewan out at the Model Farm and a seven-mile drive out to Jajmau to watch a sham battle between the Volunteers and the Madras Infantry. Alfred Butterworth led the attacking party, which had to capture the old Jajmau fort – 'rather a formidable place to take, never the less they succeeded.' Great-Aunt Emma with Polly and the

Great-Aunt Emma (left) with the Butterworths, Kitty and Cyril at The Palms, Christmas Day 1897.

children joined the defeated garrison and climbed the mound to stand looking out over Oude, a 50-foot drop to the Ganges below. Two days later the roles were reversed but still the Volunteers succeeded in out-manoeuvring the Madras Infantry.

In March the weather was beginning to warm up and the Civil Lines Tennis Club held their 'At Home'.

A gay scene, & where there was no lack of good things in the way of cakes – sweets – fruits – creams – tea – coffee – claret cup, & cherry brandy. Three sets of Tennis, & three of Badminton could be played at once, to the strains of sweet music from the Volunteer Band, at the band stand in the pretty Queen's Park, where the At Home was held. Presently the sun went down – lamps were lit around the reception building, quickly followed by the moon appearing above the horizon like a ball of fire; rackets were discarded and dancing commenced. The Washington Post was all the rage.

Each Sunday the Butterworths attended a different church but Great-Aunt Emma was most impressed by the Westcotts at Christ Church and chose to attend there as often as possible.

> I enjoyed the service greatly. A Mr Westcott is the Vicar with a twin brother to assist him; they are the sons of the Bishop of Durham. Are most energetic workers combining mission work with the ordinary diocesan duties; devoting much time & money to the cause, while living themselves on the bare necessaries of life. The only time those brothers have ever been separated in their life, was when one took a trip home lately after a spell of sickness.

Great-Aunt Emma heard about the college and the homes and workshops for the orphan children that the Westcotts had established but repeated the generally prevalent reservations about the benefits of conversion to Christianity.

> Some of the men & boys work in the Mills during the day. But it is a general complaint, both in the Mills, & in private service, that when these people are Christianized & educated, they make very inferior work people, contending constantly they should have greater privileges granted them, living under the impression because they are Christianized they are on an equality with their employers, in private service intolerable, disobedient, insolent, & frequently far more dishonest. It is a well know fact that missionaries themselves will avoid employing Christianized native servants, & instead of it being a recommendation, it is a badge to be avoided. This sounds very dreadful & probably incredible, but it has come under my own notice; it is to be hoped, however, there are exceptions to this rule, as to all others.

In Mrs Anderson Great-Aunt Emma found a lively companion eager to show her Indian life. The Andersons' bungalow was on the river bank and from the garden they could watch the bathers 'saying their prayers while in the water, washing their extremely dirty garments and afterwards drinking of the water. . .'; but what surprised her was that they wrung out the wet clothes and put them on again. Mrs Anderson drove her to Nawabganj, where the old Broken Bridge spanned what had once been the road out to Bithoor, and they explored the hamlet of old Kanhpur, the village from which modern Cawnpore had grown. They walked round the ruins of the rajah's palace and Mrs Anderson, in conversation with a young Brahmin priest, asked him why the people

Behind the bungalow.

were not afraid of taking cold by putting on wet garments after bathing. He smiled. 'They are strong and do it for God,' he replied. Then,
back at home, Great-Aunt Emma was delighted by a visit to the servants' quarters to watch the coachman's wife knead and bake *chapattees*.
Much to the pleasure and satisfaction of the coachman's wife, Great-
Aunt Emma pronounced them delicious when dipped in a spiced *dal*.

Another excitement was an eclipse of the moon, followed almost
immediately by an eclipse of the sun which lasted three hours from
midday. It was not quite total, just a thin crescent visible. Thousands of
Indian people crowded the river *ghats* to see it, some protecting their eyes
by holding up exposed and developed photographic plates.

It has greatly upset the natives, most of them believing the world is
to come to an end today; yesterday drums were sounded through
the bazaar warning the people to be prepared, & told them to leave
their houses & remain in the open during the night, which advice
they carried out to the letter; the city deserted today, not a shop
open, so the cook had to buy in for the two days, yesterday morning, informing us he knew nothing could be bought today. The
Hindus will fast from last night to tomorrow morning, the sun not
being considered clean again till he rises afresh. And after the eclipse
they would all go to bathe in the Ganges to purify themselves; in

many instances remaining there for hours for safety. The *dhursee* (sewer) here begged us all to come out of the houses and shelter under the trees; said he was trembling all over, begged off for the rest of the day that he might find safety in the Ganges. All works have been closed, all sorts of rumours are afloat, terrible earthquakes are to take place, worse than any known before, by the end of this month only 10% of the people will be left alive in Cawnpore.

Three Indians in the river were reported drowned.

On the evening of 25 March Great-Aunt Emma accompanied her brother to a full-dress reception given by Lala Madho Ram – the same man who had been closely associated with William Cooper and who appeared to him in later life in spirit form:

> Madhoram, a venerable native banker, to honour the occasion of just having had conferred upon him the title of Rai Bahadur – something resembling knighthood. It has been conferred upon him by Government on account of his hard work, & great benevolence during the late famine. Before the Government commenced relief, he set apart a large building as a kind of refuge & fed as many as 700 daily, besides going himself constantly amongst the people to ascertain their condition, & relieve them. The proceedings opened with a little entertainment by a humourist in the Theatre, the Bahadur standing at the entrance to receive his guests. Alfred congratulated him & introduced me, he shook hands with both. After the entertainment we adjourned to the grounds surrounding the Theatre which were brilliantly illuminated, & where a large open tent was created, & made comfortable with carpet, chairs & lounges, & where refreshments were served; friends sitting in groups, or roaming about at their sweet will, to the strains of the Madras Infantry Band, altogether a bright & gay scene.

On Great-Aunt Emma's last Saturday a final party took place at the Andersons' – tennis, dinner out in the open, followed by whist. Great-Aunt Emma, partnering Mr Shewan, defeated Mrs Anderson and Mr Priestley, while the others looked on and applauded. On the Sunday the usual gathering of friends took place at the Priestleys' after church, where they enjoyed the novelty of the gramophone. Monday morning, packing done, Alfred and Polly, with nine other friends, came to the station to see Great-Aunt Emma safely into the train for Agra and the next part of her tour.[26] Four friends had called at the bungalow before she left to say goodbye. She noted in her diary that it had been a delightful visit and that she left Cawnpore with many regrets.

Bhagwatdas Temple: bathers at the ghat.

15

Empire at Its Zenith

The Plague Riot, 1900

Since 1896, the year Gavin Jones failed to raise the capital for his Imperial Leather Manufacturing Company, India had been experiencing a crop of natural disasters. Poor monsoons and widespread drought caused famine so severe that conditions in 1899/1900 were described as the worst for 200 years. This coincided with an outbreak of bubonic plague that started in Bombay, probably carried by rats on ships from the Far East. Very little was known about the disease except that it was highly infectious and resulted in a painful death in a matter of days. Government brought in stringent isolation measures by setting up plague hospitals and segregation camps. These measures, which often entailed entering people's homes to remove those who had been in contact with plague victims, were seen as a violation of privacy and deeply resented by the Indian people. Many ugly incidents took place in protest against them.[1]

In drawing up rules and guidance for dealing with plague conditions, Government had given much thought to the importance of taking the people into its confidence. The leaders of the Hindus and Muslims were consulted and the crucial need for quarantine and segregation explained to them. If segregation proved impractical in the patient's own home, it must be accepted that the plague victim had to be housed and cared for in a nearby hospital or temporary plague camp. But it was always understood that 'success depends mostly on the patience and dexterity of the officer in charge and his power over the people'.

Unfortunately in Cawnpore in 1900 neither the collector, Mr Hope, nor the civil surgeon, Colonel Barry, had patience or tact. It is true that in many cases plague victims came from homes where it was thought unlikely they would be properly cared for, but the civil surgeon had over-reacted. He had segregated an elderly lady, Manbhari, who could have been isolated with her grandchildren in her own large house even though other families were living there as well, and he had also unwisely insisted on sending a sick man, Bansi, all of three miles on a stretcher to the hospital camp, instead of allowing his family to set up a private hospital nearby.

The public in Cawnpore were alarmed, workers stayed away from the mills and meetings took place to discuss getting up a petition against this oppression. Some of the Europeans thought the leaders of the unrest were the leather workers, the *chamars,* others that it was the influential Marwaris, afraid that the privacy of their homes would be violated. This extract from a letter to the *Pioneer* from an anxious Indian is an indication of unease felt among the majority of Indian people at that time.

> . . . The Plague Act is in force but the doctors do not know what plague is. Fever, cold, ague, stomach ache, boils, &c., are all included in the diagnosis of plague. The ryot is oppressed on account of plague. No one hears the grievances and the Government punishes the aggrieved. This is great injustice.
>
> Of the Europeans, specially the inhabitants of England are known for their kindness and sympathy, and strange in their reign the ryot is so much oppressed. Government says it supports the ryots and protects them from plague, but in the eyes of serious consideration it kills them. No one fears plague but fears its law which is so much killing. Sick men die from fear only. An oppression on a friend of mine at Cawnpore was very great. His wife and daughter were taken from the train and burnt. God will decide whether they were really sick or Government forcibly burnt them. The Government exults over the oppression done at Cawnpore now-a-days.
>
> The youngsters are snatched away to hospitals and killed there and their parents cry at home. Wives of respectable men are taken to hospitals and their husbands are not allowed to see them. Up to this India was wanting to see that the Government will show mercy, but now it is evident that the intention of Government is to insult the respectable and non-respectable men, carry their valuables to their treasury, and kill as many as they could possibly help to reduce the population. For certain there is no plague at Cawnpore and for nothing doctors torment the people. There is the sickness of the season only.[2]

The mention of Cawnpore was prophetic. The very day the letter appeared in the *Pioneer* a plague riot took place at Cawnpore. An infuriated mob set out from the city soon after midday and marched to the plague camp on the Grand Trunk Road at Anwarganj. They set fire to the huts, overpowered the police guard, beating them over the head with lathis and throwing their bodies onto the flames, and set the patients free. One head constable and four constables were killed. A clerk in the hospital whom the mob mistook for a doctor had to run for his life. He escaped to the BB & Cl railway station where the station master telegraphed news of the riot to Cawnpore. The collector received the news about 1.30 p.m.

Having destroyed the plague hospital the mob returned to the city. Huge crowds led by agitators assembled at Parade and threatened to attack the factories. The collector took speedy action, calling on the officer commanding the station to send out troops. Piquets of fifty soldiers were posted at the Victoria Mills, the Bank of Bengal, Christ Church, the Kotwalee and the Canal Bridge. Disregarding all established procedures, the collector appealed directly to the commandant of the Volunteers, with the result that a troop of the Cawnpore Light Horse and Volunteer Rifles took up their places in Halsey Road and along Parade. Most of the rioters dispersed quietly but as night fell bricks and stones and *kunkar* were thrown at the Volunteers who retaliated by firing over the heads of the crowd. Thirty rounds in all were fired but no one was injured. The collector, fearing an attack on the jail, which was near his official residence, now appealed directly to the colonels of the King's Own Scottish Borderers and the 5th Bengal Cavalry, thereby incurring the wrath of the authorities. His order was grossly irregular; the official report took six days to reach Government and awkward questions were asked, not only by the Viceroy but in the House of Commons as well.

The lieutenant-governor, Sir Anthony MacDonnell, arrived early next morning 'and stepped out of his railway carriage like a god descending from a machine, bringing peace to the perturbed citizens'. He was given a military escort to the collector's house, where he had separate interviews with the committee of the Chamber of Commerce and the municipal commissioners, who represented all sides of the community. Troops were withdrawn and the city patrolled by a strong force of armed police; the protests from the Indian people were meanwhile given careful consideration. To protect their workpeople – as much from blackmail at the hands of the police as from the plague regulations – mill managers put forward a scheme of H. D. Allen's whereby each man would receive a ticket, a talisman to identify him, and in the event of his falling sick they, the mill managers, would provide nearby hospital treatment.

The entire business community of the city came to a halt. The cotton mills and leather factories were deserted. The Cawnpore Woollen Mills persuaded a few hands to come in with the inducement of double wages. 'The city was silent, there was no wheeled traffic and natives sat about quietly with a preoccupied air and the usual sounds of toil and trade were not heard.' All shops were shut and it was extremely difficult to get any food supplies.

Mr Wishart, wishing to see for himself what had happened, drove out in a *ticca ghari* to Anwarganj. The driver was too frightened to approach the scene of the outrage and drew up at a nearby village. Wishart got out with his camera to investigate.[3]

> I was confronted by a group of three brawny individuals with lathis who inquired whether I was the doctor. I hurriedly explained that I was not and never had been, and retired swiftly but in good order upon my ticca which was about 500 yards off. I was escorted to it by my friends with the lathis who objurgated my gharrywallah to such purpose that he kept his tats at full gallop till we were out of sight.

Gussie Anderson had a vivid recollection of the plague riots. Gussie, the teenage daughter of Great-Aunt Emma's friend Mrs Anderson, had travelled out to India just after the Boer War had started. At Bombay she, like everyone else travelling up-country, was examined by Indian doctors, and had her temperature checked before being given permission to travel by train. She was examined again on arrival at Cawnpore. Notwithstanding these precautions, it was two travellers taken ill with plague, seized at the railway station and rushed to a doctor at the segregation camp at Cawnpore, who sparked off the riots that April.

> And then some of the folk went round the bazaars and said, these men haven't got plague and their caste has been broken and they have been taken there for some purpose and they stirred up the people and they said that they aren't ill and there's something shady going on and the camp was attacked. And the sepoys were killed and these two men sat in chairs and they had to be tied in be-cause they were too ill to sit up and they were taken shoulder high right through the bazaars, sitting up, dying in their chairs. And the plague was disseminated and from that day the plague spread in Cawnpore like wildfire. The small village on the way to the big station was absolutely wiped out. It was a small village you drove

through and there were always children and women and men and dogs haring about the place. The village was always teeming – well ever after that we would go through an absolutely dead village. There wasn't a soul alive in it from the plague, the houses empty. And plague used to run down one side of the street and up the other and the explanation was given to us that the rats didn't easily cross the road but they very easily went from house to house, so the rats travelled and gave it to each other and they gave it to the humans, all the way up one side of the street and then along the other or by the time it came to the end of the street they were so terrified they probably went dashing off to another place and took the plague somewhere else. But that was the start of the plague in Cawnpore and Cawnpore had a terrible lot of plague.

Gussic recalled that Mr Shewan came over to the Andersons and sat with their mother, a gun across his lap. When things had quietened, Mrs Anderson drove out in her trap to buy what bread she could find to distribute among her friends. Mr Shewan accompanied her, his gun loaded. Meanwhile the Andersons' enterprising cook went foraging for food and returned with potatoes hidden in the folds of his turban.

The latest dodge of the mob is to waylay the servants of Europeans on their way back from the bazaar, thump them well with lathis and loot them of everything in their possession. Such outrages have become very common and the police appear powerless to suppress them. In not every case, however, does the servant come off second best. One prominent factory manager sent a man for bread, but was disappointed to see him return empty-handed. On asking him what had happened, to his master's horror, the man with a bland smile produced two small loaves from his puggri. Inasmuch as the gentleman was the proprietor of a large family, the advent of these supplies did not help matters much, and he was compelled to drive to the baker's himself and bring back bread in his trap.

The hotels are in sad plight. No meat is to be had and on Saturday even the faithful moorghi failed us. We were reduced to fried German sausage and cold cross buns of the previous day, which were, at all events, satisfying. One sporting manager provided his guests with 'mutton' by the simple expedient of buying a goat and slaying it in the compound. The famine has given great impetus to sport in the neighbourhood. The usual dinner for the last few days has been soup of a sort, tinned fish and three courses of game. This is a luxury. At the other end of the scale we find buns.[4]

The lieutenant-governor made considerable concessions – some thought too many – and his proposals to amend the plague restrictions were printed in the vernacular for all to read. In essence he promised minimum official interference; each community would be allowed to make its own arrangements. No sick person would be removed from his residence against the will of his family; if it proved necessary to isolate a patient he would be housed as close to his home as possible. A *baid or hakim* at Government expense could attend the patient if the family objected to treatment by European methods; ladies, and particularly purdah ladies, would be examined only by lady doctors.

Life in the city slowly returned to normal. It was a time when there was no friction between the two communities – some wealthy Hindus sent a large quantity of sweetmeats to the mosques for distribution to the Muslims after prayers. Foss Westcott preached a sermon at Christ Church that Easter Sunday alluding to the failure of justice which we commemorate on Good Friday when a weak Roman governor was overruled by the rabble of a subject race. 'The moral of Mr Westcott's remarks being to point out that *Vox populi* was not necessarily *Vox Dei* and that a just attitude towards the native should be kept by his congregation, each within his own area of influence.'

The sad episode came to an end eight months later when seven of the rioters were hanged at the jail. The *Pioneer* reported on 17 December:

The last stage of the tragedy that commenced on the 11th April last, took place on the morning of Saturday, the 15th instant. The seven condemned rioters, after unsuccessful appeals to the High Court, the Lieutenant-Governor, and the Viceroy, in succession – paid the extreme penalty of the law – in the jail of Cawnpore. They all appear to have met their death with fortitude, except Karim Elahi, the one who is looked on as their ringleader, and he had to be supported at the last moment. A small and orderly gathering of relatives and friends had collected outside to receive the bodies after the execution – but although in some cases these corpses were carried through the city, covered only with a cloth, the populace for the most part remained apathetic and showed no signs of sympathy. In the case of Karim Elahi some sort of funeral procession seems to have been arranged which was followed by many Mahomedans, with whom Karim Elahi's brother, Abdul Karim,

Hospital staff: Nurse Walden, Dr Wynne-Edwards and Dr Alice Marval.

has, in the past, been a man of influence. But at the mosque, where prayers were uttered over the dead body, the Moulvi is reported to have used the words showing complete absence of sympathy with the actions that led to the violent end of the lifeless man before him.

Overcrowding and poor sanitation had long been serious problems in Cawnpore and outbreaks of plague continued for several more years. One of my mother's earliest memories was of being taken with little May Silver, the girl next door, to a high platform on the parade ground so that they could be publicly inoculated, to encourage the crowd to come forward for similar treatment. 'May cried,' my mother commented scornfully. 'The exercise did not have the desired effect.' There was an unjustified suspicion that they used different *suis* – needles – on the little girls. A young woman doctor, Dr Alice Marval, who had trained in London, came out to work at St Catherine's Hospital. She left a note of her plague experiences and how difficult it was to help the people.

It would be difficult to exaggerate the dirt and untidiness of some of the houses. Moreover the sick people are often not allowed to take any medicine until after the fever has lasted three days for fear of 'driving it inwards'. Sometimes even water is not allowed the poor sufferers. They lie in a low, dark room, the acrid fumes of the fire close beside them and surrounded by ten or twelve squatting figures,

Commemorative window in Liverpool Cathedral; Alice Marvel top left.

who comment loudly upon the bad symptoms and relate how so-and-so died with just such, so many days ago. They often howl and wail over the patients, while they are all quite conscious and sometimes not really ill and they constantly ask me before them whether it is going to be death or recovery.

The doors of these rooms are often so low that I have to stoop quite double in order to get in. I like to begin by ordering out as many people as possible. Then I crawl in and try to make out the patient in the darkness, until my eyes get used to it and the smoke or the people bring a wee taper floating in oil. The patient is generally lying entirely covered up under a thick quilt, well tucked in over the face, so that one feels that even in a well-ventilated room no fresh air could reach the mouth.

Up to December 26th there have been 32 patients treated in a hut and in a small isolated ward in the Hospital. Of these many came in after several days of illness and neglect, and 15 died here while three were removed and died at home. The two who are in now seem absolutely friendless and destitute, and if they recover, I cannot tell what will become of them. There must be many such in the city, for I have found several entirely forsaken. Even so, they cling to their homes and we find it difficult to persuade them to come in, though there may be no one to give them even a drink of water. I once asked after a woman lying helpless on the floor of her house, and the reply was 'How can I give her drink when she is a Muhammadan and I am a Hindu?'[5]

After only two years Dr Alice Marval[6] died of plague, along with her English nurse, Sister Walden, and two Indian members of the staff – Nancy, a nurse, and Pudmoni, the dispenser. William Cooper built a new wing at St Catherine's that included a little chapel dedicated to the memory of the four women who died trying to help plague victims. In Liverpool Cathedral Alice Marval is depicted in a stained-glass window.

Lord Roberts

To many in India, and in Cawnpore in particular, the man whose name and reputation was most closely linked with glorious empire was 'Bobs Bahadur' – Lord Roberts. Over the years and the various Afghan campaigns Roberts had gained a name for winning battles and for showing compassion towards his soldiers, working tirelessly to improve their conditions and performance. The march from Kabul to Kandahar in 1880 was celebrated, as were the tactics he employed at the Battle of Kandahar, the forward thrust that was a holding feint and the decisive flanking attack that won the battle. At the end of the day, when Ayub Khan and the Afghan army were defeated, Roberts went personally to each regiment and battery to ask after the men, and was received with cheers. In 1885 Roberts, now a baronet, became Commander-in-Chief India.

He had a horror of the effects of liquor and introduced the Army Temperance Association and regimental institutes into every cantonment in India. 'What is required is a sufficient number of good-sized, well-lighted rooms, where soldiers can amuse themselves in a rational manner, and where they can have their supper and glass of beer with comfort and decency.' It was the measure for which more than any other he hoped his name would be remembered in India, although for years he campaigned for better conditions in the Indian Army for both the European and the Indian soldiers – improved pay, better sanitation, establishment of dairies, prizes for cooking, better care of horses, and, dear to every Indian soldier's heart, a grant of land to pensioners for distinguished service. Lady Roberts, too, identified closely with her husband's care for the troops. She put up a scheme for an Indian Nursing Service and backed it by establishing convalescent homes for soldiers in the hills.

Roberts's last visit to Cawnpore was in March 1893, shortly before he retired and left India for good. A farewell tour in the Punjab took him to Lahore where he was presented with addresses by the Hindu, Muslim, Sikh and European communities. At each station along the way wellwishers gathered to express their admiration and speed him on his way. Bands played 'Auld Lang Syne', he was cheered wherever he went. In Lucknow the *talookdars* presented him with a sword of honour and a splendid address.

In Cawnpore he was fêted at the Cawnpore Club with people proudly reminding him that Cawnpore was the city of his birth and the place where he had seen thrilling fighting during the Mutiny and where he had won his VC. Mill managers competed with each other to shake him by the hand – with good reason, as much of the success of their mills was linked with the Army campaigns and his patronage.

Lord Roberts arrived here early on Saturday morning and held an inspection parade of the troops at 7 o'clock the same morning. He

Farewell to Lord Roberts, seated centre, at the Cawnpore Club, 1893.

expressed himself thoroughly satisfied; the charge of the 4th Bengal Cavalry was particularly noteworthy. The Volunteers turned out fairly well, mustering 28 of the Cawnpore Light Horse and 72 of the Cawnpore Rifle Volunteers.

A garden party to meet His Excellency was given by the officers of the garrison, in the afternoon, at the Station Club. It was largely attended, and the inevitable photograph was, of course, taken. Lord Roberts left this evening at 7.25 for Delhi.

Yet another dance is to come off before we subside into hot weather inertia. The popular Commandant of the Volunteers has issued invitations for the 3rd Proximo, prior to his leaving for England early in the month.[7]

The Allen family were personal friends. In summer months at Simla the Robertses spent as much time as possible away from their official house and out their cottage at Mashobra where they were close neighbours of George Allen of the *Pioneer*. The paper kept its readers informed of all Lord Roberts's exploits and now wrote a glowing eulogy.[8]

Lord Roberts has won the highest distinction that it is possible to achieve in India short of the Governor-Generalship, and the honours he has gained shine with the greater lustre, inasmuch as he has gained them solely in the military service of the Crown. His career is one that the Indian Army may well be proud of; it is that of a soldier among soldiers, skilful in martial exercises, brave to a fault, imbued with the true spirit of English manliness and proud of his profession; of a leader endowed with those personal qualities which command the enthusiastic devotion of the men whom he commands in the field, their admiration and affection in time of peace; of a General whose ability and power impress themselves upon all who come within their range; and of a Commander-in-Chief unsurpassed for his capacity for work and his talent for administration.

His last night in India he was honoured at a dinner given at the Byculla Club, Bombay, and in reply to the many speeches he concluded:

> Gentlemen, I must not detain you longer; indeed I am afraid I have already trespassed too long on your patience; but I find it difficult to stop when I begin talking about India and the Indian Army. Ties which it is not easy to loosen bind me to India, and to the gallant comrades with whom I have served so long. I leave India with the deepest regret. Almost all my most valued friendships have been made out here, not only amongst my own countrymen, but amongst the Natives in various parts of India, to many of whom I am greatly attached. From every one with whom I have been associated, whether European or Native, whether Civilian or Soldier, I have received invariable and unfailing kindness, sympathy and support. My interest in the progress and welfare of this country will continue unabated, whatever the future may have in store for me. To the Army in India I bid farewell with feelings too deep for words. To its discipline, bravery and devotion to duty both in peace and war I owe whatever success it has been my good fortune to achieve.

Next day he sailed from India.

On his arrival in London the British public took him to their hearts. Kipling's ballad-ditty, 'Bobs Bahadur', caught the ear of the music-hall goers and wherever Roberts went he was hailed a hero.

> Then 'ere's to Bobs Bahadur – little Bobs, Bobs, Bobs,
> Pocket-Wellington *an' arder*★ –
> Fightin' Bobs, Bobs, Bobs!
> This ain't no bloomin' ode,
> But you've 'elped the soldier's load,
> An' for benefits bestowed,
>   Bless yer, Bobs!

★sc. 'half'.

His autobiography, *Forty-One Years in India*, was an instant success; it ran into thirty-five editions and was translated into German, Italian and Urdu. For the celebrations for Queen Victoria's Diamond Jubilee she appointed Roberts to command the Colonial Contingent, soldiers from every part of the empire. Roberts led the contingent mounted on his famous grey arab, Vonolel, the small pony that had carried him through the Afghan campaigns and had been decorated personally by Queen Victoria with the Afghan medals the year before.[9]

In the Boer War, in which his son won a posthumous VC, he acquitted himself with distinction. In Cawnpore news of the campaign in South Africa was closely followed. General French was Gavin Jones's brother-in-law and when the relief of Kimberley was announced Cawnpore felt a sense of personal pride. Jones's son Leslie was serving as second-in-command of Kitchener's Horse. He wrote to his mother:

My dearest Mother,

By the time you get this you must have arrived at dear old Cawnpore, how I wish I could be there to meet you at the station as I did, it seems years ago. I feel as if I shall be an old man before this is finished. . .

I've nearly completed 3,000 miles from camp to camp over the veldt and have been everywhere except Pietersburgh way up North and I don't like any of it. Give me India with its wealth of trees and animals and men, not this endless rolling prairie and its beastly kopjes, only burnt farmsteads, few buck and bird life, dirty water dams and Africanders Dutch and English descent, I dislike them both, both boast and both lie and neither a patch on an Australian, Canadian or Home bred man.

These African winds are detestable, no wonder the Cape is called Cape of Storms.

The Indians who had settled in the Cape had no quarrel with the British and to show their appreciation for Lord Roberts's success in defeating the Boers they presented him with an address. The last name among the signatories is that of M. K. Gandhi.

In Cawnpore L. B. Kennedy,[10] a colourful personality, reputed to be the finest *shikari* in India, who worked for Cooper Allen overseeing the mounting and preserving of game trophies, stole a march on other admirers of Roberts by writing to the great man and asking permission to call his Cawnpore bungalow Paardelberg after Roberts's victory over the Boers. Roberts graciously consented.

THE GREAT

Authority

LORD GEORGE HAMILTON speaking at the Imperial Institute remarked that there was a growing tendency for the Government Contracts to be placed in India, and stated that he hoped this would still further develop the **LEATHER TRADE** there Already India had supplied many of the Saddles and Leather Articles of equipment, and when he told

LORD ROBERTS

that Government were placing contracts for such things in the hands of Indian Manufacturers his Lordship remarked :—

"YOU CANNOT GET BETTER SADDLES OR BETTER LEATHER."

THE WENSE TANNERY have surpassed the finest manufactures in leather goods and their productions are acknowledged to be even **"Better than the Best."** Catalogues, samples, and all information promptly supplied on application to the Secretary.

Wense Tannery, Cawnpore, advertisement.

Perhaps the best example of Cawnpore's enthusiasm and hero worship of Roberts is the incident of the birthplace telegram. The normally restrained McRobert was so carried away with the excitement of the victory at Paardelberg that he composed and sent off a cable to Lord Roberts, using his authority as president of the Chamber of Commerce to do so without consulting the other committee members.

The Sheiling, Cawnpore
3rd March 1900

The Secretary,
Upper India Chamber of Commerce,
Cawnpore

Dear Sir,

On 28th ultimo on arrival of the news of Cronge's surrender I took the liberty of wiring to Field Marshal Lord Roberts at Paardelberg: 'Your birthplace salutes you.'

I did this as President of the Chamber of Commerce representing the Commercial Community. The following reply has just been received from Lord Roberts:

'Many thanks for your welcome message.'

I shall be obliged if you will kindly circulate this among the Members of the Committee for information.

Yours sincerely
A. MCROBERT

Sammy Johnson, the man who took over at the Muir Mills when Gavin Jones first retired, had been an implacable detractor of McRobert and lost no opportunity to belittle him. Their quarrel now surfaced over the birthplace telegram.

The first intimation of the cable came in an announcement in the *Pioneer*. This was immediately followed by an explanatory letter from McRobert circulated by the unfortunate secretary, Wishart. Johnson was beside himself that McRobert should send such a message and advise the press of it, making use of his position as president without the knowledge and approval of the committee. He poked fun at McRobert's 'peculiar form of greeting' and suggested it exposed him to ridicule. Other members sided with McRobert. 'Cawnpore', wrote one, '. . . should be proud to be the birthplace of a general who has so materially changed the outlook of the war for the better. In a matter of such universal rejoicings, amongst Englishmen at any rate, and which I share, Mr Johnson's note of dissent certainly does not sound well. . .' As for the powers of the president, McRobert grumbled: 'The committee might just as well set themselves to regulate the colour of the President's waistcoat as to determine the questions Mr Johnson wants raised.'

Death of Queen Victoria: The End of an Age

The Boer War brought to the surface an extraordinary manifestation of patriotism and loyalty throughout the British Empire. Volunteers from Canada, Australia and India fought alongside the regular soldiers and volunteers from the 'Mother Country'. In India there was a remarkable spontaneous expression of loyalty uniting both the Hindus and the Muslims. It was the personality of the Queen Empress that drew forth this feeling of loyalty to the ruling power and it was never more apparent than with the death of the old queen.

Worn with nearly seventy years of royal duty and tired from the strain of the war in South Africa, she died peacefully on the Isle of Wight at Osborne House. Lord Roberts was the last person outside the family to visit her, only eight days before she died. News of her passing flashed by telegram to all corners of the empire and was received with shock and genuine sorrow. In India telegrams poured in expressing the grief felt at her death; the people of India had lost a mother figure. Meetings were called and attended by people of all castes. Shops, schools, offices and law courts were closed and all festivities suspended. There was talk of 'profoundest sorrow'. In Lahore purdah ladies, dressed in deepest mourning, attended a dinner and gave alms to the poor 'for the benefit of the soul of the Queen Empress'. The following resolution was passed:

> That this meeting of the Mohamedan parda ladies of Lahore put on record its deepest sorrow and grief at the demise of her late Majesty Queen Empress Victoria and feel that in Her Most Gracious Majesty the women of the whole world lose the brightest ornament of their sex, of whom they are rightly proud . . . this meeting which is the first of its kind in Lahore, especially among Mohamedan parda ladies, believes that the privilege of mourning at a meeting of their own such a good and beloved Empress as Queen Victoria would not have been possible for them in India without the influence brought about in this country by Her Majesty's rule and therefore prays for the blessing of God on Her Majesty's departed soul.[11]

In Cawnpore the secretary of the Chamber of Commerce, Wishart, sent round an urgent memo to the committee members: 'You are probably aware that the death of Her Majesty Queen Empress of India was announced this morning 23 January 1901.' All mills and factories stopped work and banks, *mahajans* and traders closed the bazaar.

The state funeral took place in London on 1 February amid scenes of great solemnity. The chief mourners walked three by three in procession, led by a piper playing 'The Flowers of the Forest'. There were forty massed bands with muffled drums to play Chopin's Funeral March. As the cortège slowly drew level with the silently waiting crowd, off came every hat and every woman curtsied. The troops lining the route stood with heads bent over their reversed arms. The coffin was taken to the mausoleum at Frogmore that Queen Victoria had had built for her Prince Albert. Forty years earlier she had commissioned statues of Prince Albert and herself from Baron Marochetti, the sculptor of the Angel of the Well at Cawnpore.

Three weeks later McRobert, addressing the annual meeting of the Chamber of Commerce, spoke eloquently of the late Queen:

> It may truly be said that the Queen has died full of years and full of honours, and that she will go down to history as the greatest and best of constitutional sovereigns. But to us who feel that the privilege of having been her subjects is something to glory in all our days, she was much more than a mere sovereign. Her unswerving patriotism, her unfailing sympathy with every form of suffering, and her tact on all occasions and at every crisis, made us feel that she had a personal interest in each one of us. So much so that now to speak of our *King* almost grates upon the ear. No calamity ever happened but she was the first with a message of sympathy couched in language that was never stereotyped, but always so simple and transparently sincere that it went straight to the heart. A woman of noble character and blameless life, she will live in our affections to the end. There have been many touching tributes to her memory from all the corners of the earth, but could she now return to this world, there are none she would esteem so highly as those that have been humbly and reverently offered by the natives of that land of which she was the beloved Empress and Mother. Our King and Emperor has solemnly undertaken that he will endeavour to follow

OPPOSITE: *The monument to Queen Victoria in Queen's Park, Cawnpore.*

in the footsteps of his revered mother, and we his loyal subjects can ask for no higher standard of attainment. Long may he be spared to reign over us with his devoted Consort, loved and esteemed by the nation as Princess of Wales, and now our honoured Queen.

I ask you to pass the following resolution and propose that a copy of it be forwarded in due course through the proper channel: 'That the Members of the Upper India Chamber of Commerce desire to express their feelings of deep grief and heartfelt sorrow at the death of their much loved and never-to-be-forgotten Sovereign, Queen Victoria, the first Empress of India, who, during her long and glorious reign, devoted herself unfalteringly and unceasingly to her people, and they most respectfully tender to Their Majesties the King and Queen and the Royal Family their sincere sympathy and condolences in the great loss that has befallen them.'[12]

The question everyone in India was asking was what sort of memorial would be suitable to honour the memory of the late Queen Empress. Lord Curzon proposed a magnificent scheme for a national Victoria Hall to be built in Calcutta, to which cities and towns all over India eagerly subscribed. Cawnpore, however, also wanted its own memorial. The firm of Baijnath Ramnath, the wealthy bankers who had financially backed the Elgin Mills, came forward 'in the most public-spirited manner' with a proposal to put up a statue in the Queen's Park.[13] The ladies of Cawnpore collected funds for new wards at the Dufferin Hospital. McRobert himself was more in favour of an industrial museum 'where models and designs of all kinds appropriate to the industrial life of Cawnpore could be exhibited'. But as a first step it was agreed a public meeting should be held for all to express their views.

A large gathering assembled at the Station Theatre at the invitation of the collector. Seated on the stage were several European and native gentlemen, including several magistrates, members of the legal profession and representatives of the leading commercial and industrial interests of Cawnpore. A committee to collect subscriptions was elected and a sum of Rs. 47,946 collected. McRobert made an allusion to 'the striking fact that Cawnpore was unique among the cities of the Empire in its method of observing the day of the Queen's funeral, inasmuch as in Cawnpore, and in Cawnpore alone, did all races, creeds and sects combine to attend the religious service in her memory held in the open air'.[14]

McRobert, the 'Uncrowned King of Cawnpore'

At the turn of the century the *Pioneer* invited a number of celebrities to give their opinion on dangers for the future. Their forecasts included the following: 'The pursuit of money and the gauging of everything by a money standard' (Walter Crane); 'The influence of the irresponsible press' (Stanley Weyman); 'Trade unions, the relation of workmen and employers' (Arthur Pinero); 'The collision of the Western Powers in the East' (Ian Maclaren); 'Widespread materialism and the growing influence of mere money' (John Rhys); and ominously, 'Enormous armies, fleets and military resources now accumulated by the Powers of Europe to tempt their rulers and peoples to struggle for ascendency. . .' (Frederic Harrison).'[15]

But if Cawnpore had fears for the future there was no evidence of its apprehension. *Thacker's Bengal Directory,* which for years had charted the growth of commerce and industry in Cawnpore, suddenly in 1900 blossomed out into pages of illustrated advertisements. The Elgin Mills, Empire Engineering Company and the Muir Mills vied with one another; Mr M. X. de Noronha and the Cawnpore Brush Company and the North West Tannery displayed their wares. Elgin even had the astute idea of printing their name along the pages of the volume. The commercial importance of Cawnpore was not in dispute.

McRobert's comments and reports appeared regularly in the pages of the *Pioneer.* It was he who was behind the proposal for model villages for the workforce. He believed that these would go a long way towards resolving the problem of irregular labour at the mills. The men could earn sufficient in one week for their modest needs and would choose to take off the rest of the month. If they were rebuked they merely went to the next mill where they were certain to find employment. McRobert Ganj and Allen Ganj were the first in India, followed a few years after by Maxwell Ganj. These model villages with sanitation and clean water supply escaped completely when the plague next struck Cawnpore and decimated the city.

Cawnpore also prided itself on being the first provincial town to have electricity and a tramway. The tramway ran from Sursaya Ghat to the East Indian Railway station. When the trams were first introduced it became a popular outing to board the tram at Sursaya Ghat and ride through the city to the EIR station to meet friends who might be passing through on one of the fast night trains. The restaurant was excellent and dinner and drinks could be ordered in advance. You then returned to the terminus at Sursaya Ghat where traps and phaetons would be waiting.[16]

The war in South Africa brought Cawnpore into prominence as the chief source in India of army supplies. 'It is quite refreshing to find the papers reporting week after week that such and such a large consignment of boots, tents and warm clothing had been forwarded to South Africa.' The mills of Cawnpore were making good profits, putting aside prudent sums for depreciation yet paying handsome dividends. The leather industry could not disclose its figures but it was said that 'out of 100,000 pairs of boots required annually, 60,000 were to be supplied by Cawnpore'.[17] Elgin, also being private, did not disclose its accounts but Cawnpore Cotton Mills paid a 10% dividend on ordinary shares, Muir Mills 3%, Victoria Mills 5% and the recently set up (1895) Cawnpore Sugar Works 16%. But it was the Cawnpore Woollen Mills that were the most consistently thriving source of wealth with a distribution of 10% and a 5% bonus.[18]

The shareholders of the Cawnpore Woollen Mills were so gratified at the results McRobert had achieved that they arranged for a formal presentation to be made to him. Fittingly it was Gavin Jones, the 'Father of Cawnpore', who was chosen to give the address and make the presentation. From the *Pioneer of* 19 March 1902:

> An interesting ceremony took place yesterday afternoon at the Lal Imli Club rooms, when very handsome testimonials were presented by the shareholders of the Cawnpore Woollen Mills Company, Limited, to the Hon'ble Mr A. McRobert and Mrs McRobert. Mr Gavin-Jones was most appropriately chosen as the shareholder personally to make the presentation, for he not only was the founder of the mills (which originally were the property of a private company) but also he may be considered the father of the Spinning and Weaving Mills of Cawnpore. He was concerned in the starting of the Elgin Mills, the Muir Mills (which, indeed, he managed for a number of years), and the Cawnpore Woollen Mills (of which he was originally a proprietor). This all took place long before the large leather concerns had come into existence. Out of the European staff of the Elgin Mills came the founders of what are now (like the Muir and Woollen Mills) still larger concerns, viz., the Cawnpore Cotton Mills Company, Limited, and the Victoria Mills Company, Limited. So that in a sense Mr Gavin-Jones may be

Sir Alexander McRobert.

said to be indirectly responsible for these later creations also. How the Cawnpore Woollen Mills Company, Limited, have developed since they commenced may be gathered from the fact that (as a private concern) they began with a capital of only Rs. 20,000.

In presenting the testimonial, Mr Gavin-Jones said: 'Ladies and Gentlemen, – As most of you know, this meeting has been convened for the purpose of presenting a testimonial to Mr and Mrs McRobert, and to give effect to a resolution unanimously carried at the 22nd general meeting of shareholders in February, 1900, when it was proposed that the shareholders should show their gratitude in some measure by voting to Mr McRobert a handsome testimonial. The particular form that the keepsake should take was to be left to the Directors, in consultation with Mr and Mrs McRobert.

'Amongst old friends who have worked with me in days gone by, it is a pleasure to me to be asked to take a prominent position in a meeting of this kind, and they will, I know, pardon me for saying only a few words as I am not practised in the art of speaking. You all know the able manner in which our friend Mr McRobert has brought the Woollen Mills to the high standard it has now attained. He has had a great many difficulties to contend with: in fact in the early days, I believe, he hardly looked upon its pioneers as his friends in giving him such a task to tackle. However, with true Scotch energy and perseverance, he worked on undaunted, under the most depressing circumstances, when it seemed almost hopeless to pull the concern through.

'When Mr McRobert undertook the management of the Company, the subscribed capital was only three lakhs, and its operations confined to the manufacture of coarse blankets made out of the common wool of the country. Now, as we all know, the capital is eighteen lakhs, the larger part of which has been earned and accumulated from profits, while the finest quality of goods is produced from imported wool. A sum of fifteen lakhs has also been put away, which gives the Company practically an impregnable position. This splendid result of fifteen years' labour, speaks for itself. It shows how admirably the business has been managed by Mr McRobert, and those who work with him. Now that we shareholders are reaping bountifully the fruits of his labour, it is fitting that we should acknowledge the gratitude due to him. It is with the sincerest pleasure that, in the name of the shareholders, I ask Mr McRobert to accept these tokens of their respect and gratitude.

'Before ending, I would like also to express thanks to those who have worked so efficiently with Mr McRobert and helped him to be successful. I, amongst others, have often noted an excellent tone of good fellowship amongst the working members of the Woollen Mills. May it long continue, bringing with it in the near future another surprising bonus.'

Mr McRobert, in returning thanks for himself and Mrs McRobert, alluded to the appropriateness and pleasure to himself in the fact that Mr Gavin-Jones made the presentation. Mr McRobert recalled an incident which, he said, had been remembered by him as redounding greatly to the credit of Mr Gavin-Jones, in that in the early and troublous days of the Mills as a joint-stock concern, Mr Jones had come forward and voluntarily surrendered the shares that had been part of the good-will of the original proprietors, an example subsequently followed by his partners.

The testimonial took the form of a handsome gold watch and chain to Mr McRobert, and a silver tea and coffee set to Mrs McRobert, the latter bearing (on the tray) an inscription stating that it was given 'in grateful recognition of her helpfulness'. A singularly felicitous expression!

Alexander McRobert was now indeed the 'Uncrowned King of Cawnpore'.

Epilogue

——

Gavin Jones spent his last year in India writing a history of Cawnpore. He was keenly aware of all that had been achieved in the short space of a single life and his own part in that remarkable achievement. But he also looked beyond, to a vision for India itself.

> The introduction of the railway has been the most potent factor to waken the people and spread its civilising influence, it is silently but surely improving the intelligence and mode of life of the inhabitants, the stone wall barrier of caste, that has enslaved the millions of centuries, is gradually melting away & education & increasing contact with the white man & the increasing facilities of access to Europe, is destined to revolutionise & accomplish the change which is the goal of British rule. The rapid, safe & cheap transport of goods & the widening intercourse with the outside world is changing the habits of the people & the increase & distribution of wealth is creating new wants & a taste for improved living & luxuries undreamt of by their forefathers. They are better clothed & the perfect freedom & sense of security they enjoy is uplifting them to higher levels of life. The momentum imparted is gathering force, which if wisely directed will bring unfathomable benefits in its train, ignored & misdirected will engender trouble, ending in discord, disaffection, disloyalty & rebellion. The firm hand & mailed fist must always remain in evidence till the people are sufficiently advanced to appreciate the blessing of the benevolent rule of England & can be trusted to stand safely on their own feet.[1]

He died in 1913. The last photograph taken of him shows a tall figure carrying a grandchild on his shoulders. I have talked with this granddaughter who as a little girl sat on Gavin Jones's knee and looked with awe at the scar on his shoulder, shaped like a star, and learnt it was from the wound Jones sustained that day when, escaping from Fatehgarh,

Gavin Jones with granddaughter Mollie (Mallaby).

The Stewarts' golden wedding anniversary card.

he swam for his life during the Great Mutiny. In Cawnpore the story is still repeated that whenever Gavin Jones was visited by the old zemindar who had saved his life by employing him as a woodcutter, Jones would have him sit in his chair while Jones sat on the floor.

His son, Tracy Gavin Jones, carried on his work in Cawnpore and played a political role, a delegate to the 1930 Round Table Conference representing British business interests which earned him in 1936 the knighthood that had eluded his father. In 1949, after partition, Tracy Gavin Jones fought a bitter dispute with the leading worthies of Cawnpore who wanted to play safe and tactfully move the Angel of the Well to another site out of harm's way. Tracy argued for the truth of history – better the Angel be destroyed on the very site of the dark deeds than sanitised in the compound of All Souls Memorial Church. Tracy was shouted down and the Angel now stands with part of the gothic screen close to the church but far from the Bebee Ghur and the well in which the murdered women and children were thrown, 'the living with the dead'.

John and Millie Stewart celebrated their golden wedding anniversary at Ardvorlich in 1907. A charming card incorporating their engagement picture and a recent one was sent out to mark the occasion. Millie died in 1910 and four years later John Stewart, the 12th Laird of Ardvorlich, was laid to rest with his Stewart ancestors in the little graveyard of the chapel at St Fillans while the piper played a lament.

The family interests at Elgin had been served for many years by Ralph Maxwell and the Dunbars. Now they were joined by Major William Tracy, Hugh Maxwell's grandson, who left the Army to enter the family business. But not for long. Ralph Maxwell put the Elgin Mills in the hands of Begg Sutherland & Co. Ltd[2] as managing agents and left India for good in 1912. One of my father's first experiences of Cawnpore was when as a newly arrived *chokra* at the Elgin Mills he joined the Cawnpore Light Horse and was proud to take part in escorting Ralph Maxwell to the station to bid him farewell, honouring the Maxwell family's 106 years in Cawnpore. Ralph Maxwell lived modestly, enjoying the shooting and fishing in Scotland and the cricket at Lord's. Invariably when he was in London he met La Reine once a week to reminisce about their years in Cawnpore.

Gavin Jones, Hugh Maxwell and John Stewart were the pioneers but it was William Cooper who was the first to carry off high honours, the CIE in 1897 and a knighthood at the 1903 Durbar. We know he was the first president of the Chamber and their representative on the Legislative

Ralph Maxwell.

Mrs Gavin Jones.

Cawnpore Light Horse: winners of the All India Tent Pegging Competition, 1901. Standing: Trooper F. W. Hart, Sergeant Jardine, Trooper O. Briscoe, Corporal Collinson, Trooper A. R. Black. Seated: Lieutenant C. T. Allen, Captain Begbie.

Assembly for seven years and for many years the commandant of the Cawnpore Volunteers. Yet there is something elusive about him as a person during his time in India. There are many references to his philanthropy and generosity, particularly to children. His Christmas parties were famous and on one occasion he threw open the grounds of his house to the Sunday School fête, inviting all children of English descent and every denomination; over 400 children enjoyed themselves to the background of the band of the Staffordshire Regiment. At Volunteer sports he donated many of the prizes and he gave the two hard tennis courts for the Club house. When his wife died he commissioned a marble tomb of the finest workmanship from the Italian sculptor Professor Villa of Genoa, famous for his funerary statues, and endowed it handsomely with Rs. 5,000. His wife was buried at Cawnpore's Mirpur cemetery beside her mother and sister.[3]

Two years before his knighthood the McRoberts on home leave visited William Cooper at Hume Towers.

> *6 July 1901* We met Mr Cooper at Waterloo and reached B'mouth at 6 p.m. Hume Towers is a very fine place and Mr Cooper has improved it very much. The grounds are beautifully laid out and fine pine trees everywhere. After dinner played patience and I went to bed leaving Col Cooper and Alec playing billiards. It is a hot night. There are some lovely pictures, vases and furniture in Hume Towers. Mr Cooper seemed very glad to have us in his nice home. I wonder what Mrs Cooper would have thought of it all, had she been alive.[4]

A friend[5] recalled how Sir William, when electricity was first installed, would take great delight in bustling everyone into a darkened room and then suddenly switching on the lights.

When he was seventy Sir William married again, repeating the formula of his first marriage, taking pity on an attractive widow with a young daughter. They lived an exotic life, with a 'doll's house' in London close to the Spiritualist Church of which he was co-founder with the medium Percy Beard. Later he moved from Hume Towers to Castle Carey on the island of Guernsey where visitors were met in style from Weymouth, given the best cabin and ushered first off the ship with the flag flying to greet them. He wrote a number of learned books, expressing his convictions on psychic matters, much influenced by his years in India, and on social and political problems: *The Murder of Agriculture, Socialism and Its Perils, Britain for the Briton, England's Need, Spiritual*

Sir William Cooper.

H. D. Allen, his wife Nella, Mrs Kirkman and G. B. Allen at The Retreat.

St Catherine's Hospital for Women.

Science and *England's Fatal Land Policy*. He believed that England's return
to prosperity lay in agriculture and that no economic system could be
satisfactory if it failed to give equality of opportunity.

He died at Castle Carey in 1924. India was not forgotten in his will.[6]
He made donations to the Allahabad Free Schools and Orphanage, the
Ramsay Hospital at Naini Tal for the maintenance of the Cooper Wing
for non-paying and poor patients and for the Summer Home of Soldiers'
Children at Mussoorie. His bungalow at Cawnpore became the Circuit
House where the Governor and his Lady stayed on official visits and
where society went to write their name in the Book. Mysteriously, after
his death his fortune disappeared.

Sir George Allen was taken ill in Paris and died at his London home in
1900. His health had never recovered from the terrible exposure he endured when the P & O liner *Tasmania* was wrecked off the coast of
Corsica. He had bought a large property called Free Chase, close to
where Kipling was to settle at Bateman's in Sussex. Georgina described it
as 'a lovely refined home'. Both the sons of his first marriage, George
Berney and Henry Deacon, were to die in their fifties.

George Berney Allen's contribution to Cawnpore was his passion and
talent for landscaping which led to his creation of Allen Bagh. It is Allen
Forest that is his memorial. In 1902 Government made a grant of bare
scrubland beyond the old East India Company gardens to the Allen
family in perpetuity and this gave GBA the opportunity to create a wild
area of natural beauty.[7] A huge lake of dammed water stretched from

the Allens' new house, The Retreat, to a bay at the far end where a small gem of a house built with imported stone and designed by an Italian, modelled on the classic Greek Tower of the Winds, made a perfect picture. The upstairs rooms were open on three sides to the elements. The whole area was planted with forest trees and undergrowth. It was possible to ride or walk for four miles under the tall jungle trees in deep soft dust with peafowl or porcupine for company, while overhead parrots screeched and small brown monkeys rustled in the tree tops.

GBA understood to perfection the art of pleasing the eye, that the vista must never be revealed all at once but lead first to one corner or along one avenue to another. The Allens' house at Mashobra, near Simla, also bears testimony to GBA's genius and eye for beauty. When McRobert came to lay out the estate at Douneside he consulted GBA, a trusted friend, and his reply gives a clue to his working.

I have been thinking more about Douneside and as you are visiting the nursery people give you my views. The tree planting I indicated when I was with you is in my opinion *the very minimum* that should

Lake House, Allen Bagh.

be undertaken. If the place was mine – more particularly as you are going to be away much these next two years – I would, while keeping the best trees for the positions I have indicated, at the same time plant the *whole of the foreground* (every damned square yard of it) with cheap trees with a view to cutting out later. They would all help each other up, whereas my fear is that the permanent planta-tion may, owing to the bleak position, grow up stunted and not give you the desired results quickly. A thick plantation bang in front of you would not block your view at all for several years and when it began to the trees you decided to leave would (much as you may think otherwise) actually heighten the effect of your beautiful mountain landscape. Have I made myself clear? Do as you think right. All I wish to emphasise is that under the existing conditions you cannot possibly make the mistake of planting too much - it is *so easy* to cut down at any time. I should be inclined to plant all the fields in front, high and low – it will be done at the expense of your farm but will reduce your responsibilities in that direction. You would make much more money out of planting 'douglas' and larch than you ever will out of farming!

On a low stone bridge close to Lake House GBA's initials and the date of his birth and death are recorded.

H. D. Allen, Harry Allen, married Nella Jacob, whose father had built the canals in the Punjab. They were serious-minded people and dedi-cated Plymouth Brethren and their lives touched many of the young children in Cawnpore who attended their Sunday School classes, first at the Chamber and later out at The Retreat.[8] My mother never forgot the favourite hymn they taught her, 'Jesus wants me for a sunbeam. . .'

It was Sir George's third son, Charles Turner Allen, CTA, who would play a distinctive role in Cawnpore. With 'a reputation which for wealth, for honour, for credit stood second to none in the whole of India',[9] he was utterly charming – but he had no head for business. Reputedly he had fagged at Eton for the future Viceroy Lord Wil-lingdon, while the boy who in turn fagged for him became the Viceroy Lord Irwin. Certainly when Queen Mary was touring India after the Delhi Durbar the royal train was discreetly stopped at Cawnpore in order that she might lunch with the Allens at Fairlawn.[10]

CTA made and lost two fortunes. When he left Cawnpore he sold the *Pioneer,* while The Retreat was sold to Sir Padampat Singhania, grandson of Juggilal. When the Test cricket matches were first played in

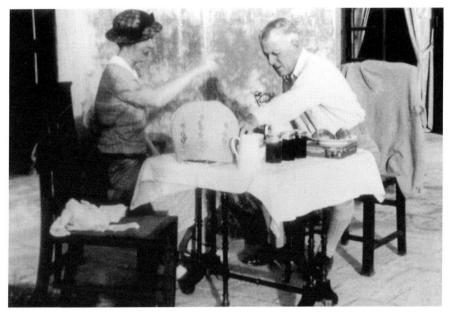

C. T. Allen and his wife breakfasting at Lake House.

Cawnpore the cricketers always stayed at The Retreat. Soon after GBA's death Allen Bagh was sold to the Forest Department on condition it was always kept open for the people. Lake House Charles Allen intended to keep but it stood empty all through the war years. Everything was just as he had left it, suits and coats hanging in the almirahs and papers arranged under paperweights on his study desk as if at any moment he would walk in. It was left in the safe keeping of the half-crazed *chowkidar,* Lal Khan, and many were the moonlight picnics my husband and I enjoyed in the grounds of Lake House, paddling out in a flat-bottomed skiff to the tiny cormorant island under a velvety sky filled with stars of unforgettable brilliance. But CTA never returned and Lake House is now part of the Cawnpore Zoo.

Soon after CTA first arrived from Eton, Georgina McRobert became almost a mother to him. A diary note records: '9 Nov 1901. Drove Charlie Allen home from Church and promised to dine with him at the Club and go to the Fancy Dress Ball on Thursday.' When Logie Watson was suddenly taken ill with an abscess on the liver it was CTA who drove Georgina about so that she could arrange nursing for the sick man. Doc Fuller, the mill doctor, operated, McRobert stayed the last hour and made Logie's will for him; but he made a good recovery.

Sir Thomas and Lady Smith.

Logie Watson, McRobert's neighbour at Pirie and Sons' Stoneywood Works, was knighted; so was Henry Ledgard, who prospered once he had thrown over the restraints of working under Gavin Jones. One of his daughters, Elsie, married an up-and-coming agent at the Bank of Bengal, Thomas Smith, who would become the highly successful director of the Muir Mills and play a leading part in public affairs. He was one of four Europeans to sit on the Hunter Committee to inquire into the case against Brigadier-General Dyer for the 'monstrous events'[11] of the Jallianwala Bagh shooting at Amritsar. Dyer was relieved of his command. Many Europeans in India felt Dyer had been unfairly treated and a fund of £26,000 was raised, and a golden sword presented to Dyer as 'Defender of the Empire'. In Cawnpore, with its memories of the massacre at the Bebee Ghur, Smith had to put up with being snubbed and ostracised at the Club for the next three years. The only comment he made was 'Dyer never gave us a chance.'[12]

Smith was knighted in 1920 and he and his wife set a standard that none dared mock. Lady Smith's children's parties were the high spot of

Christmas week and many was the four-anna piece I cherished for running an egg and spoon race or a sack race that ended up among the huge baskets of ferns hung beneath the peepul tree in her garden. Sir Thomas died in 1963 and members of the Dyer family attended his memorial service.

Old man Horsman had to wait to see his dream realised but it came about in 1911 with the help of his sons Harry and Albert. They had a sensitive ear to the times and called their cotton mill Swadeshi ('of the country') – a choice that was looked on askance as not quite 'pukka'[13] – and made it one of the finest mills in India, equipped with modern machinery and a showplace. Frank Horsman died in Bombay in 1922 and was brought back to be buried in Cawnpore. His estate was so colossal that the Treasury office had to send to Allahabad, the headquarters of the Board of Revenue, for sufficient stamps of the right value to cover the stamp duty on the letters of administration.[14]

The Horsman brothers (Harry was knighted) built two public hospitals, endowed and run for the people of Cawnpore – the Ursula Horsman Memorial Hospital, in memory of Albert's daredevil wife who

Albert and Ursula Horsman and Rani.

Ursula Horsman, 1932, 'off to Lucknow'.

Nick Pocock with Albert and Harry Horsman at Swadhesi Mills.

died in a flying-boat accident off Alexandria, and the Alec Horsman and Dufferin Hospital in memory of their mother. During the war I did some volunteer nursing at the UMH and watched as a man with gangrene had his leg sawn off and thrown into a bucket.

Wishart, who loved Cawnpore so much he could hardly be persuaded to take any home leave, fell ill and was sent up to Naini Tal to recover; but he died and was buried there in 1904, although he had always spoken of leaving his bones in Cawnpore.

Gussie Anderson fell in love with the blue eyes of Harry Bevis, the son of W.G. Bevis. He was to die of a burst appendix, operated on by the civil surgeon on the dining-table at Chapman's bungalow.

For Georgina McRobert perhaps the highlight of her experience in India was attending the 1903 Delhi Durbar when Lord Curzon

Interior of Durbar tent, 1903.

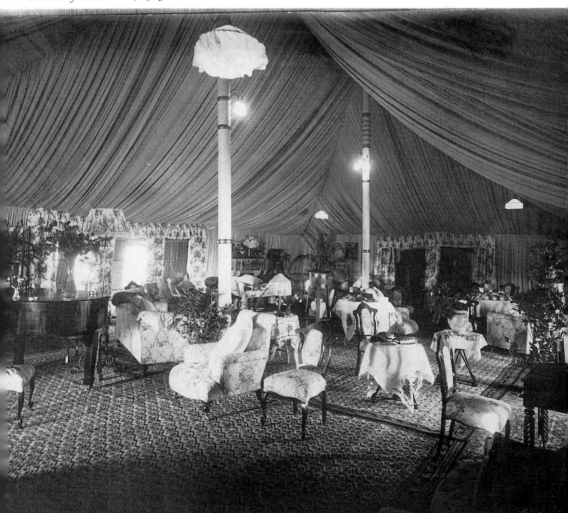

proclaimed Edward VII Emperor of India. Self-consciously aware of the importance of the occasion, she noted details in large handwriting in a hard-backed notebook. The McRoberts travelled from Cawnpore as guests of Sir James and Lady La Touche in a special train, accompanied by the *khitmagar* and *ayah*. They found a magnificent camp laid out with everything, even to sumptuous drawing-rooms under canvas. They watched the state entry from chairs in the south gallery. Lord Curzon had a gold umbrella held over him, the Maharajah of Bikaneer rode in a camel cart, the Maharajah of Kapurtala on an elephant, massed bands played Scottish airs and, when the Mutiny veterans passed, 'See the Conquering Hero Comes'. 'We all cheered and shouted till we were hoarse, I could not keep back the tears, some of the veterans were so old and bent, scarcely able to walk. A place on the opposite side to where we sat was reserved for them. Good old Lancers.' An elephant carrying a *chowrie* saluted with it as it passed the colours. When the Begum of Bhopal passed, the Viceroy uncovered his head.

Honours were presented at the Dewan-i-am in the Red Fort, the Viceroy placing the honour round the neck of Europeans and the Foreign Secretary investing the Indians. Georgina registered the distinction uneasily. This was when William Cooper went up for his knighthood.

> We had supper in the Dewan-i-Khas in the Red Fort, the private hall of audience of Shah Jehan, the Old King of Delhi. It was like fairy land with the electric light, every detail of the roof shown up with the rows of small lights all round. I could not but think of our eating ham in this lovely room – in a Mohommedan's eyes that would have defiled it for ever and the old king was of that faith. 'If there is a paradise on earth it is this.[15]

When they dined at Viceregal Camp, Georgina found it pleasant but very formal, with gold-printed menu cards each with a correct name and engraved with an elephant and howdah. There were presentations and speeches. 'Beating on the table I broke my wine glass.' 'I shall ever be grateful to God', Georgina remembered, 'for permitting us to see the Durbar under such favourable surroundings.'

Back home her writing changes and she is in her own world, the glamour of the Durbar almost unreal. Her little dog Judy had died. 'The house seemed empty without Judy. I went over and saw where her little remains were laid and my heart felt very sore at the thought that never again would I see her dear affectionate face and hear her sharp little bark.' Poor Georgina, time was running out for her too.

She was to the a most painful death from cancer, tenderly nursed by Alex.

The following entries are from Alex McRobert's diary:

9th Nov 1905 Gave me her Bible today inscribing it 'To dear Alec from Georgina', the last she ever wrote. She said she had composed something nice in her mind to put into it but found she could not write more than the words above. Yet she has her bright days with flashes of her old spirit. This morning her countenance showed the effect of yesterday's suffering. The soothing draught in the evening makes the night easier than the day. Now there is a spell of fine weather it is of no use to her. She sometimes fears she will linger a long time yet.

14th Nov Just before sleeping time she broke down and clung to me like a fluttering frightened bird might. She said she was afraid to go away into the unknown, but presently she calmed, recovered her composure and fell asleep like a baby.

19th November Have had to increase the doses of nepenthe as the pain has increased and also become more general. The flesh is almost gone from her arms once so rounded and her face is pinched. She is not repining but she would like those who love her to pray that her release may be soon if God so wills it. Even a linnet came into her room through the window after dark and we kept it in a box all night. It must have wanted a refuge.

29th Nov Today I asked her what message I would give to Kirkie [Mrs Kirkman], and she threw her arms round my neck and kissed me, not able to say anything. I sat up with her till near midnight and went upstairs without awaking the nurse after the normal sleeping draught had taken effect.

30th Nov In the morning I talked with her about Foss's consecration and she understood it was taking place at this moment in Allahabad between 8 and 9. I then read to her the Collect, Epistle and Gospel for St Andrew's Day and followed with the passage from Daily Light. Our attention was specially attracted when I came to the words 'My presence shall go with thee and I will give you rest'. This was about half past eight and at 11.15 she was taken home to Jesus.[16]

Alexander McRobert endowed the University of Aberdeen with a generous cancer research fund and in Cawnpore built the Georgina McRobert Hospital in her memory, which became the hospital for all

Amir of Afghanistan at Cawnpore Woollen Mills, 1907.

mill personnel. I was born there and so were two of my children. Georgina's bust stood in the staff duty room. The night Georgina died Foss Westcott was ordained Bishop of Chota Nagpur. He went on to become the Metropolitan of Calcutta, immensely respected. He died in Darjeeling at a great age in 1949. I remember seeing him play a fine game of tennis, albeit from the back line, only a few years before his death. George Westcott reluctantly left Christ Church College and the SPG Brotherhood to become Bishop of Lucknow in 1910. He died in 1928 and was buried at Allahabad in the shadow of the cathedral. No roses bloom on his grave now, only a few straggling vincas.

McRobert tried to put Georgina's death behind him, concentrating on his work. He was proud to be called upon to escort the Princess of Wales round the mill, and built an impressive relationship with the Amir of Afghanistan. There was a memorable trip with Logie Watson into Afghanistan and later he entertained the Amir in Cawnpore, treasuring the medal the Amir gave him. In 1911 he was married again to a formidable young woman half his age, Rachel Workman, the daughter of well-known American explorers of the Himalayas. She presented him with the three sons he had always wanted. McRobert's energy and vision carried him to many parts of the world and earned for him a knighthood in 1910, a KBE in 1919 and a baronetcy in 1922. In 1920 he persuaded six concerns[17] to amalgamate as the British India

---

WANTED.

MANAGER wanted for an important manufacturing concern up-country. Must be a man of ideas with a passion for work and in the prime of life and health. Possessed of unlimited driving power and a sound knowledge of accounts. A born organizer and administrator equipped with a liberal education and a sterling character. Capable of dealing with big business. Must have well developed the faculty of handling men tactfully. No objection to a Service man if otherwise qualified. Not a mere, *sab-janta-walla* but a sort of Admirable Crichton. Remuneration offered Rs. 3,000 to Rs. 6,000 per month according to equipment, with tempting prospects of advancement. Men who want the pay only but do not fill the bill to at least 75 per cent. are warned off. Fullest particulars of education, training and career, in strict confidence, *by letter only* (Registered Post), to—THE CHAIRMAN, British India Corporation, Ld., Cawnpore.   637

Corporation, the BIC. An advertisement he worded himself (above) gives an insight into the man he was.

Lady McRobert preferred to remain in Scotland with the children. Her husband meanwhile became increasingly withdrawn and solitary, working constantly at furious pressure. He went out of his way to preserve the personal touch with his employees, particularly at the Lalimli Club, and the McRobertganj workers' settlement where he was sometimes to be seen in his shirtsleeves sitting on a *charpoy* talking with the men.[18]

He died suddenly. For several months after an operation for appendicitis he had not been well. The day of his death, on home leave at Douneside, he had been impatient because the chauffeur had not been able to start the Standard. 'Seizing the crank Mackie furiously turned the handle but it was too much for his heart condition. He went upstairs and sat at his desk where he had a heart attack and died.'[19] Tributes to his life and work poured in and there were references to his many benefactions, often most unobtrusively made, both in India and in Scotland. At his funeral four of the pallbearers were Cawnpore friends – Sir Logie Watson, Sir William Cooper, C.T. Allen and Doc Fuller.

Unlike Cooper's, McRobert's immense fortune was safeguarded. Lady MacRobert (as she now spelt her name) played a leading role in bringing up the boys and administering the estate. Later she set up the Alexander MacRobert Memorial Trust[20] and fulfilled her husband's wish for a hall at Robert Gordon's College. When each of the three sons was killed in turn in flying accidents, two in wartime, Lady Mac-Robert presented a bomber in their memory, 'MacRobert's Reply'. This was followed by a gift of four Hurricane fighters and setting up Alastrean House as a convalescent home for RAF personnel, gestures that caught the imagination of the public and attached celebrity to the name MacRobert.

Alfred and Polly Butterworth enjoyed over forty years in Cawnpore. My grandfather's memorial is the Lalimli clocktower, known in our family as the 'Dog Tower', since he designed it while in Kasauli with his son who was undergoing the painful course of injections for rabies after being bitten in the face by a pet monkey.

At the Delhi Durbar of 1911 when George V was proclaimed King Emperor, Cawnpore's contribution to India was such that a special train was commissioned to carry all the Cawnpore Woollen Mill staff, their wives and children, and 1,000 of the workforce to attend, entirely due to the esteem in which McRobert was held. My mother, thirteen years old, proudly wearing a rather heavy unbecoming overcoat made specially for the occasion from a Lalimh blanket, was among the excited throng. The

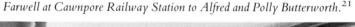

Farwell at Cawnpore Railway Station to Alfred and Polly Butterworth.[21]

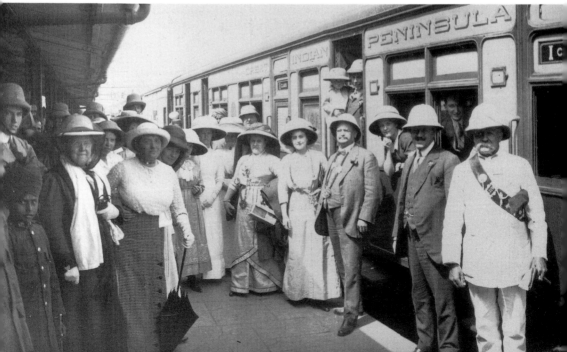

To our most respected Patron
Mr. A. Butterworth Senior.

IT is with a feeling of deep sorrow that we approach you to bid your goodself a fare-well address on the occassion of your departure from our midst.

We take this opportunity of expressing our deep gratitude towards you for the constant self-denial you have shown for our improvement and our hearty appreciation of your paternal care over us.

It is now with painful feelings that we come to bid you fare-well, yet our sorrow is somewhat alleviated when we see' our benevolent and generous master Mr. A Butterworth Jr. over us.

Your continued untiring efforts to bring this mill in such prosperous and flourishing condition.—Your generous and sympathetic treatment towards us and above all; your intense and immense feelings for the poor and suffering have produced deep regard and cherished a life-long memory into our hearts.

Words fail to express the gratitude we feel. If we had thousand tongues we could not but justify of the good works done to us.

We now earnestly request you to accept this small token of our great love and respect for you, and we bid you fare-well with our hearty wishes for a safe and prosperous voyage home.

May you prosper eternally and may God rain down the best of His Blessings in profusion upon you, and may you enjoy peace and tranquility of mind at your dear native land

We ever beg to remain,
Our most respected Patron,
Your most obedient servants,
Engineering Department,
Lalimli Mills,
Cawnpore.

train was so heavily laden that the engine was unable to pull the load up a slight gradient. My Grandpa Butterworth saw the dilemma and gave instructions for all level-crossing gates to be closed. Then the engine was backed slowly towards the Victoria Mills where on a more level track it had a chance to get up steam. This time it mastered the gradient, with much chugging and snorting, as hats and handkerchiefs were waved and the happy party went off cheering.[22]

Every member of the party was presented with a medal that McRobert had had struck to mark the occasion. On one face it showed 'King George V, King and Emperor, Delhi 1911 Durbar', and on the reverse Lalimli Mills, Cawnpore. An aerial view of the mill, chimneys smoking, flags flying from both the clocktowers – his pride and joy; and below, the trademark he made famous, the Lalimli tree.

Lalimli Durbar medal,

When Grandpa Butterworth first retired in 1914 the mill workers at Lalimli were given the day off. Alfred Butterworth sat beside the driver in the large open car with Polly Butterworth and my mother, a young flapper of sixteen, at the back. As they drove out of The Palms, past the Lalimli Club and slowly along the Mall, the scene was extraordinary. Men were there in huge numbers, throwing flowers over the car, throwing coins, while some of the older men who had known Alfred Butterworth since the early days of the mill prostrated themselves in front of the car and banged their heads on the ground. As the car edged forward tears were running unashamedly down my grandfather's face.

Because of staff shortages during the Great War my grandfather was persuaded to return to Cawnpore for a further four years. When he finally retired it was a very different send off; the special relationship between the Indians and the British had come to an end with the war.

Not surprisingly perhaps, the Mawari firm of bankers that came to the financial aid of the Elgin Mills in the 1870s went on ultimately to become industrialists in their own right, though not until after the Great War. Operating under the name of Baijnath Ramnath, one of the brothers, Moolchund, was the first to make his mark publicly. In December 1901 an elaborate ceremonial marriage in the Mawari tradition took place between Moolchund's son, aged eleven years, and the daughter of Lala Daichund of Calcutta. 'The scene at the house of the bridal party was unique ... so many Europeans were there, the lofty hall in which it took place and in the adjoining rooms opening on to it, that they positively filled the place.'[23] Moolchund later made an abortive attempt to seize control of Cawnpore Cotton Mills but he was ousted and the family regrouped to trade as Baijnath Juggilal. Juggilal, the friend of Atherton West and Horsman and Duckworth, was content to remain a banker, but with his son Kamlapat laid the foundations for the JK Empire, reputed at one time to be the fourth largest business house in the private sector in India.[24] It was Juggilal's grandson, Padampat, who gained a knighthood and as a respected figure in business circles attended my wedding and called me his 'daughter'.

Lord Roberts, 'Bobs Bahadur', died in France. It was the early days of the Great War and the field-marshal had gone to review the troops of the Indian Division in France. He died in November 1914, fittingly among the Indian soldiers he loved and who loved him. General Rawlinson described him as 'the greatest and most lovable man I have ever known'.[25] In his funeral procession his coffin was placed on the gun carriage his son had died trying to save in the Boer War. He was buried in St Paul's, close to those other great British heroes, Nelson and Wellington.

Among the many personalities jostling to play their part in twentieth-century Cawnpore was the romantic figure of 'Lady June' Thomson. Born in 1883 in Cawnpore, the daughter of a railway driver with the East Indian Railway, her real name was Marie Frances Grindolph.

Mrs June Thomson.

Beautiful, determined to get on, with a lively imagination, she 'reinvented' her past in a convenient fusion of fact and fiction. Many stories were told about her. She married in 1901 a man called Herbert O'Brien, assistant manager of a colliery, who gave her three daughters and died in a road accident in Jubbalpore when he was thrown out of a dogcart close by the offices of Frizzoni and Co.[26] Henry Thomson, a contemporary of McRobert and a fellow Aberdonian, for nineteen years the chief engineer at the Cawnpore Woollen Mills, had recently joined Frizzoni and Co. at their head office at Allahabad; and he was now persuaded to marry the lovely young widow and take her children under his protection. A few years later Henry and Marie Thomson returned to Cawnpore and settled down with the children of both marriages. Henry Thomson was dour and silent, absorbed in his work. Marie Thomson's warm-hearted impulsiveness was forty years ahead of her times. Her eccentricities were soon the talk of the station. Cawnpore was shocked and fascinated by her, men found her irresistible. Things became so serious that after the death of Henry Thomson discreet arrangements were made to persuade her to stay away from Cawnpore so that her young family might grow up respectably. Without exception they all did well. The eldest daughter, Vera O'Brien, married at sixteen a major in the Sikh Pioneers. My grandmother Polly Butterworth was one of the witnesses at the civil ceremony. Henry Thomson had been a friend and associate of my grandparents for nineteen years, at the mill, as a fellow Mason and as a Volunteer.

The second daughter, Clare, married Alex Shakespear,[27] a man over twice her age, greatly respected in Cawnpore, who introduced her to the high society that led on her third marriage to her becoming the Duchess of Sutherland. Marie Thomson was overjoyed and insisted that she was now related to royalty and called herself 'Lady June'. Another daughter, it was always incorrectly rumoured, had become Merle Oberon. 'Lady June' never returned to Cawnpore until she was dead. She is buried at the Cantonment Cemetery beside the little son who died of measles many years earlier. The entry in the lych gate register charmingly gives – 'a lady'.

Atherton West, with the reputation of being a white Marwari, continued as secretary and manager at the Victoria Mills until in complicated circumstances it was sold in 1921. At last he had the opportunity to put up his own mill, Atherton West and Co. and Atherton Mills. The mill started work in 1924 but sadly only a few months earlier old Atherton West had died. His son Bert took over the running of the mill and in that same year married May Silver, the girl who had lived next door to The Palms, who was publicly inoculated with my mother at the Parade. May's parents were the young couple fêted at the Lalimli Club on return from honeymoon when Great-Aunt Emma visited Cawnpore. May wore Mary Duckworth's wedding veil and the cake was decorated with treasured favours. Mrs West, in mourning for her husband, would only allow her daughters to attend as bridesmaids if they wore black

ABOVE *Mall Road* en fête *for the visit of the Viceroy, Lord Irwin, in 1926. Whiteaway Laidlaw on the right.* BELOW *Lord and Lady Irwin at the Elgin Mills looking down at the author (who disgraced herself by refusing to curtsy) presenting a bouquet made by her mother.*

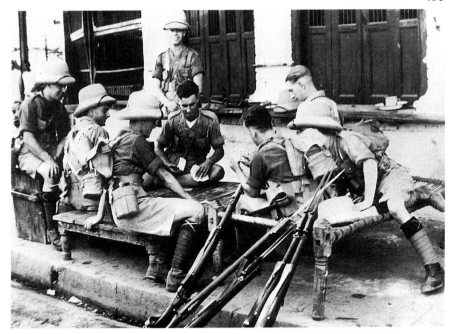

Soldiers playing cards: Cawnpore riots, 1903.

ribbons to their bonnets. At the reception a large crowd gathered for the
formal photograph. Among the many faces is that of a young Indian
lady, Kailash Srivastava, the first Indian lady in Cawnpore society to
appear out of *purdah*.[28] She had recently returned from Manchester with
her husband, J. P. Srivastava. He was later knighted and both he and
Lady Srivastava were celebrities in Cawnpore and well-known political
figures in India.

Cawnpore with its huge population of mill workers saw more than its
fair share of riots and strikes and severe communal violence during the
political agitation for Home Rule and the Quit India campaign in the
1930s. It had such a reputation as a trouble spot that the authorities kept
very tight control and only the most senior administrators were sent to
hold office at Cawnpore between the wars.

At the outbreak of war in 1939 the younger generation of English
families came out to India to join their parents for the duration, my
brother and I among them. The Quit India campaign was brought home
to me personally when one early morning, the dew still on the grass,
I cycled to Green Park for my daily ride and an unseen student

in the DAV Hostel shouted out 'Go home, white monkey.' As the war progressed, things quietened politically; mills were fully stretched making boots and tents and army uniforms and now silk parachutes for the war against Japan. Apart from the occasional – hushed up – bomb outrage and the movement of regiments, life continued as if the old ways would last indefinitely. But we all knew that once the war was won India would gain her freedom from British rule.

After the death of Sir Alexander McRobert and a fierce boardroom battle, Sir Robert Menzies emerged as the second 'uncrowned king' of Cawnpore. He and his wife Jenny were the leaders of Cawnpore society during the war years. There had always been rivalry between the BIC and Begg Sutherland. The Scots doctor at the McRobert Hospital once told me that McRobert's BIC directors were businessmen and Begg Sutherland's were gentlemen. In 1946 the gentlemen bowed out. Begg Sutherland, in a well-kept secret, was sold to the BIC. It was a triumph for Sir Robert Menzies but it was a short-lived one. The BIC in their turn fell to the Mawari, Haridas Mundhra.[29] It proved to be a sorry tale of forged share certificates, shady deals and a prison sentence for

Independence, 1947: A. P. Wattal, chief engineer of the United Provinces Public Works Department, State Irrigation Branch, taking over the Kanpur Electricity Supply Corporation, in the presence of (left to right) R. N. Mookerjee, I. O. Hamilton, R. L. Powell and D. Dare.

Mundhra, with Government intervention and a receiver for the BIC. Cooper Allen was sold off for a single rupee.

On the stroke of midnight on 15 August 1947 India became independent. In Cawnpore at the Power House, a symbol of all that was being handed over, a simple ceremony took place. Ian Hamilton and R. L. Powell – Ron Powell, my husband – representing the managing agents Begg Sutherland, were photographed with A. P. Wattal, chief engineer UP, as he signed acceptance of authority for the Power House on behalf of the Government of India. Cawnpore became Kanpur. At the Residency, Lucknow, the Union Jack that had flown day and night since the Mutiny was ceremoniously lowered and the flagstaff cut down. The flag was presented to King George VI.

One by one the Europeans sold up their mills and left. The last mill to remain in European hands was Atherton Mills, run by Tony West, son of Bert West and grandson of Atherton West who had been friends with Juggilal. The special relationship with Juggilal Kamlapat is demonstrated by both families building identical mills side by side at Anwarganj. The chimney of JK Cotton Spinning and Weaving bears the words 'Juggilal West 1921'. Juggilal put up 25 per cent of the capital for the Atherton West Mills and Atherton West purchased their spinning machinery for them from Tweedale and Smalley of Accrington.

Towards the mid-fifties, with mill after mill passing into Indian ownership, the close relationship somewhat soured when the Singhanias were reluctant to purchase part of the West family holding at a previously agreed price. The mill was forced to close with over 6,000 bales of unsold cloth stock. Pant-ji, for many years Chief Minister of the UP, now one of the dominant figures along with Lal Bahadur Shastri in Nehru's Cabinet, at the instigation of the influential Dr Jawaharlal Rohatgi, looked into matters. Pertinent questions were asked at the Lucknow Secretariat, to such effect that it was reported 'dhotis were flying'. The result after eighteen months was Government controllership for five years and eventually Suraj Bhan and Son, who had been linked with the original West enterprise in Victoria Mills, bought out the shares at Rs. 5/-.[30]

When Tony West, the last of the West family, the last Englishman to own a mill in Kanpur, came to leave in November 1970, the staff asked to give a party for him on his last evening. The usual speeches and presentations were made – a silver tea set, a framed speech and so on. Tony expressed a wish to go round the mill to take his farewell next day of each and every department. The staff pleaded that he should time his visit between two shifts, at eleven o'clock, so that two shifts of men might see him. Tony inquired if this would entail any loss of work and they assured him not. It was agreed he should be at the mill at 11 a.m.

The hooters blared out and the machines were switched off. The men for the second shift came in and took up their places beside their machines and the men from the first shift remained where they had been. The mill was silent in curious anticipation. As Tony went through each department it was as if the workers had agreed on some age-old ritual, unspoken yet known to all, of honour and farewell. Everyone seemed to have come in his newest clothes, or if not new then newly washed, *puggris* freshly bound. Each man standing by his machine wanted to shake Tony by the hand and place a garland of marigolds round his neck. Some could only afford a few strung on a slender thread, others presented thick wet garlands of petals and tinsel smelling sweetly of wild roses. The handshaking and the garlanding completed, the second shift man started his machine. Machine after machine roared into life as Tony passed until the whole shed reverberated. The garlands round his neck accumulated; three *chaprasis* walked behind him ready to receive them each time they became too many for him to wear comfortably. One man had forgotten to bring a garland and tried to press a ten-rupee note into Tony's hand, and when Tony smilingly refused it said 'Nai Sahib, hum kuch dena mangta' – 'I want to give you something.'

By the time they reached the last department Tony's hand was limp and he could barely speak. His eyes were red with incipient tears, sleepless nights and the alcohol that had made the last few weeks possible. Honour had been done. The workmen would go home and tell their families, 'Today the Sahib left. He shook hands with me.'

Tony West slipped away from Kanpur, alone and unnoticed, to catch a plane from Lucknow on his way back to England, wife and children. It was some time before he could bring himself to speak about his last visit to the mill that had been his and his father's and his grandfather's before him. Sometimes at night he would wake and think he could smell the nutty stench of cotton and hear the hooters calling out to the men from first one Kanpur factory and then another. But now it was only a dream.

Envoi

Those days are over. Gone forever. Yet from time to time I hear on the radio the announcement of a concert to be held at the MacRobert Centre, Stirling, and with a thrill realise the past is still very much part of the present. The descendants of the pioneering families of Cawnpore continue the legacy of hard work and endeavour.

The Trust funds set up by Sir Alexander MacRobert and later augmented by Lady (Rachel) MacRobert are famous for their generous donations to hospitals and the RAF; their charitable projects reach into the future. The Stewart family continue to enjoy their estate at Ardvorlich and I was privileged on several occasions when transcribing the Stewart letters to enjoy it too. When I visited the grandson of Ralph Maxwell we sat in a room adorned with trophies and mementoes of the Grand Old Man of Pigsticking. The son of Sir Harry Horsman continues to make regular visits to Kanpur to oversee the wellbeing of the two hospitals built and endowed by his forebears for the people of Kanpur. Sir George Allen's talent with the *Pioneer* is inherited by his great-grandson Charles Allen, author, journalist and broadcaster, well known for his series of books on India, including *Plain Tales from the Raj.* The Butterworth connection with India continues through my cousins who live on the top of a beautiful mountain near Dharamsala and organise treks into Kulu. Occasionally I meet Tony West, the last of the English mill-owners in Kanpur, and then we exchange stories of our grandparents and our parents and our own childhoods while the great-grandson of Lala Juggilal, Mr Vijaypat Singhania, was recently fêted when he arrived in his twin-engine aircraft, Tiger, at Quebec having won the 1994 Round the World air race.

Perhaps the most prophetic of all is the Gavin Jones connection. When the Channel Tunnel opened in 1994 a picture of Sir Christopher Mallaby, KCMG, 'our man in Paris', striding out into the future that links England to Europe, appeared in the papers. I could not help thinking his great-grandfather Gavin Sibbald Jones must be looking on with quiet satisfaction.

Ap ki topiyan par salamat rahi
The blessing of heaven be upon their heads.

Notes and Sources

PROLOGUE

1 Emma Butterworth, born in 1849, married in 1872 James Mellor of Thongsbridge, near Huddersfield, and after his death Rowland Archer. She died childless on 4 June 1926, aged seventy-seven. Notes on the Butterworth family by my father, Harold Wilkinson, 1958.

2 'The syce stood at the back of the carriage and at the Memorial Gardens would get off at one gate and meet the carriage at the second gate as they were coming out. This was because in those days only one Indian was allowed in the Memorial Gardens at a time.' Ruby Wilkinson, *Memoires*.

3 This marble statue, the Angel of the Resurrection, was executed by Baron Marochetti from a design by Lady Canning. He altered it by placing two branches of palms in the arms – the original drawing had only one and was more graceful. It is possible Lady Canning had seen the illustration that appeared in the *Illustrated London News* (May 1856) of the Angel of Scutari, the monument to the Crimean dead where each angel holds one palm frond.

4 *Sherriff's Illustrated Route Charts and Travellers' Hand Book to Egypt and India*, London, 1882.

5 Joe Lee, *The Indian Mutiny: A Narrative of Events at Cawnpore*, Victoria Press, Cawnpore, 1893.

CHAPTER ONE

1 BL: 9057 i 16 Gavin S. Jones, *The Story of My Escape from Fatehgarh*, Pioneer Press [Cawnpore?], 1913. Published in *Blackwood's Magazine* 1859, under title 'Reminiscences of the Mutiny'.

2 William Edwards, *Personal Adventures*, Smith, London, 1858.

CHAPTER TWO

1 Sullivan died shortly after, of cholera. When the Memorial Well Gardens

were established Private Murphy was appointed custodian. Mowbray Thomson and Delafosse went on to become major-generals.

2   NAI: Home Public Proceedings of the Governor General in Council, vol. 8, January 1858, nos. 278 and 278B.

3   Khaki comes from the Persian word for 'earth' or 'dust'. This was the colour of the uniform worn by some of the Punjab regiments at the siege of Delhi and became very popular for the first time in the Army during the 1857-58 campaigns. Cloth was dyed with a mixture of black and red office inks to take the place of the red uniforms that had given the soldiers the name of 'Lal Coortee Wallahs'.

4   To my way of thinking this is how we held power, not by setting Hindu against Muslim, but by encouraging the 'people', the lower castes.

5   *The Mofussilite,* 27 November 1857.

6   Lieutenant George Cracklow. Born 1832, died 1878.

7   Brevet-Major O. H. St G. Anson, *With HM 9th Lancers during the Indian Mutiny*, privately printed, Malcolmson and Co. Ltd, London and Redhill, n.d. Information James and Barbara Anson.

8   On the Revd Moore's map (BL: ADD 37151) General Wheeler's bungalow is shown situated within a large triangular compound flanked by the canal, Duncan's Hotel and what was to become the H & S Factory.

9   Archibald Spiers, CS, had been a witness at their wedding.

10   Lieutenant George Cracklow's papers.

11   Fred Roberts was born in Cawnpore in 1832, at a bungalow on the site of what became the Lalimli Club (next door to The Palms where Great Aunt-Emma stayed with my Butterworth grandparents). He was the son of General Sir Abraham Roberts who at that time was stationed at Cawnpore in command of the Bengal European Regiment and had married as his second wife a widow, Isabella Maxwell. Their infant was a sickly baby and there is a story, believed in Cawnpore, that when the baby had smallpox his life was saved when his grandmother took him to be bathed in the Ganges. The fact that his grandmother believed in such Indian remedies may have given rise to the rumour that Frederick Roberts was himself Anglo-Indian. General Sir Abraham Roberts had three children born to *bebees* before he married for the first time but I have not been able to trace any direct Indian relationship in Fred Roberts's descent. If the grandmother was an Indian lady, she was a grandmother through stepbrothers and not a blood relation.

12   Field-Marshal Lord Roberts, *Forty-One Years in India,* 2 vols., Macmillan, 1897.

13   Rebel sepoys were called 'Pandies', after Mungal Pandy, who ran amok on the parade ground of the 34th Native Infantry at Barrackpore, the first spark of the Mutiny.

14   H.E. Marshall, *Our Island Story,* T.C. & E.C. Jack, Edinburgh, n.d.
    The story of Jessie's Dream was debunked by Richard Collier in *The*

Sound of Fury: 'As a ballad, as a poem by John Greenleaf Whittier, as a box-office draw at Wallack's Theatre, New York, "Jessie's Dream" echoed, round the world, yet the truth was more prosaic. The romance, composed by a French governess to divert her pupils, reached the Calcutta papers even before word had come of Lucknow's first relief. Accredited by Parisian papers, it was featured by the *London Times* on 14th December, but the pipers, Pipe-Major Alexander M'Kellar later affirmed, were silent until Havelock reached the Residency. And Jessie Brown, allegedly a 78th Highlander's wife, could never have been present to hear them. The womenfolk of the 78th were then 800 miles away in Poona, enjoying free beer and rations in token of their husbands' service.' Information Mrs Shirley Tomlinson.

15 William Forbes-Mitchell, *Reminiscences of the Great Mutiny*, Macmillan, London, 1893.

16 The gallant and beautiful young widow Lakshmi Bai, Rani of Jhansi, was the Boadicea of India. Driven into rebellion by the injustice of the annexation of Jhansi, she led her army with 'bravery, cleverness and perseverance', fighting valiantly like a man, 'the most dangerous of all rebel leaders'. Her example inspired many in the freedom struggle that led to Independence 1947. (Antonia Fraser, *Boadicea's Chariot.*)

17 George Vickers, *Narrative of the Indian Revolt*, London, 1858. Published in weekly parts.

18 Thomas Lewin, *A Fly on the Wheel,* Constable, London, 1912. Cawnpore was riddled with *nullahs* and waterways which in the rainy season turn into regular rivers. Each was spanned by a bridge. This particular bridge was near the theatre and the Assembly Rooms. Information Mrs Betsy Macdonald.

19 Thomas Lewin went on to make his name working among the Lushai tribes. His grandson Tommy Macdonald joined Begg Sutherland's sugar factories in the 1930s.

20 John Kirk and Co., long established in Cawnpore as traders in country produce and agents to the Maxwell family, had, according to information supplied by Dr Nigam, a huge compound. It was conveniently situated near the Custom House and Permit Ghat Bazaar and their offices included the Cawnpore Bank. The whole area of the compound included what became the Upper India Chamber of Commerce, the McRobert Hospital and its grounds, the original office of Begg Sutherland and the Muir Mill bungalows of Smith Square and Johnson Square.

   Information supplied by Mrs Holland of Muir Mills states that Smith Square was built about 1920. A pre-Mutiny thatched bungalow belonging to the Maxwells stood where Smith Square now is. During the Great War this bungalow was used as a Red Cross depot and was in the charge of Joe Kendall who was awarded the MBE for his work.

21 John Percival, *For Valour, The Victoria Cross, Courage in Action,* Methuen,

London, 1985. 'Part of the 64th Regt which had been badly upstaged by young Lieutenant Havelock remained at Cawnpore, most of the time under siege, for many months. On 28 November 1857, the same Major Stirling who had suffered the humiliation of watching another officer lead his men to glory, again had a charge against the guns. This time he was firmly to the fore, but as he reached the Indian battery Stirling was shot dead. Again the glory went to another – this time a fifteen-year-old Irish drummer boy named Thomas Flinn, who was wounded early in the action, picked himself up and pressed forward with his comrades. At the battery Flinn was seen to take on two of the enemy artillery men in hand-to-hand combat, and his courage was so impressive that he was awarded the VC. Two days after the investiture in Karachi Flinn was imprisoned for being drunk and disorderly, and for the rest of his time in the army his service record is simply a calendar of the years he spent in military prisons. He was discharged finally in 1869 and returned to Achlone, Ireland, where he lived in total obscurity, dying a pauper in the workhouse in 1892. He was just fifty. Sadly his drunken decline following the highest award for courage is not unique in the history of the VC.' Thomas Flinn was one of the two youngest boys ever to win the VC. Information Mrs Margaret Cooke.

In Lichfield Cathedral there is a brass tablet accompanied by the regimental badge of 64th Foot (later 2nd Staffordshire Regt). 'Colonel Nicholas Wilson K. H. Killed at Cawnpore Nov XXVIII MDCCCLVII. Major Thomas Stirling. Killed at Cawnpore Nov XXVIII MDCCCLVII. Capt. Richard C. M. Crea. Killed at Cawnpore Nov XXVIII MDCCCLVII.' Information Paul Norris.

22   J.W. Sherer, *Havelock's March on Cawnpore,* Nelson, 1911.
23   The Noronha family possess a certificate of appreciation issued to M. X. Noronha by Mr Sherer for his work in arranging a buggy . . . 'and I should employ Noronha again if I had another job of the kind.' Information supplied by Dr M. Nigam.
24   The Revd Moore's diary, *op. cit.*
25   OIOC: photo EUR 59, Francis Collins papers.
26   Information Mr Gash, a relative.
27   Forbes-Mitchell *op. cit.*
28   Lewin, *op. cit.*
29   The Revd Moore's diary, *op. cit.* Things were sufficiently returning to normal for christenings to take place. 'I have 200 cheroots for nothing. Sandy sent them as a Xening present. I hope Mrs S. will have twins next time, and soon!'
30   Cracklow papers, *op. cit.*
31   Forbes-Mitchell, *op. cit.*
32   Cracklow papers, *op. cit.*
33   Forbes-Mitchell, *op. cit.;* Forbes-Mitchell's story of 'Jamie Green'.

34 In later years, being near the railway colony and difficult to protect, the tablets and monuments were constantly looted and vandalised. Even in 1970 when I tried to find Peel's grave, there was no sign of it. A willing urchin pointed out what he swore had been the very spot which once had marked a hero's grave. Now the entire cemetery has been built over.

35 Collins papers, *op. cit.*

36 One of the hospitals Collins was describing had been set up in the big old bungalow next to the entrenchment. Partly fortified, it had once housed General Windham and Bruce but in the palmy days of Cawnpore, long before the Mutiny, that house had belonged to Adam Maxwell and been bought by Nawab Rooshum ood Dowlah when he retired from the Court of Oude – see *Traders and Nabobs*. Ultimately it became the bungalow of the Superintendent of the Harness and Saddlery Factory which was to be built on the site of the entrenchment. It was reputed to be haunted, a link with the time when it had been a hospital. A beheaded sepoy was reported seen on many occasions, asking for food, begging for *roti,* a *chaupatty.* It has recently reverted to being a hospital. Information Mrs Larmour.

37 Information Humphry Peppé.

38 Moore's map.

39 Information Antony Werner.

40 OIOC: 88D 22 (a) 1859. Official Report on Cawnpore Mutiny, Colonel G.W. Williams.

CHAPTER THREE

1 Stewart family papers. Lieutenant John Stewart, RA, was to become a key figure in the development of the leather industry in Cawnpore.

2 Sherer, *op. cit.*

3 Roberts, *op. cit.*

4 OIOC: L/MIL/17/COLL 205/14. Sherer's report.

5 Sherer, *op. cit.*

6 Information Colonel C.H.T. MacFetridge.

7 Sherer, *op. cit.*

8 OIOC: *The Englishman.*

9 See *Traders and Nabobs.*

10 Recently I was given this reference that suggests the authorities took the part of the Peishwa against Adam Maxwell and sentenced him to prison.
    Asiatic Journal, New Series XXIV, 1837, 'Asiatic Intelligence' Sep 1837, p. 8. 'Mr Adam Maxwell, of the late house of Maxwell Bennet and Co [*sic*], and his accomplice Oomrad Ali, having been tried before the Sessions Court of Cawnpore, for swindling Rs. 11,500 from the Peishwa, at Bithoor the former has been sentenced to six months' imprisonment in the gaol of

Cawnpore, and to pay a fine to Government of Rs.1,000, or, in default, to three months' further imprisonment; and to the latter, five months' imprisonment has been awarded. (Original report from the Agra Ukbhar.)'

A further report appears on p. 46: 'It appears that Maxwell claimed he had been appointed mukhtar to Bajee Rao with the intention of furthering his return to power and restoration of his rank, wealth and powers. Maxwell was accused of having pretended through his influence that representations could be made to the Governor General. The Agra Ukhbar commented that Maxwell had returned from England after the failure of Maxwell's and had acted as mukhtar to the late Mujumud-ud-Doolah and the King of Oude.

'It concludes that his intriguing to be made mukhtar to the Peishwa is no crime, and that he had a right to set what value he pleased on his services in that capacity; in short, it considers the charges absurd, and the sentence illegal, and declares that the native assessors first found a verdict of "not guilty", and ultimately said "guilty". Mr Maxwell has appealed to the Sudder.'

Case continued p. 70. Discusses Baji Rao's evidence. He denied that he had appointed Maxwell as his mukhtar . . . said he did not agree a fee . . . but still gave Maxwell Rs. 11,500. Cross-examining Baji Rao, Maxwell asked why, if he had not appointed him as his mukhtar, he had paid him. Information supplied by Christopher Hawes.

11   OIOC: L/AG/34/27/162 p. 153. Peter Maxwell's will attested by Hugh Maxwell at Cawnpore 30 April 1858.

12   NAI: Home Public Proceedings, nos. 91-3, 4 June 1858.

13   Allahabad Archives: Mutiny File 653, no. 12, 26 July 1858.

14   NAI: Home Public Proceedings, nos. 1 and 2, 14 May 1858. Amelia Horne's claim.

15   NAI: Home Public Proceedings, no. 175, January 1885. Churcher claim.

16   Allahabad Archives: Mutiny File, *op. cit.*

CHAPTER FOUR

1   A nickname for old India hands taken from the usual manner in which servants were summoned – 'Koi-hai?', 'Is anyone there?'

2   Lewin, *op. cit.*

3   Stewart family papers. John Stewart writes to his sister Tina, married to William Roberts, BCS. John Stewart and his brothers and sister were descended on their mother's side from John Athanass, the son of one of the first Greek traders in Calcutta, and himself a successful and wealthy businessman. The name Athanass was proudly included in family names for two generations and it seems possible that this charming story of the Greek father was handed down through the Athanass connection.

4   Extract from a letter from E.A. Reade (the man who had hounded Adam

Maxwell) from Agra 28 June 1957 to Tina's husband Roberts about the murder of William Stewart:

Poor Stewart, Alas! was one of the first victims. As far as I can learn he had mounted his horse to see what the disturbance was, and was shot down with other officers, who had similarly gone towards the lines, by parties of mutineers stationed at various points for this purpose. The mutineers of this contingent appear to have been less bent on murder of females and children than at other places, and several of these unfortunates were hidden by them or carried by the back of the lines, towards the residency. Poor Mrs Stewart was, with other ladies, hidden, but hearing from a servant, as some say, or, as others say, seeing her husband's riderless horse, rushed out with one of her children towards the lines, and both fell victims. Little Charlotte was detained by a Mrs Hawkins, and how, or by what means, I know not, was carried off to the residency, and sent by the Rajah towards Agra, where they were brought in, in carriages sent from hence. Mrs Hawkins lost two of her children, and is still almost demented. But dear little Charlotte has found a mother in Charlotte Alexander (Blair), grand-daughter of our dear friends the Kennedys. Alexander's detachment mutinied also in the Jaloun district, and they came into Agra, only with the clothes on their backs, protected by Jourdain's [?] equestrian troops. I have got clothes for them and assisted this good dear girl to provide for little Charlotte, whom I trust God will be pleased to spare. His sustaining hand should increase our faith. On the road from Gwalior the fugitives were detained by Mrs Gilbert being confined. Yet she and her baby have reached in safety and are doing well.

5   This was when Lieutenant Roberts joined him to start organising Lord Canning's triumphal tour.
6   John Stewart writes to his sister Tina.
7   The agents of Tod Heatley and Co.
8   OIOC: *The Pioneer*, Monday 15 July 1867.

THE EAST INDIAN RAILWAY

In one district the railway brought to light a system of praedial slavery as firmly rooted as when the English had entered the country ninety years before. It had continued safer for the poor man to be the slave of the rich man than to be his hired workman. Bondage was profitable to the people: our laws did not interfere directly with the institution; and so during the long years that Exeter Hall was declaiming on the African, slavery flourished unmolested under the sanction of the British Government in Bengal. It was reserved for the railway to do naturally for the hill people of the San-thal country what English philanthropists had done spasmodically for the blacks of Jamaica. Coolie recruiters were let loose on the country; the value of labour rose; every able-bodied man and woman could earn an ample livelihood by the work of their hands, and freedom became an object of ambition. But in proportion as the labour of the serfs became valuable to themselves, so also did it become profitable to their masters. Complications arose, the local officials bungled, the Calcutta statesmen could not make out what was wrong, and during a year of unexampled prosperity a peaceable tribe rose in revolt. Then came enquiry and explanation, remedial measures followed, and the nation which the railway found slaves it left free men.

9   OIOC: MSS EUR B 212.

10 Some idea of the discomforts is conveyed by the following letter written from Aezenghur on 27 March 1868, by Delia Peppé to her husband, a near neighbour of the Debnams and fellow grantee in the Goruckpore district.

We came in here this morning about an hour ago, that is ten o'clock, after a night of trouble and harassment I hope never to experience again.

We left Benaris last evening about 6 p.m. by dak gharry, and about nine or ten a storm came on which nearly smothered us. The horse would not face it, and after an hour or two of discomfort we started afresh and again stuck several times, expecting every instant to be put into the ditch . Annie had been a little out of sorts during the day and now got worse – got sick at stomach, when all at once the coachman called out that a man had jumped off the top of the gharry with two of my boxes, and was running away.

I got out at once but could not see a thing, the night was dark. But sure enough my little portmanteau was gone with all my trinkets, Edward Bridgman's *three* watches, and goodness knows what else. The other box contained a pair of bronze piano lamps I had just bought from Lewis Steward. I strongly suspect the coachman who called for the choukedar of a village and strange to say, not only a choukedar but a policeman in blue clothes made their appearance. But to little use, for we had only the satisfaction to hear the former say, 'Where am I to look for anything in such a dark night?'

Poor Annie was getting worse and I had to hurry on the best way I could. However as we were only two cosse [approximately four miles] from Jaunpore, I went to the Thanna there and made a statement of my losses, which one of the constables took down in writing. And then we came on for I was most seriously alarmed about Annie. She was very ill for several hours, vomiting and purging. I had to get her out several times. First she took sherry, then some gin, but as neither seemed to do her good I gave her chlorodine twice before it gave her any relief. At present she is quiet and I hope asleep. Poor child her mouth is like a stick, so dry and parched. She had something to drink but could not retain it at first but the last cup of tea has remained.

I have reported the case of the robbery to the Superintendent of Police at Jaunpore and have also written to Benaris about it but I fancy there will be little redress and I must bear it. [Peppé family papers.]

The following extracts from the *Pioneer* amplify the theme:

ON FRIDAY NIGHT LAST, ABOUT 10 O'CLOCK, A special train, bringing the 102nd Regiment (*en route* from Kamptee to Lucknow) from Jubbulpore, came to a stand still, on account of the engine breaking down, at about the 48th mile below Allahabad Under the impression that the train had arrived at a station, the wife of one of the Serjeants got out of a carriage. There being no proper landing place at that spot, she fell headlong down a bank some thirty-five feet high. Her husband, seeing her disappear, jumped out also and met with a like accident. On getting to his feet he found his wife lying insensible. His cries to his comrades above induced six others to jump from the carriage, who all fell more or less precipitately down the incline. The Assistant Surgeon, Dr. Tyrrell, hearing the cries for help, jumped out also, and reached the bottom of the cutting with only a few slight bruises. At this stage, the engine having been temporarily repaired, the driver blew his whistle as a signal to proceed. On hearing the whistle, the Colonel and all the men in the carriages shouted to him to stop. The driver refused, asserting that the Colonel had no right to give orders, that he was only a passenger, and that he (the driver) was in charge there. Meanwhile the train moved on, leaving the unfortunate people below in the dark and in the jungle, all more or less contused—the woman being insensible, and terribly cut about the head and shoulders, and one of the men with a compound fracture of the arm.   Dr. Tyrrell made his way in the dark to where he saw a number of natives seated round a fire, and from them learnt that a bungalow, occupied by Mr. Vice, the Assistant Engineer, was close at hand.   The poor sufferers were soon removed to Mr. Vice's house, and to that gentleman's prompt and friendly succour were eventually indebted for food and shelter as well as some medical comforts.

Such are substantially the facts of the case as they have been reported to us on the best authority.   The official inquiry usual in such cases will doubtless tell us more.

———————◆———————

WE HAVE SELDOM HEARD OF ANYTHING IN the way of narrow escapes to equal the follow_ ing :—One day last week a jemadar of points- men at Sutna station was going along by the side of the rails to let a down-train out of the station, when he was seen to stagger wildly about for a few moments, and then fall down close to the rails just as the train was coming on. As soon as the train had passed he was seen lying quite still in the same place, and everyone of course supposed he had been killed by a blow from some part of the engine.   Two or three men accordingly came running up, but found the jemadar alive, prostrate on the ballast, with an enormous cobra twined about his legs.   Fortunately one of the men had a . stick and began hitting at the cobra with all his might, regardless of the bare shin of the poor jemadar. The snake was finally killed, and then the jemadar picked himself up, rather ruefully, and explained the whole affair. It appeared that in getting out of the way of the train he trod on the snake, and in trying to dodge the snake he tripped over the wire that works the distant signal, and rolled back towards the train in company with the venomous reptile. The latter was probably frightened at the train, and writhed about the man's legs for protection; the man himself lay as still and flat as possible, and had the satisfaction of seeing the projecting part of the cow-catcher pass about an inch above his nose. His feelings may be better imagined than described when he found himself saved from both perils, uncrushed and unbitten, and none the worse for the adventure, saving for the fright and a hearty belabouring about the legs with a stout bamboo. The above may be relied on.

WE REGRET TO HAVE TO RECORD A FATAL ACcident, which occurred to the Down Mail Train at the Cawnpore Station, East Indian Railway, on the morning of the 2nd. This Train, due at about 3 A. M., when it ·arrived at the Goods Shed, about three or four hundred yards from the Station, and consequently was still going at a considerable speed, left its own line for the Goods siding, and ran into the Goods Train which was being unloaded at the sheds. It appears that, at the place of junction between the main rail and siding, the point had been carefully locked by the two pointsmen stationed there, so as to permit the Goods Train to proceed, without disturbing them from the sleep to which they betook themselves. The Jemadar, who ought to have satisfied himself that the pointsmen were on the alert for the Down Train, thought it sufficient to tell a chuprassie to see to the mat_ter, and the chuprassie contented himself with giving a shout from near the passenger station, without seemingly thinking any answer requisite. Thus the two Trains came into collision, the engines were locked fast together, and three carriages behind either engine were piled one on the other. Six natives were killed on the spot, and one died shortly after. The latter was an Honorary Magistrate in the Cawnpore District, named Kinder Sing, and two of the others were his servants. The head of one of the victims was completely severed from his body. A native, who was unloading oil-casks from the Goods Train, was crushed, and is not expected to live; others, who had received more or less injuries, were taken to hospital. There were only two English travellers by the Train, one of whom, Sir William Hamilton, was slightly injured.

Not five hours after the above, another native lost his life at the same station. Standing with the chain of a carriage in his hand to hook on to an approaching Engine, he was not careful to avoid the buffers, between which he was immediately crushed, and death was almost instantaneous.

11 Major Aitken, formerly 13th NLI, now Inspector General of Oude Police, was presented with the VC by Sir Hugh Rose at a ceremony at the Residency to mark his heroism in guarding the Baillie Guard Gate during the siege.
    OIOC: *The Pioneer,* 11 January 1865.

12 The future Lord Roberts.

13 Summary of his career prepared by John Stewart, Ardvorlich, March 1899. Letter to Richmond I. W. Ritchie, CS, Private Secretary to the Right Honourable Secretary of State for India.

14 'The Headman of Leather': 'mochee' is one who works in leather, a shoemaker or a saddler, a man of low caste – it is a somewhat back-handed compliment.

15 W. B. Wishart, *Commercial History of Cawnpore, 1863-1902,* privately printed.

16 Gavin Sibbald Jones, 'The Rise and Progress of Cawnpore'. Unpublished MS, Cawnpore, 25 November 1906.

17 OIOC: L/AG/34/27, p. 648.

18 OIOC: L/AG Bengal Inventories 1807/8.

19 Emma Roberts, *Scenes and Characteristics of Hindostan: Sketches of Anglo-Indian Society,* London, 1835.

20 CC: Captain J. de Wend, 44th Regiment, personal papers.

21 Fanny Parks, *Wanderings of a Pilgrim in Search of the Picturesque,* Richardson, London, 1850.

22 Gavin S. Jones, *op. cit.*

23 Robert Montgomery, *Statistical Account of Cawnpore,* published by Government, 1849.

24 Examples of John Stewart's 'commissions':
    [Stewart to Roberts. Cawnpore, 5 June 1861] I write to say that I despatched yesterday by *Bangy Coolies* to your address the following:
                    A set of Buggy Harness
                    2 Large tins of Salmon
                    2 Small ditto
                    1 Ham lbs 11 3/4
                    2 Tin cases of oil
    The Harness is Rs 25- the two tins of oil being one maund also Rs 25- and the Ham and Salmon Rs 30-1- as per memos accompanying. I paid Rs 2 for coolies hire so my share of expenses has been Rs 82-1- You have to pay the coolies Rs 5 on arrival.
    Coolie is an expensive item but Tina found it the most satisfactory way of getting things from Cawnpore – as the Bullock Train has no direct service between Fattehgarh and Bareilly and often stores etc are delayed many days and not too much care taken of them.
    As the coolies will be returning empty handed could you without much trouble make one load for one of them of some dozens of Bareilly jail towels

and Jharans – Tina once sent us some Jharans – beauties such as dear Millie loves. . . If the Mangoes have come in and Bareilly has many, the other coolie might bring a load of them – we have very few mangoes at Cawnpore.

[John to Tina. Cawnpore 25 March 1865] I send you today by the train leaving tonight a package containing Mrs Bayley's stay irons, George's cheroot box, Mrs Edwards's child's shoes etc., Mrs Reasson's slippers, Robert's Boots and lasts – I am going to the train to see Mrs St George Tucker and her sister Miss Letitia off to the Hills and I'll book your Packages – so you can send down your servant with a note for it.
    The prices of the articles sent are as follows:

Mrs B's stays	Rs 2.0
George's Cheroot Box	0.9
Mrs P's slippers	1.0
2 pairs children's Boots	3.0
1 pair " shoes	0.8
1 pair " shoes patent	1.4

You have already paid Rung Loll for Robert's Boots. Mrs Edwards's Boots will cost Rs 4 each so that Mrs Edwards's order will come to 12/12.
    The Tusser Silk and Tub and chair came down all right and were in time to send with heavy luggage. The chair is a capital thing. If I meet anyone at the train I know going up I shall entrust him with your package so you'll get it free.

Tina was to give a Ball for the whole of Agra society and Stewart promised to supply her with cloth to transform her drawing room into a dancing floor.

[John to Tina. Cawnpore 20 January 1866] The Brown Holland is too thin and flimsy I think for so large a room as yours. It would not stand the stretching. The best cloth for Dancing is Rupia Duck 1/8 a yd!! out of the question. Next to that comes Bolt Canvass or sail cloth. It is 9 annas per yard width 2 ft and would cost 80 or 90 for your room – but I can't get enough of it here. Next to that comes American Drill which is very dear and I think too dear for the quality. The next best is Doosootie (of course I am putting Holland out of the question).
    At the 88th Ball the other day they tried to get Canvass but could not, so they put down Doosootie [cheap cotton fabric woven with double threads] with *nails* only and waxed and chalked it – and I never danced on a better floor – so I think you had better go in for Doosootie – it should be as close woven as possible. If you can get it at Agra good and well – but if not I can get the same man that furnished the 88th cloth to furnish yours – the Doosootie sells at 3/- per than [length of fabric] of 11 yards.
    Perhaps you can get good Doosootie from Moir of the Jail. If you have

time I am in favour of the lacing – because you can leave the side pieces down and take up the cloth at any time for washing it. Have the eyeholes close enough and there's no fear of the cloth tearing. The Doosootie won't cost you more than from 40 to 50 or 60/-. Canvass would cost 100 or more and Holland the same. Drill 120/-.

I think I'll be able to wax the cloth for you and French chalk it – Get some soap stone powdered down.

25 Fanny Maxwell's letters and Tom Tracy's diary. Kind permission of Antony Werner, transcribed by Joanna Motion.

26 Dr Begg's (the planters' doctor) brother-in-law.

27 Hobson-Jobson gives 'Post, i.e. properly transported by relays of men and horses, and thus "the mail" or letter-post, as well as any arrangement for travelling, or for transporting articles by such relays.' In this case an arrangement for travelling.

28 While Gavin Jones was at Cawnpore he received his Mutiny Medal 'for service during the disturbances'. It arrived on 16 May 1861. He received and acknowledged it the same day.

29 OIOC: *The Mofussilite,* 8 January 1861.

30 OIOC: *Calcutta Gazette,* v / 11 / 393, 1861.

31 Roberts, *op. cit.,* vol.1, p. 375.

32 Police officers were drawn from the Army and many were captains. Even today a senior policeman is greeted as 'Captain Sahib'.

33 Also his background of being an indigo planter and a zemindar, 'the business of which is more like that of a magistrate or collector's office'.

34 Har Chand Rae, Ramanand Goro Pershad Sukul, Muflis Rai Gunga Sahai, Babu Nanu Mal, an employee of A. Warwick from Hingunghat. The link with Hingunghat, famed for its high-quality cotton, was to prove providential. Also associated with them were Captain Aitken (later awarded the VC) and Captains Tovey and Coghill. For years Tovey's name has been incorrectly written as Toby.

35 S. P. Mehra, *Cawnpore Civic Problems,* Citizen Press, Cawnpore, 1952.

36 John Chapman, *The Cotton and Commerce of India,* London, 1851.

37 James Forbes, *Oriental Memoirs,* London, 1813.

38 Arnold Wright, *Annesley of Surat and His Times,* Melrose, London, 1918.

39 Norman Longmate, *The Hungry Mills* 1861-1865, Temple Smith, London, 1978.

40 OIOC: 'Cotton Crisis 1861'. NWP 216/4, 30 March, no. 77, p. 193.

41 Gavin Jones, *op. cit.*

42 Letter to Messrs Anderston Foundry Co., Glasgow, from Dymes and Co., Madras, 19 January 1861. Information Theon Wilkinson.

43 *The Pioneer,* 26 April 1865. 'If General Lee can win a battle and thereby send cotton up the rueful faces of Bombay Banias will be lightened up at the renewed glimmer of prosperity. They are praying fervently for a

continuation of the American War as it would not matter to them if every man in America were destroyed, provided cotton rose sufficiently high to admit a remunerative rate.'

44   Mrs Margaret Vemon, *née* Trickett, wife of William Vernon, mill manager at the Elgin Mills from 1905 for twenty years, was a keen photographer. She won the Kaisar-i-Hind medal in June 1918 for organising the Red Cross war effort at Cawnpore. Thanks to Madge Vernon and Peggy Vernon, *née* Catterall.

45   'A Short History of the Family', compiled by Fanny Bell and Gavin Jones in 1891.

46   A School will be opening at this House, which stands in a very healthy and pleasant situation by the side of the river.
Terms including board and washing, per month.
Reading, Writing, Arithmetic, Book-keeping, Geography etc. Sa Rs 30/-
Latin, Greek, Hebrew, Persian and Sangscrit 35/-
Regular attention will be paid to the correct pronunciation of the English language. A Persian and Sanscrit Moonshi will be employed.
        Letters addressed to Mr Carey will be immediately attended to.
        Mission House School, Serampore, 1 May 1801. (Seton Karr, *Selections from the Calcutta Gazette*, vol. 1.)

47   Minden Wilson, *History of the Behar Indigo Factories*, Thacker Spink and Co., Calcutta, 1908.

48   In the copy of Gavin Jones's story of his escape from Fatehgarh deposited at the British Library, his son Tracy Gavin Jones, writing in 1913, notes that his father was working with the GIP Railway and on leave, staying with his brother John Moore Jones at Mendhi Ghat, when the Mutiny broke out. This is contradicted in Gavin Jones's own notes on family history and by a contemporary biography that states that after the death of their mother Gavin had been working on the indigo estate with John Moore Jones and did not join the GIP Railway until 1862.

49   Andro Linklater, *An Unhusbanded Life: Charlotte Despard, Suffragette, Socialist, and Sinnfeiner*, 1980.

50   They were married at Holy Trinity, Brompton, London on 14 November and sailed almost immediately for India. Rather oddly, GSJ gives his father as Captain HM Service as if his grandfather was more important to him than his father.

51   Edmond Jones and Clinton Kemp were buried at the roadside at Gopi Ganj, not far from the Palee bungalow. In 1970 when I passed that way the two crosses had been freshly whitewashed and a few marigolds threaded together placed around them. Each year there is a boat festival at Mirzapore at which the ballad of the murder of Moore, Jones and Kemp is recounted.

52   Information Jean Butterworth.

53   OIOC: *The Pioneer*, 8 May 1865.

CHAPTER FIVE

1 Letters and diaries of Mrs Edmonia Hill published in the *Atlantic Monthly* in April 1936 under the title of 'The Young Kipling'.
2 OIOC: *The Pioneer,* 18 July 1866.
3 OIOC: *The Pioneer,* 3 May 1866.
4 OIOC: *The Pioneer,* 3 December 1866.
5 OIOC: *The Pioneer,* 30 September 1868.
6 OIOC: *The Pioneer,* 9 February, 14 May and 23 May 1866.
7 Now part of the Beecham Group.
8 OIOC: *The Pioneer,* 4 December 1868.
9 'On the 27 June 1866 Moteewallah a Printer was convicted at the Supreme Court, Calcutta of Counterfeiting the *Labels* of Messrs Crosse and Blackwell, London, and was sentenced by Mr Justice Plear to Two Years Rigorous Imprisonment and on the 30th of the same month for selling Spurious Articles.' *The Pioneer,* 7 April 1871
10 OIOC: *The Pioneer,* 20 November 1867
11 OIOC: *The Pioneer,* 16 February 1870.
12 OIOC: *The Pioneer,* 17 December 1866.
13 *Memorials of Old Haileybury College and Haileybury 1806–1987.* Information supplied by Alastair Macpherson, hon. archivist.
14 OIOC: *The Pioneer,* 3 January 1866.
15 IOC: *The Pioneer,* 18 January 1869.
16 OIOC: *The Pioneer,* 8 November 1865.
17 Among them was the old 'Thomason' locomotive, which was employed originally on the embankment of the Solani aqueduct of the Ganges Canal, then lay for some years in the Roorkee workshops and was used occasionally for sawing up timber. It has now not unworthily helped to pump out water from the foundations of a railway bridge, and when thoroughly repaired has still some work left in it yet. I have mentioned this engine because I believe it was the first locomotive introduced into this Presidency, if not in all India.
18 OIOC: *The Pioneer,* 7 July 1869.
19 OIOC: *The Pioneer,* 24 March 1869.
20 OIOC: *The Pioneer,* 6 October 1869.
21 OIOC: *The Pioneer,* 15 July 1867. In the past year the East Indian Railway had carried ½ million tons of freight and 2 million passengers and made a net profit of £683,147

CHAPTER SIX

1 Gavin Jones, *op. cit.*

2 Power, Capt Sievewright . . . General Forrest, an old Dragoon officer, relative of Stacey and friend of Aunt Fanny, Dr Orton, both the Halseys, and Captain Sanderson, Cantts magistrate and cousin of the Stewarts.

3 Letter to William Cooke, Bastee, from Begg Maxwell and Co. (Peppé papers):

Cawnpore, 19 March 1868

Dear Sir,

We have the pleasure of your favour of 17 Instant enclosing currency notes and postage stamps for Rs 30-8-, in all of the Bill for the Harness ordered for you, for which we thank you.

We hope your sowing prospects arc favourable. – The sowings seem to, be doing well in Tirhoot and Chuppra -

Yours faithfully,

BEGG MAXWELL & CO

4 Maxwell letters.

5 One of the largest firms to crash was T. Palmer and Co. No one knows where Palmer sprang from nor why he settled at Cawnpore, but he quickly made a name for himself manufacturing machinery at Cawnpore, carrying off many prizes and at the Allahabad Exhibition in 1866 second only to Thomson and Co. of Calcutta. He negotiated the important and lucrative contract for building the pontoon bridge across the Ganges. When he failed, details of his crash and details of his considerable property in houses and machinery were reported in the *Pioneer,* giving useful information about his business.

6 Gavin Jones, *op. cit.*

7 At the Agra Exhibition in April 1867 Cawnpore again won many prizes. Halsey won several prizes for his pure Indian-bred bulls and cows, also for cross-bred cattle. The Model Farm won prizes for fowls, turkeys, ducks and rabbits. Heera Lal won second prize for his brass articles while the First Class medal for Lithographic Printing went to Abdool Rahman Khan. Cawnpore leather carried off the top prizes. First prize to Captain John Stewart and second prize jointly between his ex-tanner, now running his own business, Deacon and Co., and Bhawanee and Thakoor Deen. It seems it was too soon for the Elgin Cotton Spinning Co. Ltd to compete. There is mention of a prizewinning printed dress cotton from Cawnpore but the best sample of cotton sent by A. O. Hume, 'the Father of Congress', came from Banda and Etawah. Tina's husband won a prize for his collection of insects!

8 OIOC: *The Pioneer,* 8 March 1870.

9 OIOC: *The Pioneer,* 23 June 1870, the Cawnpore Sewerage Complaint:
Dear Sir, The Contract of the sewerage of the Cawnpore city, given to a Mr Warwick, Secretary of the Elgin Mills in Liquidation, has seemingly caused not a little commotion among the European and Native mercantile community of the Station, contending as they do, and very justly, that the

contract should have been put up to public competition and not so quietly handed over to Mr Warwick.

There are some who are both able and willing to have given ten to twelve thousand rupees more than Mr Warwick, and were tenders called for doubtless a saving of twenty to twenty-five thousand rupees might be effected. Is this so small a sum, Mr Editor, that it should be passed over summarily? In these days of taxes the public have a right to demand the competition system as the only means of decreasing Government expenditure by which the imposition of an increased tax might be avoided. There is of course, as is usual in such cases, much speculation as to how Mr Warwick obtained the contract, or why he should have had the preference, and the natural conclusion drawn in answer supposes the action based on the cousinship of Mr Warwick with the collector, in whose gift the contract was, nor is rumour satisfied with this solution, for it adds that one of the municipal staff who seemingly has been dismissed to make room for Mr Warwick offered to take up the contract on terms more favourable to Government, but was refused on the plea that 'he was not a man of capital'. A capital excuse and a capital offence to pervert public capital into capital for a cousin. Why, Sir, there are several able and wealthy men in Cawnpore and out of it, who would have been glad to have tendered for the contract, and even the ex-engineer could have readily raised the required capital from more than a dozen bankers had he met with a show of fair play.

There are other evils existing in the Cawnpore municipality, which will not stand, though they require, ventilating, and it is time the public should strain every nerve to check these growing evils, as their infection seems to affect other departments under Government in this station; – a slight allusion to one of them I was glad to see in a late issue of the *Pioneer* referring to the supply of wheat.

AN EX-COUSIN

10 Murray and Co. regularly advertised *jharans* manufactured by prisoners in jails. *The Pioneer,* 9 June 1871.
11 Gavin Jones, *op. cit.*
12 The Cawnpore Chamber of Commerce. Extracts from speech made by the Hon'able Mr H. Ledgard on 19 March 1915: 'All the cotton mills and the woollen mills today are traceable to the joining of forces by Mr Hugh Maxwell who owned the Elgin Mills, then in its infancy . . . and Captain Chapman who was in charge of the Govt Clothing Factory here. The two joined forces and the Elgin Mills became strengthened by the clothing and tent-making work for Government Departments.'
13 Information Gussie Allan, formerly Gussie Bevis.
14 Dated 1870; in the possession of Mrs Lesley Thomas, *née* Bevis.
15 Charles Ker, ICS.
16 Maxwell letters lent by Joyce Umfreville, transcribed by Joanna Motion.

17 Aunt Fanny still thinks of the Viceroy as the Governor-General.

18 We know RWM returned with Hugh Maxwell in 1865, but an article in *Business and Sporting* gives 1863. Mr Shakespear in an article in the *Hog Hunter's Annual* also gives 1863 but he may have taken it from *Business and Sporting*.

19 He married Florence West in 1885.

20 'Field Rules' of the club:

Cawnpore Tent Club Rules.

COMMITTEE:—Capt. Jennings, 6th B. C., A. McL. Hutchison, Esq., 14th Regiment, and R W. Maxwell, Esq.

1. The Entrance Donation to be Rs. 16, with an optional subscription of Rs. 10 for the season. Non-subscribing members to pay Two Rupees to the Fund for each meet they attend.

N. B.—The season to commence 1st September.

2. The affairs of the Club to be managed by a committee consisting of three members, including the Secretary, to be elected as vacancies occur.

3. The Committee are responsible for the general management of the Club, and it is their duty to arrange for meets—as often as sport can be procured—and for the renting of jungles.

4. Two days' notice of each meet shall be given and posted at the Club and Regimental Messes.

5. Any member desirous of joining a meet should send his name to the Secretary, at least 36 hours before, after which he will be responsible for his share of the messing at the discretion of the Committee. Any member joining a meet without giving the required notice to pay a fine of Rs. 2 to the Fund.

6. For each meet the Committee shall appoint a member to transact the business of the day, and his arrangements as regard placing the spears, the number to ride each pig, beating, &c., must be adhered to, he also shall be responsible for seeing the coolies paid.

7. A general meeting shall be held at the beginning and close of each hunting season for the inspection of accounts, &c.

8. Beaters shall be paid for by the members present at each meet, but extra expenses, such as presents to men cut by pigs, shall be paid by the Fund.

9. Any member of another Tent Club visiting the Station shall be considered an Honorary Member of the Cawnpore Tent Club.

21 OIOC: MSS. EUR D 915, vols. 1, 2 and 3. Cawnpore Tent Club Log Book.

22 Standing: W. S. Halsey, officiating magistrate and collector; H. C. Barstow, assistant magistrate and conllector; E. C. Buck, assistant magistrate and collector; Capt. K. J. W. Coghill, brigade major; Capt. T. W. R. Boisragon, 30th NI; Lieut. A. J. T. Welchman, 14th Bengal Cavalry. Centre

row: A. W. Brind, executive engineer Ganges Canal; F. Halsey, agent, Bank of Bengal; Capt. T. Tovey; R. W. Maxwell, Begg, Maxwell & Co.; Lieut. J. R. Wilmer, RA; H. Farrell, veterinary surgeon, RA; Lieut. J. T. Camilleri, 7th Dragoon Guards. Front row: Lieut. R. H. Grant, RA; H. B. Goad, officiating district superintendent of police; Cornet W. R. Truman, 7th Dragoon Guards.

23 From the *Pioneer,* 7 September 1866: 'To Mr Francis Halsey, our Bank of Bengal Agent, we are indebted for giving us timely notice to witness some wrestling matches which took place the other day, and in the absence of something better, were certainly not to be despised. The arrangements were excellent indeed, and though the wrestling matches had a monotony and weariness attached to them, yet on the whole every body went away satisfied: the entrance fees were 1 rupee 8 annas and 4 annas.'

24 From the *Pioneer,* 3 April 1868: 'On Thursday evening last Mr Farrell, veterinary surgeon at Cawnpore, was returning on horseback from the camp of a battery of artillery which he had accompanied out of Cawnpore, in the direction of Lucknow, when he passed five men sitting on a bridge by the roadside. He asked them if they had seen his second horse. They replied that it was a little further on, and he passed them. He had not gone far when his horse was struck by a stick from behind, and plunging, threw his rider, who then saw that the five men he had passed were attacking him. He ran to meet one of his opponents, but was immediately felled by blows of the *lattees* of those who were behind him, and became senseless. When he next recovered his senses, he was being carried towards Cawnpore on a *charpoy.* He had been robbed of a few rupees and a ring. No trace has been found of his assailants. The above occurred between Oonao and Cawnpore. Such a daring assault would hardly have been ventured on in 1858.'

25 RWM says he referred to Richardson for dates of Mayo's visit and mentions 1870 but the Log Book gives 1871. R.W. Maxwell, 'Reminiscences of a Secretary', *Hog Hunter's Annual,* vol. 2, 1929, Times of India Press.

26 Information Mrs Mollie Mallaby.

27 Information Major P. J. A. Mallaby.

28 Rai Bahadur Ram Narain, *Cawnpore Past and Present,* Citizens Press, Cawnpore, 1945-7.

29 Information Mrs Mainwaring.

30 The panels were given to a church in Gravesend to be incorporated into the pulpit, but the church was bombed during the war. Information Mrs Margaret Gavin Jones.

31 Information Mrs Mainwaring.

32 Stewart writes: 'I have gone against Mr Maxwell and think him a horrid hard man who deserves to be badly served for not being indulgent to those who make money for him.'

33 Gavin Jones, *op. cit.*

34 Cloaks.

35 In 1872's terrible hot weather, the worst he had ever known, Stewart lost two of his community of fifteen European subordinates and their wives, both from heat.

36 This was the house that had belonged to John Maxwell and was sold by his son Adam Maxwell to Rooshun-ood-Dowlah, an ex-minister from the court of Oude, in 1839 for Rs 30,000.

37 The work of Colonel (Sir) Henry Yule (1820-89) of the Bengal Engineers.

38 These were engraved by a local sculptor, Mr White.

39 Mackillop's father had been the man who had unwittingly contributed to George Ravenscroft's downfall by lending him funds too easily. See *Traders and Nabobs.*

40 Information Theon Wilkinson.

41 The Angel was called by various names: The Angel of Resurrection, The Angel of Peace, The Angel of Forgiveness.

CHAPTER SEVEN

1 Dr Condon was civil surgeon and in charge of jails. His daughter married William Knighton who wrote *Private Lives of an Eastern King,* describing the court of Oude before 1856.

2 Emery Churcher and David Churcher were brothers-in-law of James Maxwell, Hugh Maxwell's youngest brother, who married into the Churcher family.

3 Information Muir Mills minute book, and thanks to Mr Chopra.

4 OIOC: *The Pioneer,* 17 March 1874.

MUIR MILLS CO. LTD. CAWNPORE

Subscribers are informed that 10 per cent is payable in allotment of Shares. They are therefore requested to remit Rs 20 per share to the Bank of Bengal, Cawnpore or to the undersigned, to whom also apply for Prospectus and all other information.

E. J. CHURCHER, Managing Director

5 The bank later forced him to resign.

6 Information supplied by Mrs E. Balshaw, widow of Sir William's gardener. Thanks, too, to Mrs Desmond Young for her help.

7 J. Southwood and Co., Exeter, *Spiritual Manifestations.* Information J. Stanley Beard, JP, FRIBA.

8 Information Gussie Bevis.

9 First mentioned in Muir Mill minutes on 19 June 1874 as Madhoram Chorewal.

10 Sir William was associated with Ernest and Percy Beard in the building and

establishment of the London Spiritual Mission at 13 Pembridge Place, London, W2, and commissioned the young Stanley Beard to build the flat above the stables. The Coopers owned 4 Pembridge Villas.

11 The directors considered the existing arrangements for cotton purchase unsatisfactory, with large sums of money being at times in the hands of the broker without apparent security. They therefore decided to entrust the purchase of all cotton for the Muir Mills to Messrs Cooper Allen and Co., Cawnpore. Terms were to be the same as then paid to Shambul Badrupa Hard, i.e. 2% on purchase at Hingunghat or other adjacent market. Messrs Cooper Allen and Co. undertook to 'supply all necessary capital for the purchase of the same and draw on the company against railway receipts on demand or otherwise as may be at time of purchase to be mutually decided upon'. Messrs Cooper Allen and Co. were asked to accept this arrangement by letter stating terms in detail.

12 There had been an occasion when an outing was planned to Nujjafgarh, Gavin Jones and Stewart each travelling by canoe, while the ladies and the children went by carriage. Stewart letters.

13 OIOC: *Pioneer Supplement 1865–1940*: Clive Rattigan, 'Men Who Made *The Pioneer'*.

14 Rudyard Kipling, *Something of Myself,* London, 1937.

15 The only reference I have found to his being in Cawnpore is in Lady Allen's letter of condolence to McRobert in which she says they were in Cawnpore at the time of McRobert's arrival. Information the late Ian Mitchell, archivist MacRobert Trusts.

16 Mr Bishop joined Allen Bros as a boy of fourteen in 1916 and was told this by an old man of eighty who had worked all his life at the London office.

17 Information Major Idris Morgan-Williams, OBE.

18 All that is known about Charlotte Ludlam is her red gold hair and very tiny wedding ring. She had three children in quick succession and is believed to have died about 1866.

19 OIOC: *The Pioneer,* Monday 23 October 1865:
A short time back your Lucknow correspondent affirmed that the Punjab Trading Company had sold ice there, during the present hot season, to the value of Rs 9,20,000(!!) The *fact* is that the Machine for producing it was got into working order on the 10th July; that about 1,800 maunds have been sold up to 15th October (a fair result enough), yielding a gross return of between 9,000 and 10,000 rupees, out of which, however, the cost of material and twelve months' expenses will, of course, have to be deducted.

I should not have noticed the ridiculous twaddle alluded to, but that I hear it has been copied into both the *Indian Daily News* and *Lahore Chronicle.* And as the exaggeration is at strange variance with the sober statement on the subject, which has just appeared in the Company's Half-yearly Report, issued by its Directors, while the public might regard it as a bait held out to assist the disposal of an impending issue of new Shares, I am in justice called on to contradict it. Your Lucknow correspondent would appear, from his recent effusions, to consider criticisms upon Trade his *forte*. Might I be allowed to express my belief, that would he desist, the shopkeepers, who carry on without the aid of his criticisms, the proprietor of this paper who perhaps has to pay for, and the public who are expected to read them, would probably be grateful.

20   OIOC: *The Pioneer,* 1 March 1867.
21   Kipling, *op. cit.*
22   Comment by Sir Roper Lethbridge in *Journal of the East India Association,* 1914, new series, vol. 5, pp. 276-81.
23   Margarita Barns, *The Indian Press,* Allen and Unwin, London, 1940.
24   Stewart family papers.
25   From his home at Biarritz 12 May 1921. Information Ian Mitchell.
26   Letter to his brother Bob.
27   Major Evelyn Baring (later Lord Cromer), the Finance Member from 1880 to 1883, had introduced a free trade budget and was a strong supporter of Ripon and the Ilbert Bill. He was replaced by Sir Auckland Colvin who was ready to compromise and surrendered to the agitators. See Sir Penderel Moon, *British Conquest and Dominion of India,* Duckworth, London, 1989.
28   Moon, *op. cit.* p.867.
29   OIOC: *The Pioneer,* 27 April 1868.
30   Moon, *op. cit.*

CHAPTER EIGHT

1   19 August 1874.
2   Anthony was a younger brother of John Stewart. Uncle Geo was George Debnam.
3   Gavin Jones's wife.
4   John Stewart's maternal grandfather. He is buried at Kensal Green Cemetery, London, and the epitaph reads: 'Robert Joseph Debnam born on the 12th of June 1781 at Chatham, died on the 18th April 1876 at his residence 15 Kensington Gate. Major late of HM 13th Light Infantry entered the army in 1803 in HM 65th Regiment. He served in the Mahratta campaigns in Burmah and Afghanistan. An honoured life 37 years spent in India was closed in his native land. . .' Information John Stewart of Comrie.
5   Moon, *op. cit.*
6   Screens of the fragrant *khus khus* grass are hung at doorways and windows, kept constantly wet so that when the hot dry winds blow, evaporation takes place and the whole house is deliciously cooled. But they are only effective in the dry heat.

7   *Khurref* – the crop sown just before the rainy season, in May and June and reaped after the rains in November and December, usually rice, maize and the tall millets. *Rubbee* – the crop sown after the rains and reaped the following spring or early summer: wheat, barley, gram, linseed, tobacco and vegetables.

8   Information T. F. G. Hepburn, MBE, Superintendent 1946-59.

9   Not until shortly after the Mutiny did Naini Tal become the summer head-quarters of the North Western Provinces. Stoneleigh, on the site of the present Ramsay Hospital, was the first Residence of the Lieutenant-Governor c. 1862 and probably in this year the Government offices moved for the first time to Naini Tal. Some years later Government House was moved to Maldoon House on Sher-ka-dande, above the site of the landslip, until in 1895 it was declared unsafe. In 1900 the present Government House was completed and occupied. Information from a book on Naini Tal, compiled in 1927 by (Sir) J. M. Clay, then Deputy Commissioner Naini Tal, under the directions of the Governor, Sir Malcolm Hailey. Thanks to Mrs Audrey Baylis.

10 Information Brian George in *Family Tree*.

CHAPTER NINE

1   Information Accrington Public Library. Richard S. Crossley, *Captains of Industry*, 1930.

2   Peter Crookson, 'Death of the Pals', *Sunday Times* Colour Supplement, 1988.

3   Information Mrs Ruby Wilkinson, *née* Butterworth.

4   Born at Long House, Grane, Haslingden, Atherton West was the son of a weaver, James West, who was unable to sign his name in the baptismal register and merely made his mark.

5   *Thames* was a single-screw steel vessel, with a speed of 15 knots, cabins for 120 first and 46 second class passengers, and a large cargo capacity. She could also carry troops or emigrants in her 'tweendecks.

6   From India came sugar from the Rosa Factory (that had once belonged to John Maxwell), clay toys from Lucknow, artistic pieces sent from Lahore by Lockwood Kipling, durries from jails. Begg Sutherland won prizes for their leaf tobacco and their cigars from Tirhoot. Among the official awards in Jury Section XIV, First Order of Merit Silver Medal was won by both the Elgin Mills and Muir Mills for tents and camp equipment. The experts reported: 'Ingenuity of construction, actual usefulness, strength, lightness, portability, capability of being speedily set up, or speedily taken down, and packed in a minimum space. They are admirably adapted for the use of surveyors, explorers, travellers, or those whose occupations necessitate

frequent changes of residence. I consider this exhibition of camp equipage to be entitled to a first class award.' (Melbourne State Library, SLT 606-49451 M 480.) There was also a Fifth Order of Merit for unbleached calico won by Elgin.

The *Argus* of 29 October 1880 carried two columns of adulation for the wonders on display: 'The articles illustrate the growth, produce, arts, sciences of the whole world and testify to the wealth and culture, energy and enterprise of the colonists.'

7 Information Charlie Tosh.

8 James Macdonald Dunbar, Hugh Maxwell's son-in-law.

9 Faruckhabad was the cotton-growing area in the Agra district.

10 Information George Dickson.

11 Information Alice Horsman.

12 Information Major Nick Pocock.

13 Information Mabel Ridsdale.

14 Information Major Nick Pocock.

15 Sir Stanley Reed, *The India I Knew 1897-1947*, Odhams Press, 1952.

16 Photographer S. H. Dagg, Mussoorie and Allahabad. Information Theon Wilkinson and thanks to Michael Garnett.

17 Fred Riley, *A Trip Round the World in 1898*, privately printed. Thanks to Peggy Vernon, *née* Catterall

18 N. N. Sen writing in *Indian Mirror,* quoted in Briton Martin, *New India,* University of California, 1969, p. 114.

19 A. H. Harrington to Lord Dufferin, quoted in *New India, op. cit.,* p. 127.

20 *Cawnpore Volunteer Magazine,* December 1900.

CHAPTER TEN

1 *The Pioneer,* 22 April 1887.

2 Gavin Jones, *op. cit.*

3 Havelock and Neill have disappeared but the nails around which the figures were moulded were clearly discernible in 1970.

4 Muir Mills minute book covers information in this chapter.

5 Henry Ledgard was born on 20 December 1854 in Teddington, Middlesex. He was one of several sons of a Yorkshire family: one brother stayed at home, another went to Australia, and another to Lima in Peru, and the only sister eloped to America. Ledgard was twenty when he arrived in India.

One Christmas Day he was in Lahore visiting friends and on entering the drawing room saw a young girl standing in tiny stockinged feet on the grand piano hanging up Christmas decorations. Her name was Florence Robertson, she was seventeen. They were married in Naini Tal in 1881 and she kept her white wedding stockings in her 'treasure' box. They had four daughters, one of whom, as the wife of Sir Thomas Smith, became a Cawnpore *burra mem*. Information Lady Smith.

7   Walter Butler, partner in Ford and Macdonald, contractors and engineers.
8   Arnold Beer introduced the jute industry to Cawnpore but the venture failed.

CHAPTER 11

1   Lady Allen's letter, see note 16, chapter 7.
2   Obituary by Canon Fisher, *Cawnpore Quarterly*, July 1922.
3   James Cruickshank, 'McRobert of Douneside', *Deeside Field Club,* 2nd series, vol. 2.
4   Information Dr C.G.S. Milne, FRCS.
5   Information F. Brightman.
6   Information F. Brightman.
7   Back row: J. W. Staines, assistant; W. S. Brunning, master tailor; W. Cole, assistant dyeing master; P.C. Stowell, assistant; D. H. Binns, worsted overlooker; Mrs Logie Watson; H. Sanderson, carding and spinning manager; Mrs Silver; W. Walker, assistant; G. Hodgkinson; J. Ednie, engineer and electrician. Second row: A. Butterworth, Jun., assistant engineer; A. J. Mitchell, finishing manager; W. Vickers, accountant; ?; A. Butterworth, Snr., mill manager; Mrs Kitty Lilley; A. McRobert, manager; Mrs Polly Butterworth; J. Measures, hosiery overlooker; ?; ?; ?; A. H. Silver, assistant; W. H. Lockwood, milling manager. Third row: ?; ?; ?; L. p. Watson, Cooper Allen; Peter Scott, weaving manager; ?; Mrs Binns; A. W. Lilley, assistant; ?. Front row: James Scott, dyeing manager; C. A. Watts, assistant; A. H. Fraser, assistant; W. H. Howard, assistant; MacRobert archives.
8   Information Dr C.G.S. Milne, FRCS.
9   Information F. Brightman.
10   These rectangular stone-built cottages were thatched either with heather or broom. The two rooms were separated by a timber-framed partition and on either side of this was a built-in wooden bed with doors – the box bed or press bed. Each room had its fireplace, a wide open stone one in the 'but' (kitchen) and a smaller one in the 'ben' (parlour).
11   James Cruickshank, *Memoirs of a Wayfaring Man*. Information Aberdeen Central Library.
12   Information Dr Alexander Cormack.
13   James Cruickshank, *Alex. Pirie and Sons Ltd, Paper Manufacturers, Stoneywood, and Waterton 1770-1945*, 1946.
14   His lodgings in Blackfriars Street were almost next door to Robert Gordon's College where he had a post as lecturer in chemistry. Not far away was the Mechanics Institute in Marischal Street. There he became Neil Arnott lecturer in physics and chemistry. Information *The Gordonian*, 19 March 1931.

15 *An Appreciation* signed 'D' – probably Mr Dawson of Allen Bros, July 1922.

16 This was the Great Comet which had not been seen since 1807 and returned now to be seen between 26 June and 16 July.

17 Gladstone was debating the Land Law in Ireland. *Hansard*, 3rd series, vol. 262.

18 *An Appreciation* signed G.N.C. [Cave]. *Aberdeen Free Press,* Tuesday 4 July 1922.

19 Roberts, *op. cit.*

20 See note 14 above.

21 'The Russians were persistent in their attempts to encroach on Afghan territory, in order that they might be in a position to control the approach to Herat, a Russian occupation of which fortress we could not permit.' Roberts, *op. cit.* The Amir was friendly towards the Indian Government while not wishing their army in his country; he looked to them for support with arms and ammunition against the Russians.

22 Thomas A. Rust and Julian Rust, photographers Mussoorie and Allahabad, 1870-90. Information Theon Wilkinson.

23 When my school became the UKCA School in 1953 it moved to rooms in Sheiling House. Morning prayers took place in the McRoberts' billiard room. Later when the Indian parents took over the running of the school the name was changed to Sheiling House. It continues to this day with over 800 pupils and is highly successful.

24 The Cawnpore Club, the Burra Club, dates from 1833 when it was started as a reading room for Army officers. It was officially listed in *Thacker's Bengal Directory* in 1888.

25 The firm of White and Co. had been the resident monumental masons for many years. Albert Priestley's name first appears in 1888 when he joined Mr White as sculptor. A year later Priestley had struck out on his own and is described as 'sculptor and photographic artist'. His skills were demonstrated by the charming memorial card he designed on the death of his young wife in childbirth. Many of the beautiful monuments in the Cantonment Cemetery are Priestley's work.

26 Chamber of Commerce Reports. Thanks to H. K. Srivastava.

27 Chamber of Commerce Reports.

28 The Cawnpore Woollen Mills and Army Cloth Manufacturing Co. Ltd: 11th Ordinary General Meeting, Saturday 23 February 1889.

29 Information F. Brightman.

30 The Cawnpore Woollen Mills and Army Cloth Manufacturing Co. Ltd: 12th Ordinary General Meeting, Saturday 22 February 1890.

31 Information Ian Mitchell.

32 Information Mrs Ruby Wilkinson.

33 MacRobert archives at Tarland.

CHAPTER TWELVE

1 G. O. Trevelyan, *The Competition Wallah,* London, 1864, p. 288.
2 Briton Martin, *op. cit.*
3 Helena Petrovna Blavatsky was a Russian-born religious mystic. She went to America after touring Europe for several years and founded the Theosophical Society in 1875. She arrived with Olcott in India in 1878 was based in Madras. Aims of the Society were: 1 to form a nucleus of the universal brotherhood of humanity without distinction of race, creed, sex, caste or colour; 2 to encourage the study of comparative religion, philosophy and science.
4 Private letter from Hume to Ripon quoted in Briton Martin *op. cit.,* p. 67.
5 Moon, *op. cit.*
6 *Bombay Gazette,* 31 December 1885; 'Political Progress in India', *The Times,* 11 February 1886, p. 13.
7 This was the time when Annie Besant, an ardent Theosophist, had led the match girls' strike. 1889 also saw the Great Dock Strike.
8 Sir Auckland Colvin, Governor of the North Western Provinces.
9 Moon, *op. cit.*
10 The *Tasmania* was a one-funnel three-masted passenger steamship with a single screw. Information Stephen Rabson, P & O archivist.
11 The inherited fighting spirit of the Hearseys had brought him up against the authorities and persuaded him to throw in his lot with the supporters of New India.
12 'As a journalist Rudyard Kipling was far from being a great success. His father had induced my own father, Sir George and the other proprietors of the two papers to give the young Rudyard a post on the Lahore paper. There he had produced a number of his stories and sketches and poems, all of which had displayed remarkable literary ability for so young a man. But in the day to day business of journalism Kipling did not by any means shine. He had little taste for mere routine duties; he was apt to neglect the rather tedious assignments that inevitably fell to the lot of the junior members of a very small staff.

'It was Sir George who suggested Kipling's removal to *The Pioneer* at Allahabad. *The Pioneer* had then become India's leading English-edited newspaper and Sir George felt it would afford greater scope for Kipling's talents as a writer. He, of course, once more proved to be right. Much of Kipling's best work was produced while he was on *The Pioneer* and in the back files of the paper can, I have reason to believe, be found buried even now verses, sketches and stories by Kipling that have not been unearthed and republished.' Clive Rattigan, *op. cit.*
13 NAI: Home Judicial B Dept., January 1890, nos. 33-5.

14 Information Edward S. Bishop.
15 Information Edward S. Bishop.
16 Information Malcolm Barnes, Allen and Unwin.
17 Built about 1884.
18 Information T.V. Baddeley, CBE.

CHAPTER THIRTEEN

1 The SPG Mission received its charter from William Ill in 1701 (*The Pioneer*, 21 February 1901).
2 *The Story of the Cawnpore Mission*, Society for the Propagation of the Gospel in Foreign Parts, London, 1909.
3 Revd R.G. Slater in *Christ Church College Diamond Jubilee*.
4 'At first 27 members met each Friday for an hour and a half to stitch useful garments while Foss Westcott read aloud from some edifying book.' Extract from the *Cawnpore Mission Society*, 1888. Information Revd Reg Messenger.
5 *The Story of the Cawnpore Mission, op. cit.*
6 *Christ Church College Diamond Jubilee, op. cit.*
7 'Some Reminiscences' by Shri Debi Prasad Shukla, BA, an old student and ex-professor of the college. *Christ Church College Diamond Jubilee, op. cit.*
8 *Christ Church College Diamond Jubilee, op. cit.*
9 A. A. Blair and O. W. Stallard.
10 The Rt Revd Charles Saunders, who worked with the Brotherhood and eventually became Bishop of Lucknow, told me that after five years with the Brotherhood he returned to England in 1916, penniless, and his father had to pay the taxi!
11 Information Charles Saunders.
12 *The Story of the Cawnpore Mission, op. cit.*
13 SPG Mission, Cawnpore: *A Short Account of the Industrial Work*, Rhodes House, Oxford, 1895.
14 In response to my query 'Did any of the boys make a special mark in life?' Charles Saunders replied: 'No, indeed, they were the poor remains of famine years and their achievement in learning to read and write and to learn a trade was a great advance. Only one I remember was musical and he died of consumption at about twenty years old. I remember a hymn he wrote and composed – it is only a fragment I'm afraid: "Purabse Majasi ate Jesu pasmuki rahnumayi ck sitara Khass . . . the Wise Men came to Jesus from the East, their guide was a special star." '
15 W. E. Burrows 1896 and W. T. Huett 1903.
16 21 September 1898 by Colonel Armstrong, IMS, the civil surgeon, a warm and generous supporter of the Mission. He gave his own bungalow, White

House, to the SPG. This, set in a beautiful garden on the banks of the Ganges, was to be for fifteen years my parents' home, from where I was married.

17 *The Story of the Cawnpore Mission, op. cit.*
18 Information Dr M. Nigam.
19 This was a historic achievement. 80–90,000 Durham coal miners went on strike on 9 March 1892. 200 trains of the NER were suspended, business among tradesmen declined, the families of the miners suffered and the loss to the country was generally computed at about £3,000,000. The Bishop of Durham intervened and by the sheer weight of his personality called together three representatives of the owners of the pits, three representatives of the miners and three businessmen unconnected with the mines to a conference at his own house where the disagreements were thoroughly discussed and compromise agreed upon. The meeting took place on 1 June. On 3 July the miners went back to work amid great rejoicing. See Arthur Westcott, *Brooke Foss Westcott, Life and Letters,* Macmillan, London, 1903; Geoffrey Best, *Bishop Westcott and the Miners,* Cambridge University Press; and *The Bishop Westcoll Memorial Lecture, 1966.*
20 Brooke Foss Westcott had been a master at Harrow School, Canon of Westminster, Regius Professor of Divinity at Cambridge and Bishop of Durham. Interestingly his feeling for India stemmed perhaps from his great-grandfather, Foss Westcott, who had been a member of Honourable East India Company's Madras Establishment during the years 1741-57.
21 Revd R. G. Slater's concluding remarks in *Christ Church Diamond Jubilee.*

THE SOCIAL SCENE

1 Back row: Mr Moore, Miss Anderson, Lu Butterworth, Gussie Anderson, Samuel Ball, Molly McCarthy. Front: Harry Bevis, Bee Butterworth. Butterworth album.

CHAPTER FOURTEEN

1 They were married at Cawnpore in 1887 just before the Stewarts left India for good.
2 A series of letters from Gavin Jones in the Stewart family papers.
3 Hume Towers.
4 The proprietor of the Agra factory also wrote to Stewart for financial aid, 4 August 1896. Stewart family papers.
5 It was widely believed in Cawnpore that many years earlier, at the time of the Mutiny, the Wisharts' *ayah* had saved the life of her memsahib when she

hid the family in the bazaar but that ultimately they had died at the boats. That *ayah's* name was Uluma, her son Stephen John was a well-known old Indian Christian and his mother lived on into her nineties, dying in 1932. Information John Bannerman. It is interesting to speculate that possibly Wishart's romantic attachment to Cawnpore stemmed from that tragic episode.

Maud Diver tells the story in 'An Echo of the Mutiny' in the *Cornhill Magazine* (June 1937, vol. 155, no. 390). In 1914 a Cawnpore family on home leave took a house in Somerset. There in the library, framed under double glass, was the letter dated 9 June written by Mrs Larkins, wife of Major George Larkins, commanding a battery of the Bengal Artillery at Cawnpore, to her sister-in-law Henrietta. The siege had already raged for four days and their faithful *ayah* who had accompanied them into the barracks now wished to escape. Mrs Larkins gave her this letter and a ring and made Uluma promise to carry them to the Governor of Bombay, who was her brother. When word came that the besieged garrison had been promised safe conduct to Allahabad, Mrs Larkins and her children made their way down to the boats where they died. Uluma, in trying to fulfil her task, was denied admittance to the Governor. When the letter reached him she was nowhere to be found.

It is interesting that both Maud Diver and the Cawnpore legend state that the Larkin family was hidden in the *ayah's* hut in the bazaar. Since it was virtually impossible, and no mention is made of it in any account, for any European to leave the entrenchment once the siege had begun, perhaps the family had hidden with Uluma and later joined the rest of the Europeans sheltering in Wheeler's entrenchment. The Cawnpore couple's own ayah had been the daughter of Uluma and recalled how as a girl of sixteen her mother had sheltered an English lady and her children in the year of The Great Trouble, 'till all went out to be killed'.

See also OIOC: Photo EUR 233.

6   Sir Edward Buck, Secretary to the Government of India, Revenue and Agricultural Department. Wishart had got to know Buck when he was a young settlement officer in Cawnpore and a keen member of the Cawnpore Tent Club. He was responsible for renovating the Reading Room (now the Cawnpore Club) in 1864. Information Dr M. Nigam.

7   A is George Allen, proprietor of the *Pioneer*.

8   The second boot contract expired in 1900.

9   Literally 'the kingdom', in this context the area around the Fort.

10   Rai Bahadur Ram Narain recalled buying his first bicycle from Gavin Jones shortly after they started in production.

11   'Empire Engineering Company', p. 318, Arnold Wright (ed.), *History, People, Commerce and Natural Resources,* Somerset Playne, 1920.

12   Information Shri Atma Prakash Gupta.

13 Members of the Cawnpore Tent Club and guests: Capt R. W. H.
Ronaldson, HLI; Lieut. H. G. Stainforth, 4th Bengal Cavalry; E. W. S.
Douglas, ex. eng PWD canals; Warre; Col. p. F. M. Baddeley, H & S Fty;
G. B. Allen, Cooper Allen and Co; Maj. W. G. Yate, 4th Bengal Cavalry; J.
Reeve, asst Elgin Mills; Lieut. F. V. Smith, 4th Bengal Cavalry; H. Cherry,
asst. Elgin Mills; Col. J. Armstrong, Civil Surgeon; R. W. Maxwell,
partner Elgin Mills; Lieut. W. Neilson, HLI; Mrs Head; Mrs Waller; Mrs
Armstrong; Miss Dunbar; Miss Read; Mrs Douglas; Miss Baddeley and
friend; Mrs Hall-Flower; Miss Beadon and the famous *shikari,* Prag.
Maxwell family album. Noronha took the group photograph on 23 May
1895, so it is probable he also took this Christmas meet of 1896.

14 'Reminiscences of a Secretary', *Hog Hunter's Annual,* vol. 2, 1929. Thanks
to E. T. H. Alexander.

   The following note on the Cawnpore Tent Club was written for me by
Pop Fuller, for many years an active member. Thanks also to Charles Ker,
ICS, for information on pigsticking.

The origin of hoghunting, or pigsticking as it is also called, is not known to
the writer but there are several references in Tod's *Annals and Antiquities of
Rajasthan* which indicate that the Rajputs hunted the boar from very ancient times. It is not surprising therefore to find in *Notes on Early Hoghunting*
by A. P. Collett (late ICS) remarks on hoghunting in Bengal, Behar and
Cawnpore and 'the conditions in the twenty years preceding 1807'. The
description 'tent' was presumably adopted because most meets were carried
out, even more in the old days, from camp.

   The records of the Cawnpore Tent Club date back to 1869 and I think it
was Colonel Norrie (10th Hussars) who told me his father had killed a boar
in The Mall about 1870. Reviewing the yearly bags from 1869 to 1940, one
is struck with their consistency: in 1869 forty boar were killed, in 1940
thirty. The years in which the bag exceeded a hundred were 1875, 1897,
1899, 1911 and 1927-30, while those in which less than twenty bit the dust
were 1871, 1872, 1882, 1909 and 1938. Probably various factors to some
extent cancelled each other out. Earlier, pig may have been more plentiful
and covers nearer to hand, but the mounts, according to Baden-Powell and
others, although handy were small, expensive and not fast. Then in some
years pig would be more numerous than spears and in others just the opposite, while the advent of the rains determined the length of the season.
Another factor, in later years, was diminishing cover due to increased cultivation and here credit is due to the Tent Club for helping the 'under-
developed areas'. We were often implored to hunt a patch, containing
crusty old porkers, into which no one dared venture, only to return the
following year to find it all cultivated.

   Enough of facts and figures. Pigsticking took one across country (willingly or unwillingly!) that one would otherwise never have seen and effectively dispelled the worries of the working week. Sometimes the line would be started soon after dawn, men and horses half-awake, and then there was that moment, still before sunrise, when all *were* awake. Before long, a shout from the line, 'wuh jata' and, assuming a rideable boar, the hunt was on with the horse developing that wonderful 'fifth leg' across unseen country. It should perhaps be mentioned that our main covers were 'jhow' (a giant gorse or tamarisk) so the rider could see little of the ground and in any case was intent on following the pig. It was therefore left almost entirely to the horse, unlike fox-hunting, to negotiate the ground – which varied from 'bilkool maidan' to 'poached-egg' country and irrigation drains.

15 Back row: Apsley, Constance. Centre row: William Cherry, Surgeon Captain RN; Norah, Bertie, Maggie, *née* Maxwell. Front row: Maxwell and William. Cherry family photo.

16 For RWM to use a Latin tag in the confidence that his reader would understand it is a reminder that the nineteenth century was a time when privileged families enjoyed a classical education. The study of Greek and Latin was the key to Greco-Roman culture and a knowledge of the basic shared culture uniting France, England and Germany. In spite of the difficulties of travel RWM thought nothing of travelling to London via Budapest.

17 Alexander Blake Shakespear, CIE, was a partner in Begg Sutherland and Co. and their sugar director at Mahowrah.

18 Joe Lee, *op. cit.*

19 Forbes-Mitchell, *op. cit.*

20 Great-Aunt Emma's diary, author's possession.

21 He had married again.

22 Social calls were limited to twenty minutes. This was considered the longest time that you could keep a carriage standing at a door. If you were staying longer the horse would have to be unharnessed and stabled or walked up and down. With this slow pace of life there were nice details: for instance there was always one extra place laid at table, for the unexpected guest. It was cleared away after everyone sat down. Information Dr Stanley Black.

23 This is also where Forbes-Mitchell was taken to view Cawnpore.

24 The Noronha family had been settled in Cawnpore since the Mutiny, based at Manuel House, their handsome mansion on the Mall Road. In 1897 they are listed as 'De Noronha and Son, government auctioneers, merchants and photographers, stone, lime and surki mills, kunkar quarries and brick fields'.

25 Information Gussie Bevis, the Andersons' daughter.

26 This was typical of Cawnpore hospitality.

CHAPTER FIFTEEN

1 Details of the riots taken from NAI: Home Department Simla Records Public A, June 1900, nos. 291-302.
2 OIOC: *The Pioneer,* 11 April 1900.
3 When Harry Horsman gave the speech before the Governor, Sir Harry Haig, at the Jubilee Dinner in 1935 to celebrate fifty years of the Chamber of Commerce, heralded by *The Pioneer* as CAWNPORE'S PROUD RECORD, he made special mention of Mr Wishart and the regard in which he was held.

'Mr Wishart, despite the fact that he could, when necessary, give very forcible expression to his views, occupied a high position in the regard, not only of the members of the Chamber but in that of his workmen, and also of the Indian population of Cawnpore in general. An amusing example of the influence he exerted over the minds of the Indian public was furnished during the first Cawnpore riots in 1900. Undeterred by the fact that murderous rioting had been active and that there was a considerable abullition of feeling within the City, Mr Wishart passed through the City in his closed office juan. This was held up by the rioters at one place but on hearing the flow of expletives which issued from within, the mob laughed and allow the carriage to proceed, saying "Let him go; it is the *galliwala saheb.*" '

4 OIOC: *The Pioneer,* 18 April 1900.
5 Quarterly Paper, *SPG Mission Notes,* 1905.
6 Alice M. Marval, born 26 January 1865, died 4 January 1904. All four were buried at Subadar-Ka-Talao Cemetery.
7 OIOC: *The Pioneer,* 30 March 1893, under 'Cawnpore'.
8 OIOC: *The Pioneer,* 8 April 1893.
9 Vonolel, the last famous war charger the world would know, died peacefully in 1899 aged twenty-seven and was buried in the military pensioners' cemetery, Dublin. (J. M. Brereton, *The Horse in War,* Newton Abbot, 1976.) Information Elizabeth Talbot Rice and Salli Dyson.
10 Kennedy died mysteriously of arsenic poisoning in Kenya on a big game hunt.
11 OIOC: *The Pioneer,* 28 January 1901.
12 OIOC: *The Pioneer,* 21 February 1901.
13 Baijnath Ramnath commissioned Cawnpore's own sculptor, Albert Priestley, to build a statue of Queen Victoria. The 8-foot aluminium statue was erected at Sursaya Ghat and formally unveiled in 1907. The subscriptions collected were so handsome that it was decided to commission an even larger statue of the Queen, to be modelled by Thomas Brock (who

sculpted the Victoria memorial outside Buckingham Palace). This was shipped out from England and put up at the corner of Queen's Park, where it stood gazing in the direction of Memorial Gardens and the Angel of the Well, a substantial landmark to all passers by on the Mall Road. Information Mary Ann Steggles.

 After Independence both statues were dismantled and a statue of Mahatma Gandhi now stands on the original pedestal. For a while Brock's statue lay shrouded in tarpaulin in the police lines. It now rests in the basement at the Lucknow Museum. Information Dr M. Nigam.

14   OIOC: *The Pioneer,* 13 March 1901.
15   OIOC: *The Pioneer,* 28 January 1901: 'Dangers of the New Century'.
16   Information Mabel Ridsdale.
17   OIOC: *The Pioneer,* 12 February 1902: 'Cawnpore'.
18   OIOC: *The Pioneer,* 3 March 1902: 'Industries at Cawnpore'.

EPILOGUE

1   Gavin Jones, *op. cit.*
2   (Sir) George Sutherland, a partner of the company, as Sheriff of Calcutta had the honour of proclaiming the accession of King Edward VII to the throne in 1901.
3   The exceptionally beautiful marble tomb stood close to the entrance to the Mirpur Cemetery and the caretaker's small house, so escaped the vandalism that most of the cemetery experienced over the years. In the 1970s, however, an unfortunate dispute arose over the land. An attempt to remove the marble was made and the angel, not without some damage, was taken to the south porch of All Souls Church. The remains of the tomb were incorporated into the housing development that took place.

 The inscriptions read: 'A tribute of love to the memory of Hannah Poole, Relict of the late G. H. Poole who died on the 24 February 1880 in the 80th year of her age.' 'In loving memory of my beloved sister Anne Grace Poole who died at Cawnpore June 13 1896, daughter of George Hacking and Hannah Poole.' 'In ever loving memory of my dear wife Harriet Frances Cooper who died on Christmas Morning 1897. The last of the family of George Hacking and Harriet Poole.'
4   Georgina's diary. MacRobert Trust archives.
5   Mrs Haskell.
6   His bungalow became the Circuit House where the Governor of the UP and his lady stayed on official visits and where Cawnpore society went to write their names in the Book, signifying their call and hoping to ensure an invitation to the long-white-gloved functions.
7   Information Tommy Lowe.

8   The Retreat was built as two houses, one for living and one for sleeping. The children had to put their topees on to cross from one to the other. Information P. G. Moore.

9   Rai Bahadur Ram Narain, *op, cit.*

10   Information P. G. Moore.

11   Sir Winston Churchill.

12   Information H. Finch.

13   Information Dr Stanley Black.

14   Information P. G. Moore.

15   Georgina's diary, *op. cit.*

16   Alexander McRobert's diary. MacRobert Trust archives.

17   Cawnpore Woollen Mills, Cooper Allen, NW Tannery, New Egerton Woollen Mills, Dhariwal, Cawnpore Cotton Mills and Empire Engineering.

18   Information Mr Chopra.

19   Information Dr C. G. S. Milne, FRCS.

20   This was a charitable trust and thereby exempt from tax. Among its investments was a controlling interest in the BIC and one of its objects was 'to perpetuate the ideals of our race and empire'. Information John Christie, 'A Taste of Freedom', *Blackwood's Magazine,* November 1970, no. 1561, vol. 308.

21   From left: Harry Horsman, Mrs Horsman, Mrs Silver, Mrs Bee Briscoe, *née* Butterworth, Mrs Polly Butterworth, Mrs Kitty Lilley, *née* Butterworth, Alfred Butterworth, sen; standing on train: Arthur Lilley and baby son; at window: Ruby Butterworth; Mr Silver; at carriage window: Alf Butterworth, jun; the guard. Photo Mrs Vernon.

22   Information Ruby Wilkinson.

23   OIOC: *The Pioneer,* 16 December 1901.

24   Information S. P. Mehra.

25   Lord Rawlinson.

26   Mr Stromeyer.

27   They were married at St James's, Spanish Place, Manchester Square, London, on 21 October 1922. He was fifty-one and she was nineteen. Alex Shakespear spent fifty years working in India. He came from a family with long associations with India and an earlier Shakespear had married a daughter of Thackeray. Educated at Berkhamsted Grammar School, he came out to India in 1894 as an indigo planter but soon joined Begg Sutherland of Cawnpore, working under Wishart (who was distantly related) and following him as secretary of the Chamber until 1912, when he was made CIE and a partner in Begg Sutherland. It was said he would have received a knighthood but that he was 'reported' for keeping Indian women. His father had been a colonel in the Indian Army and after his death his mother made her home with 'Shakes'. He was devoted to her and it was not until

the year after her death that he married the charming young daughter of Mrs Marie Thomson, Clare O'Brien. 'Shakes' died in Colombo in 1949.

28 Information Queenie Hirdey Narain.

29 The tax exemption on the thirty per cent shares of the BIC held by the MacRobert Trust was withdrawn. The shares came on the open market and were bought by Haridas Mundhra who became Chairman of the Board in 1956. The transaction involved forged share certificates in his Calcutta companies, owned and controlled by him to raise advances for his new acquisition and ended in a prison sentence for Mundhra and the intervention of the State Bank who put in a receiver. Cooper Allen was sold for Rs 1–; an offer from Batas to buy Cooper Allen was turned down and it re-emerged as The Tannery and Footwear Company of India Ltd. Information Kenneth Wilcox.

Mundhra's definition of success was: 'First you speak him sweet words and get him in your foothold. And then you screw.' I personally heard him ask our six-year-old daughter, 'Who loves you best? Your father or your mother?' She registered her startled expression at the idea of such divisiveness.

30 Neil Bonnarjee, Secretary of the Upper India Chamber of Commerce and past Secretary to Pant-ji in Lucknow, also played his part. After five years of Government controllership an arrangement was made with the Bajoriay family. This failed and it was then in 1970 that Suraj Bhan and Son stepped in. But Suraj Bhan was an old man and did not live long. The mill was subsequently run by the National Textile Corporation.

APPENDIX

First Annual Report of Elgin Cotton Spinning & Weaving Co. Ltd

———

Elgin Cotton Spinning & Weaving Company Limited,

CAWNPORE.
___

DIRECTORS.

Hugh Maxwell, Esq., *Chairman.*
Joseph Strong, Esq.
Lalla Ishack Lall.
Lalla Guneshee Lall.
Frederick Buist, Esq., *Secretary* and *Manager.*

———

BANKERS.

Agra and Masterman's Bank, *Calcutta.*

———

Capital, Rs. 4,00,000, in 1,600 Shares of Rs. 250 each.

———

FIRST ANNUAL REPORT.

PROCEEDINGS of the First Ordinary General Meeting of the Shareholders of the Elgin Cotton Spinning and Weaving Company Limited, held at the Office of the Company, at Cawnpore, on Monday, the 6th February 1865.

Present.

Hugh Maxwell, Esq., Captain S. Chalmers, Captain K. Coghill, J. Strong, Esq., Colonel Bruce, J. Westmorland, Esq., Captain H. Chalmers, J. M. Tritton, Esq., D. Kennedy, Esq., Lalla Guneshee Lall, Lalla Ishack Lall and Lalla Chota Lall, and by Proxy, Major Aitkin, Colonel Wilson, Dr. Innes, G. A. Wilson, Esq., and Lalla Sook Nundun.

The Chairman read to the meeting the Report of the Directors since the formation of the Company, as follows, at the same time submitting the accounts closed to 31st January 1865.

DIRECTORS' REPORT.

The Directors of the Elgin Cotton Spinning and Weaving Company Limited have the pleasure of laying before the Shareholders the following report of the Company's proceedings since its formation.

1. The Company was registered on 5th May 1864 with a Capital of Rupees (3,00,000) three hundred thousand, which was afterwards increased to Rupees (4,00,000) four hundred thousand by resolutions passed and confirmed at extraordinary general meetings of the Company, on 31st July and 4th October 1864, respectively. The increase was formally registered on 3rd December 1864; 75 per cent of the capital has for the present, been called up.

2. Arrangements for the supply of the necessary machinery were entered into with Messrs. Platt Brothers, of Hartford Works, Oldham, and B. Hicks and Sons, of Bolton, through their agent, Mr. R. Newton, of Bombay, who has had much practical experience in this description of business there. One-third of the estimated cost was remitted to the above-named firms with the orders, and the remaining two-thirds of the cost has been transferred by the Agra Bank, Calcutta, to our credit with the head office in London to meet the manufacturers' bills, in full, on presentation of invoices, and bill of lading, according to agreement. A portion of the machinery was shipped in the "Vanguard" in December last, and Messrs. Platt Brothers have undertaken to engage and send out the European staff necessary to fit and work the machinery.

3. Contracts have been entered into with Messrs. Doyle and Co., of Calcutta for the erection of the factory, and bungalows of the European staff. The foundation stone of the mill was laid on the 8th December last in the presence of a numerous assemblage of the residents of Cawnpore and neighbouring stations.

4. The Directors have made satisfactory investments, as will be seen by the accounts placed before you, of such portions of the capital as there is no immediate employment for, and these are all convertible on demand.

5. The Directors, in the interest of Shareholders, thought it proper to send their Secretary and Manager to Bombay in November last to observe the working of the cotton mills there, and they have to state that that gentleman's report, which now lies open for Shareholders' inspection, is most satisfactory, and confirms the opinion of your Directors as to the soundness, and probable pecuniary success, of the undertaking.

6. Directors retire from office according to the terms of the Limited Liability Act.

7. The Auditors' report and accounts, closed to the 31st January 1865, are submitted herewith.

HUGH MAXWELL, *Chairman*.
FREDRICK BUIST, *Secretary*.

CAPITAL AND LIABILITIES.

For value of 1,600 shares at 250 each	4,00,000 0 0		
Less 25 per cent uncalled	1,00,000 0 0		
		3,00,000	0 0
Amount of Interest from Banks	634 10 5		
„ overpaid calls from Shareholders	12 11 5		
		647	5 10
Messrs. Doyle and Co., Security Deposit in Agra and Masterman's Bank Calcutta		5,000	0 0
Total Rs.		3,05,647	5 10

CREDITOR.

PROPERTY AND ASSETS.

Amount of outstanding calls due up to date by Shareholders			12,875 0 0
Land purchased from Cawnpore Municipality, including compensation for standing crops ...	1,146	0	0
Less realized on ditto ...	309	2	0
			836 14 0
Charges General, Advertizing, Printing and Postage, Stationery, House Rent, Stamp Paper, Law Charges, Exchange, and Building, and clearing rubbish			4,333 5 6
Office Furniture			461 7 6
Establishment			3,505 4 9
Suspense—Advance to Secretary, proceeding to Bombay Rupees 1,850, and Sundries Rupees 153			2,003 0 0

INVESTMENTS.

Government 5½ per cent Promissory Notes in custody of Agra and Masterman's Bank, Calcutta, amounting to Rupees 70,000, including interest and charges			81,426 11 6

CASH.

Gooropersaud Sookul, Cawnpore, deposit payable on demand on security of Government paper bearing interest at 6 per cent ...	50,000	0	0
Agra and Masterman's Bank, Calcutta, bearing interest at 2 per cent ...	918	15	2
Agra and Masterman's Bank, London ..	98,123	8	0
Bank of Upper India, Cawnpore, bearing interest at 2 per cent ...	923	4	0
			1,49,965 11 2
Messrs. Platt Brothers and Co., Oldham, remittances to account Machinery for £3,720-0-11			36,628 2 2
Messrs. B. Hicks & Son, remittance to account for Machinery for £1,365, ...			13,440 0 0
Messrs. Doyle and Co., for law expenses			108 0 0
			3,05,583 8 7
Cash Balance in hand on 31st January 1865			63 13 3
Total, Rs.			3,05,647 5 10

HUGH MAXWELL, *Chairman.*

JOSEPH F. STRONG, *Director.*

Examined and found Correct.

D. KENNEDY,
GEORGE D. WALKER, } *Auditors.*

FREDERICK BUIST, *Secy.*

*List of Shareholders of the Elgin Cotton Spinning and
Weaving Company Limited, Cawnpore, on
31st January 1865.*

Aitkin, R. H. M., Major.
Alexander, G., Captain.
Bruce, L. G., Colonel.
Bhugwandoss Bahadoormul.
Buist, W.
Birney, J., Lieutenant.
Burlton, N. R., Lieutenant.
Bond, H. F., Captain.
Boyce, J. H.
Blunt, A., Captain.
Chalmers, S., Captain.
Chalmers, M. J., Mrs.
Chalmers, H. B., Captain.
Coghill, K., Captain.
Chunsook Hurrydoyal.
Clerk, M. G., Lieutenant.
Choteloll Shaw.
Conlan, T.
Campbell, H. L., Major.
Cadell, A.
Chundernauth Chowdry.
Elahebux, Sheik.
Fawcus, J., Doctor.
Fraser, E. G.
Goode, C. B.
Grant, R. G., Captain.
Gaussen, D., Lieut.-Col.
Gavin, J. F. A., Reverend.
Hill, P., Brigadier General.
Hurchund Roy Ramanund.
Herschell, J., Lieutenant.
Hume, J., Major.
Isback Lall.
Innes, J. H. K., Doctor.
Johnson, J.
Jogindronauth Mullick.
Kennedy, D.
Loyd, F. R., Doctor.
Lance, F., Lieutenant.

McCarthy, W.
Moolchund.
Murray, K.
Maslen, G. B.
Maxwell, H.
McDonald, J. D., Major.
Miller, T.
Marshall, H. I. W.
Ouseley, R., Captain.
Osborne, H.
Osborne, G.
Obbard, H. S., Major.
O'Brien, Major.
Prinsep, J. H.
Peacock, H. P., Lieutenant.
Reay, J., Captain.
Reilly, J.
Reilly, C. H., Lieutenant.
Strong, J.
Saxton, G. H., Colonel.
Sooknundun.
Sheett, J., Doctor.
Simpson, A., Captain.
Sparks, B., Lieutenant.
Shakespeare, I. T., Lieut.-Col.
Shore, R. N.
Sladen, J. R., Captain.
Thullier, H. R., Lieutenant.
Tritton, J. M.
Taylor, J. W., Lieutenant.
Westmorland, J. P., Lieutenant.
Wood, E. S., Captain.
Wilson, T. F., Lieut.-Col.
Warburton, R., Lieutenant.
Wild, E. J., Captain.
Walker, J.
Wilson, G. A., Cornet.
Wooma Churn Bose.
White, E. H., Doctor.

HUGH MAXWELL,   *Chairman of Directors.*
JOSEPH F. STRONG   *Director*
FREDERICK BUIST,   *Secretary.*   (289)

Glossary

atta	flour, ground grain
babool	thorny mimosa tree
baboo, babu	clerk in an office
bandobast	efficient arrangement
bania	trader, shopkeeper
bebee, bibi	lady, wife or mistress
beegah	measure of land, approx 5/8 acre
bhai band	brotherhood
bheesty, bhistie	man who sprinkles water from a goatskin
bungay, bunggys	yokes for carrying loads, labourers
burkha	full-length veil used by Muslim ladies
burra	senior
burra khanna	dinner party
burtans	pots and pans
chabutra	raised garden terrace
chal	move speedily
chamar	leather worker
chaprasie, chuprassie,	office peon
charpoy	Indian string bed
chillum	hukka bowl that contains the tobacco
choola	clay oven
chokra	boy, youngster
chota hazari, hazri	early morning tea
chowdrie	headman in village
chowkidar	watchman
chowrie	ornamental fly flapper
chaupatty	unleavened bread
cutcherry, kacheri	law court
dak, dak gharry	post, mail carriage
dal	lentil
dechi	cooking pot
dhai, dhaee	wet nurse
dher	distaff spinner

dhoti	loincloth
dhursee, darsie	tailor
Doab	land between the Ganges and Jumna
doolie	litter
Doorga Poojah	Hindu festival, worship of Durga
fenoose	wall oil lamp bracket
feringhi	European
galliwalla	foul-mouthed
gareb	poor, humble
ghat	steps down to the river, landing stage
go-down	store room
goosul	bath
gora	European soldier
gurrah	earthenware water pot
gwallor	cowherd
hackery	two-wheeled bullock carriage
hakim	an authority, doctor
hamara	my
hukah, hooka	Indian pipe
jemadar	native officer
jhanpanies	men carrying dandy (open litter)
jharan	duster
jheel	a reedy lake
jhow	giant gorse or tamarisk
Kabir panth	followers of Kabir, a saint
kanat	colourful tent lining
kapra walla	cloth merchant
keddah	elephant enclosure
kelat	ceremonial gift
khansama, khansamah	head servant, cook
khabar, khubbar	news, of game
khurref	autumn crop
khus khus tattie	screen of sweet-smelling vertiver
kila	fort
kismut	fate
kitmagur, khitmagar	servant, table waiter
koi hai	'is anyone there?' nickname for up-country European of the old school
kothi, koti	mansion
kotwalee	police station
kutcha	raw, crude, not brick built
kuttri	crops on a sandy bank
lakh, lac	approx £10,000

lala	title of respect
lal-imli	red-flowered tamarind tree
lathi	iron-tipped bamboo weapon
Lat Sahib	Governor-General
luggao	to moor a boat
lumber igarah	number eleven
lungee baja	'skirted music', bagpipes
ma-bap	mother and father
mahajun	banker, merchant
maidan	open space, a park
maula	oak-like tree
maund	Indian measure of weight
mela	festival, fair
mistri	skilled workman, mason, bricklayer
moochee	leather worker, cobbler
molly, mali	gardener
moorghee khanna	hen house
moorghi	hen
mukhtar	authorised agent
munshi	clerk, writer, teacher of language
mussel	dish washer
mussack	inflated goatskin
nam	name
nullah	ditch
nuzzur hog gye	'the gift has gone'
palkee	palanguin
pandies	rebels, after Mungal Pandy
pariah	outcast
pergunnah	a district
peshkar	court official
pie	small copper coin
puggri	cloth bound turban
pukka, pucka	ripe, mature, substantial
punka	overhead fan
purdah, parda	curtain, especially screening women from the sight of men
raj	kingdom, government
roti	bread
rubbee	spring crop
sephai	sepoy soldier
seirkee, surki	thatched
shikari	sport, hunting
shoke	a fancy, favourite pastime

shook'r Khooda	'thanks be to God'
sirdar	bearer
sudder	chief court
sui	needle
talookdar	landed gentry
tamasha	a spectacle
tatties	grass screens
tehseeldar	chief revenue officer
thali	metal tray
thannadar	police chief
tiffin	luncheon
ticca gharri, tikka	hired box-like carriage
tope	grove of trees
topee	pith helmet, hat
toshikhana, tokhanna	government treasury for gifts received, go down
zemindary	farming an estate

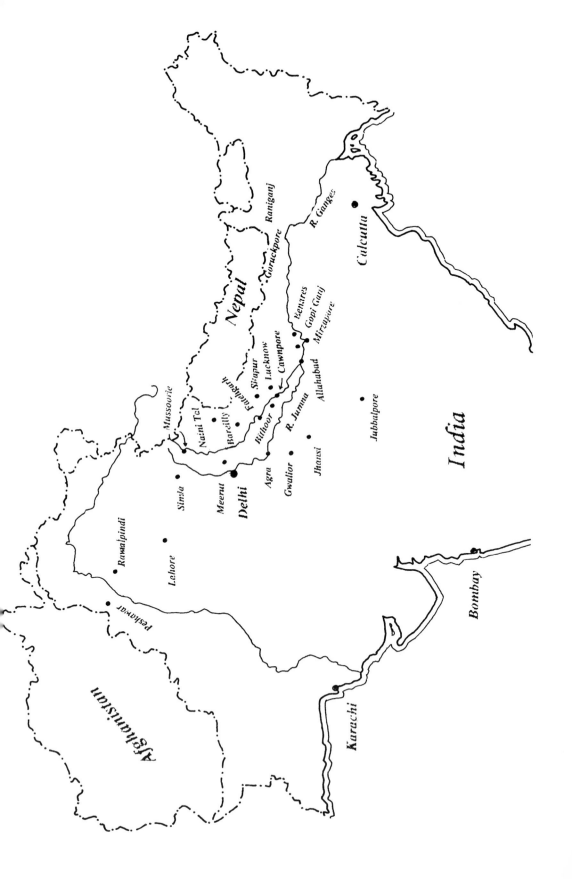

Nepal

India

Afghanistan

Raniganj

R. Ganges

Goruckpore

Calcutta

Benares
Gopi Ganj
Mirzapore

Sitapur
Lucknow
Cawnpore

Futteghur

Allahabad

Mussoorie

Naini Tal

Bareilly

Bithoor

R. Jumna

Jubbulpore

Jhansi

Simla

Meerut

Delhi

Agra

Gwalior

Rawalpindi

Lahore

Peshawar

Bombay

Karachi

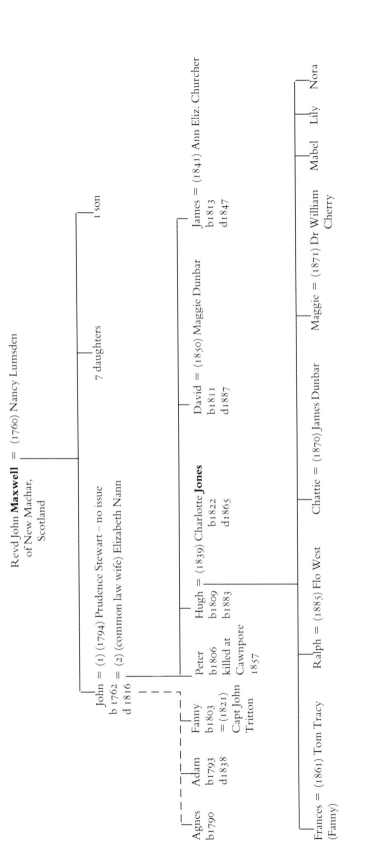

Revd John **Maxwell** = (1760) Nancy Lumsden
of New Machar,
Scotland

John = (1) (1794) Prudence Stewart – no issue
b 1762 = (2) (common law wife) Elizabeth Nann
d 1816

7 daughters   1 son

Agnes   Adam   Fanny   Peter   Hugh = (1839) Charlotte **Jones**   David = (1850) Maggie Dunbar   James = (1841) Ann Eliz. Churcher
b1790   b1793   b1803   b1806   b1809   b1822   b1811   b1813
         d1838   = (1821)   killed at   b1883   d1865   d1887   d1847
                 Capt John   Cawnpore
                 Tritton   1857

Frances = (1861) Tom Tracy   Ralph = (1885) Flo West   Chattie = (1870) James Dunbar   Maggie = (1871) Dr William   Mabel   Lily   Nora
(Fanny)   Cherry

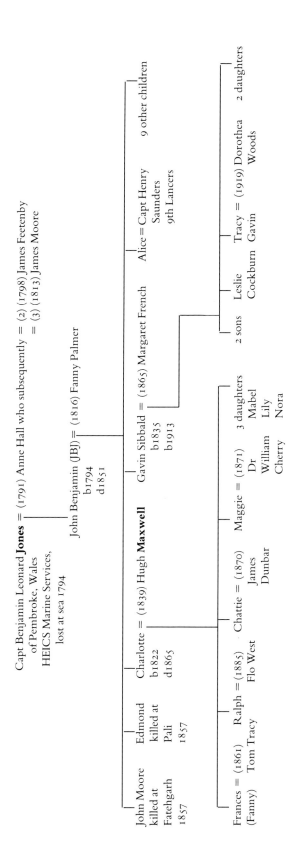

Capt Benjamin Leonard **Jones** = (1791) Anne Hall who subsequently = (2) (1798) James Feetenby
of Pembroke, Wales   = (3) (1813) James Moore
HEICS Marine Services,
lost at sea 1794

John Benjamin (JBJ) = (1816) Fanny Palmer
b1794
d1851

Edmond
killed at
Pali
1857

John Moore
killed at
Fatehgarh
1857

Charlotte = (1839) Hugh **Maxwell**
b1822
d1865

Gavin Sibbald = (1865) Margaret French
b1835
b1913

Alice = Capt Henry   9 other children
        Saunders
        9th Lancers

Frances = (1861)   Ralph = (1885)   Chattie = (1870)   Maggie = (1871)   3 daughters
(Fanny)   Tom Tracy   Flo West   James   Dr   Mabel
                                      Dunbar   William   Lily
                                                       Cherry   Nora

2 sons   Leslie   Tracy = (1919) Dorothea   2 daughters
                Cockburn Gavin   Woods

Index